Blackstone's

Prison Law Handbook
2014–2015

Blackstone's
Prison Law
Handbook
2014–2015

Margaret Obi

OXFORD
UNIVERSITY PRESS

OXFORD
UNIVERSITY PRESS

Great Clarendon Street, Oxford, OX2 6DP
United Kingdom

Oxford University Press is a department of the University of Oxford.
It furthers the University's objective of excellence in research, scholarship,
and education by publishing worldwide. Oxford is a registered trade mark of
Oxford University Press in the UK and in certain other countries

© Margaret Obi, 2013

The moral rights of the author have been asserted

First Edition published in 2013
Impression: 1

Crown copyright material is reproduced under Class Licence
Number C01P0000148 with the permission of OPSI
and the Queen's Printer for Scotland

Published in the United States of America by Oxford University Press
198 Madison Avenue, New York, NY 10016, United States of America

British Library Cataloguing in Publication Data
Data available

ISBN 978–0–19–967173–1

Printed by
L.E.G.O. S.p.A.–Lavis TN

Links to third party websites are provided by Oxford in good faith and
for information only. Oxford disclaims any responsibility for the materials
contained in any third party website referenced in this work.

Preface

This book is my attempt to demystify prison law, which is set within a statutory framework and tightly governed by an ever changing range of detailed regulations and guidance. The aim is to equip the reader with the essentials for advising on the full range of issues that are likely to arise whilst a prisoner is on remand, a serving prisoner, or on licence under supervision until the sentence expiry date. I have tried to keep the text as practical, user-friendly and portable as possible, without sacrificing some of the finer points and intricacies that can arise in practice.

Inevitably, a book such as this can only ever be a detailed introduction. The reader will have to grapple with the case law, and Rules themselves and regularly check whether the PSIs and PSOs which govern the exercise of the prison authorities' decision-making powers have been modified or changed.

I am grateful to the many people who have assisted me with this endeavour along the way, with special thanks to the editorial team at Oxford University Press for their incredible patience and understanding.

This book is dedicated to Iweka.

Margaret Obi
September 2013

Contents

Part A The Prison System

Part B Public Funding

Contents

Part C The Prison Regime

Part D Formal Discipline

Part E Informal Discipline

Part F Release and Parole

Contents

Part G Judicial Review

Contents

Icons List

The following icons are used throughout this book:

KD Key Document

📖 Cross reference to *Blackstone's Criminal Practice 2014*

Table of Cases

Table of Cases

Table of Primary Legislation

Table of Primary Legislation

Table of Secondary Legislation

Table of Secondary Legislation

Table of Conventions

Table of Practice Directions

Abbreviations

ACCT	Assessment, Care in Custody, Teamwork
ACR	automatic conditional release
ADA	additional days awarded
ARD	automatic release date
AUR	automatic unconditional release
BCU	Briefing and Casework Unit
CALM	Controlling Anger and Learning to Manage It
CARATS	counselling, assessment, referral, advice and throughcare
CED	custodial end date
CPS	Crown Prosecution Service
CRD	conditional release date
CRL	Childcare Resettlement Licence
CSC	Close Supervision Centre
CSCP	Cognitive Self Change Programme
DACU	Data Access and Compliance Unit
DCMF	design, construct, manage and finance
DCR	Discretionary Conditional Release
DDC	Deputy Director of Custody
DDHS	Deputy Director of High Security
DHS	Director of High Security
DPA	Data Protection Act
DPSP	Directorate of Public Sector Prisons
DSPD	dangerous and severe personality disordered
DTO	Detention and Training Order
DYOI	Detention in a Young Offender Institution
EDS	Extended Determinate Sentence
EPP	Extended Sentence for Public Protection
ERS	Early Removal Scheme
ETS	Enhanced Thinking Skills
FNP	foreign national prisoners
FOIA	Freedom of Information Act

Abbreviations

FRS	Facilitated Return Scheme
FTR	fixed term recall
GOod	Good Order or Discipline
HDC	home detention curfew
HMP	Her Majesty's Prison
HSU	High Security Unit
IAR	information access representative
ICC	International Criminal Court
ICTY	International Criminal Tribunal for the Former Yugoslavia
IEP	Incentives and Earned Privileges
ISP	indeterminate sentence prisoner
IMB	Independent Monitoring Board
IMR	inmate medical record
IPP	Imprisonment for Public Protection
ISHS	Initial Segregation Health Screen
LAA	Legal Aid Agency
LAP	Local Advisory Panel
LASCH	Local Authority Secure Children's Home
LED	licence expiry date
LSS	Local Security Strategy
MAPP	Multi-Agency Public Protection
MAPPA	Multi-Agency Public Protection Arrangements
MBU	Mother and Baby Unit
MDT	Mandatory Drug Testing
MHRT	Mental Health Review Tribunal
NOMS	National Offender Management Service
NOS	National Operation Services
NPD	non parole date
NPS	National Probation Service
NSF	National Security Framework
OASys	Offender Assessment System
OMM	Offender Management Model
PADAs	prospective additional days awarded
PCA	Parliamentary Commissioner for Administration

PCS	Probation and Contracted Services
PDP	Prison Disciplinary Procedures
PED	parole eligibility date
PIN	personal identification number
PPCS	Public Protection Casework Section
PPO	prolific or priority offender
PPU	Public Protection Unit
PSI	Prison Service Instruction
PSO	Prison Service Order
RDR	resettlement day release
ROR	resettlement overnight release
ROTL	Release on Temporary Licence
SCSL	Special Court for Sierra Leone
SDS	standard determinate sentence
SED	sentence expiry date
SLED	sentence and licence expiry date
SOTP	Sex Offender Treatment Programmes
SPL	Special Purpose Licence
SSU	Special Security Unit
STC	Secure Training Centre
TERS	Tariff Expired Removal Scheme
UAL	unlawfully at large
VDT	voluntary drug test
VPU	Vulnerable Prisoner Unit
YOI	Youth Offender Institution

Part A
The Prison System

A1 National Offender Management Service (NOMS)

A1.1 Overview

NOMS is an executive agency of the Ministry of Justice. It incorporates HM Prison Service and the National Probation Service (NPS). NOMS is responsible for delivering reduced re-offending and public protection, which it aims to achieve by integrating policy and offender management services within the public, private, voluntary and community sectors.

NOMS is divided into directorates which include:

- Directorate of Public Sector Prisons
- National Operation Services
- Probation and Contracted Services

A1.2 Directorate of Public Sector Prisons (DPSP)

There are currently 120 public sector prisons (shortly to be reduced by 6), including 3 immigration removal centres operated by NOMS on behalf of the UK Border Agency.

The Director delegates the general management of prisons to Deputy Directors of Custody (DDC) who cover 11 regions across England and Wales. In addition there are Deputy Directors responsible for supervising Youth Justice and the High Security estate.

The Deputy Director of High Security (DDHS) has responsibility for the 8 high security prisons, centrally manages the highest security prisoners, provides tactical support for all prisons, and is responsible for delivering the Close Supervision System and Managing Challenging Behaviour Strategy.

A1.3 National Operation Services (NOS)

The NOS is responsible for operational services across NOMS including prisoner population management, parole, recall and other casework, security, safer custody and public protection services.

A1.4 Probation and Contracted Services (PCS)

The PCS contract manages the National Probation Service, privately operated prisons, a range of system wide contracts and third sector providers delivering offender services, including over 100 Attendance Centres.

A2 The National Probation Service (NPS)

A2.1 Overview

The NPS comes under NOMS. Probation services are provided by 35 Probation Trusts across England and Wales. The Trusts are responsible for commissioning services from the public, private and third sectors in addition to being providers of court services and offender management.

The Offender Management Model (OMM) requires each offender to have a single named Offender Manager, who works with them during their sentence and assesses their needs whether they are in custody or in the community.

A2.1.1 Key points

- The OMM includes an Offender Supervisor to deliver the day-to-day supervision and to drive through implementation of the sentence plan.
- The Offender Manager will usually be the offender's home probation officer (based in the prisoner's home area), who will also perform the role of Offender Supervisor for offenders under supervision in the community.
- For offenders in custody the Offender Supervisor is likely to be a seconded probation officer (working within the prison) or an appropriate member of the prison staff.

A2.2 Custody Based Offender Supervisor

The role includes:

- preparing information and risk assessments for prisoners being considered for early release eg advising on curfews;
- assisting the prisoner with work on offending behaviour within the sentence planning process;
- assisting prison staff in the prison's bail information scheme for prisoners on remand awaiting trial.

A2.3 Community Based Offender Manager

The role includes:

- working with prisoners during and after sentence to assist in resettlement;

- implementing licence condition requirements;
- assisting in sentence management;
- making arrangements for the prisoner's release;
- acting on concerns of the victim;
- supervising the prisoner while on licence.

A3 **Multi-Agency Public Protection Arrangements (MAPPA)**

A3.1 **Key Documents**

KD Public Protection Manual (PPM)

MAPPA Guidance 2012

A3.2 **Overview**

Section 67(2) of the Criminal Justice and Court Services Act 2000 requires all 42 criminal justice areas in England and Wales to establish Multi-Agency Public Protection Arrangements (MAPPA) to assess and manage the risk posed by sexual and violent offenders on their release from prison. The involvement of the Prison Service was put on a statutory footing with the implementation of sections 325–326 of the Criminal Justice Act (CJA) 2003.

Collectively the police, Probation Service and Prison Service are known as the 'Responsible Authority', and are required to publish annual reports. The 'Responsible Authority' discharges its function through the Strategic Management Board (SMB), which must include senior representatives from each service and Duty to Co-operate agencies.

A3.3 **MAPPA Offenders**

The CJA 2003 specifies that MAPPA principally applies to the following offenders:

a) any person convicted of murder;
b) any person sentenced in England and Wales to a term of imprisonment or detention of 12 months or more, for a sexual or violent offence as set out in Schedule 15 of the Act;
c) any other offender who may cause serious harm to the public (wherever the offences were committed).

Prisoners who may pose a significant risk may be identified from the following groups:

• MAPPA offenders (as just described);
• offenders subject to harassment procedures;
• offenders who present a risk to children (if not within the scope of MAPPA);
• offenders disqualified from working with children;

- offenders identified as being dangerous and severe personality disordered (DSPD);
- potentially dangerous offenders.

The list is not prescriptive or exhaustive.

Offenders who fall outside these criteria, but who present a risk of harm, may still be made subject to multi-agency risk management. However, these offenders will not be managed within MAPPA.

A3.4 Offender Categories

MAPPA offenders fall into one of the following categories:

- Category 1—registered sexual offenders

This category includes offenders convicted or cautioned for sexual offences listed in Schedule 3 of the Sexual Offences Act 2003, and required to comply with registration requirements as set out in Part 2 of that Act. The identification of such offenders is primarily the responsibility of the police. These prisoners are often referred to as being on the 'Sex Offenders Register'.

Public Protection Manual, Chapter 1, paragraph 2.3

Sexual Offender Notification

Section 82 Sexual Offences Act (2003) provides the period of time an offender is required to comply with the notification requirements.

Sentence	Adult	Juvenile (under 18)
Is sentenced to 30 months or more imprisonment (inc. life)	An indefinite period	An indefinite period
Is admitted to a hospital subject to a restriction order	An indefinite period	An indefinite period
Is sentenced to a imprisonment for a term of more than 6 months but less than 30 months	10 years	5 years
Is sentenced to imprisonment for 6 months or less	7 years	3 years 6 months
Is admitted to hospital, without a restriction order	7 years	3 years and 6 months
Is cautioned	2 years	1 year
Is given a conditional discharge	The duration of the conditional discharge	The duration of the conditional discharge
Received any other disposal (e.g. a fine or community punishment)	5 years	2 years 6 months

---

During the period when offenders must comply with the notification requirements, they must notify their home address to the Police within three days of
the date of conviction, caution or finding, unless they are detained or outside
the United Kingdom, in which case the three days runs from the end of that
period of detention or return to the United Kingdom.

"Home Address" is defined in section 83(7) as meaning the address of his/her
sole or main residence in the United Kingdom or, if there is no such residence,
the address or location of a place in the United Kingdom where he/she can
regularly be found and, if there is more than one such place, one of those
places as the person may select. Changes to their home address must be also
be notified within three days. This includes where an offender is away from
their home address for a period of seven days either in one period or collectively
over a twelve-month period. The offender is required to verify their address to
Police every 12 months.

Restrictive Orders

Where offenders pose a continuing risk of serious harm, the Police will consider
whether the risks posed by such an offender are sufficiently high to justify
applying for one of the following orders introduced in the Sexual Offences
Act (2003):

- Notification Order (sections 97–101)
- Risk of Sexual Harm Order (sections 123–129)
- Sexual Offences Prevention Order (sections 104, 106, 107, 108, 110 and 113)

- Category 2—violent and other sexual offenders

This category includes violent offenders and sexual offenders convicted of a specified offence (murder or any of the offences in Schedule
15 to the Criminal Justice Act 2003) who are sentenced to at least
12 months' imprisonment and applies equally to determinate, indeterminate and suspended sentences. This category also includes those
detained under guardianship or hospital orders.

There will be a small number of cases where the sexual offence does not
attract registration or where the sentence does not cross the threshold
for a Disqualification Order (disqualifying the offender from working
with children) under sections 28–29A of the Criminal Justice and
Court Services Act (CJCSA) 2000. Although the offenders are not
required to register with the police, all offenders will be subject to
statutory supervision by the Probation Service or the Youth Offending
Team (YOT), with the exception of the small and ever decreasing
number of offenders sentenced prior to the Criminal Justice Act 1991
or those recalled until their Licence Expiry Date.

The legislation in respect of violent or sexual offenders is not retro-
spective. It therefore only includes offenders who were sentenced or
received a Disqualification Order since April 2001 or who were serving a similar offence on that date. Such prisoners remain in Category

2 only for so long as the relevant sentence or Disqualification Order
is current.

• Category 3—other offenders

This category is not identified by the sentence or other disposal of
the court.

The 'Responsible Authority' must:

1. establish that the offender has committed an offence which indicates that he/she is capable of causing serious harm to the public.
   It includes not only convictions, but cautions, and juveniles who
   have been reprimanded or warned;
2. reasonably consider that the offender may cause serious harm to
   the public and that a multi-agency approach at Level 2 or 3 (see
   A3.5) is necessary to manage the risks.

Information is shared between other agencies (including Youth
Offending Teams, Jobcentre Plus, housing authorities, education
authorities, social services, NHS Trusts and the UK Border Agency)
known as Duty to Co-operate Agencies, and may result in recommendations for additional licence conditions on release.

A3.5 Levels of Management

All offenders to whom MAPPA applies must be managed according
to three levels of risk:

• Level 1 (low or medium risk): where the risk can be managed by one
  agency, usually the Probation Service or Youth Offending Team.
  Most MAPPA offenders are managed at this level.
• Level 2 (high or very high risk): where active involvement of more
  than one agency and regular Multi-Agency Public Protection
  (MAPP) meetings is required.
• Level 3 (highest risk): where the risk requires multi-agency involve-
  ment and more frequent MAPP meetings.

Although there is a correlation between the level of risk and the level
of MAPPA management not all high risk cases need to be managed
at Level 2 or 3. The central issue is for the 'Responsible Authority' to
determine the lowest defensible risk management plan.

📖 *Blackstone's Criminal Practice 2014* **B3** and **E23**

A4 **Types of Prison**

A4.1 **Male Adult Prisons**

There are broadly five types of prison for male adults:

- *Local Prisons* are closed prisons, which tend to be located in towns and cities. They accommodate men aged 21 or over who are sent from the court either when remanded in custody before trial, after conviction, or at the sentence hearing. Each court has an arrangement with a local prison, which makes them susceptible to over-crowding. Following assessment and categorization some prisoners will serve their sentence in local prisons while others will be transferred elsewhere.

- *High Security Prisons* accommodate Category A or Category B prisoners. There are currently 8 high security prisons—Belmarsh, Frankland, Full Sutton, Long Lartin, Manchester, Wakefield, Whitemoor and Woodhill.

- *Category B Training Prisons* aim to offer sentenced prisoners opportunities for education, training, work or offender programmes. Security levels between Category B prisons vary. Allocation will depend on the prisoner's security category and the availability of appropriate training opportunities or offender behaviour programmes.

- *Category C Prisons* make up the majority of prisons in the prison estate. They are closed prisons but have less internal security. The staff ratio is much lower than in Category B prisons, and control is often maintained by stricter application of the Prison Rules.

- *Open Prisons* have the most liberal regimes. Open prisons hold Category D prisoners, and work or study is mandatory. Most lifers spend 2 or 3 years in an open prison before being considered for release.

In addition to these prisons, there are a number of different prisons or units within prisons designed to accommodate dangerous or vulnerable prisoners:

- *Resettlement Prisons/Units* are located within some Category C and D prisons. Prisoners coming to the end of long sentences are transferred to resettlement prisons to engage in work or a community placement outside the prison and to re-establish links with family in preparation for release.

- *Special Security Units (SSUs)* are also known as High Security Units (HSUs). At present there are 3 SSUs at Belmarsh, Full Sutton and Whitemoor for exceptional risk Category A prisoners. The unit at Belmarsh also holds prisoners detained under the Prevention of Terrorism Acts.

- *Close Supervision Centres (CSCs)* tend to be units within particular prisons. They are effectively prisons within prisons. Security is intense as they provide a limited number of places for inmates who pose a significant threat to the safety of other inmates and staff.

- *Vulnerable Prisoner Units (VPUs)* separate sex offenders and other vulnerable prisoners (eg informants or former police/prison officers) from the main prison population for their own protection. Some prisons have specific wings for such prisoners, while others hold them on normal location.

- *Dangerous and Severe Personality Disorder Units* treat psychopaths or those suffering from severe personality disorders. At present there are 5 units: Frankland, Whitemoor, and the high security hospitals, Ashworth, Rampton and Broadmoor. Offenders are eligible for treatment if they are considered likely to commit an offence that could cause serious physical or psychological harm from which a victim would find it very difficult to recover. There must be evidence of a severe personality disorder and a link between that disorder and the risk of violent offending. Most referrals are from high security prisons, and places are allocated on the basis of priority need.

A4.2 Women's Prisons

There are currently 13 women's prisons. The local closed prisons (Bronzefield, Eastwood Park, Foston Hall, Holloway and New Hall) hold remand prisoners, those awaiting allocation following conviction and those serving short sentences. Holloway also holds Category A remand prisoners, and some long-term prisoners. The other closed prisons, Downview, Drake Hall, Low Newton, Peterborough, Send and Styal are the female equivalent of Category B and C prisons for men. There are no longer any semi-open women's prisons. The only open prisons are Askham Grange and East Sutton Park. Young female offenders are accommodated in Youth Offender Institutions (YOIs) which are discrete units, within the adult female estate.

A4.3 Young Offender Facilities

There are three types of facilities for the detention of young offenders:

- *Young Offender Institutions (YOIs)* hold the vast majority of young offenders. These facilities are run by the Prison Service and accommodate young offenders aged 15–21. YOIs accommodate large numbers, and have lower ratios of staff to young people than STCs and LASCHs. Male young offenders aged 14–16 are normally allocated to the juvenile only establishments (Ashfield, Werrington and Wetherby) or the juvenile units within YOIs. Female young offenders aged 18–20 are normally allocated to the discrete YOIs at Askham Grange, Drake Hall, Eastwood Park, East Sutton Park, Low Newton and New Hall, while those aged 17 are normally allocated to the special juvenile units at Downview, Eastwood Park, Foston Hall and New Hall.

• *Secure Training Centres (STCs)* are purpose-built privately run centres for young offenders up to the age of 17 years. There are currently four STCs—Hassockfield (County Durham), Oakhill (Milton Keynes), Medway (Kent) and Rainsbrook (Rugby). They hold vulnerable young people who are sentenced to custody or remanded to secure accommodation. STCs are much smaller than YOIs. The regimes aim to be constructive and education-focused, providing tailored programmes for young offenders.

• *Local Authority Secure Children's Homes (LASCHs)* are run by local authority social services departments which are overseen by the Department of Health and the Department for Education. LASCHs accommodate young male offenders aged 12–14, girls up to 16 years and vulnerable boys aged 15–16. They aim to focus on individual needs, and have a high ratio of staff. The homes tend to be small, accommodating between 6 and 40 young people.

A4.4 Private Prisons

Following the implementation of sections 84–87 of the Criminal Justice Act (CJA) 1991 and successive amendments, the Home Secretary was given the power to 'contract out' the running of prisons and contract with the private sector to 'design, construct, manage and finance' (DCMF) new prisons. Currently, the management of 14 prisons is contracted to private sector partners.

Doncaster, Wolds and Oakwood were built and financed by the public sector but are run by private companies under management-only contracts, while the following are DCMF prisons: Altcourse, Ashfield, Birmingham, Bronzefield, Dovegate (including YOI), Forest Bank, Lowdham Grange, Parc (including YOI), Peterborough, Rye Hill and Thameside.

A4.4.1 Key points

• All private prisons have a contract with the Government which sets out the 'performance criteria' to be applied.
• Although private prisons must comply with the Prison Rules, they are not required to comply with Prison Service Orders (PSOs) and Prison Service Instructions (PSIs) unless directed to do so by the Secretary of State.

- In practice most of the operational PSOs and PSIs apply to private prisons, other than for personnel matters which are only of relevance to the Prison Service itself.
- Private prisons are fully integrated into the penal system. Allocation to a private prison is administered in the same way as allocation to a state prison. Over and above the admission criteria of the particular establishment there are no special allocation requirements.

A5 **Prison Personnel**

A5.1 **Public Sector**

The management hierarchy in state prisons is as follows:

- Governing governor—Grade A
- Senior operational manager—Grades B to D
- Operational manager—Grades E to F

The role of the Governing governor varies according to the size and type of establishment but will usually involve supervising security arrangements, writing reports, conducting disciplinary hearings and managing other disciplinary procedures.

The prison officer ranks in public sector prisons are:

- principal prison officer
- senior prison officer
- prison officer

Section 8 of the Prison Act 1952 confers on prison officers whilst exercising their duty the same 'powers, authority, protection and privileges', as a police constable, including the power to use reasonable force, and conduct strip searches. Most prison officers work in small teams, either assigned to a specific duty, or to a particular wing within the prison. Each team is led by a senior prison officer, and where several teams are working together (eg, different staff shifts on a wing) they will be supervised by a principal prison officer. All uniformed prison staff are under the supervision of a junior grade prison manager.

A5.2 **Private Prisons**

In private prisons the day-to-day management is overseen by a Director who performs a very similar role to the Governing governor in the public sector.

The officers in private prisons are known as prison custody officers. They do not have the powers of a constable under the Police and Criminal Evidence Act (PACE) 1984. Their powers and duties are derived from section 86 of the CJA 1991. These powers were extended when the Offender Management Act (OMA) 2007 came into force and are now similar to the powers of prison officers.

A6 **Non-governmental Organizations**

A6.1 **Prisons and Probation Ombudsman**

The Prisons and Probation Ombudsman is appointed by the Secretary of State to investigate complaints from prisoners, those subject to supervision, and those for whom reports have been written. The Ombudsman also has responsibility for investigating deaths in custody, and probation hostels (Approved Premises). The Ombudsman, who is independent of the Prison Service and the National Probation Service, works with a team of deputies, assistants, investigators and other staff.

A6.2 **Parole Board**

The Parole Board was established in 1968 with the implementation of the Criminal Justice Act 1967, and became a non-departmental public body in 1996 when the Criminal Justice and Public Order Act 1994 came into force. The Board's role is to assess risk to determine whether it is safe for certain prisoners to be released into the community. The work of the Board is supported by casework teams.

See *R (Brooke) v Parole Board and others* [2008] EWCA Civ 29 where the Court of Appeal dismissed the Secretary of State for Justice's appeal against the Divisional Court finding that the Parole Board was not objectively independent from the state and was therefore in breach of the English common law and Article 5 of the European Convention on Human Rights (ECHR).

A7 **Sources of Prison Law**

A7.1 **Overview**

Prison law is derived from a number of different sources:

- Statute
- Prison Rules 1999, SI 1999/728 (Prison Rules) and Young Offender Institution Rules 2000, SI 2000/3371 (YOI Rules)
- Prison Service Orders (PSOs) and Prison Service Instructions (PSIs)
- Case law

A7.2 **Statute**

A7.2.1 *The Prison Act 1952*

This Act is the only statute that deals exclusively with the prison system and is in essence an enabling act. It sets out the legal responsibility for managing the penal system, giving the Secretary of State maximum discretion and general 'superintendence of prisons'. The Act creates two statutory watchdogs:

- Chief Inspector of Prisons (section 5A)
  The Chief Inspector of Prisons reports directly to the Secretary of State for Justice on prison conditions and the treatment of prisoners in England and Wales. There are inspection teams specializing in men's prisons, women's prisons, Young Offender Institutions and immigration removal centres. The Chief Inspector is required to produce an annual report which is laid before Parliament.
- Independent Monitoring Board (IMB) (sections 6–9)
  Each prison establishment is required to have an IMB. Members of the Board are appointed to monitor day-to-day life in prisons to ensure that proper standards of care and decency are being maintained. Members have unrestricted access to the prison at any time, can talk to any prisoner out of sight and hearing of members of staff, and prisoners can make a confidential request to see a member of the IMB. The Board has no statutory authority to change policy or overturn adverse decisions of the Governor or prison staff.

A7.2.2 *Criminal Justice Acts*

The Legal Aid, Sentencing and Punishment of Offenders Act (LASPO) 2012 came into force on 3 December 2012. Following the implementation of LASPO, the CJA 2003 continues to govern the release of determinate sentenced prisoners. All prisoners sentenced after commencement of LASPO are now subject to the CJA 2003 irrespective of the date of the offence. Prisoners already serving sentences imposed under CJA 1991 (offences committed before 4 April 2005, and prisoners serving less than 12 months) and CJA 1967 (sentenced before 1 October 1992) will continue to be released according to those arrangements. However, LASPO has brought these provisions within CJA 2003 so all release provisions for determinate sentenced prisoners are now contained within the same statute.

As well as simplification and consolidation of the release provisions, LASPO, amongst other things:

- abolished Imprisonment for Public Protection (IPP) and Extended Sentence for Public Protection (EPP);
- introduced a new automatic life sentence;
- introduced a new Extended Determinate Sentence (EDS);
- changed the test for release for existing Discretionary Conditional Release (DCR) 1967 and 'old style' extended sentence cases; and
- amended arrangements for determinate recalls.

A7.3 **Prison Rules**

The Secretary of State has rule-making power under section 47 of the the Prison Act 1952. The current Prison Rules (see **Appendix 1)** include general provisions, specific rights, prohibitions and obligations, prison discipline and rules governing prison officers and visitors. The equivalent rules for Young Offender Institutions are contained in the Young Offenders Institution Rules 2000 (YOI Rules— see **Appendix 2**).

The Rules are regulatory only. It is not possible to bring an action for breach of the Rules themselves, as prisoners must prove that they suffered loss or injury as a direct result of the breach (see the important House of Lords case: *R v Deputy Governor of Parkhurst Prison ex p Hague; Weldon v Home Office* [1992] 1 AC 58). However, the *Hague* case affirmed that implementation of the Rules is susceptible to judicial review.

A7.4 **Prison Service Instructions (PSIs) and Prison Service Orders (PSOs)**

The Prison Act 1952 and the Rules confer significant discretionary powers on the day-to-day operation of the prison system and, in an attempt to achieve a consistent approach, the Prison Service has developed policy guidance to flesh out the detail. The most important policy documents for legal advisers are PSOs and PSIs. All new Prison Service operating instructions issued after 1 August 2009 are published as PSIs and have fixed individual expiry dates. Existing PSOs remain in force until replaced.

Although the policies have no statutory authority, they are susceptible to Judicial Review as they guide the exercise of discretion. Successful challenges are likely to be based on the failure to comply with a lawful policy or on the failure to depart from a policy where it results in a breach of the prisoner's basic rights.

A7.5 Case Law

Court judgments have a substantial impact on prisoners' rights as they 'fill in the gaps' by clarifying rights and entitlements. The judgments of the European Court of Human Rights and the implementation of the Human Rights Act 1998 have had a substantial impact on prisoners' rights.

The case of *Golder v United Kingdom* (A/18) (1975) 1 EHRR 524 led the way as the first case against Britain to reach the ECtHR. It was held that the right to a fair trial under Article 6(1) ECHR included the right to have access to a court.

Following a domestic challenge, the House of Lords in the landmark case of *Raymond v Honey* [1983] 1 AC 1 affirmed that prisoners retain all civil rights other than those expressly removed by parliament or implied by their imprisonment.

All lifers are entitled to a review of detention once their minimum term has expired, in compliance with Article 5 rights (right to liberty and security): *R (on application of Anderson) v Secretary of State for the Home Department* [2003] 1 AC 837.

Parole Board reviews of recalled prisoners are subject to much higher standards of procedural fairness with the introduction of the right to an oral hearing: *R (on the application of Smith and West) v Parole Board* [2005] UKHL 1, and another major step forward came with the decision in *Ezeh and Conners v United Kingdom* [2004] 39 EHRR 1 which established that Article 6 rights are engaged whenever a prisoner faces the prospect of additional days, and as a result prisoners are entitled to legal representation at disciplinary hearings before an independent adjudicator (District Judge).

More recently the Court of Appeal upheld important decisions relating to the function of the Parole Board: *R (Brooke) v Parole Board and others* [2008] EWCA Civ 29) and *Secretary of State for Justice v Walker* [2008] EWCA Civ 30 where the court dismissed an appeal by the Secretary of State for Justice arising from a ruling by the High Court that failure to provide adequate funding for offending behaviour programmes (which had led to an increase in the number of prisoners serving indeterminate terms of Imprisonment for the Protection of the Public (IPP) beyond their minimum term) was 'arbitrary, unreasonable and unlawful'. In the House of Lords case of *Secretary of State for Justice v James* [2009] UKHL 22, the failure to provide resources to enable prisoners to demonstrate to the Parole Board that their detention for public protection is no longer necessary was described as 'deplorable'.

In both *Walker* and *James* the court stopped short of finding the detention to be unlawful in and of itself. However, in *James, Wells and Lee v UK* [2012] ECHR 1706, the court found the post-tariff detention was unlawful pursuant to Article 5(1) and as there was no meaningful review of detention it also violated Article 5(4).

A8 **Access to Information**

A8.1 **Key Document**

KD PSO 9020

A8.2 **Overview**

Each establishment is required to appoint at least one information access representative (IAR) to handle requests for documents or information (PSO 9020, paragraph 2.7.1). All requests made directly to the prison (including those addressed to specific departments) must be passed to the IAR who will either meet the request by collating and copying the documents or will forward it to the Data Access and Compliance Unit (DACU) of NOMS.

A8.2.1 **Key points**

- DACU is responsible for implementing freedom of access to information across the Prison Service.
- Information kept by the Prison Service will fall into two distinct categories: personal data covered by the Data Protection Act (DPA) 1998 or non-personal data which is covered by the Freedom of Information Act (FOIA) 2000.
- If a request for disclosure is refused, an application for an internal review may be submitted and ultimately a complaint may be made to the Information Commissioner and Information Tribunal.

A8.3 **Personal Data**

All prison records from reception to release relating to a specific prisoner fall into this category. This includes factual information, indications of intent and expressions of opinion. Simple and straightforward requests for documents relating to matters the prisoner has already been a party to or is entitled to as of right, eg reasons for categorization decisions and the documents that informed the decision, can be requested informally (no fee) on an ad hoc basis by writing to the prison, and will often be disclosed at local discretion.

There is no prescribed format, and there is no need to specify that the request is being made under the DPA 1998. Most requests can be made this way. Some documents, if requested, must be provided free of charge, eg the Notice of Report and witness statements in relation to an adjudication hearing. Others can attract an administration charge (£10), eg the parole dossier, although this will not be levied if the request is met at local level. See *R (on the application of Stephenson) v Secretary of State for Justice* [2010] EWHC 3134 (Admin).

In emergencies an urgent request may be made without a signed authority, on the basis that the prisoner will provide prison staff with the necessary consent directly. Legal representatives unsure whether the documents they are requesting will be disclosed on an ad hoc basis may contact the IAR for advice.

A formal 'subject access request' should be made if any of the following circumstances apply:

- The request is for a large amount of information;
- The request will require a fee to complete (photocopying charges or £10 DPA 1998 fee);
- The IAR does not have immediate access to all of the information requested;
- The IAR has concerns over disclosing the information or believes any part of it may be covered by an exemption;
- Additional information is required to complete the request;
- The request includes information under FOIA 2000 (see **A8.4**);
- The request relates to medical reports or security information.

If it is clear that the information will not be disclosed informally the formal request can be sent directly to the DACU (by post or email). If the formal request has been sent to the prison it will be forwarded to the DACU by the IAR. Requests, whether directed to the IAR or to the DACU, should include:

- the prisoner's full name and prison number;
- the establishment where the prisoner is being held;
- the date of sentence (if known);
- a description of the personal data being sought and the relevant dates or period;
- a signed authority from the prisoner (unless there is none on file and it is an emergency);
- £10 cheque or postal order made payable to HM Prison Service (formal requests only).

The IAR or DACU must comply with the request as soon as possible and within 40 days (PSO 9020, paragraph 1.21.1). If the request falls to be considered by the DACU, they will liaise with the IAR with regards to any documents which are held locally. The only exceptions are requests for inmate medical records (IMRs) and security information. For these documents the DACU will make direct contact with the relevant department, who will be responsible for considering whether the material can be disclosed in full or in part before sending it to the DACU via the IAR. Most personal data will be disclosable, however, responses to requests for all prison records are likely to take longer than a request for specific documents.

Only the DACU can refuse requests for information outright, and only if the document or information is exempt. The most common exemptions relied on by the Prison Service are:

• information that would prejudice the prevention or detection of crime (which includes crimes committed in prison);
• information that is legally privileged.

A8.4 Non-Personal Data

Any request for information that does not contain information about a specific individual eg policy documents, will be covered by FOIA 2000.

Legal representatives should check whether this information is already in the public domain before making a written request for disclosure, as most policies are published in the resources section of the Justice website; a notable exception being sensitive security policy which has restricted access and is only available to staff on the Prison Service intranet. However, the minimum guidelines in the National Security Framework (NSF) are available on the website and will be replicated in the prison's local security strategy, which ought to be disclosed upon request.

The request should be addressed to the IAR. There is no prescribed format. If for any reason the IAR is unable to comply with the request, the legal representative will be advised to make the request to the DACU. The Prison Service should respond within 20 working days (PSO 9020, paragraph 1.16.1), and will usually process the request free of charge, but there may be a fee for photocopying and postage.

Under FOIA 2000, certain information may be exempt from disclosure. Some exemptions are absolute, while others are known as 'qualified exemptions', and require the Prison Service to consider whether disclosure is in the public interest. Qualified exemptions include information held with a view to publication on a future date, maintenance of security and good order in prisons and information relating to the formulation and development of government policy. Absolute exemptions include information reasonably accessible by another means, personal information (gateway to the DPA), and information provided in confidence (PSO 9020, paragraph 1.9.4).

Part B
Public Funding

B1 **Overview**

The Legal Aid Agency (LAA) is an executive agency within the Ministry of Justice, and it replaced the Legal Services Commission in April 2013.

Prison Law is a Class of Work within the Crime Category of the 2010 Standard Crime Contract (as amended). The Part A Specification is of general application to all Classes of Work. Where there is any conflict with specific rules in Part B, the latter takes precedence (Contract Specification, Part A, Rule 1.6). Judicial Review proceedings are administered through Associated Civil Work.

Public funding covers:

- Advice and Assistance
- Advocacy Assistance
- Associated Civil Work (Legal Help and Civil Legal Representation)

Funding only covers Sentence, Discipline, Parole Board and Treatment Cases (Contract Specification, Part B, Rule 12.4).

B1.1 **Application Forms**

The appropriate forms for Advice and Assistance are CRM1 and CRM2. For Advocacy Assistance the forms are CRM1 and CRM3. The forms must be fully completed, signed and dated by the client. Copies must be kept on file.

In addition Form PL1 is required if seeking Prior Approval to offer Advice and Assistance on a Treatment Case.

B2 **Devolved Functions**

Devolved Functions must be exercised in all appropriate cases (Contract Specification, Part A, Rule 4.5). Reasons must be given, justifying the exercise of the Devolved Function on CRM2 or a file note (as appropriate) in accordance with the relevant Rule in the Contract Specification.

The relevant Devolved Functions in the context of Prison Law are:

B2.1 **Application from a Child or Protected Party**

- *Accepted an application from a child or protected party or someone on their behalf (Contract Specification Part A, Rules 4.24 to 4.27)*

B2.1.1 Key points

- Instructions may be accepted directly from a child (person under 18) in proceedings where the child is entitled to defend without a Litigation Friend.
- Direct instructions may also be accepted where there is good reason why a parent/guardian cannot make the application on the child's behalf, and the child is old enough to give instructions and understand the nature of the advice and proceedings.

B2.2 **Previous Advice**

- *Previous Advice & Assistance (Contract Specification, Part B, Rule 12.60)*

Advice and Assistance can only be provided to a client who has previously received such advice on the same matter within the last 6 months if:

(a) there is a gap in time and circumstances have changed materially between the first and second occasions when the Advice and Assistance, or Advocacy Assistance was sought; or
(b) the client has reasonable cause to transfer from the first Provider; or
(c) the first Provider has confirmed that they will be making no claim for payment for the Advice and Assistance or Advocacy Assistance given.

B2.2.1 `Key points`

- Reasonable enquiries must be made to ascertain whether the client has previously received Advice and Assistance or Advocacy Assistance and if so, when (Contract Specification, Part B, Rule 12.65).
- Further advice should not be provided merely because the client wants a second opinion, if there is less than 6 months between the first and second request for advice and there is no material change in circumstances, or if the client is unable to provide a reasonable explanation for seeking Advice and Assistance from a new solicitor (Contract Specification, Part B, Rule 12.62).
- If Advice and Assistance is provided it may only be reasonable for limited costs to be incurred (especially following a second or subsequent change) and a detailed note must be placed in the file justifying the further advice (Contract Specification, Part A, Rule 4.37).
- Any claims made in contravention of these Rules will either be reduced or disallowed on audit.

B2.3 **Advocacy Assistance**

- *Grant or Refusal of Advocacy Assistance (Contract Specification, Part A, Rule 4.32)*

An application is granted when the solicitor or category supervisor signs the 'Declaration and Grant' section of a properly completed CRM3 which has been signed by the client. The application cannot be granted retrospectively. Refusing to grant Advocacy Assistance is also a Devolved Power.

B2.4 **Counsel**

- *Instruction of Counsel (Contract Specification, Part A, Rule 4.35)*

Counsel may be instructed (in accordance with the Rules) where it is in the interests of the client.

B2.5 **Other Powers**

- *Given telephone advice before the signature on the form (Contract Specification, Part B, Rule 12.19)*

A claim can be made for advising clients over the telephone, provided that:

(a) the client meets the Financial Eligibility Test and the Sufficient Benefit Test, or

(b) the client subsequently signs the CRM1 and 2 or CRM1 and 3
application forms, and is financially eligible.

B2.5.1 `Key points`

- After providing initial advice over the telephone, it will be necessary
  to consider whether to delay any further work until receipt of the
  completed forms.
- A claim cannot be made for ad hoc telephone advice to a client on
  an issue which develops no further or is resolved during the course
  of the telephone call or is resolved by writing an ad hoc piece of correspondence (Contract Specification, Part B, Rule 12.22).
- *Postal Rules (Contract Specification, Part B, Rules 12.17 to 12.18)*

The Part B postal rules override the postal rules in Part A.

B2.5.2 `Key points`

- Wherever possible the client should be sent the relevant application forms by post after instructions are received and before work is
  commenced.
- Advice and Assistance cases should wherever possible be conducted
  by correspondence with the client, or by video-link or telephone if
  such facilities are available.

B3 **Qualifying Criteria**

B3.1 **Means**

All units of work are subject to the client being financially eligible (unless the client is a child) according to the Criminal Legal Aid (Financial Resources) Regulations 2013 (Criminal Financial Regulations 2013).

B3.1.1 **Key points**

- It will always be 'impracticable' for clients in custody to provide proof of income (see Contract Specification, Part A, Rule 3.6). There should be a note on the file.
- Proof of income must be obtained from the client's wife (or partner if they were living together prior to the client's imprisonment) unless the relationship has broken down.
- Prison wages are nominal and as the work is non-contractual prisoners are not provided with wage slips; nonetheless the income should be included on CRM1 and certified as correct on CRM 2.
- Clients in custody will be eligible if their wife or partner is in receipt of a 'passporting' benefit.

B3.2 **Merits**

The Sufficient Benefit Test is the merits test which applies to both Advice and Assistance and Advocacy Assistance. The test must be satisfied before commencing or continuing to work on a matter which falls within its scope. The test is as follows:

> Advice and Assistance and Advocacy Assistance may only be provided on legal issues concerning English and Welsh law and where there is sufficient benefit to the Client, having regard to the circumstances of the Matter, including the personal circumstances of the Client, to justify work or further work being carried out.
>
> There should be realistic prospect of a positive outcome that would be of real benefit to the Client.

B3.2.1 **Key points**

- In all cases there must be a brief note on the file justifying how the Sufficient Benefit Test has been met and continues to be met. This will be checked on audit (Contract Specification, Part B, Rule 12.7).
- Files which do not have a note setting out how the Sufficient Benefit Test has been met and which do not objectively appear to satisfy

the test may be nil-assessed on audit (Contact Specification, Part B, Rule 12.8).

- The Sufficient Benefit Test must be applied as a cost–benefit test ie whether a notional reasonable private paying client of moderate means would pay for the legal Advice and Assistance or Advocacy Assistance (Contract Specification, Part B, Rule 12.10).
- Cases that have minimal or borderline prospects of success but still have some benefit to the client under Advice and Assistance or Advocacy Assistance must be clearly justified on a file note (Contract Specification, Part B, Rule 12.12).
- Cases that have minimal benefit/impact on the client will not satisfy the Sufficient Benefit Test and cannot be claimed as Contract Work (Contract Specification, Rule 12.13).

B4 **Scope**

B4.1 **Sentence Cases**

This Unit of Work can be claimed under Advice and Assistance. The Sufficient Benefit Test is only capable of being satisfied if the work done is in connection with the client's progression through the prison system or concerns issues directly relevant to the client's sentence. A non-exhaustive list of the types of work which could meet the Sufficient Benefit Test includes:

(a) Indeterminate/life sentence planning
(b) Determinate sentence planning
(c) Challenging adverse sentence calculations (not within 6 months of conviction if client represented in the Crown Court under a Representation Order)
(d) Challenging adverse licence conditions
(e) First categorization and allocation arising from initial sentence
(f) Category A reviews
(g) Security categorizations (excluding Category A)
(h) Re-categorization
(i) Re-setting of minimum terms
(j) Accessing offender behaviour courses
(k) Legal issues arising out of Home Detention Curfew, Release on Early Conditional Licence, Release on Temporary Licence and Early Removal Scheme
(l) Challenging transfers to Close Supervision Centres under Prison Rule 46
(m) Matters concerning formal procedures involving consideration of documentation and written representations (Contract Specification, Part B, Rule 12.101)

B4.2 **Discipline Cases**

This Unit of Work covers Advice and Assistance and Advocacy Assistance in proceedings before a Governor/Director or Independent Adjudication and only applies to eligible prisoners post conviction or on remand (Contract Specification, Part B, Rule 12.108).

Advocacy Assistance under this Unit of Work must not be provided if:

(a) It appears unreasonable that approval should be granted in the particular circumstances of the matter or case;
(b) Permission to be legally represented has not been granted by a Governor or other prison authority, where appropriate (in which case the client may only be assisted under Advice and Assistance

by preparing written representations) (Contract Specification, Part B, Rule 12.116).

Advocacy Assistance under this Unit of Work must only be provided where:

(a) Permission for legal representation is granted by the Governor or prison authority; and
(b) There is a note on file confirming that the Sufficient Benefit Test has been met (Contract Specification, Part B, Rule 12.117).

B4.2.1 Key points

- In disciplinary cases (Advocacy Assistance) the Sufficient Benefit Test will not be satisfied where there is no risk that the client will have additional days added to their sentence (Contract Specification, Part B, Rule 12.113).
- For indeterminate or life sentence prisoners the Sufficient Benefit Test is capable of being satisfied where there is a real likelihood that they will be penalized in a way which will have a damaging impact on a future parole review. A note must be placed on the file justifying the grant of Advocacy Assistance (Contract Specification, Part B, Rule 12.114).
- A notional 'interests of justice test' must be applied, in particular, whether:
  (a) The client would, if any matter arising in the proceedings is decided against him/her, be likely to have additional days added to their sentence;
  (b) The determination of any matter arising in the proceedings may involve consideration of a substantial question of law;
  (c) The client may be unable to understand the proceedings or state their own case;
  (d) The proceedings may involve the tracing, interviewing or expert cross-examination of witnesses on behalf of the individual;
  (e) There would be a negative impact on a subsequent parole review or categorization decision.

B4.3 Parole Board Cases

This Unit of Work may only be undertaken on behalf of eligible clients who are convicted prisoners and who require Advice and Assistance and/or Advocacy Assistance in relation to:

(a) Parole Board hearings; or
(b) mandatory life sentences; or
(c) other parole review; or
(d) breach of licence conditions; and
(e) licence recall (Contract Specification, Part B, Rule 12.123).

B4.3.1 Key points

The Sufficient Benefit Test may only be satisfied on a pre-tariff review for a Category A prisoner if it is clearly stated to be in order to protect the client's position, or to prevent a detrimental effect on a subsequent Parole Board review (Contract Specification, Part B, Rule 12.126).

B4.4 Treatment Cases

Prior Approval (Form PL1) is required to provide Advice and Assistance to a client on legal issues relating to their treatment in prison. Few treatment cases are approved. A refusal to grant approval will not prevent a legal representative from providing Advice and Assistance, but the work will either have to be pro bono or on a private basis.

B4.4.1 Key points

- Complaints that are objectively trivial or minor and matters which do not raise significant legal or human rights issues will not be funded (Contract Specification, Part B, Rule 12.86).
- Complaints relating to living conditions in prison will not ordinarily be funded. Such cases should be addressed through the prison internal complaints scheme and the Prisons and Probation Ombudsman (Contract Specification, Part B, Rule 12.87).
- Complaints relating to living conditions may be funded if the client has a severe mental health problem or severe learning difficulties, such that even with the help of other prisoners or staff they will be unable to formulate their complaint adequately (Contract Specification, Part B, Rule 12.88).
- Unless there is a serious human rights dimension or serious mental health problem or severe learning difficulty complaints relating to the following will not be funded:
  (a) Entitlements to rights and privileges;
  (b) Issues arising out of correspondence (except legally privileged correspondence);
  (c) Food (where there is no religious dietary requirement involved);
  (d) Exercise;
  (e) Lost or damaged property;
  (f) Issues arising out of the Incentives and Earned Privileges (IEP) scheme (except where an IEP warning could have a serious impact on parole or progression).

B5 New Matter Starts

B5.1 Overview

Only one Sentence Case or Parole Board for a client can be started at any one time. If Sentence Cases and Parole Board Cases are opened concurrently, each matter must be claimed separately (Contract Specification, Part B, Rule 12.35). Concurrent Treatment Cases and Disciplinary Cases may be commenced provided that they are unrelated and distinct issues or cases. There must be a note on the file justifying the commencement of the second case (Contract Specification, Part B, Rule 12.36).

B5.1.1 Key points

- Disciplinary Cases and Parole Board Cases where it is clear there will be an oral hearing must be started as Advocacy Assistance (Contract Specification, Part B, Rule 12.37).
- Disciplinary Cases and Parole Board Cases, where it is not clear there will be an oral hearing, must be started as Advice and Assistance. If the matter is subsequently listed for an oral hearing the Advice and Assistance costs should be claimed and a fresh Advocacy Assistance started (Contract Specification, Part B, Rule 12.38).
- Advice and Assistance in relation to a review or an appeal is not a new matter if Advice and Assistance has already been provided (Contract Specification, Part B, Rule 12.71).

B6 **Payment**

B6.1 **Advice and Assistance**

Advice and Assistance is paid as a Fixed Fee. Profit and waiting costs (core costs) are calculated using hourly rates as set out in the Criminal Legal Aid (Remuneration) Regulations 2013. Core costs in excess of the Escape Fee Case Threshold are claimable as an Escape Fee Case (Form CRM18A).

B6.1.1 `Key points`

- Escape Fee Cases are assessed and paid at hourly rates.
- Escape Fee Cases must be claimed on Form CRM18A, together with the full file of papers (or photocopy), original CRM11, original completed CRM1 and CRM2 if the claim includes freestanding Advice and Assistance, and original invoices for disbursements.
- To claim a Fixed Fee, costs must equate to 8 Units of Work or more.

B6.2 **Advocacy Assistance—Disciplinary Cases/ Parole Board Cases**

Fees are paid either as a Lower Standard Fee, Higher Standard Fee, or Non-Standard Fee. Profit and waiting costs (core costs) are calculated using hourly rates as set out in the Criminal Remuneration Regulations 2013 to determine the appropriate fee.

B6.2.1 `Key points`

- Core costs below the lower limit will be paid as a Lower Standard Fee.
- Core costs above the lower limit but below the higher fee limit will be paid as a Higher Standard Fee.
- Core costs above the higher fee limit will be assessed and paid as a Non-Standard Fee at hourly rates (Form CRM18A—see **B6.1.1**).
- Different limits apply to Discipline Cases and Parole Board Cases (see Criminal Remuneration Regulations).
- To claim a Lower Standard Fee costs must equate to 8 Units of Work or more.

B6.3 **Disbursements**

Disbursements (including travel disbursements) are payable in addition to the Fixed and Standard Fees, subject to the contract rules including reasonableness. Any single disbursement in excess of £500 requires an application for Prior Authority on Form CRM4.

Counsel's fees (and Agent fees) must be agreed and paid for out of the appropriate Fixed or Standard Fee, and are not claimable as disbursements. Counsel's time should be recorded as part of the claim using the same hourly rates. However, where an Advice and Assistance matter has become an Escape Fee Case Counsel's fees can be claimed as a disbursement.

B6.4 Travel and Waiting Time

Travel time is not included in the calculation to determine whether a case is an Escape Fee Case or a Non-Standard Fee (Contract Specification, Part B, Rule 12.44). It may only be claimed separately on an Escape Fee Case or a Non-Standard Fee Case. Once a case becomes eligible for payment as an Escape Fee Case travel time is claimable but is limited to one hour each way for all journeys (Contract Specification, Part B, Rule 12.45). If the client is moved to another prison further away travel time of up to 3 hours each way may be claimed for any journeys made after the case became eligible for payment as an Escape Fee Case (Contact Specification, Part B, Rules 12.46 to 12.47).

Waiting time only counts towards the calculation of costs to determine whether the case has reached the Escape Fee Case Threshold, or to determine whether the case is a Lower, Higher or Non-Standard Fee.

B7 **Associated Civil Work**

B7.1 **Key Documents**

KD Prison Law Judicial Review 2013

Civil Procedure Regulations 2012

Civil Merits Regulations 2013

Civil Remuneration Regulations 2013

Applications for Judicial Review or Habeas Corpus arising from any matter within the Crime Category are funded as either Controlled Work or Licensed Work. The relevant Civil Contract is the one in force at the time the civil work is commenced. The LAA's Special Cases Unit is responsible for managing Judicial Review cases involving prisoners. Detailed guidance on their approach can be found in the Prison Law Judicial Review 2013.

It is important to be familiar with the Civil Legal Aid (Merits Criteria) Regulations 2013 (Civil Merits Regulations 2013) and Civil Legal Aid (Procedure) Regulations 2012 (Civil Procedure Regulations 2012) and Civil Remuneration Regulations 2013, as specific tests apply to Judicial Review funding applications. Clients in receipt of a 'passporting' benefit automatically satisfy the means test for all levels of funding.

B7.2 **Controlled Work—Legal Help**

Legal Help (CW1) covers Advice and Assistance and case preparation. The Sufficient Benefit Test must be met:

> Help may only be provided where there is sufficient benefit to the client, having regard to the circumstances of the matter, including the personal circumstances of the client, to justify work or further work being carried out.

The Standard Fee is inclusive of profit costs, and travel and waiting time. Disbursements may be claimed separately. If the amount of the claim is likely to exceed the Escape Fee Threshold (calculated on the basis of hourly rates), an application can be made for the claim to be treated to as an Escape Fee Case. The application to extend the financial limit must be made before the limit has been reached. Escape Fee Cases are remunerated on the basis of hourly rates (see Civil (Remuneration) Regulations 2013). If the application is refused an appeal can be submitted to an Independent Costs Assessor and/or the Costs Appeal Committee on a point of principle.

B7.3 Licensed Work—Investigative Help

Investigative Help is designed to bridge the gap between Legal Help and Full Representation. An application for Investigative Help (using CIVAPP1 and CIVMEANS1) will be appropriate in cases where the prospects of success are unclear and substantial investigative work will be required before an application for Full Representation can be submitted. There must also be reasonable grounds for believing that when the investigative work has been carried out the claim will be strong enough in terms of prospects of success and costs benefit (see **B7.4.1**) to meet the criteria for Full Representation.

Certificates for Investigative Help will usually be limited to making further enquiries, if appropriate obtaining Counsel's opinion on the merits, sending a full Letter Before Claim, and responding to the Reply. In straightforward cases an application for Investigative Help may be refused if it is reasonable for the Letter Before Claim to be sent under Legal Help.

B7.4 Licensed Work—Representation Certificate

Applications for Judicial Review are made on CIVAPP1 and CIVMEANS1. The application will need to include sufficient details of the facts of the case. If a witness statement has been obtained this should be attached to the application form together with a copy of any Letter Before Claim in accordance with the Pre-Action Protocol, the response if applicable, and any other relevant material.

B7.4.1 Key points

- Judicial Review must be available (ie the challenge must relate to a decision of a public body exercising a public function and must be submitted within time);
- Any genuine alternative remedies must have been exhausted;
- The respondent must have been given a reasonable opportunity to respond to the challenge or to deal with the applicant's complaint unless this was impracticable in the circumstances;
- Full Representation will be granted if these criteria have been met and the prospects of successfully obtaining a substantive order are:
  - (a) Very good (80% or more)
  - (b) Good (60–80%)
  - (c) Moderate (50–60%)
- Full Representation will be refused if the prospects of successfully obtaining the substantive order sought are:
  - (a) Unclear (consider application for Investigative Help);

   (b) Borderline (prospects of success are not poor but, because there are difficult disputes of law, fact or expert evidence it is not possible to say prospects of success are better than 50%) and the case does not appear to have significant wider public interest, to be of overwhelming importance to the client or to raise significant human rights issues; or

   (c) Poor (prospects of success are clearly less than 50%) (Civil Merits Regulations 2013, Rule 58(3)).

- Full Representation may be refused unless the likely costs are proportionate to the likely benefits of the proceedings, having regard to the prospects of success and all other circumstances (Civil Merits Regulations 2013, Rule 58(2)).

Certificates for Full Representation will initially be limited to applying for Permission on the papers and, if granted all steps up until receipt of the respondent's evidence and Counsel's opinion. If Permission is subsequently granted, the Certificate will be extended to cover the oral hearing.

B7.5 Emergency Applications

The tight timescale for making Judicial Review claims may require an application for funding to be made as an emergency. Urgent applications can be made by fax on forms CIVAPP6 and CIVMEANS1. This is only justified where work must be completed within days rather than weeks.

Part C
The Prison Regime

C1 **Overview**

Within a few weeks of sentence, categorization and allocation decisions will be made, sentence planning will have begun and for determinate prisoners the sentence will have been calculated. Categorization decisions are of critical importance as they determine entitlements, parole decisions and the prison regime.

These decisions frequently form the basis of complaints. Other complaints tend to relate to the day-to-day living conditions within prisons, which vary significantly between institutions.

All prison establishments have a duty to deal with prisoners' complaints. The Prison Rules vest this duty in the Governor and the Independent Monitoring Board (IMB) under Rule 11 and Rule 78.

Each prison has its own IMB, which must decide its own detailed procedures taking into account statutory requirements, best practice, PSI 02/2012 and local circumstances. The IMB's statutory duty is to ensure that prisoners are being treated properly, which includes hearing requests and complaints. At any stage a prisoner can ask the IMB to consider a request or a complaint, or to review a response to either. Prisoners can also complain directly to the Chair of the IMB about any matter covered by 'confidential access'.

C2 **Prisoner Categories**

C2.1 **Key Documents**

KD PSI 05/2013 (Initial Categorization—Category A and Restricted Status)

PSI 39/2011 (Adult Females)

PSI 40/2011 (Adult Males)

PSI 41/2011 (Young Adult Males)

PSI 56/2011

The Secretary of State is required to categorize prisoners (Prison Rules, rule 7(1)). There are four main categories for male adult prisoners:

- *Category A* for prisoners whose escape would be highly dangerous to the public, the police or the security of the state, and for whom the aim must be to make escape impossible. This is the only category that applies to all prisoners: remand, male, female, adult and juvenile. These prisoners are centrally managed by the Director of High Security (DHS). Recommendations for upgrading or downgrading are made by the Category A Team. Within Category A there are three escape risk classifications:
  - *Standard Escape Risk* prisoners who have been charged with a serious offence which would make them highly dangerous if at large. However, there is no specific internal or external intelligence that suggests that an attempt to escape is likely. Most Category A prisoners are standard risk.
  - *High Escape Risk* prisoners who meet the standard risk classification however, there are one or more factors present which suggest that the prisoner may pose an enhanced risk. The factors include:
    - access to finances, resources and/or associates that could assist an escape attempt
    - position in an organized crime group
    - nature of current/previous offending
    - links to terrorist network
    - previous escape(s) from custody
    - at least one of the above factors plus predictable escorts to be undertaken (eg court production, hospital treatment)
    - length of time to serve (where any of the other factors noted are also present)
  - *Exceptional Escape Risk* prisoners who meet the high risk classification however, there is recent internal or external intelligence that suggests that an escape is being planned and the threat is such

that heightened security conditions are required to mitigate this risk (PSI 05/2013, paragraph 2.8).
- *Category B* for prisoners who do not require the highest conditions of security, but for whom escape must be made very difficult.
- *Category C* for prisoners who cannot be trusted in open conditions, but who do not have the resources or will to make an escape attempt.
- *Category D* for prisoners who can be reasonably trusted in open conditions and for whom open conditions are appropriate.

C2.2 Young Offenders

Young adult prisoners may be held in four security categories:

- *Category A* for prisoners whose escape would be highly dangerous to the public, the police or the security of the state, and for whom the aim must be to make escape impossible.
- *Restricted Status* for prisoners whose escape would present a serious risk to the public and who are required to be held in designated secure accommodation. Although potentially highly dangerous they are seen as lacking the capacity or propensity to plan or effect an escape from secure conditions.
- *Closed Conditions* for prisoners for whom the highest conditions of security are not necessary but who present too high a risk for open conditions or for whom open conditions are not appropriate.
- *Open Conditions* for prisoners who present a low risk, can be reasonably trusted in open conditions and for whom open conditions are appropriate.

C2.3 Female Prisoners

Women prisoners may be held in the same four security categories as those described for young adult prisoners at **C2.2**.

C2.4 Escape List Prisoners

Prisoners who have recently escaped from prison or where there is intelligence that they are likely to mount an escape attempt may be placed on the Escape List, also known as the 'E' List, by the Governor.

Although it is not a security category in itself, it affects categorization decisions as 'E' List prisoners must be at least Category B. Such prisoners are subject to stringent security measures and are required to wear distinctive marked clothing. Reasons for being placed on the 'E' List must be given in writing and reviewed at least every 28 days (PSI 56/2011, paragraph 5.1).

C3 Initial Categorization and Allocation—Category A

C3.1 Key Documents

KD PSI 05/2013 (Initial Categorization—Category A and Restricted Status)

PSI 39/2011 (Adult Females)

PSI 40/2011 (Adult Males)

PSI 41/2011 (Young Adult Males)

C3.2 Provisional Category A or Restricted Status

Remand prisoners, prisoners received into custody for the first time and prisoners in custody at any other time may be classified as potential Category A, provisional Category A, or confirmed Category A prisoners on reception into prison if charged with serious violent, sexual or drug-related offences (PSI 05/2013, paragraph 2.4). A Restricted Status is any female, young person or young adult prisoner convicted or on remand whose escape would present a serious risk to the public and who is required to be held in designated secure accommodation (PSI 05/2013, paragraph 2.5).

Prison staff must obtain as much information as possible to determine the prisoner's suitability for provisional Category A or Restricted Status. This information is primarily obtained from the officer in charge of the case and may include whether the victim was known to the prisoner, possible motives, extent of any violence, whether weapons were used, drugs and alcohol consumption and any information known about the prisoner's mental state.

Having considered this information prison staff are required to report to the DDHS any prisoner who is believed to meet the criteria for potential Category A or Restricted Status.

C3.3 Indicative Offences

Offences which contain features indicative of consideration for Category A are set out in the following extract:

PSI 05/2013 The Identification, Initial Categorisation and Management of Potential and Provisional Category A / Restricted Status Prisoners

Criteria for reporting in a Potential Category A / Restricted Status Prisoner 3.2

Offence Type	Offences	Indicative of Consideration for Category A
Violence	• Murder • Attempted Murder • Manslaughter • Rape • Attempted Rape • Sexual Assault • Robbery (firearm) • Robbery • Wounding with intent • Kidnapping	• Victim unknown • Random/unprovoked attack • Extreme/sadistic/frenzied violence • Life threatening violence/injuries • Firearm discharged in a public place • Carried out for financial gain • Serial/repeat offences • Escalation in offending behaviour
Sexual Offences	• Rape • Attempted Rape • Buggery • Sexual Assault	• Victim unknown • Random/unprovoked attack • Extreme/sadistic/ritualistic violence • Life threatening injuries • Weapons used • Repeat/serial offences • Previous sexual offending • Escalation in offending behaviour
Robbery and Offences	• Robbery • Conspiracy to rob with firearms • Possession of a firearm • Possession of ammunition	• Firearms present or found subsequently • Firearm discharged in public place • Firearm discharged at person(s) • Significant amount of money stolen • Significant standing in an Organised Crime Group • Professional armed robbery • Serial/repeat offences • Escalation in offending behaviour
Importation of Class A Drugs (including conspiracy)	• Importation of class A drugs • Conspiracy to import class A drugs • Possession of drugs with intent to supply	• Drugs valued in excess of £10M • Conspiracy to import drugs in excess of £10M • Firearms used/present • Significant standing in an Organised Crime Group • Repeat Offences

Possession WI to Supply Explosives	• MUST BE REPORTED IN	• MUST BE REPORTED IN
Offences Connected with Terrorism	MUST BE REPORTED IN	MUST BE REPORTED IN
Offences Under the Official Secrets Act	MUST BE REPORTED IN	MUST BE REPORTED IN

C3.4 Non-indicative Offences

Prisoners who are not charged or convicted of any of the offences listed at **C3.3**, may nonetheless be reported to the DHS if at any stage special features are identified which justify consideration for Category A or Restricted Status.

PSI 05/2013 The Identification, Initial Categorisation and Management of Potential and Provisional Category A / Restricted Status Prisoners

These might include a prisoner:

3.9.1 who, during a sentence, is charged with or convicted of any offence which meets the criteria set out in the table at 3.2;

3.9.2 who is the subject of new information or intelligence which suggests that Category A must be considered regardless of current offence/ charges;

3.9.3 who is behaving in prison in a way which suggests that escape would be highly dangerous to the public, the police or the state;

3.9.4 where there are reasonable grounds to believe a prisoner is under suspicion / investigation of an offence that meets the Category A / Restricted Status criteria;

3.9.5 where there is intelligence that a prisoner holds a significant position in an organised crime group; has links to terrorist networks; or would otherwise be highly dangerous if at large.

3.9.6 who is the co-defendant of another prisoner who has been made Category A / Restricted Status.

C3.5 Pending Decision

While a formal decision is pending the prisoner may be treated as if they are provisional Category A or Restricted Status prisoners in agreement with the Category A Team. Prisons outside the high security estate usually hold such prisoners in the segregation unit whilst awaiting a decision from the DDHS (PSI 05/2013, paragraph 4.13).

C3.6 **The Decision**

The Category A Team will consider the report and decide within 3 working days whether the prisoner should be placed provisionally in Category A or Restricted Status (PSI 05/2013, paragraph 3.14). The decision will be communicated to the prison together with any special instructions about security.

C3.7 **Allocation**

If, as a result of the classification, the prisoner needs to be moved to a high security prison, this transfer should take place as soon as possible, and no later than 3 days after the classification has been made. The Category A Team will make arrangements to move high or exceptional risk prisoners as a priority.

C4 **Re-categorization and Re-allocation—Category A**

C4.1 **Key Documents**

KD PSI 08/2013 (Initial Categorization—Category A and Restricted Status)

PSI 39/2011 (Adult Females)

PSI 40/2011 (Adult Males)

PSI 41/2011 (Young Adult Males)

C4.2 **Preliminary Reviews**

The Category A Team will review the security category of each provisional Category A or Restricted Status prisoner on remand:

> **PSI 08/2013 The Review of Security Category – Category A / Restricted Status Prisoners**
>
> **Reviews of Provisional Category A and Restricted Status Prisoners General**
>
> 3.1 The Category A Team will ensure that the following reviews of Provisional Category A and Restricted Status prisoners take place:
> - <u>During remand periods</u> - review of security category every 12 months, or sooner if there is new information to indicate that Category A or Restricted Status may no longer be warranted; and reviews of escape risk classifications every 6 months for high risk and every 3 months for exceptional risk.
> - <u>Immediately following conviction and sentence</u> - review of security category; if the prisoner remains Category A, this will be followed by:
> - <u>First Formal Review</u> - this normally takes place approximately 3 months after conviction and sentence. If the decision is that the prisoner should continue to be Category A/Restricted Status, then the prisoner is a confirmed Category A/Restricted Status.

The Category A Team should send the prisoner notification of the decision within 4 weeks of the review. Any recommendations to downgrade must be forwarded to the Director for a final decision (PSI 08/2013, paragraph 3.7).

C4.3 **First Formal Review**

All provisional Category A and Restricted Status prisoners must be reviewed as soon as practicable after conviction and sentence.

The Category A Team will prepare a review dossier based on the court records (including serious charges not resulting in conviction, and convictions based on a lesser role than previously indicated), the judge's sentencing remarks, the prisoner's previous convictions, if any, and information from the police. The prisoner will be given a copy of the disclosure and normally allowed a month to submit representations (PSI 08/2013, paragraph 3.19).

The prisoner should be notified of the outcome of the review within 4 weeks of the panel meeting (PSI 08/2013, paragraph 3.27). It is highly likely that the prisoner's Category A/Restricted Status will be confirmed at this stage, as the decision will be based on much of the same information that was used to determine the prisoner's provisional status.

Downgrades at this stage are only likely if the charges were reduced or a significantly lesser sentence was imposed.

C4.4 First Annual Review

The first annual review of categorization must take place 2 years after completion of the first formal review unless:

- the Director ordered at the first formal review that the prisoner's first annual review should take place earlier; or
- the Governor of the holding prison decides the prisoner's first annual review should take place earlier on the basis of exceptional risk reduction (PSI 08/2013, paragraph 4.8).

Prison staff will prepare individual reports using the forms at Annex B of PSI 08/2013. The assessments include offending history, prison history, offence-related work, psychology, mental health, security information and drugs. The authors cannot make any recommendations. The reports are disclosed to the prisoner who is invited to submit representations within 4 weeks, although this can be extended at the prison's discretion. Sensitive information relevant to the issue of categorization will be included in section 7 of the forms, but will be withheld from the prisoner (PSI 08/2013, paragraph 4.21). Information should only be withheld if it falls within an exemption under the Data Protection Act (DPA) 1998, eg disclosure would prejudice the prevention or detection of crime, which includes crimes committed in prison.

C4.5 The Decision

The initial recommendation will be made by the Local Advisory Panel (LAP) which should be made up of the Governor and appropriate report-writing staff (PSI 08/2013, paragraph 4.22). The LAP will consider the reports and the prisoner's representations. See *R (on the application of Ferguson) v Secretary of State for Justice* [2011] EWHC 5 (Admin) where it was held that the LAP was entitled to rely upon further internal advice from a prison psychologist, which had not been disclosed to the prisoner.

The final decision will be based on the Category A Review Team's consideration of the documents and the Governor's recommendation. Any factual errors identified by the prisoner ought to be resolved (if possible) by the time the matter is referred to the review team. If the Category A Review Team supports a recommendation for maintaining Category A status the decision will be made and issued by the head of the review team (PSI 08/2013, paragraph 4.27).

The final decision will be referred to the DDHS and an advisory panel (who normally meet once a month) in the following circumstances:

> ### PSI 08/2013 The Review of Security Category – Category A / Restricted Status Prisoners
> #### Referral of Annual Reviews to the DDC High Security
> 4.29 The Category A Team may alternatively refer a case to the DDC High Security (or delegated authority) and the next available monthly Category A panel if:
> - the LAP or Category A Team recommends the prisoner should be downgraded;
> - the DDC High Security (or delegated authority) has made a special request at the previous review that the case should be referred to the DDC High Security (or delegated authority) and the DDC's panel;
> - the prisoner has recently moved from Restricted Status within a YOI to Category A status within a high security prison;
> - the DDC High Security (or delegated authority) has not reviewed the prisoner's case for five years. This will ensure that the DDC High Security (or delegated authority) considers all Category A / Restricted Status prisoners for downgrading at least every five years.

The notification must provide detailed reasons for the decision. In exceptional circumstances frailty and ill-health may justify placing a high-risk prisoner in Category B (*R (on the application of Pate) v Secretary of State for the Home Department* [2002] EWHC 1018). However, see *R (on the application of Roberts) v Secretary of State for the Home Department* [2004] EWHC 679 (Admin) where Elias J held that it was a legitimate policy for the Home Office to seek to eliminate any risk of escape.

See also *R (Lynch) v Secretary of State for Justice* [2008] EWHC 2697 (Admin) where the High Court found the re-categorization decision to be flawed as the decision-makers failed to take material factors into account.

C4.6 Oral Hearings

The DDHS can grant an oral hearing of a Category A or Restricted Status prisoner's annual review if there are exceptional circumstances that suggest that oral submissions would be the fairest means of determining the prisoner's suitability for downgrading (PSI 08/2013, paragraph 4.7). The appropriateness and format of an oral hearing is at the Director's discretion. However, common law principles of procedural fairness may make an oral hearing necessary—see *R (DM) v Secretary of State for Justice* [2011] EWCA Civ 522. In *R (Fox) v Secretary of State for Justice* [2012] EWHC 2411 the Category A Team considered that 'there were no exceptional circumstances which necessitated an oral hearing in the interests of fairness'. The court held that the 'exceptionality test' was wrong; the test is fairness. Although oral hearings are likely to be rare, in the circumstances of this case procedural fairness required an oral hearing as the claimant was 68 years old, had served 18 years against a 10-year minimum term and had initially been granted approval for a particular programme.

A decision to refuse a request for an oral hearing will only be interfered with if it is wrong (not unreasonable or irrational)—see *R (Lynch) v Secretary of State for the Home Department* [2012] EWHC 1597 (Admin) QBD.

C4.7 Further Reviews

After the first annual review Category A and Restricted Status prisoners must be reviewed annually. The procedure is the same as for first annual reviews. Categorization reviews are often timed to coincide with other reviews such as sentence planning and parole reviews. Category A and Restricted Status reviews may be deferred in exceptional cases, subject to the consent of prison staff and the Category A Team, eg, to enable the prisoner to complete an offender behaviour programme. A deferred annual review should not normally affect the timing of subsequent annual reviews (PSI 08/2013, paragraph 4.13).

C5 Initial Categorization and Allocation—Non-Category A

C5.1 Key Documents

KD PSI 39/2011 (Adult Females)

PSI 40/2011 (Adult Males)

PSI 41/2011 (Young Adult Males)

C5.2 Remand Prisoners

All prisoners on remand awaiting trial are presumed innocent. The prison's sole function is to hold them in readiness for their next appearance at court. Prisoners on remand or convicted and awaiting sentence, other than those provisionally classified as Category A are unclassified. Most adult male remand prisoners will serve their remand time in a Category B establishment, although in theory there is no reason why they could not be allocated to a Category C prison. Remand prisoners and un-sentenced prisoners remain unclassified, regardless of their current location until they have been given a definite category, following which they may be reallocated.

C5.3 Convicted and Sentenced Prisoners

The categorization of all non-Category A prisoners is carried out by prison staff. Prisoners are categorized according to the likelihood that they will seek to escape, the risk that they would pose should they succeed, the safety of others within the prison and the need to maintain good order.

All convicted and sentenced prisoners including those serving indeterminate sentences must be categorized within 4 working days of all essential documents being received. Documents essential to the categorization process are:

(i)   Previous convictions (if any)
(ii)   Details of current offence(s)
(iii) Current custodial record
(iv)   Previous record (if available)
(v)   Prisoners security file
(vi)   Public protection information (MAPPA) if available
(vii) Person escort report (PER form)
(viii) Offender Assessment System (OASys) (if opened prior to sentence)
(ix)   Request for information from UK Border Agency

Any documents other than those in this list, which are referred to as part of the assessment, must be listed on the form. This is to ensure the prisoner is aware of the information that was considered in the event that he or she chooses to challenge the categorization decision. A copy of the categorization form must be disclosed to the prisoner if he or she requests it. If the prisoner has difficulty understanding the form, the reasons for the decision must be explained to him or her verbally.

C5.3.1 Key points

- All prisoners must be placed in the lowest category consistent with the needs of security and control.
- A prisoner must be assigned to the correct security category and no adjustment must be made to match prisoners to available places.
- Categorization decisions must be fair, consistent and objective.
- Categorization decisions are individual risk assessments which must be reached in line with current policy and without bias or any other irrelevant factor.
- Prisoners sentenced to determinate sentences of less than 12 months must be considered for categorization to Category D.

C5.4 Allocation

C5.4.1 Key points

- Allocation and categorization are separate processes, although the same form will be used by the same officer, often on the same day.
- Where it is in the prisoner's own best interests (eg, to access offender behaviour courses) or where there is overcrowding, a prisoner may be allocated or retained in a prison of a higher category than his or her classification.
- Prisoners sentenced to determinate sentences of less than 2 months must be considered for allocation to open conditions as soon as possible after sentencing, subject to a requirement that they spend at least 7 days in closed conditions.

C6 **Re-categorization and Re-allocation—Non-Category A**

C6.1 **Key Documents**

KD PSI 39/2011 (Adult Females)

PSI 40/2011 (Adult Males)

PSI 41/2011 (Young Adult Males)

C6.2 **Purpose**

The purpose of re-categorization is to determine whether, and to what extent, there has been a clear change in the risk the prisoner presents since the last review and to ensure he continues to be held in the most appropriate conditions of security.

Allocation is a separate process, the purpose of which is to assign the prisoner to a suitably secure establishment which best meets his or her needs insofar as the pressures on the estate allow.

C6.2.1 Key points

- Risk levels may increase or decrease depending on individual circumstances and the prisoner's security category must reflect this.
- Re-categorization to a lower security category is not an automatic progression or right but must be based on clear evidence of reduction in previously identified risk levels to a level that is manageable in an establishment of the lower category.
- Decisions to re-categorize a prisoner to Category D/Open Conditions must be based on the prisoner's proven trustworthiness and manageable risks.
- Two years is considered to be the maximum time a prisoner should spend in open conditions. However, assessment of a prisoner's individual needs may support an early re-categorization.
- Young adult male prisoners must be risk assessed in the months preceding the attainment of adult status, the aim being to transfer the prisoner on, or soon after his twenty-first birthday save for exceptional or compassionate reasons. However, the prisoner must be transferred to the adult estate before he reaches 22.

See *R (Adetoro) v Secretary of State for Justice and Parole Board* [2012] EWHC 2576 where the Secretary of State's attempt to rescind the initial acceptance of the Parole Board's recommendation of a transfer to open conditions without inviting submissions was found to be inherently unfair.

It is the practice of the Secretary of State to accept recommendations for open conditions unless the recommendation was based on erroneous material or entirely unreasonable. See *R (Wilmot) v Secretary of State for Justice* [2012] EWHC 3139.

C6.3 Timing of Reviews

All prisoners (other than those already categorized as Category D or Open Conditions, those serving less than 12 months, prisoners serving indeterminate sentences and young male adult prisoners) must have their status reviewed at regular prescribed intervals.

Prisoners in the open estate, Category D prisoners held in the closed estate and young male adult prisoners will be reviewed only if there is a change in their circumstances, their behaviour gives cause for concern, or when new information or intelligence suggests an increase in risk levels.

The timing of a prisoner's recategorization review must not be withheld or delayed to await the outcome of a Parole Board hearing, as it could unfairly prejudice the prisoner's chances of success.

C6.3.1 *Annual review*

The following prisoners will be reviewed annually:

- Prisoners serving indeterminate sentences
- Determinate sentence prisoners serving 4 years or more
- Extended Sentence for Public Protection prisoners (EPP) serving 4 years or more

C6.3.2 *Six-month review*

The following prisoners will be reviewed at 6 monthly intervals:

- Prisoners serving a determinate sentence of 12 months or more but less than 4 years
- EPP serving less than 4 years
- Prisoners in the last 24 months of their sentence

C6.4 Recalled Prisoners

Recalled prisoners must be reviewed within 4 working days of the Parole Board or Justice Secretary making a decision in their case.

Where possible it is preferable for recalled prisoners to remain in the prison of their reception until the completion of their first recall review. Once the Parole Board or the Justice Secretary has made a decision, recalled prisoners may be categorized in the normal way. In addition to the normal procedures and risk assessments carried out at the review stage, the assessment must take account of:

(i)   The prisoner's security category at original release;
(ii)   The circumstances resulting in the recall;
(iii) The length of time the prisoner was on licence prior to recall;
(iv)   The number of times the prisoner has been recalled;
(v)   Comments (specifically relating to risk) made by the Parole Board;
(vi)   Time to serve.

C6.5 Non-routine Categorization

A significant change in circumstances could justify a review outside the normal cycle or for prisoners who are not subject to routine reviews. Significant changes may include:

PSI 40/2011 Categorisation and Recategorisation of Adult Male Prisoners

SECTION 5: RECATEGORISATION AND ALLOCATION

5.1 The purpose of the recategorisation process is to determine whether, and to what extent, there has been a clear change in the risks a prisoner presented at his last review and to ensure that he continues to be held in the most appropriate conditions of security.

Allocation often follows immediately after recategorisation but is a separate process, the purpose of which is to assign the prisoner to a suitably secure establishment which best meets his needs insofar as pressures on the estate allow.

. . .

5.9

- there is a change in circumstances or behaviour which indicates an urgent threat to prison security or the good order of the establishment
- intelligence indicating involvement in ongoing serious criminality
- further charges of a serious nature indicate that the prisoner requires a higher level of security
- a notice of deportation is served
- a Confiscation Order is enforced
- a Serious Crime Prevention Order (SCPO) is imposed
- new or additional information comes to light. For example, during completion or updating the OASys assessment which highlights additional risk factors
- there is cause for concern that the current categorisation decision is unsound. *(There must be corroborative evidence to support that concern)*
- the prisoner has completed a successful ROTL
- serious ROTL failure

- a sentence/tariff is reduced on appeal
- a key piece of offending behaviour work is completed, or there has been a successful detoxification or opiate substitute maintenance regime
- a prisoner is recalled to custody
- a prisoner is returned to prison custody from a Special Hospital.

Similar criteria apply to female adult prisoners (PSI 39/2011) and young adult males (PSI 41/2011).

The RC1 form must be completed even in an emergency. If as a result of an urgent re-categorization, the prisoner is reallocated, the documentation should be forwarded to the new prison as soon as possible. This policy was introduced following *R v Governor of HM Latchmere House, ex p Jarvis* (unreported, 20 July 1999) where it was held that a transfer for good order or discipline was unlawful as the re-categorization procedure had not been followed. The court also noted that there did not appear to be any emergency which justified dispensing with the normal procedure.

Discretionary lifers who have served the minimum term should be given the opportunity to make formal representations when re-categorization is being considered. If the decision is taken in an emergency the prisoner should be given the opportunity to make representations as soon as reasonably possible thereafter: *Hirst v Secretary of State for the Home Department* [2001] EWCA Civ 378. The Court of Appeal in the *Hirst* case concluded that the transfer (from a Category C to a Category B prison) could have taken place for operational reasons and therefore the re-categorization could have been delayed which would have given the prisoner the opportunity to make representations. The ruling in the *Hirst* case is very narrow and does not apply to other categories of prisoner.

Prisoners who are not post-tariff discretionary lifers will not have the opportunity to make representations, which was held to be lawful in *R (on the application of McLeod) v HM Prison Service* [2002] EWHC 290 (Admin). In *Palmer v Secretary of State for the Home Department* [2004] EWHC 1817 (Admin) the submission that determinate prisoners should also have the right to make representations prior to re-categorization was rejected on the grounds that the right to be provided with written reasons and to appeal an adverse decision, adequately safeguard procedural fairness.

C6.6 Foreign National Prisoners

The categorization procedure applies equally to British citizens and foreign national prisoners. However, in assessing whether a foreign national prisoner should be downgraded to Category D/Open

Conditions, the decision-maker must assume that deportation will take place and the effect that would have on the risk of escaping or absconding, unless a decision not to deport has already been taken.

The policy guidance on the categorization and allocation of foreign national prisoners is in PSI 52/2011.

C6.7 Mother and Baby Units

Rule 12(2) of the Prison Rules (YOI Rules, rule 25) gives the Secretary of State the authority to allow women prisoners to keep their babies with them, subject to appropriate conditions. The policy on Mother and Baby Units (MBUs) is in PSI 54/2011. Pregnant women and women with children under the age of 18 months are eligible to apply for a place in an MBU. This applies to both remand and convicted prisoners.

There are currently 7 MBUs. The units in Askham Grange, Bronzefield, Eastwood Park, Peterborough and Styal accommodate mothers and babies up to 18 months old. The age limit for babies at Holloway and New Hall is 9 months.

As part of the application procedure a dossier will be compiled, which will include a report from social services. The application will then be considered by a multi-disciplinary admissions board. The mother should be present at the board meeting, but if she is unable to attend she should be given the opportunity to make a full written submission. Applications must be considered on the merits of the individual case, but admission will only be granted if the following criteria are met:

- It is in the best interests of the child/children to be placed in an MBU.
- The mother is able to demonstrate behaviours and attitudes that are not detrimental to the safety and well-being of other unit residents (or the good order and discipline of the unit).
- The mother has provided a urine sample that tests negative for illicit drugs.
- The mother is willing to sign a standard compact, which may be tailored to her individual needs.
- The mother's eligibility and eligibility to care for her child is not impaired by poor health, or for legal reasons such as the child being in care or on the Child Protection Register as a result of the mother's treatment of that child, or other children in care (PSI 54/2011, paragraph 2.2.5).

PSI 54/2011 reflects the decisions of two important cases. In *R (on the application of P and Q) v Secretary of State for the Home Department* [2001] 1 WLR 2002, the Court of Appeal held that rigid adherence to the 18-month age limit may contravene the Prison Service's own policy to promote the welfare of the child and breach ECHR Article 8 (right to family life), as there will be exceptional circumstances where it would be in the best interests of the mother and child to remain in the MBU beyond the child's eighteenth month. The court ruled that the decision with regards to *P* was not disproportionate as she was serving a long sentence and had a significant proportion of that sentence left to serve, and would therefore have to be separated from her child at some stage. However, Q's appeal was allowed, as she was serving a short sentence, and did not have adequate childcare arrangements in place.

Contested separations are referred to the central management team and Separations Boards for consideration.

C7 Challenging Categorization and Allocation Decisions

Some of the common categorization and allocation complaints raised by prisoners are as follows:

- refusal to downgrade;
- an emergency upgrade;
- no reasons given;
- dissatisfaction with reasons;
- factual errors in reports or documents;
- refusal to conduct early review;
- dissatisfaction with allocation.

C7.1 Obtaining Disclosure

Challenging adverse categorization or allocation decisions will often require more information than the client is able to provide in an initial phone call or letter, and therefore the document which informed the decision will need to be obtained.

Disclosure in the form of a 'gist' was introduced following the decision in *R v Secretary of State for the Home Department, ex p Duggan* [1994] 3 All ER 277. However, following the case of *R (Lord) v Secretary of State for the Home Department* [2003] EWHC 2073 (Admin), Category A prisoners became entitled to full disclosure of the reports subject to public interest immunity under section 7 DPA 1998, and it was held that in rare cases where it was appropriate to withhold certain information the 'gist' should, in compliance with the principles set out in *Duggan*, state whether the views expressed are unanimous or not, indicate the numbers of views for or against if opinions are divided, and summarize each of the reported views. As a consequence (except where security information and reports from the police are concerned), all Category A convicted prisoners are able to make meaningful representations and challenge contradictions or inaccuracies where necessary.

Non-Category A prisoners do not have the same rights and entitlements. There is a duty to give reasons for adverse decisions, but the courts have argued that to adopt the procedural fairness requirements that apply to Category A prisoners (eg automatic disclosure and the right to make representations) would add an unnecessary and disproportionate administrative burden on the Prison Service. The only exception applies to the re-categorization of discretionary lifers who have served the minimum term, following the decision in *Hirst v Secretary of State for the Home Department* [2001] EWCA Civ 378.

The court in the *Hirst* case recognized that re-categorization of a discretionary lifer from Category C to Category B would have an adverse effect on the prisoner's release prospects. Although the impact of this case is confined to discretionary lifers post-tariff, the arguments in favour of the right to make representations equally apply to other categories of prisoner, and therefore this distinction is somewhat artificial and may not be sustainable.

Notwithstanding the distinction between Category A and non-Category A prisoners, categorization and allocation are open processes and there should be no difficulty in obtaining disclosure. An authority should be enclosed with the written request for disclosure, however if the matter is urgent the letter of request should explain the reason for its absence, and ask for the consent to be obtained directly from the client. The following should be obtained:

- copies of the relevant forms (ie First Review, Annual Review, ICA1/ICA2/ICA3, RC1/RC3);
- copies of any other reports which informed the decision;
- clients instructions;
- witness statements, if appropriate.

C7.2 Non-disclosure

PSI 40/2011 Categorization and Recategorization of Adult Male Prisoners

3.5 Withholding Information

- Information relevant to the categorisation decision may be withheld from the prisoner in certain circumstances:
  (i) in the interests of national security;
  (ii) for the prevention of crime or disorder, including information relevant to prison security;
  (iii) for the protection of a third party who may be put at risk if the information is disclosed;
  (iv) if, on medical or psychiatric grounds, it is felt necessary to withhold information where the mental and or physical health of the prisoner could be impaired;
  (v) where the source of the information is a victim, and disclosure without their consent would breach any duty of confidence owed to that victim, or would generally prejudice the future supply of such information.
- *In such cases, the information to be withheld must be recorded separate from the main form. Consideration must be given to disclosing a summary of the information or an edited form that protects the anonymity of the informant. Where information that impacts on the categorisation decision is withheld from the prisoner, the form must nonetheless record that other information has been considered along*

with a brief description of the type of information (i.e. SIR) as far as is compatible with maintaining security / protecting other persons.
- Under the Data Protection Act 1998, prisoners are entitled to request a copy of all of their personal data. The Prison Service has a statutory duty to disclose such data subject to a number of exemptions. PSO 9020 Data Protection gives further information.

C7.3 Complaints Procedure

Appealing a decision through the complaints procedure is the main and often the only way that a prisoner can seek redress. If there is some substance to the complaint clients should be encouraged to utilize the Requests and Complaints procedure. It may be appropriate to submit written representations in support of the complaint, subject to funding limitations. For publicly funded cases the Sufficient Benefit Test should continue to be applied. If it is not appropriate to make written representations, the client will be free to pursue the complaint without legal assistance.

No prisoner has the right to be allocated to a particular prison of his choice, although the Prison Rules, rule 4(1) provides that 'Special attention shall be paid to the maintenance of such relationships between a prisoner and his family as are desirable in the best interests of both.' Requests for transfers should be made through the Requests procedure, or through whatever local arrangements are in place. Routine applications for transfer are less likely to be granted in the present climate of severe prison overcrowding. However, the application should be given priority if, eg, the client is the victim of bullying, or the main visitor has medical problems that make normal visiting impossible (a medical report should be obtained).

Domestic courts are reluctant to interfere with decisions made for operational or security reasons, and applications to the European Court under ECHR Article 8 (right to private and family life) have been rejected on the grounds that interference with this right is justified, in the interests of national security, public safety or the economic well-being of the country.

C7.4 Judicial Review

In general the courts are reluctant to interfere with administrative decisions of prison Governors, particularly decisions that do not appear to have a direct impact on liberty. They have shown more readiness to interfere with decisions relating to Category A prisoners serving indeterminate sentences, as the longer they remain in that category, the longer they are likely to serve.

The following is a non-exhaustive list of the circumstances that may justify a claim for Judicial Review:

- *Failure to give reasons.* Provisional Category A and Restricted Status decisions are outside the formal review procedures that apply to convicted prisoners. Prisoners will not be served with a dossier, nor will they be invited to make representations. However, if written reasons are requested they must be provided. A failure to give reasons will be susceptible to Judicial Review, but it is highly unlikely that the reasons themselves will give rise to a claim as it would be difficult to argue that it was unreasonable for the prison to rely on information from the police.

- *Inadequate reasons.* A full set of prison reports will not have been prepared by the time the first formal review takes place; therefore the decision will be based on the original information, trial records and the order of imprisonment. Reasons based on these documents are unlikely to offer much scope for challenge, unless they have been carelessly drafted. Subsequent reviews will be based at least in part on subjective prison reports. Factual errors should be addressed through the Requests and Complaints procedure. Adverse decisions based solely on the prisoner's denial of guilt would be unlawful. As it would be inappropriate for the decision-maker to second guess the Court of Appeal, guilt must be assumed. However, there will be circumstances when continual denial of risk will have a negative impact on the assessment of risk, resulting in a refusal to downgrade (see *R (on the application of Roberts) v Secretary of State for the Home Department* [2004] EWHC 679. As long as the reasons themselves demonstrate that proper consideration has been given to significant matters in the client's favour, that irrelevant matters have not been taken into account, and that undue weight has not been given to a denial of guilt, they are unlikely to give rise to grounds for Judicial Review.

- *Inflexible interpretation of the policy.* A rigid application of policy may make a decision susceptible to Judicial Review, if it fails to properly take into account exceptional circumstances. See, eg, *R (on the application of Pate) v Secretary of State for the Home Department* [2002] EWHC 1018 Admin, where the inflexible application of the old definition of Category A was successfully challenged. The court criticized the failure to consider that escape could be made impossible for that particular prisoner in a less secure prison.

- *Procedural errors.* Failure to follow the re-categorization procedures, eg, even in an emergency is likely to result in a successful claim for Judicial Review (see *R v Governor of HM Prison Latchmere House, ex p Jarvis* (unreported, 20 July 1999).

C8 Sentence Planning

C8.1 Key Documents

KD PSO 2205

PSI 41/2012

C8.2 Introduction

Sentence planning within the Prison Service and supervision of offenders by the Probation Service are both centred on the IT-based Offender Assessment System (OASys). Instructions and guidance on OASys for the purposes of sentence management is contained in PSO 2205. ASSET is the equivalent assessment tool used by the Youth Justice Board for young offenders, which records training plans and objectives in much the same way.

OASys is a risk and needs assessment tool. It includes an interview process and a self-assessment questionnaire to be completed by the prisoner. Based on these assessments sentence plans are drawn up within OASys to manage and reduce these risks. In addition management plans must be completed for offenders who are assessed as Medium, High or Very High risk. Those that remain High or Very High risk prior to release will be made subject to the Multi-Agency Public Protection Arrangements (MAPPA) (see **A3**).

> ### PSO 2205 Offender Assessment and Sentence Management – OASys Chapter 3
>
> **3.1 Outline of OASys**
>
> 3.1.1 OASys includes the following components:
>
> - **Likelihood of reconviction and offending-related factors OASys 1 – short version; OASys 2 – full version**
>   case identification
>   offending information (Section 1);
>   offence analysis (Section 2);
>   offending-related factors (Sections 3-12);
>   health and other considerations (Section 13)
>
> - **Risk of serious harm, risks to the individual, and other risks**
>   screening section
>   full risk of harm analysis
>   harm summary section
>
> - **OASys summary sheets (one each for OASys 1 and OASys 2)**
>   scoring schedule
>   risk of reconviction score
>   offending-related factors summary

risk of serious harm summary
risks to the individual, and other risks

- **Supervision and sentence planning (SSP)**
  Outline plan, *for use with PSRs only*
  initial plan
  review plan, *including transfer and termination if applicable*
  Request for information form (RFI)

- **Self-assessment questionnaire SAQ**
  This is a questionnaire to give the offender an opportunity to record their views

- **Information not be disclosed to the offender (INTBDTTO)**
  This is a confidential section where information is held which would not be disclosed to the offender but would be available to general users. *Confidential information of a sensitive type must be held else-where and only a reference to its location entered here.*

- **Transfer & Termination (TT)**
  This is completed when an offender is discharged from custody with no further supervision plan or completes a period of supervision in the community.

- **Request for Information (RFI)**
  All completed and submitted requests for information are available in this section. RFIs automatically attach themselves to assessments on submission. Ad-Hoc RFIs will also be located in this section.

3.2 The likelihood of re-offending assessment

3.2.1 Likelihood of reconviction and offending related factors (OASys 1 and 2)
This includes:
- case identification
- offending information (Section 1)
- offence analysis (Section 2)
- assessment of factors linked to offending
  o accommodation (Sections 3)
  o education, training & employability (Section 4)
  o financial management & income (Section 5)
  o relationships (Section 6)
  o lifestyle & associates (Section 7)
  o drug misuse (Section 8)
  o alcohol misuse (Section 9)
  o emotional well-being (Section 10)
  o thinking & behaviour (Section 11)
  o attitudes (Section 12)
  o health & other considerations (Section 13)

3.3 The risk of serious harm assessment

3.3.1 This includes:
- a screening section
- a full analysis section
- a harm summary section.

3.3.2 The risks addressed are:
- risk of serious harm to others
- risks to children
- risks to the individual
  - suicide
  - self-harm
  - coping in custody / hostel setting
  - vulnerability
- other risks
  - escape/abscond
  - control issues
  - breach of trust.

3.3.3 The risk of harm summary includes management issues and the risk management plan.

C8.3 Aims of Sentence Planning

The aim is to identify and classify offender-related needs, such as homelessness, poor education, employment, thinking skills, substance misuse and relationship problems. It also assesses risk of harm to others, using a scale from low to very high.

PSO 2205 Offender Assessment and Sentence Management – OASys Chapter 3

2.1 Aims of sentence management

2.1.1 For the Prison and Probation Services:
- to provide information to assist prison establishments and probation service areas to target resources more effectively, in order to ensure that prison regimes and probation service programs more closely match the identified needs of offenders.

2.1.2 For the Public:
- to reduce the likelihood of re-offending by offenders by identifying areas of criminogenic need or offending related factors and providing action plans aimed at reducing that likelihood during custody and while under supervision in the community.

2.1.3 For the Offender:
- to enable offenders to make constructive use of their time in prison.
- to provide strategies to avoid further offending and consequent further periods of imprisonment.
- to provide a more structured resettlement into the community.

C8.4 OASys and Decision Making

Many decisions and underlying judgements upon which they are based, are dependent on the accuracy of the OASys assessment. These can be divided into three main categories:

1. Formal Processes: induction, categorization and allocation; Incentives and Earned Privileges (IEP) Scheme; resettlement.
2. Release Decisions: home detention curfew (HDC); Release on Temporary Licence; parole review; preparation for release on licence.
3. Interventions: offender behaviour courses; therapeutic communities; drug and alcohol treatment; work; education.

C8.5 Community-based Offender Managers

PSI 41/2012 Sentence Planning

Mandatory actions

1.9

- Community-based Offender Managers must produce the assessment and sentence plan and oversee delivery for the following groups of offenders:
  i. All those subject to suspended sentence orders and community orders (NB whilst a sentence plan is not required for single requirement curfew and exclusion, risk information should be obtained prior to sentence and sent to Electronic Monitoring suppliers)
  ii. Those subject to IPP sentences
  iii. Those subject to extended determinate sentences introduced by the LASPO Act 2012
  iv. PPO offenders serving custodial sentences
  v. Those serving custodial sentences who are assessed as posing a high or very high risk of causing serious harm to others

C8.6 Custody-based Offender Supervisors

PSI 41/2012 Sentence Planning

1.9

- Custody-based Offender Supervisors must produce the assessment and sentence plan and oversee delivery for the following groups of offenders:
  i. Those subject to life sentences
  ii. Those subject to a determinate sentence of 12 months or more, where the offender is assessed as posing a low or medium risk of causing serious harm to others

C8.7 Procedure

OASys assessments are mandatory for the following:

- young offenders (sentenced when aged 18–20) with at least 4 weeks left to serve;
- prisoners serving between one and 4 years with at least 6 months left to serve up to the conditional release date;
- prisoners serving 4 years or more;

C8 Sentence Planning

- all offenders sentenced under the CJA 2003 (12 months or over);
- life sentence offenders;
- extended sentence recall offenders, if they will be recalled for more than a year;
- licence recall offenders, if they will be in custody for more than a year (PSO 2205, paragraph 6.1).

Eligible prisoners must be assessed as part of the induction process or within 8 weeks of sentence. The OASys assessment must be reviewed at least annually and whenever a significant milestone has been completed (PSO 2205, paragraph 6.4).

Prisoners should be aware of the information in the assessment. However, sensitive information will be kept separate and will not be disclosed. A copy of the completed assessment must be provided on request. A Sentence Planning Board must be held for Discretionary Conditional Release prisoners and may be held for automatic conditional release prisoners depending on the circumstances and local arrangements. The prisoner will have an opportunity to be present for at least some of the Board meeting in accordance with the open procedure. If the prisoner refuses to attend this should be recorded.

C8.8 Risk Assessment

PSO 2205 Offender Assessment and Sentence Management – OASys Chapter 4

4.1 Risk of Harm

4.1.1 The risk of harm part of OASys is divided into three sections:
- screening
- full risk of harm analysis
- harm summary.

4.1.2 *If the screening process suggests that there are indications of risk, then the relevant parts of the full risk of harm analysis will normally be completed. If it is decided this is not necessary, the reasons for not doing so must be recorded.*

4.1.3 The risks addressed are:
- risk of serious harm to others
- risks to children
- risks to the individual
- suicide
- self-harm
- coping in custody / hostel setting
- vulnerability
- other risks
- escape / abscond
- control issues
- breach of trust.

4.1.4 The risk of harm summary includes management issues and the risk management plan.

4.1.5 Details of how to complete the risk of harm may be found in the OASys help section on the OASys website on the Intranet.

Background

4.1.6 There is limited evidence about which factors predict the risk of serious harm. When assessing the risk of further offending, the best predictor of future behaviour is considered to be past behaviour. This is also a good starting point when considering the risk of harm.

4.1.7 Identifying risk of serious harm requires a holistic approach. The assessment must explore the offender's situation and behaviour, as well as their criminal convictions. The current offence and the previous convictions may not, on their own, indicate risk. It is also important to remember that risks may change over time and must be kept under review.

4.2 Risk of serious harm – definitions

4.2.1 Risk of serious harm can be defined as a risk which is life-threatening and/or traumatic, and from which recovery, whether physical or psychological, can be expected to be difficult or impossible.

4.2.2 Because of the duty of care when assessing risk in relation to staff and prisoners, assessors considering the risk of harm to these two groups will be concerned with both serious harm as defined here, and harm that is less serious in impact.

4.2.3 The levels of risk of harm used in OASys are:
- **Low** – no significant, current indicators of risk of harm.
- **Medium** – there are identifiable indicators of risk of harm. The offender has the potential to cause harm but is unlikely to do so unless there is a change in circumstances, for example, failure to take medication, loss of accommodation, relationship breakdown, drug or alcohol misuse.
- **High** – there are identifiable indicators of risk of harm. The potential event could happen at any time and the impact would be serious.
- **Very high** – there is an imminent risk of harm. The potential event is more likely than not to happen imminently and the impact would be serious.

4.2.4 In order to support risk management and public protection work in establishments, a flag has been added to LIDS to record the level of risk of harm. *OASys Clerks must input the risk level on LIDS using one of the following codes:*
L - Low / **M** - Medium / **H** - High / **VH** - Very High

4.2.5 Risk is categorised as risk to:
- the public
- prisoners
- known adults
- children
- staff
- self.

Risk to public

4.2.6 Harm, either of a general nature or directed to a specific group, for example, a minority ethnic group, women, the elderly.

Risk to prisoners

4.2.7 Harm to other prisoners in custody.

Risk to a known adult

4.2.8 Harm to a particular individual, for example, a previous victim, partner, someone against whom the offender has a grudge.

Risks to children

4.2.9 Any kind of harm to children, including violent and sexual behaviour, emotional harm and neglect.

Risk to staff

4.2.10 Harm to those working with the individual, for example, prison or probation staff, police, other agencies, partnerships, public officials. It can include any incident in which an employee is abused, threatened or assaulted in circumstances arising out of the course of their employment. It includes violence committed against an employee outside the work situation, physical force, verbal abuse and threats (with or without weapon) and any sexual or racial harassment. There does not have to be a physical injury.

Risk to self

4.2.11 This includes:
- **Suicide:** possibility that the offender will take their own life.
- **Self-harm**: possibility that the offender will deliberately harm himself or herself irrespective of method, intent or severity of the injury. Self-harm will include injuries ranging from a self-inflicted scratch or cigarette burn, to a potentially life-threatening act such as hanging.

4.3 Management of risk and action plans

4.3.1 For those offenders who have received a rating of **very high**, **high** or **medium** in relation to risk of serious harm, risks to the individual and other risks, a management plan must be completed.

4.3.2 The management of this group of offenders must be in line with the Prison Service Public Protection Standard.

Low risk

4.3.3 There is a need to check whether any procedures in the public protection standard apply. Low risk of serious harm cases are unlikely to require specific risk management work to be done unless there is a change of circumstances that increases the risk.

Medium risk

4.3.4 Where a prisoner has been assessed as presenting medium risk of serious harm in custody or the community prison staff will need to check whether any procedures in the public protection standard apply. It is anticipated that these cases will be managed as part of the normal process of sentence management, but staff will need to consider whether any additional action is required.

High risk or **Very high** risk of serious harm

4.3.5 Where prisoners are assessed as presenting a high or very high risk in custody, and/or the community, *consideration must be given to whether any action needs to be taken immediately to minimise the risk in the prison environment.* Staff will need to check whether any procedures in the public protection standard apply.

4.3.6 *The risk of harm assessment must inform assessments and decisions about the management of the prisoner, for example, allocation, work allocation, re-categorisation, release on temporary licence etc. Sentence plans must be developed which work to minimise the risk.* The Prison Service *Dangerous Offender Strategy* may also inform the management of this group of offenders. Close and effective liaison with the supervising service will be crucial in these cases.

4.3.7 *Prior-to-release cases must be referred to the multi-agency arrangements provided by Section 67 of the Criminal Justice and Court Services Act 2000.*

Contents of the management action plan

4.3.8 The plan will include the following:

- Interface with other assessments, procedures and decisions
  o *The risk of harm assessment must inform all relevant assessments, procedures and decisions, for example:*
    ■ *the type of cell accommodation*
    ■ *transfer decisions*
    ■ *arrangements for escort and visits.*
  o In the light of the risk of harm assessment prison staff may need to invoke specific procedures, for example:
    ■ review of re-categorisation
    ■ inform managers of concerns
    ■ submit a security information report.
- Multi-agency arrangements (see also Chapter 15, section 15.2 on Public protection and dangerous offenders)
  o *The plan must indicate which agencies are involved with the case. Where appropriate it must identify individuals and contact points. The role of each agency in managing the risk must be clear.*
    ■ Has there been a public protection panel meeting?
    ■ Are there mental health issues which require liaison with health professionals?

4.3.9 Staff need to ensure that there are good channels of communications with the offender's supervising officer. *All information about victims must be stored in the confidential section of OASys (INTBDTTO) and regularly reviewed.*

4.3.10 *Offending behaviour work must focus on victim awareness if this has been highlighted as an issue.*

C8.9 Offender Behaviour Assessments

OASys will trigger further risk assessments targeted at specific risk factors, including violent offences, sex offences and general offending. The outcome of these assessments forms the basis for referrals to offender behaviour programmes.

Offender Behaviour Programmes

(source: <http://www.justice.gov.uk>)

ART (Aggression Replacement Training) – A groupwork programme for people convicted of violent offences or who have problems controlling their temper. It challenges offenders to accept responsibility for their behaviour; the aims are to reduce the incidence of assault, public order offences and criminal damage, increase public protection and challenge offenders to accept responsibility for their crime and its consequences.

ARV (Alcohol Related Violence Programme) – An alcohol programme which aims to reduce alcohol related violent offending. This medium intensity cognitive behavioural group programme is designed for hazardous drinkers (i.e. NOT severely dependant drinkers) in custody for alcohol related violence. It challenges the way individuals think towards drinking and violence, examines lifestyles and decision making, primarily (but not exclusively) in younger men.

ASRO (Addressing Substance Related Offending) – A drug and alcohol cognitive behavioural intervention designed to assist offenders address drug and alcohol related offending and to reduce or stop substance misuse.

Belief in Change – A year long programme for medium to high risk general offenders. It focuses on reintegration and building skills and support networks for release. It uses a range of methods including community living, structured group work, individual coaching and mentoring. It places high emphasis on building links in the wider community and increasing employability. Belief in Change encourages participants to think about their personal faith and spirituality and how this might support their process of change.

BSR (Building Skills for Recovery) – This is a psychosocial programme which can be delivered in a group setting or on a one-to-one basis. It aims to reduce offending behaviour and problematic substance misuse with an eventual goal of recovery. This is achieved through the exploration of previous and current substance use and the acquisition of a skill set to prevent future relapse into former patterns and behaviours – in essence the formulation of a person centred 'Recovery toolkit'.

CALM (Controlling Anger and Learning to Manage it) – An emotional management programme designed for those whose offending behaviour is precipitated by intense emotions. The goals are to assist offenders to understand the factors that trigger their anger and aggression and learn skills to manage their emotions.

Choices, Actions, Relationships and Emotions (CARE) – This is a course for female prisoners whose offending is related to difficulties with emotion regulation. The course aims to help participants identify and label emotions and develop skills for managing emotion. In addition, the course aims to foster a positive self-identity that will enable participants to live the kind of life they would like to on release.

CDVP (Community Domestic Violence Programme) – A Domestic Violence programme aimed at reducing the risk of violent crime and abusive behaviour towards women in relationships by helping male perpetrators change their attitudes and behaviour and to reduce the risk of all violent and abusive behaviour in the family.

Chromis – This is a complex and intensive programme that aims to reduce violence in high risk offenders whose level or combination of psychopathic traits disrupts their ability to accept treatment and change. Chromis has been specifically designed to meet the needs of highly psychopathic individuals and provides participants with the skills to reduce and manage their risk.

COVAID Programmes (Control of violence and anger in impulsive drinkers) – A series of programmes aimed at reducing violence and anger in impulsive drinkers. The different versions of the COVAID programme can be delivered as groupwork or on a one to one basis, in either secure or community settings. All the programmes are aimed at reducing re-offending primarily by young men with a repeated history of violence whilst intoxicated.

CSB (Cognitive Skills Booster) – Designed to reinforce learning from other general offending programmes (ETS, Think First and R&R) through skills rehearsal and relapse prevention.

Democratic TC (Therapeutic Community) – Democratic TCs provide a residential, offending behaviour intervention for prisoners who have a range of complex offending behaviour risk areas, including emotional and psychological needs and Personality Disorders. Democratic TCs provide a 24/7 living-learning intervention for offenders whose primary criminogenic risk factors need to be targeted whilst simultaneously addressing psychological and emotional disturbance.

DID (Drink Impaired Drivers Programme) – DID challenges attitudes and behaviour, aiming to reduce drink driving. Through self monitoring of an offender's drinking it aims to increase the knowledge of alcohol and its effects; promote safer driving and create a change in behaviour and attitude towards alcohol use and driving. It also aims to raise awareness and the effects on victims, victims' families and the offender themselves.

FOCUS Substance misuse programme – A cognitive behavioural treatment programme designed to assist prisoners to address factors relating to substance (drug and alcohol) misuse that links to their offending behaviour.

FOR (Focus on Resettlement) – This is a resettlement intervention designed to give a kick-start to the process of change It is a brief cognitive-motivational programme the primary objective of which is to increase the motivation of prisoners to become committed and active participants in setting their own agenda for change. This programme is designed for those serving sentences under 4 years and is only available in custody.

Generic Booster Programme GBP – This is a booster programme for candidates from TSP, BSR and the new violence programme. It is currently in development and will be piloted over the next year.

HRP (Healthy Relationship Programme) – A programme for men who have committed violent behaviour in a domestic setting. The aim is to end violence and abuse against participants' intimate partners. Participants will learn about their abusive behaviours and be taught alternative skills and behaviours to help them develop healthy, non-abusive relationships. There are two versions of HRP – the moderate intensity programme for men assessed as having a moderate risk/moderate need profile and the high intensity programme designed for high risk/high need offenders.

IDAP (Integrated Domestic Abuse Programme) – A domestic abuse programme designed for men who have committed violent behaviour in an intimate relationship. The aim is to end violence and abuse against participants' intimate partners. Participants will learn about their abusive behaviours and be taught alternative skills and behaviours to help them develop healthy, non-abusive relationships.

JETS (Juvenile Estate Thinking Skills Programme) – The JETS programme is based on the ETS cognitive skills programme but has been specifically re-developed for use with a juvenile age group (14-17 years). The JETS programme addresses thinking and behaviour associated with offending.

Kainos 'challenge to change' – This programme is a full time, twenty four week, therapeutic community based programme targeted at medium to high risk offenders with criminogenic needs that match those targeted by the programme. It uses a hybrid model - combining elements of cognitive behavioural programmes provided in four main intervention modules with learning, and delivered through a therapeutic community approach. The programme is partly facilitated by mentors who have already completed the programme. The Kainos Community is a registered charity and currently runs programmes in three prisons: HMP the Verne, HMP Stocken and HMP Swaleside.

LIAP (Low Intensity Alcohol Programme) – Provides motivation for behaviour change through alcohol misuse awareness to assist relapse prevention.

OSAP (Substance Abuse Programme) – This programme addresses drugs or alcohol misuse, using cognitive methods to change attitudes and behaviour to prevent relapse and reduce offending.

P-ASRO (Prison - Addressing Substance Related Offending) – A Drug intervention, P-ASRO addresses how thought processes and socio-economic situations contribute to the development of problematic levels of substance use and crime in individuals over their life span. Uses full assessment, programme material, individual key work sessions and a post programme review to evaluate progress and identify further support and treatment needs.

Priestley One to One Programme (Priestley OTO) – A cognitive and motivational programme focuses on changing behaviour to reduce offending, including problem-solving, self-management and social skills; to increase public protection and challenges offenders to accept responsibility for their crime and its consequence. This programme only runs in the community.

PPTCP (Prison Partnership Therapeutic Community Programme) – An abstinence based substance misuse programme based on a total immersion model. Participants take responsibility for self, and mutual, help in making lifestyle modifications within a three phase treatment model designed to mirror wider community living. Participants are responsible for the day to day running of the programme which consists of work roles, leisure time, group and 1:1 sessions, challenging behaviour and support. Can also be referred to as hierarchical or concept based TC's.

PPTSP (Prison Partnership Twelve Step Programme) – A drug and alcohol high intensity intervention programme aiming to highlight loss of control over an individual's substance use, offending and other dysfunctional areas of life. The aim is to develop a commitment to change whilst gaining the support of a Higher Power. Unhelpful thought processes are replaced with more pro-social models with ongoing support linked to the Fellowships of Narcotics Anonymous, Alcoholics Anonymous and Cocaine Anonymous.

RAPt (Rehabilitation of Addicted Prisoners Trust) – including Alcohol Dependency Treatment Programme (ADTP) – These are Drug & Alcohol interventions that aim to highlight loss of control over an individual's substance use, offending and other areas of life and develops a commitment to change whilst gaining the support of a higher power. Follows the 12 step NA fellowship programme.

RESOLVE – A moderate intensity cognitive-behavioural intervention that aims to reduce violence in medium risk adult male offenders. The programme includes group and individual sessions and is suitable for offenders with a history of reactive or instrumental violence.

RESPOND – This is an individual cognitive skills programme for offenders who are eligible for TSP but not suitable for the group format for a variety of reasons. It is currently in development and will be piloted next year.

SCP (Self Change Programme) – Aims to reduce violence in high risk repetitively violent offenders. The programme targets offenders' patterns of anti-social thinking and beliefs that support violence.

SDP (Short Duration Programme) – A structured 4 week intervention, based on a CBT/Harm Minimisation model. Looking at substance awareness, harm minimisation and the treatment services available in prison and the community. Also focusing on harm minimisation, the cycle of change and relapse prevention and on high-risk situations, coping with cravings and relationships as well as problem solving, reviewing the programme and each individual's relapse prevention plan. The intervention concludes with a post programme review to evaluate progress and identify further support and treatment needs.

Sex Offender Treatment Programmes (SOTP) – A range of programmes are available for sexual offenders, providing a menu which are offered according to the level of risk and need of the offender.

C-SOGP (Community Sex Offenders Group Programme) – helps offenders develop understanding of how and why they have committed sexual offences. The programme also increases awareness of victim harm. The main focus is to help the offender develop meaningful life goals and practice new thinking and behavioural skills that will lead him away from offending.

NSOGP (Northumbria Sex Offenders Group Programme) – helps offenders develop understanding of how and why they have committed sexual offences. The programme also increases awareness of victim harm. The main focus is to help the offender develop meaningful life goals and practice new thinking and behavioural skills that will lead him away from offending.

NSOGP (Northumbria Sex Offenders Group Programme) – Community Better Lives (RP) BL and RP (Community) - A sex offender treatment programme that follows on from 'core' programmes such as NSOGP or SOTP. Its aim is to reinforce and consolidate core learning and to develop and practice skills essential in assisting men to formulate appropriate relapse prevention strategies.

TVSOGP (Thames Valley Sex Offenders Group Programme) – helps offenders develop understanding of how and why they have committed sexual offences. The programme also increases awareness of victim harm. The main focus is to help the offender develop meaningful life goals and practice new thinking and behavioural skills that will lead him away from offending.

I-SOTP (Internet Sex Offender Treatment Programme) – A programme designed to explore and address the thoughts, feelings and beliefs underpinning the group members internet sex offending. Aim is to reduce the risk of further similar offending and, like other sex offender programmes, increases the offenders understanding of the impact of their offending on others, including their victims.

ASOTP-CV (Adapted Sex Offender Treatment Programme - Community Version) – Adapted Community sex offender programme similar to SOTP, but adapted for those who have social or learning difficulties. It is designed to increase sexual knowledge, modify offence-justifying thinking, develop ability to recognise feelings in themselves and others, to gain an understanding of victim harm, and develop relapse prevention skills.

SOTP Core (Sex Offenders Treatment Programme) – Core helps offenders develop understanding of how and why they have committed sexual offences. The programme also increases awareness of victim harm. The main focus is to help the offender develop meaningful life goals and practice new thinking and behavioural skills that will lead him away from offending.

SOTP BNM (Sex Offenders Treatment Programme Becoming New Me) – Covers similar areas to Core SOTP, but adapted for those who have social or learning difficulties. It is designed to increase sexual knowledge, modify offence-justifying thinking, develop ability to recognise feelings in themselves and others, to gain an understanding of victim harm, and develop relapse prevention skills.

SOTP BLB (Sex Offenders Treatment Programme Better Lives Booster) – Designed to boost sexual offenders' learning from other SOTPs and provide additional opportunities to practice personally relevant skills. It can be run in two forms—a low intensity (one session a week) helps to maintain change in long term prisoners and the high intensity, pre-release programme is particularly focused on preparation for transition into the community.

SOTP ABLB (Sex Offenders Treatment Programme Adapted Better Lives Booster) – Aimed at those who have completed the Adapted SOTP. Shares the same aims as the Core version but the treatment delivery methods are different to accommodate different learning styles and abilities. A low intensity version is for long term prisoners and a high intensity version is for those who are in the last year of their sentence, preparing them for release.

SOTP Extended (Sex Offenders Treatment Programme Extended) – Extended is targeted at high and very high risk men who have successfully met the treatment targets of the Core programme. The programme covers 4 areas; recognising and modifying patterns of dysfunctional thinking, emotional regulation, intimacy skills and relapse prevention.

SOTP HSF (Sex Offenders Treatment Programme Healthy Sexual Functioning) – Aims to promote healthy sexual functioning, mainly in high-risk sexual offenders, who acknowledge current or very recent offence-related sexual interests. Modules include developing a more healthy sexuality, patterns in sexual arousal, behavioural strategies for promoting healthy sexual interest and relapse prevention.

SOTP Rolling (Sex Offenders Treatment Programme Rolling) – Rolling provides a less intensive level of treatment with more emphasis on relationships skills and attachment styles deficits. The group rolls continuously with members joining and leaving as it rolls along so members will therefore be at different stages of treatment, depending on when they joined the group.

The Women's Programme – This is a cognitive and motivational programme specifically designed for women who have committed acquisitive offences and are at risk of reconviction for non violent crimes. It is suitable for women where there is a demonstrable history of acquisitive offending despite the current offence not appearing acquisitive in nature. The programme looks at the way women understand and deal with problems in their lives, and looks at alternative ways of dealing with them.

TSP (Thinking Skills Programme) – A cognitive skills programme which addresses the way offenders think and their behaviour associated with offending. The programme aims to reduce reoffending by engaging and motivating, coaching and responding to individual need and building on continuity. It supports offenders developing skills in setting goals and making plans to achieve these without offending.

Additionally:

A>Z – This is a short motivational non-accredited programme designed to support offenders in engaging in pro-social activities and see a reason for moving away from offending.

Motivational enhancement work designed to encourage prisoners to consider their lives up until now, choices they have made and goals for the future.

C9 **Challenging the Sentence Plan**

As the OASys assessment is an open process the client will be aware of the content of the sentence plan, and is likely to have signed it to confirm agreement with the aims and objectives. Even if the client refused to engage in the process he or she will be entitled to a copy of the assessment.

The sentence plan may be challenged either through the Complaints procedure or by way of Judicial Review.

C9.1 **Complaints**

Complaints relating to the sentence plan are likely to fall into two categories which may overlap:

- *Factual disputes.* If the client is unhappy with the content of a sentence plan a copy of the OASys assessment should be obtained. Factual disputes should have been raised by the client during the assessment, even if it was not resolved in his or her favour. If the client remains dissatisfied, he can make a complaint through the Requests and Complaints procedure. Some factual disputes can be independently checked and verified eg a previous conviction incorrectly entered on the police national computer. However other disputes are likely to involve the exercise of judgement eg a reference in the documents to a drug problem that is denied. It is unlikely to be unreasonable for the assessor to reject the client's version of events in light of other indicators.

- *Offender behaviour programmes.* The courses are not compulsory. Although no risk assessment is infallible it is unlikely to be of benefit to the client to challenge its scientific basis. In *R v Boswell* [2007] EWCA Crim 1587 the Court of Appeal dismissed an argument that challenged the risk assessment tools used by the Probation Service in the preparation of a pre-sentence report, as it was accepted that they are the product 'of a good deal of research and provide a satisfactory basis for reaching conclusions of the kind that were reached in this case'. If the client cannot be persuaded to undertake the course, consideration should be given to its suitability based on his individual circumstances, and if appropriate written representations can be submitted. Refusal to attend courses can present particular problems for indeterminate prisoners who can only be released on the direction of the Parole Board, as it may be difficult for these prisoners to demonstrate that they have addressed their offending behaviour. However, it would be unlawful for parole to be refused solely on the ground that the prisoner had not accepted guilt. Eligibility for most courses is not dependent on an admission of guilt (with the exception of the Sex Offender Treatment Programmes (SOTP), which requires the prisoner to give a full and frank account of the offence) and therefore in most cases it will be in the client's best interest to attend the course.

It may be that a particular course has been identified in the sentence plan, but that course is either oversubscribed or unavailable at the establishment where the client is currently being held. If the client has not already done so, he should submit an application for transfer to another prison. If the course has not been completed by the time parole is to be considered it may be appropriate to request a deferral. If the hearing goes ahead it would be unlawful for parole to be refused solely on the ground that the course had not been completed, although it is bound to have an impact on the assessment of risk.

See *R (on the application of Gill) v Secretary of State for Justice* [2010] EWHC 364 (Admin), where the High Court held that reasonable steps should be taken to enable disabled prisoners (which includes prisoners with learning disabilities) to participate in programmes identified as necessary to reduce risk of re-offending.

C9.2 Judicial Review

Particular problems arise if the client is a short-tariff lifer. These prisoners can only be released at the direction of the Parole Board. However, the inadequate provision of offender behaviour programmes has meant that significant numbers remain in custody beyond tariff as they cannot demonstrate that they are no longer dangerous.

The majority decision in *R (on the application of Cawser) v Secretary of State for the Home Department* [2003] EWCA Civ 1522 determined that the failure to provide resources could not in itself breach ECHR Article 5 (right to liberty and security). However, in *Walker v Secretary of State for the Home Department* [2008] EWCA Civ 30, the Court of Appeal upheld the High Court ruling, which on the basis of domestic common law had found the Prison Service's failure to provide sufficient offender behaviour programmes, arbitrary and unreasonable, and therefore unlawful. The failure to provide appropriate resources was also heavily criticized in the House of Lords case of *Secretary of State for Justice v James* [2009] UKHL 22.

The domestic courts stopped short of declaring the post-tariff detention was unlawful and it was on this basis that the applicants appealed to Strasbourg. In stark contrast the European Court of Human Rights in *James Wells & Lee v UK* [2012] ECHR 1706, in a unanimous decision, held that the failure to make appropriate provision for rehabilitation courses denied prisoners a real opportunity for rehabilitation which is a necessary element of any detention justified solely on grounds of public protection. Their continued detention was therefore found to be in breach of ECHR Article 5(1) and 5(4) which protects individuals from arbitrary detention. The decision is final as the Government's request for a review was turned down in February 2013. This paves the way for prisoners to challenge detention by way of Judicial Review and damages claims for false imprisonment and/or section 8 of the Human Rights Act 1988.

C10 **Requests and Complaints Procedure**

C10.1 **Key Documents**

KD PSI 02/2012

PSI 75/2011

C10.2 **Overview**

The Requests and Complaints procedure are dealt with separately.

The underlying principles of the current system are:

- Establishments should take full responsibility for dealing with requests or complaints internally, with recourse to Prison Service Headquarters (NOMS) only in the case of reserved subjects or confidential access to Area Managers.
- Requests or complaints should be dealt with at the lowest level at which a proper response can be provided, subject to a prisoner's right to appeal to a higher level if he or she is dissatisfied.
- Staff should take responsibility for the decisions and actions they take and be prepared to explain them.
- Requests or complaints should wherever possible be dealt with informally, with full opportunity for explanation and conciliation before formal procedures are invoked.

Complaints made by a legal representative on behalf of a client fall outside the internal requests and complaints procedure.

C10.3 **Requests**

C10.3.1 **Key document**

KD PSI 75/2011

C10.3.2 *Applications*

All prisons are required to have a local applications procedure. Requests can cover a wide range of everyday needs, and must be considered upon receipt of an oral or written application. The applications system is viewed as an intermediate process between an informal discussion with an officer and a formal complaint.

C10 Requests and Complaints Procedure

The essential elements of the local procedure are:

C10.3.3 *Reserved subjects*

Requests relating to reserved subjects (see **C11**) must be in writing and will be referred to either the Briefing and Casework Unit (BCU) or the DHS, depending on the prisoner's security category.

C10.4 Complaints

C10.4.1 Key document

 PSI 02/2012

C10.4.2 *Principles*

The complaints procedures must be well-publicized and all prisoners must know how to complain. It must be easy to make a complaint and obstacles must not be put in the way of prisoners who wish to do so. Prisoners must not be penalized for making a complaint.

C10.4.3 *Complaint categories*

Complaints are divided into four distinct categories. Each category of complaint has a separate form:

- *Ordinary complaints (form Comp 1).* Ordinary complaints are not defined. They include any complaint that does not relate to a reserved subject, and does not fall into any of the categories listed below eg lost or damaged property.

- *Appeals (form Comp 1A)*. The prisoner should use this form when appealing a response to a complaint.
- *Confidential access complaints (form Comp 2)*. Prisoners should use this form to complain about staff conduct or any sensitive matter including medical issues.
- *Appeals against adjudications (form DIS8)*.

C10.4.4 *Submitting a complaint*

The forms must be readily available on the wing. The complaint should normally be submitted within 3 months of the incident or circumstances that gave rise to the complaint or the date the prisoner was notified of the adjudicator's decision. Late complaints may be considered in exceptional circumstances, if there is good reason for the delay, or if the complaint relates to a matter that is so serious that the time limit ought not to be applied (PSI 02/2012, paragraph 2.1.4).

Complaint forms and information leaflets are available in a wide range of languages. The complaint can be submitted in the prisoner's own language, although the response will take longer, as the complaint itself and the reply will need to be translated. Prisoners with reading or writing difficulties should be assisted in completing the forms, and visually impaired prisoners should be given the opportunity to submit complaints in alternative formats such as large print forms, Braille or audio cassette (PSO 02/2012, paragraph 2.1.5). Under no circumstances should a prisoner be banned from making complaints even if he or she is thought to be abusing the system by making numerous trivial complaints or submitting multiple complaints on the same subject (PSO 02/2012, paragraph 2.1.11).

C10.4.5 *Collecting and distributing complaints*

The complaints boxes must be emptied daily (except weekends and public holidays) by the 'designated officer' who is responsible for passing the completed forms to the complaints clerk, or directly to staff for reply in appropriate cases. The complaints clerk must register and allocate a serial number to all complaints and appeals before passing them to a member of staff for reply (PSI 02/2012, paragraph 2.11.1). Complaints submitted on the wrong form should not automatically be dismissed. Where necessary the correct form should be attached to avoid confusion.

The complaints clerk or senior officer must decide who should respond to the complaint. Most responses should initially be handled by the prisoner's personal officer (or an appropriate officer at this level), unless the complaint is:

- a confidential access complaint;
- about a reserved subject;

- about a member of staff;
- otherwise inappropriate for a wing office to deal with (eg a complaint about medical treatment).

C10.4.6 *Response to a complaint*

There are two potential stages to a response. At each stage the prisoner is entitled to written reasons if the complaint is not resolved in his favour. Failure to give reasons, inadequate reasons or delay will give rise to grounds for Judicial Review.

The majority of complaints will be dealt with at Stage 1. However, if a complaint has been dealt with at a senior level at Stage 1, there will be no further internal stages.

- *Stage 1:* the initial complaint and response

  The response must be based on relevant and up-to-date information, and must not take irrelevant factors into account. Decisions should not be arbitrary, nor should they give the impression of being arbitrary. Responses should provide short explanations if the decision was based on a rule or instruction; however, a full explanation should be provided if the response contradicts the response given at the application stage. If the decision was discretionary the prisoner should be informed of the factors that were taken into account, and why that decision was reached. Even if a complaint is upheld it may not be appropriate to remedy the problem in the way the prisoner has requested. In such situations the prisoner should be provided with reasons, and informed of the action that will be taken.

- *Stage 2:* Appeal

  Prisoners dissatisfied with the Stage 1 response should complete Form Comp 1A. An appeal should normally be submitted within 7 days of receiving the initial response, although a late appeal may be considered if there are exceptional circumstances (PSI 02/2012, paragraph 2.7.1). An officer at a level higher than the officer at Stage 1 must respond to Stage 2 appeals within 5 working days of the appeal being logged. The response must add to the explanation at Stage 1 and take all relevant factors into account, assess whether the original explanation was satisfactory and whether the original decision was fair and reasonable (PSI 02/2012, paragraph 2.7.3). Reasons must be given if the original Stage 1 decision is overturned (PSI 02/2012, paragraph 2.9.1).

C10.4.7 *Confidential access complaints*

Confidential access complaints are defined as complaints involving 'a particularly serious or sensitive matter, where it would be reasonable for the prisoner to be reticent about discussing it with wing staff or have it be known to administrative and wing staff through the normal complaints procedure' (PSI 02/2012, paragraph 2.5.3). Prisoners have a right to make confidential complaints to the Governor, the Area Manager or the chairman of the IMB. The complaints clerk is responsible for forwarding the unopened complaint to the intended recipient. The reply will be sent via the complaints clerk in a sealed envelope.

Confidential access complaints addressed to the Area Manager will usually be considered by the BCU or the DHS, depending on the prisoner's security category, although the complaint can be referred to the Governor if it is urgent, or relates to a matter that would normally be dealt with by senior management. If the complaint raises a serious allegation it may be appropriate for the Area Manager to conduct an investigation.

Although the reasons for requesting confidentiality must be taken into account, it is for the officer or manager who receives the complaint to decide how far confidentiality can be maintained. However, the complaint should not be disclosed to any member of staff (or anyone else) who does not need to know about it (PSI 02/2012, paragraph 2.5.5).

The confidential access system should not to be used to fast track ordinary complaints (PSI 02/2012, paragraph 2.5.2). If confidential access is deemed inappropriate the officer will have the following options:

- Respond, if it can be dealt with quickly and easily. At the same time the prisoner should be informed that confidential access was not appropriate, and that any future complaints incorrectly submitted via confidential access will be returned to be pursued under the normal three-stage procedure;
- Refer the matter to a named operational manager or senior operational manager if the confidential complaint was sent to the Governor.
- Return the form to the prisoner, explaining why confidential access is not appropriate and offer guidance on the correct procedure (PSI 02/2012, paragraph 2.5.6).

C10.4.8 *Appeal*

There is no formal procedure for appealing a response to a confidential access complaint, other than submitting a complaint to the Prisons and Probation Ombudsman. However, if substantive new information comes to light, or there is any other good reason that clearly justifies overturning the original decision it should be reconsidered at local level, as this may avoid an appeal to the Ombudsman.

C10.4.9 *Time limits*

PSI 02/2012 Prisoner Complaints

Annex B Time Limits

Action	Time Limit
Submission of complaint by prisoner	Within 3 months of the incident or the circumstances coming to the prisoner's attention
Stage 1 response	5 working days
Stage 1 response to complaint against member of staff	10 working days
Stage 1 response to complaint involving another establishment	10 working days
Stage 1 response with an equality aspect	5 working days
Re-submission by prisoner of complaint (appeal) stage 2	Within one week of receipt of the stage 1 response
Stage 2 response	5 working days
Stage 2 response to complaint against member of staff	10 working days
Stage 2 response to complaint involving another establishment	10 working days
Confidential access complaint to governing governor	5 working days
Confidential access complaint to Deputy Director of Custody	6 weeks
Response to complaint about a reserved subject	6 weeks

Note: As stated in paragraph 2.1.5, a longer timescale will be needed where the complaint is made in a language other than English. As a rule of thumb, the timescales above will normally start once a translated version is received.

C11 **Reserved Subjects**

Requests or complaints on reserved subjects will be sifted out by the complaints clerk and dealt with by either the BCU or the DHS.

Although the list of reserved subjects is comprehensive it is not exhaustive. It includes:

- Early release due to illness or incapacity
- Parole (determinate sentences prisoners)
- Special remission
- Category A status/transfers
- Lifer transfers and allocations
- Request for access to artificial insemination facilities
- Transfer to Scotland, Northern Ireland, Isle of Man, Jersey or Guernsey
- Repatriation
- Deportation
- Mother and Baby Unit placement appeals
- section 90/section 91 Juvenile Allocations (PSI 75/2011, Annex B)

C12 **Specific Types of Complaint**

C12.1 **Complaints Against Members of Staff**

All complaints against staff should be made in writing on a complaint form under the standard or confidential access procedure. All complaints must be investigated and any member of staff or IMB member who hears an oral complaint should encourage the prisoner to put that complaint in writing. The member of staff or IMB member should make a note of the allegation and refer the matter to an appropriate operational manager to consider whether the allegation should be investigated, even if the prisoner refuses to make a written complaint. Prisoners who allege assault should be examined by a medical officer as soon as possible.

The management within the prison is responsible for initiating and conducting the investigation. For serious allegations a formal disciplinary investigation may be initiated, which is governed by PSO 1300, and on the advice of NOMS certain matters may be referred to the police.

C12.2 **Complaints about Bullying**

The standard and confidential access complaints forms contain a 'tick box' to indicate whether the complaint relates to violence, including threats and intimidation. The policy on violence reduction is contained within PSI 64/2011. All complaints with the 'discrimination, harassment or victimisation' box ticked must comply with the incident reporting arrangements in PSI 32/2011.

C12.3 **Complaints Involving Another Prison**

If the prisoner has been transferred to another prison since the submission of a complaint, the response should be forwarded to the prisoner's new prison via the complaints clerk. Complaints relating to events that took place at another prison or during transfer should be logged in the usual way and forwarded to the previous establishment with a request for information and/or a draft reply.

In general, prisons are not expected to investigate complaints or overturn decisions made in a previous establishment. However, there may be exceptions eg where the response is factually incorrect. In such cases the holding prison may overturn a response to a complaint on appeal. Wherever possible the new response should be agreed with the previous establishment (PSI 02/2012, paragraph 2.7.4).

C13 **Lost or Damaged Property**

Compensation claims for lost or damaged property either stored by the prison or 'in possession' of the prisoner are common. However, such claims do not normally attract public funding at any level (other than Judicial Review) and therefore the prisoner will usually pursue the matter without legal assistance.

Prison Service policy on the handling of prisoners' property is contained in PSI 12/2011. Liability is not normally accepted for 'in possession' property unless the prisoner was moved from their normal location without prior warning, transferred temporarily or he or she absconded/escaped, and was therefore not in a position to exercise control over his possessions. The prisoner should make a claim by submitting details of the property, the circumstances of the loss or damage and the value of the items to the Governor. If the claim is refused the prisoner may appeal through the requests and complaints procedure, and if after exhausting that procedure he/she remains dissatisfied he should complain to the Prisons and Probation Ombudsman. A complaint upheld by the Ombudsman but not accepted by the Prison Service may form the basis of a county court claim or a claim for Judicial Review.

C14 **Visits**

C14.1 **Key Documents**

KD   PSI 15/2011

PSI 16/2011

PSI 37/2010

PSO 3610

Public Protection Manual

C14.2 **Types of Visits**

Statutory visits are the minimum number of visits a prisoner will be permitted. Rule 35(2)(b) of the Prison Rules (YOI Rules, rule 10(1)(b)) provides that convicted prisoners are entitled to 2 visits every 4 weeks, which can be reduced to one visit every 4 weeks if directed by the Secretary of State.

Privilege visits are additional visits which may be authorized by the Governor or the IMB as part of the IEP Scheme, or for the welfare of the prisoner or his family (Prison Rules, rule 35(6)).

As there is no minimum number of privilege visits that may be permitted, problems arise when prisoners are transferred from one prison to another where the entitlements may be very different. Special visits from legal representatives and other professionals attending in their official capacity do not count towards the prisoner's statutory entitlement. Each prison is required to devise a local visits strategy to meet the needs of its establishment and any security considerations.

Rule 35(1) of the Prison Rules provides that remand prisoners are entitled to as many visits as they wish, although in practice this will be subject to the allocation of staff resources.

Conjugal visits are not currently permitted, and this approach has been found not to breach ECHR Article 8 (right to family life).

C14.3 **Accumulated Visits**

Convicted prisoners can accumulate up to 26 statutory visits during any 12-month period. The visits may be taken at the holding prison, or the prisoner can apply for a temporary transfer to another prison. An application can be made every 6 months as long as the prisoner has at least 6 months left to serve. Governors can refuse an application to transfer, refuse to accept a prisoner on temporary transfer or postpone a transfer on the grounds of risk to security, safety and order (PSI 16/2011, paragraph 5.8). If a transfer is authorized it will normally be for one month, but the period may be extended in exceptional circumstances.

The Governor also has discretion to allow the accumulation of privilege visits. Whenever possible, local prisons should reserve up to 2 places for use by prisoners on accumulated visits, and should maintain waiting lists for those wishing to transfer. In the current climate of severe prison overcrowding prisoners will often have to wait for long periods.

C14.4 Banning Visitors

The Governor has discretion, on authority derived from the Prison Rules, rules 35 and 73(1) (YOI Rules, rules 9 and 77) to refuse visits or determine the conditions upon which visits should take place, on the grounds of:

- maintenance of good order and discipline;
- prevention of crime;
- security;
- detriment to the best interest of the prisoner; or
- serious impediment to the prisoner's rehabilitation.

Only in exceptional circumstances should a visit from a relative be refused. Close relatives are defined as a spouse (or partner whether same sex or not with whom the prisoner was living as a couple immediately prior to imprisonment), parent, child, siblings (including half-brothers/sisters and stepbrothers/sisters), civil partner, fiancé or fiancée (provided the Governor is satisfied that there is a genuine intention to marry), or a person who has been *in loco parentis* to a prisoner or a person to whom the prisoner has been *in loco parentis*. For the purposes of social visits grandparents may be included. Any decision to refuse a visit from a close relative will be lawful only if it is reasonable and proportionate.

It does not necessarily follow that because a prisoner is in correspondence with a person or organization that they may be visited by that person or a representative from the organization (PSI 49/2011, paragraph 2.18).

C14.5 Drug Smuggling

Specific guidance on visitors and prisoners who smuggle drugs through visits is contained in PSO 3610. Clear evidence of drugs or any other unauthorized article being smuggled into the prison will normally result in a disciplinary charge for the prisoner, and arrest by the police for the visitor eg where the visitor is seen to pass an item to the prisoner who is subsequently found to be in possession of a drug or is unable to give a reasonable explanation for suspicious activity. Visitors believed to have been engaged in drug smuggling will normally be banned for at least 3 months, followed by a period on closed visits. If the intended recipient of the drugs is a convicted prisoner the visitor will normally be banned for 3 months' worth of visits, which will prevent visit entitlements from being accumulated until after the closed visit period has expired (see later) (PSO 3610, paragraph 24). In addition, the Governor will in the absence of exceptional circumstances:

- arrange targeted searches for visitors and the prisoner;
- refer the prisoner to a drug counsellor;
- consider Mandatory Drug Testing on grounds of reasonable suspicion;
- take the incident into account when reviewing IEPs, placement on voluntary testing unit, categorization, allocation and suitability for home detention curfew.

If there is reasonable suspicion of smuggling but no drugs are found, the visitor should not be banned, although in the absence of exceptional circumstances the other consequences just listed will apply. A positive indication by a drug dog will not justify a ban, although it may justify a search without consent. Intelligence can only justify a ban if the evidence is clear and persuasive (PSO 3610, paragraph 7).

Where a ban is imposed the Governor (or Controller in private prisons) has discretion to impose less than 3 months if, eg, the prisoner is serving a short sentence. A longer ban may be appropriate for repeat offences, attempts to circumvent a previous ban, the smuggling of a large quantity of drugs, any quantity of a Class A drug or where the local policy is to impose longer than 3 months (PSO 3610, paragraph 17). Any ban of longer than 3 months must be reviewed at 3-monthly intervals, to assess whether exceptional circumstances have arisen that justify revocation. Bans imposed by the Governor apply to the holding prison only. If the prisoner is transferred while a visitor is subject to a ban the Governor at the receiving prison will re-impose the ban but only for the remainder of the original period (PSO 3610, paragraph 32).

In exceptional circumstances the Governor has discretion not to impose a ban:

- if it would cause disproportionate harm to the prisoner's or visitor's right to family life (ECHR Article 8);
- if it would cause disproportionate harm to the rights of the child to have access to a parent (UN Convention on the Rights of the Child, Article 9);

- if the prisoner is a juvenile and it would to cause disproportionate harm to his rights of access to a parent;
- on exceptional compassionate or other grounds (PSO 3610, paragraph 9).

After the expiry of a ban the visitor will normally be placed on closed visits for 3 months. If a ban is not imposed as a result of exceptional circumstances the Governor may impose closed visits for the length of time a ban would have been imposed (ie 3 months) plus any further period deemed necessary.

C14.6 Protection from Harassment

There is specific policy guidance contained in the Public Protection Manual, Chapter 6, relating to prisoners on remand or convicted of offences under the Protection from Harassment Act 1997. Such prisoners, who may also be subject to an injunction or a restraining order, should be identified on reception. Their visits may be subject to closer supervision (including being held in the direct hearing of an officer), if there is a concern that others may be encouraged to continue the harassment, or refused altogether if there is sufficient evidence.

C14.7 Child Visitors

The Governor has discretion to prevent a visit from any person under 18 if it is considered that such a visit would or could potentially place the child at risk. The definition of child includes sons, daughters, brothers, sisters, stepchildren, adopted children and foster children. Grandchildren will be considered if there is a substantial case for contact, and it would be in the best interests of the child. The Governor may allow a child aged 16 or over to visit unaccompanied subject to a risk assessment and the views of all parties including the child's parent or guardian. Decisions to prevent or restrict contact should balance the risk presented by the offender with the needs of the child.

Prisoners charged with an offence against a child or who have previous convictions for such offences and prisoners assessed as posing a risk to children may apply in writing to have contact or receive visits from a person under the age of 18. Applications will be considered under the procedures set out in the Public Protection Manual, Chapter 2 and will normally be limited to children in the prisoner's immediate family, and the children of a partner if they were living together prior to imprisonment.

C14.8 Approved Visitors Scheme

Visits to Category A/Restricted Status prisoners (and provisional Category A/Restricted Status) are subject to special provisions under the Approved Visitors Scheme which are contained within PSI 15/2011. Under the scheme only closed visits will be permitted until open visits have been approved by Prison Service Headquarters. For exceptional Category A prisoners the decision must be authorized by the Director of High Security. Approval will be subject to vetting by the police, which will include a criminal record check. Details of the scheme will be in the prison's Local Security Strategy (LSS).

C14.9 Visits from Journalists

Prison Service policy on communication with the media is contained in PSI 37/2010. In compliance with ECHR Article 10 (right to freedom of expression), there is no longer a blanket ban on visits from journalists. In exceptional circumstances, where the prisoner believes that there has been a miscarriage of justice and requires the assistance of a journalist to challenge the safety of their conviction, a written application may be made to the Governor. Permission will only be granted if the Governor is persuaded that the request meets the specified criteria (see PSI 37/2010, paragraphs 3.5 and 3.6). See *R v Home Secretary, ex p Simms* [1999] 3 All ER 4000 HL, where their Lordships held that there was a fundamental right for prisoners to seek to persuade a journalist to investigate the safety of their convictions.

C14.10 Legal Visits

Visits from legal representatives are subject to the Prison Rules, rule 38 (YOI Rules, rule 16). Visits should take place in the sight of a prison officer but out of hearing. The purpose of the visit must be to:

- discuss an ongoing case or contemplated legal proceedings to which the prisoner is a party;
- discuss other legal business such as the sale of a house or instructions for a will;
- discuss a forthcoming adjudication (PSI 16/2011, paragraph 7.2).

The security arrangements, particularly in high security prisons, can be tight, but should be no more restrictive than necessary. ECHR Article 6 (right to a fair trial including access to representation, and adequate time and facilities to prepare a defence) will be breached unless the restriction is both reasonable and proportionate. For example, a blanket policy allowing only closed visits with legal advisers would be vulnerable to challenge by way of Judicial Review—see *R (on the application of Daly) v Secretary of State for the Home Department* [2001] 2 AC 532 in the context of legal correspondence.

Legal advisers may use a cassette recorder or other sound recording device, which may be subject to an undertaking that it will be used solely in relation to the proceedings and will be kept securely. Letters or documents handed to or from the prisoner will be subject to the same procedures that would apply had they been sent by post (PSI 16/2011, paragraph 7.3) (see **C15.2.3**).

C15 **Correspondence**

C15.1 **Key Document**

KD PSI 49/2011

Any decision involving the restriction of correspondence will be lawful only if it is reasonable and proportionate. Governors should give particular consideration to decisions that will restrict correspondence between close relatives.

C15.2 **Types of Letters**

Letters sent by prisoners fall into 4 distinct categories: statutory letters, privilege letters, special letters, and legal or confidential correspondence.

C15.2.1 *Statutory and privilege letters*

Remand prisoners may send up to 2 statutory letters per week under the Prison Rules, rule 35 (YOI Rules, rule 10) at public expense, and as many privilege letters as they wish (PSI 49/2011, paragraph 2.2). The postage costs of privilege letters should be paid for from prison earnings or private cash. Only privilege letters can be withdrawn as punishment. Convicted prisoners may send one statutory letter per week, and as many privilege letters as they wish unless they are in a prison where correspondence is read routinely (PSI 49/2011, paragraph 2.3). Under the Prison Rules, rule 35(4) (YOI Rules, rule 10(3) a prisoner must be given a statutory letter at public expense in place of any statutory visit the prisoner does not wish to take or accumulate (PSI 49/2011, paragraph 2.5).

C15.2.2 *Special letters*

Special letters must be permitted at public expense for convicted prisoners in the following circumstances:

- prior to a transfer to another prison or on reception at a new prison. The number of letters allowed should correspond to the number of outstanding visiting orders;
- immediately after conviction if business affairs need to be settled;
- if necessary for the welfare of the prisoner or his family;
- in connection with legal proceedings;
- to enable the prisoner to contact a relevant Offender Manager Service or an agency arranging employment or accommodation in preparation for release;

- to notify the relevant Council Tax officer of reception into custody where this has not previously been done when the prisoner was on remand;
- on a discretionary basis for additional contact with a parliamentary or consular representative;
- to contact the Prisons and Probation Ombudsman (PSI 49/2011, paragraph 2.4).

All special letters sent by remand prisoners and those under immigration detention must be sent at public expense (PSI 49/2011, paragraph 2.12).

C15.2.3 *Legal and confidential correspondence*

It is not uncommon for prisoners to complain that their legal mail has been interfered with notwithstanding the Prison Rules, rule 39 (YOI Rules, rule 17). Rule 39 prohibits legal correspondence being opened, read or stopped, unless there is reasonable cause to believe that it contains an illicit enclosure, or that the contents endanger prison security, the safety of others or are of a criminal nature (PSI 49/2011, paragraph 14.2). Each letter must be considered individually. Blanket opening or reading of correspondence to all prisoners or a class of prisoners would be an infringement of ECHR Article 8 (right to a private life). 'Confidential Access' correspondence is correspondence between prisoners and certain individuals or bodies (listed in PSI 49/2011, paragraph 14.1) eg the Prisons and Probation Ombudsman or a Member of Parliament. This correspondence is subject to the same privacy rights as legal mail.

Outgoing mail should be clearly marked 'Confidential Access', 'Prison Rule 39' or 'YOI Rule 17'. However, unmarked and unsealed letters will still be protected by the Rules if they are identified as being confidential. Incoming mail that is clearly marked and is identifiably from a legal adviser will be protected. The policy envisages correspondence being sent in a double envelope with a covering letter to the Governor. If there are grounds to suspect that a letter contains an illicit enclosure it must be opened in the presence of the prisoner, unless the right to be present has been waived (PSI 49/2011, paragraph 14.2). See *R v Secretary of State for the Home Department, ex p Daly* [2001] UKHRR 887, where the House of Lords held that a policy allowing prison staff to search a prisoner's legally privileged correspondence in his absence was unlawful. See also *R (on the application of Chester) v Governor of HMP Wakefield* [2010] EWHC 63 (Admin) where Foskett J held that the policy adopted by the prison of opening legally privileged correspondence in the presence of the prisoner was justified where intelligence received indicated that an abuse of the correspondence procedures was enabling prisoners to receive illicit enclosures, namely drugs and pornography.

C15.3 Restrictions on Correspondents

Prisoners may correspond with any person or organization, subject to the exceptions listed here:

- the recipient of a letter requests in writing to the prison that no further letters be sent (PSI 49/2011, paragraph 2.19);
- the parent or guardian of a child (under 18) has requested that the correspondence be stopped (PSI 49/2011, paragraph 2.20);
- the prisoner has been identified as posing a risk to children or a potential risk, unless an application to correspond with a child for whom they have had parental responsibility or a responsibility has been granted following a risk assessment in accordance with the Public Protection Manual. There must be compelling information to indicate that contact would be in the best interests of the child (PSI 49/2011, paragraph 2.21);
- the Governor considers that correspondence between a young prisoner aged under 18 and any other person would not be in the prisoner's best interest. The views of the parent or guardian should be taken into account. If the correspondence involves a close relative the procedures in the prison's LSS must be followed (PSI 49/2011, paragraph 2.22);
- the correspondence is between convicted prisoners (except close relatives or where they were co-defendants and the correspondence relates to their conviction or sentence) unless approved by the Governors of each prison. Approval should be given provided that correspondence will not seriously impede the rehabilitation of either prisoner, interfere with the interests of security or undermine good order or discipline (PSI 49/2011, paragraph 2.24);
- correspondence is with an ex-prisoner who is under supervision in the community unless the Governor, having taken into account the views of the supervising probation officer, considers that it would not seriously impede the rehabilitation of either party (PSI 49/2011, paragraph 2.25);
- the intended recipient is the victim or a member of the victim's family (except a close relative who wants to receive correspondence, or a victim who has already written to the prisoner since conviction) unless approved by the Governor. Approval may be withheld if it is considered that the approach would cause undue distress. This does not apply to remand prisoners unless there is evidence that the victim is being harassed, or it is an attempt to pervert the course of justice (PSI 49/2011, paragraph2.26);

- the correspondence is with a person or organization that is planning or engaged in activities that present a genuine and serious threat to security or good order (PSI 49/2011, paragraph 2.27);
- the prisoner has been prevented from writing to a person or organization (or would not be allowed to do so) and the correspondence is to another person at the same address, unless the other person is a close relative (PSI 49/2011, paragraph 2.28);
- the correspondence relates to advertising for pen-friends, unless the Governor has granted permission and approved the text (PSI 49/2011, paragraph 2.29).

C15.4 Corresponding with Journalists

Policy guidance on correspondence with journalists is contained in PSI 37/2010. The only restrictions relate to the content of the letters (see **C15.5**).

C15.5 Restrictions on Content

Prisoners in the high security estate should be informed verbally and within the induction pack that their mail will be routinely read in accordance with the prison's LSS. Other prisoners should be informed that their correspondence will not normally be read, unless they fail to comply with the restrictions on content. This may be monitored by random reading, which should not exceed more than 5 per cent of incoming or outgoing letters per prison.

Material that falls within the restrictions on content which apply to all prisoners are as follows:

PSI 49/2011 Prisoner Communication Services

Restrictions on correspondence – including publication on the Internet

11.3 Correspondence may not contain the following:
- (a) Material which is intended to cause distress or anxiety to the recipient or any other person, such as:
  - (i) messages which are indecent or grossly offensive;
  - (ii) a threat;
  - (iii) information which is known or believed to be false;
- (b) Plans or material which could assist or encourage any disciplinary or criminal offence (including attempts to defeat the ends of justice by suggesting the fabrication or suppression of evidence);
- (c) Escape plans, or material which if allowed would jeopardise the security of a prison establishment;
- (d) Material which would jeopardise national security;
- (e) Descriptions of the making or use of any weapon, explosive, poison or other destructive device;

(f) Obscure or coded messages which are not readily intelligible or decipherable;

(g) Material which is indecent and obscene under Section 85(3) of the Postal Services Act 2000;

(h) Material which, if sent to, or received from, a child might place his or her welfare at risk;

(i) Material which would create a threat or risk of violence or physical harm to any person, including incitement to racial hatred;

(j) In addition to restrictions on access to the media (see PSI 37/2010 Prisoners' Access to the Media), material which is intended for publication or use by radio, television or the Internet (or which, if sent, would be likely to be published or broadcast on these media channels) if it:

  (i) is for publication in return for payment, unless the prisoner is unconvicted. However, prisoners are permitted to receive payment for pieces of artwork or work of literary merit but only if they do not contravene any of the restrictions contained within paragraphs (ii)– (v) below and only if channelled through appropriate charitable organisations. This should not be done on a regular basis so as to constitute any form of business activity (i.e. being commissioned to write a series of books or a regular feature in a national publication). It would be for the Governor to decide if such material contravened any of these restrictions. Further guidance on this is at paragraph 2.27 of PSO 4465 – Prisoners' Personal Financial Affairs;

  (ii) is likely to appear in a publication associated with a person or organisation to which the prisoner may not write as a result of the restriction on correspondence in paragraph 2.26 above;

  (iii) is about the prisoner's own crime or past offences or those of others, except where it consists of serious representations about conviction or sentence or forms part of serious comment about crime, the criminal justice system or the penal system;

  (iv) refers to individual prisoners or members of staff in such a way that they might be identified;

  (v) contravenes any of the restrictions on content applying to letters;

(k) In the case of a prisoner against whom a deportation order is in force, material constituting or arranging any financial transaction unless the Governor is satisfied that there is a genuine need for such a transaction (i.e. if in relation to the financial support of a close relative or if seeking advice in order to petition against deportation). This restriction does not apply to a prisoner whose sentence includes a recommendation for deportation but where a decision has not been made by the Secretary of State to act upon the recommendation;

(l) In the case of a prisoner in respect of whom a receiving order or confiscation order has been made or who is an undischarged bankrupt, material constituting or arranging any financial transaction except:

  (i) on the advice of the Official Receiver;

  (ii) to pay wholly or in part a fine or debt in order to secure the prisoner's earlier release;

(iii) to defend criminal proceedings brought against the prisoner;
(iv) to meet the cost of communicating with or instructing a solicitor to act on the prisoner's behalf in bankruptcy proceedings;
(v) to meet the costs of the prisoner's production in bankruptcy proceedings.

C15.6 Restrictions on Receipt of Letters

There are no restrictions on the number of letters that the prisoner can receive if they are in a prison where most correspondence is not monitored (PSI 49/2011, paragraph 2.8). At other establishments the prisoner can receive as many letters as they are allowed to send. The Governor has discretion to return any excess letters to the sender. The prisoner should be given the opportunity to select the letters to be returned. A person who regularly sends excessively long letters may be asked to restrict future letters to no more than four sides of paper. If this request is ignored the Governor has discretion to return the letter. If a letter is returned the prisoner should be informed (PSI 49/2011, paragraph 2.9).

C15.7 Routine Reading

Correspondence (other than legal and confidential mail) may be monitored routinely. However, it must not continue for longer than necessary and should be in accordance with the guidance in the LSS.

C16 **Telephone Communication**

C16.1 **Key Documents**

KD PSI 49/2011

PSI 24/2012

C16.2 **Call Barring and Call Enabling**

Under the pin-phone system, prisoners are given an 8-digit personal identification number (PIN) number to access either call enabling or call barring services, provided they have sufficient credit on their account. Most prisoners will be subject to call barring which allows calls to be made to any number other than those specifically barred by the prison. Call enabling prevents calls being made to any numbers other than global (HMPS estate-wide) or locally (establishment based) enabled numbers, eg the Samaritans, unless they have been submitted and approved by the prison in advance. Prisoners are required to differentiate between social numbers and legal and 'confidential access' numbers.

The Governor may, in consultation with the Area Manager, place the whole prison or a wing/unit onto call enabling for operational reasons eg a high level of drugs circulating within the prison. The pin-phone system must be reviewed at least annually. Remand prisoners other than those who are classified as provisional Category A may be particularly affected by such a policy as their location is determined by the prison's proximity to the court. The more restrictive call enabling service should be linked to the level of risk, and therefore a blanket policy may be susceptible to challenge if it goes beyond the measures that are necessary. See *R (on the application of Taylor) v Governor of HMP Risley* [2004] EWHC 2654 (Admin) where McCombe J applied the proportionality test and accepted that the call-enabling regime was justified as part of the prison's anti-drugs strategy and for public protection measures.

C16.3 **Special Circumstances**

Inter-prison phone calls on an official telephone are permitted between partners or close relatives by special arrangement. The call will be recorded by the prison from where the call is being made (PSI 49/2011, paragraph 6.20). Prisoners may also apply to make a call at public expense on an official telephone for urgent legal or compassionate reasons. The request will not be granted if a visit or letter would suffice (PSI 49/2011, paragraph 8.1). Foreign national prisoners should be permitted to make international calls outside normal hours to allow for time differences, and a 5-minute phone call once a month at public expense if they did not receive a social visit in the preceding month (PSI 49/2011, paragraph 9.1). All calls by foreign nationals who are high or exceptional Category A should comply with the LSS, which will contain procedures to deal with prisoners who do not speak English or who will be calling a person who does not speak English. If the call cannot be interpreted while it is taking place, the recording should be translated within 48 hours (PSI 49/2011, Annex B).

C16.4 General Restrictions

The configuration of the pin-phone system allows Governors to control telephone use for operational reasons across the whole prison, part of the prison, in relation to individual prisoners or as part of the IEP scheme. The programmable options allow limits to be placed on:

- the maximum length of call;
- the time between successive calls;
- the maximum number of calls that can be made in a day; and
- the maximum total call time in one day (PSI 49/2011, Annex A).

C16.5 Global Restrictions

The global restrictions that can only be entered centrally include calls to or via the operator, the emergency services and known sex-line or chat-line services.

C16.6 Other Restrictions

Prisoners are free to telephone any person or organization subject to certain restrictions. Where the restriction applies, the telephone number will either be barred or not be added to a list, if the number has not already been globally or locally barred. Calls to any of the following will be barred:

- a person who has written to the prison requesting that calls from the prisoner be prevented (PSI 49/2011, paragraph 12.10);
- the victim, unless the victim is a close relative, has approached the prisoner first, or if the Governor considers that it would cause undue stress (PSI 49/2011, paragraph 12.8);
- a child under the age of 18 whose parent or guardian has requested in writing that calls from the prisoner be prevented (PSI 49/2011, paragraph 12.5);

- any person an operational manager considers a juvenile in their custody should be prevented from calling in their best interests (PSI 49/2011, paragraph 12.5);
- any particular number known in the prison eg sex-line or chat-line (PSI 49/2011, paragraph 12.1).

C16.7 Calls to Journalists

The policy on communication with the media is contained in PSI 37/2010. In exceptional circumstances calls to journalists may be approved by the Governor. The criteria that apply to visits by journalists also apply to telephone calls.

C16.8 Restrictions on Content

The content of telephone conversations is subject to the same restrictions as the content of letters (see **C15.5**).

C16.9 Recording and Monitoring

Calls from prisoners to legal advisers, the IMB, the Criminal Cases Review Commission, the Prisons and Probation Ombudsman, consular officials and the Samaritans should not be monitored or recorded. The only exception is if the Governor has reasonable grounds to believe that the calls pose a risk to prison security, the safety of others or are of a criminal nature (PSI 49/2011, paragraph 14.19).

The LSS will contain procedures to record and monitor calls either on a routine or random basis in accordance with the NSF. However, as there is no way of ensuring that only non-privileged conversations are recorded, a certain number of phone calls between prisoners and their legal representatives may be monitored inadvertently. The prison should have internal procedures in place to ensure that calls are not monitored for any longer than it takes to establish that the person the prisoner is talking to is a bona fide legal adviser.

Calls made by high risk and exceptional risk Category A prisoners will be routinely recorded and monitored. Calls by prisoners on remand or convicted under the Protection from Harassment Act 1997, and those that are considered to pose a risk to children will also be recorded and routinely monitored. The Governor will have discretion to monitor calls from other individual prisoners if it is necessary and proportionate. The listening may continue only for as long as it remains necessary based on the grounds specified in the Prison Rules, rule 35A (YOI Rules, rule 11) and is proportionate. Routine monitoring must be reviewed at regular intervals.

C17 **Searches**

C17.1 **Key Documents**

 PSI 67/2011

PSI 68/2011

C17.2 **Overview**

> ### PSI 67/2011 Annex A Authority for Searching and Powers of Arrest
>
> #### A1 Powers of Search
>
> 1. Prison Officers carry out searches under Prison Rules 64 and 71 YOI Rules 69 by reason of their constabulary powers.
> 2. Prisoner custody officers may search any person who is in or seeking entry to, the prison (or, in the case of escort PCOs, any place where the prisoner is to be held) and any article in that person's possession.

There are 4 types of personal searches:

1. Level A rub down—a cursory pat-down search;
2. Level B rub down—involves a thorough frisk of the body and a search of outer clothing;
3. Full search—a strip search involving a visual search of the body;
4. Search of other body areas ie visual inspection of the mouth.

Rub-down searches of women and strip searches may only be carried out by an officer of the same sex. Rub-down searches of men may be conducted by an officer of either sex (unless there are religious or cultural objections, in which case the search should be conducted by an officer of the same sex). Intimate searches (intrusion into a bodily orifice) by prison officers are not permitted under any circumstances. Healthcare professionals may conduct internal examinations for clinical reasons only with the prisoner's consent. The searches must be carried out in a seemly manner taking into account religious and cultural beliefs, age and any other relevant factors.

Those authorized to carry out a search of a prisoner may use reasonable force to do so, in accordance with Prison Rules, Rule 47 (YOI) Rule 50 (see **C18.2**).

C17.3 **Prisoner Searches**

Rule 41(1) of the Prison Rules requires every prisoner to be searched on reception and at any other time that the Governor considers a search to be necessary. Searches may be routine (eg prior to a mandatory drug test or cell search) or intelligence led. The frequency, type and level of searches will be defined in the LSS.

Strip searches are particularly humiliating but are a normal part of prison life, especially for Category A prisoners. It should not normally be necessary for the prisoner to be completely naked at any one time, as the upper and lower body can be viewed separately. There can be no doubt that a strip search is an interference with the prisoner's rights under ECHR Article 8 (right to a private life), and will need to be justified and proportionate to any legitimate aim. An order to bend over or squat during a strip search will only be justified if there is reasonable suspicion that an item is being concealed in the anal or genital area, anything short of that will infringe the prisoner's rights under ECHR Article 3 (right to be free from torture, inhuman or degrading treatment), and may give rise to a claim for damages for assault.

C17.4 Cell Search

The prisoner will normally be strip searched prior to a cell search and will then be taken to another location while the search is conducted. The only exception applies to the searching of any legal documents or correspondence, which should be conducted in the prisoner's presence following the decision in *R v Secretary of State for the Home Department, ex p Daly* [2001] 2 AC 532. The searching of privileged material should not continue any longer than is necessary to establish that it is bona fide and does not contain any unauthorized items. Once the documents have been searched the prisoner will be taken to another location while the cell search continues. The prisoner should be told if any articles have been removed.

If a prisoner refuses to co-operate with any type of search reasonable force may be used and a disciplinary charge may be laid (disobeying a lawful order). Policy on the use of force is contained within PSO 1600. However, if the order is successfully challenged and held to be unlawful, any related finding of guilt at a disciplinary hearing will be quashed.

C17.5 Visitor Searches

Rule 71(1) of the Prison Rules (YOI Rules, rule 75(1)) provides that anyone entering or leaving a prison may be searched. Visitors (including legal visitors) will be searched on entry to ensure prohibited items are not brought into the prison deliberately or inadvertently. The search will be either a pat-down or rub-down search depending on the security requirements of the prison. If a visitor refuses to be searched they may be refused entry or placed on closed visits. Searches (including strip searches) on leaving the prison may be conducted without consent if necessary, but only if the prison officer suspects the visitor is carrying drugs or firearms, or the officer has the powers of a constable under the Police and Criminal Evidence Act (PACE) 1984. Prison custody officers have the power to require any person to remove items of clothing but do not have the power to strip search (Offender Management Act (OMA) 2007).

PSI 67/2011 Annex A Authority for Searching and Powers of Arrest

11. *Visitors must not be full searched except where there is a power to search without consent in the circumstances outlined below.*
12. The Firearms Act 1968 (S47), Misuse Of Drugs Act 1971 (S23) and Police and Criminal Evidence Act 1984 (S32) allow those with constabulary powers (i.e. prison officers of the prison only) to conduct searches (up to and including full searches) within the context of their duties as Prison Officers, without consent, in the following circumstances:
    • if there is reasonable cause to suspect the subject is carrying a firearm (with or without ammunition) in a public place, or (in public or private) for the purpose of committing an indictable offence;
    • if there is reasonable cause to suspect the subject is carrying a class A, B or C controlled drug.
13. *If an officer of the prison has arrested the subject, a search may be conducted if there is reasonable cause to suspect they are a danger to themselves or others, or to search for anything which might be used to escape from arrest or which might be evidence relating to an offence—but: there must be reasonable cause to suspect they have such an item on them. They must not be required to remove more than a coat, jacket or gloves in public, and the search must only be to the extent that is reasonably required to find the object.*
14. Staff may search visitors under the above legislation only if:
    1. the designated in-charge governor has authorised the search; and
    2. the police will not attend, or the in-charge governor considers the delay in waiting for the police will frustrate the purpose of the search.
15. *Visitors who are subject to non routine searches must be presented with a Full Search Notice, at Annex J, together with its attached briefing.*

C18 **Use of Force**

C18.1 **Key Documents**

KD	PSO 1600
	PSO 1700

C18.2 **Overview**

Section 8 of the Prison Act 1952 and Prison Rules, rule 47 (YOI Rules, rule 50) confer on prison officers the same powers as constables, to use reasonable force in the execution of their duties. Prison custody officers' powers to use force are derived from CJA 1991, which authorizes the use of force to prevent, detect, or report an unlawful act by a prisoner, to maintain good order and discipline and to safeguard the prisoners' well-being.

Both prison officers and prison custody officers have the common law right to use reasonable force in self defence.

The use of force will only be justified if:

- it is reasonable in all the circumstances;
- it is necessary;
- only necessary force is used;
- its use is proportionate to the seriousness of the circumstances (PSO 1600, paragraph 2.2).

C18.3 **Types of Force**

C18.3.1 *Personal safety techniques*

> **PSO 1600 Use of Force**
>
> **4. TYPES OF FORCE**
>
> Staff use personal safety techniques in the correct circumstances, when it is lawful and necessary, to prevent harm to themselves or a third party.
>
> 4.1 Personal safety techniques can be used by any member of staff who works in an establishment.
> 4.2 The use of personal safety techniques must always be seen as a last resort and relevant medical considerations (see section 3 for information on medical considerations) must be taken into account.
> 4.3 Personal safety techniques are taught for use in the very rare circumstances when all methods of trying to control or evade a violent situation (e.g. by verbal de-escalation, pressing an alarm bell and awaiting assistance, running away etc) have failed and the individual concerned is acting in self

defence or for the protection of a third party (e.g. another member of staff or prisoner). These techniques should be used when C&R is impractical.

4.4 The purpose of personal safety techniques is to prevent an assault without increasing the risk of injury to the prisoner or staff.

4.5 The use of a personal safety technique must only be the force necessary in the circumstances, as the aim is always to get away from the violent situation as quickly as possible.

4.6 The use of a defensive strike must be regarded as an exceptional measure.

4.7 The actual techniques used in personal safety are detailed in the Training Manual and will be taught to staff only by qualified C&R instructors.

4.8 Only the necessary amount of force, in order to get away from the situation, can be legally justified and defended in law.

4.9 The Use of Force Form MUST be completed whenever a protective technique has been employed. The member of staff must justify their actions, why force was used and why the level of force was used.

C18.3.2 *Batons*

PSO 1600 Use of Force

TYPES OF FORCE

Batons

> Batons are used by officers in extreme circumstances as a defensive implement only with due regard to relevant medical implications.

4.10 A baton may only be carried by staff who have been trained in its use, and in those establishments in which the carrying and use of batons has been approved.

4.11 A baton must not be carried within:
- A dedicated juvenile unit; or
- A female establishment; or
- A category D establishment (open); or
- By hospital or nursing staff.

4.12 The drawing and use of a baton must be regarded as an exceptional measure. Staff will be required to justify the use of a baton.

4.13 A baton must never be regarded as anything other than a defensive implement. It may be drawn or used only when:
- It is necessary for an officer to defend themselves or a third party from an attack threatening serious injury; and
- There is no other option open to the member of staff to save themselves or another person but to employ this defensive technique.

4.14 The baton must be directed at the prisoner's arms and legs, where serious injury is less likely to result.

4.15 Officers must be aware of the medical implications of striking a prisoner with a baton see Annex E.

4.16 Officer grades that are issued with a baton MUST carry it at all times when on duty.

4.17 It is also mandatory for PEIs to carry a baton whilst on duties unless there is a risk, on the grounds of health and safety, to the individual or others. This should be decided by a risk assessment and agreed with the Governor locally.

4.18 An officer who draws or uses a baton MUST complete the Use of Force Form.

4.19 Officers must only carry a baton that has been approved for issue by Headquarters and after they have been trained in the drawing and use of a baton.

4.20 C&R advanced trained staff may be issued with a side-arm baton when asked to attend an incident as part of a tornado team. It must be drawn and used in the same way as a standard baton, in accordance with training.

4.21 There will be staff working in establishments in which the carrying and use of batons is not approved, but who may be required to attend a closed male adult or YOI establishment as part of mutual aid arrangements. These staff will be issued with sidearm batons and will receive training in their use, but will only carry their sidearm baton when deployed to a closed male adult or YOI establishment.

C18.3.3 *Basic control and restraint*

PSO 1600 Use of Force

TYPES OF FORCE

Control and Restraint (C&R)

4.24 The deployment of a Three Officer Team is the approved method of dealing with a violent or recalcitrant prisoner. It must only be used as a last resort after all other means of de-escalating (e.g. persuasion or negotiation) the incident, not involving the use of force, have been repeatedly tried and failed.

...

4.26 C&R techniques only use the force that is necessary to enable staff to cope competently and effectively with violent prisoners and potentially disruptive situations, with the minimum risk of injury to staff or prisoners.

4.27 Staff must continue to attempt to de-escalate the situation throughout the incident with the aim of releasing holds and locks. Staff must not employ C&R techniques when it is unnecessary to do so or in a manner which entails the use of more force than is necessary. The application of C&R holds may cause pain to a prisoner and if the prisoner is compliant, the holds must be relaxed.

4.28 Planned incidents involving C&R are used when there is no urgency or immediate danger. In these situations, a supervisor will prepare staff for the incident and will notify a member of healthcare in advance who will attend and observe the planned intervention (if there is any member of healthcare staff on duty).

4.29 Unplanned incidents occur when there is an immediate threat to someone's life / limb or to the security of an establishment and staff need to intervene straight away. In these situations a member of healthcare and a supervising officer will attend as soon as possible.

C18.3.4 *Advanced control and restraint*

PSO 1600 Use of Force

TYPES OF FORCE

C&R Advanced / TORNADO

> The principles of use of force are applied in serious incidents of concerted indiscipline by specially trained and equipped staff.

4.54 Control & Restraint Advanced training permits staff to be employed as part of a C&R Unit (Tornado response) and to respond to major incidents.

C18.3.5 *Ratchet handcuffs*

PSO 1600 Use of Force

TYPES OF FORCE

Use of Ratchet Handcuffs

4.39 The use of ratchet handcuffs during a C&R incident must be authorised by the supervising officer.

4.40 Ratchet handcuffs may be applied temporarily if it is necessary to remove a prisoner from one part of the establishment to another (e.g. relocation to a cell or the segregation unit). The following factors need be taken into account when making an objective decision regarding their use:
   • the distance involved
   • whether the he prisoner is continuing to be violent/aggressive and handcuffs are deemed preferable to using C&R locks during movement and relocation
   • whether the prisoner is reasonably compliant but it is not judged safe enough to permit the prisoner to walk completely independently to the relocation venue.

4.41 Factors such as age, gender, respective size and apparent strength and fitness may or may not support the justification of handcuffs, taking into account all the accompanying circumstances at the time. The physical condition of the prisoner is another consideration in deciding whether or not handcuffs should be applied or their application continued. For example, a prisoner with an arm or wrist injury may be prone to particular risk of further injury or pain if handcuffed; this might make the use of handcuffs unreasonable.

. . .

4.43 Ratchet handcuffs must NOT be used as an alternative to a body belt and must never be left on an unsupervised prisoner.

C18.3.6 *Mechanical restraints*

Mechanical restraints are body belts with metal handcuffs.

PSO 1700 Segregation

Body Belt – General

1. A Body Belt must only be used to prevent a violent or refractory prisoner causing self-injury, injuring another prisoner or member of staff or damaging property, when all other options have failed or are considered unsafe.

2. Every effort must be made to avoid the use of a Body Belt. The option to use Special Accommodation must be considered first. This does not preclude the use of a Body Belt in addition to Special Accommodation, where the circumstances of the case so demand, and where a prisoner cannot safely be left unrestrained in Special Accommodation.

3. Its use must be a last resort, when other methods (calming and de-escalation techniques, use of Special Accommodation, etc) have been tried and have failed. For further information on de-escalation techniques and communication skills...includes guidance on managing aggression, interpersonal and communication skills and diffusion strategies. If it is necessary to fit a Body Belt in an emergency, refer to these documents once the situation is under control.

4. A Body Belt may be used in conjunction with other methods of managing the risk.

5. Calming and de-escalation techniques must always be employed when a Body Belt is used and **the prisoner must be constantly observed by a member of staff in close proximity (face to face) and never by CCTV**. (see pso2700 – 8.8 constant supervision)

6. A Body Belt **must not** be used as a punishment.

7. A Body Belt **must not** be used on a prisoner under the age of 18.

8. Before, during and after the application of the Body Belt, all possible steps must be taken to preserve the prisoner's dignity. Any person that does not need to be in the vicinity of the prisoner must be moved away. The prisoner must be spoken to calmly and respectfully at all time.

9. Any prisoner who is placed in a Body Belt must be taken out of it as soon as the reasons for its use no longer exist.

C19 **Mandatory Drug Testing (MDT)**

C19.1 **Key Document**

| KD | PSO 3601

The authority to obtain a urine or non-intimate sample from a prisoner for the purposes of drug testing is derived from section 16A of the Prison Act 1952. The basic procedural requirements are contained in the Prison Rules, rule 50 and YOI Rules, rule 53.

The MDT framework covers:

- *random testing*—selection for testing on a purely random basis;
- *reasonable suspicion*—testing where there is a reason to believe that the prisoner has misused drugs;
- *risk assessment*—testing where the prisoner is being considered for a privilege eg Release on Temporary Licence, or a job with a high degree of trust;
- *frequent test programme*—where the prisoner has a previous history of drug misuse;
- *testing on reception*—either on a routine or occasional basis (PSO 3601, paragraph 4.1).

The Governor may vary the nature and frequency of non-random MDT, in line with the prison's local drug policy. A refusal to provide a sample or lack of co-operation is likely to result in a disciplinary charge being laid. However, see *R (on the application of Bashir) v Independent Adjudicator* [2011] EWHC 1108 (Admin) where the High Court held that the prisoner had been wrongly convicted of failing to obey a lawful order when he elected to maintain a 3-day fast for personal reasons, which prevented him for providing a urine sample. The prison had interfered with his ECHR Article 9 rights by requiring him to perform an act that depended on him breaking his fast.

Prisoners ordered to attend an MDT suite should be informed of the authority to request a sample, the reasons for the request and the consequences of refusal. Prisoners will be made subject to a thorough rub-down search or a full strip search prior to providing a sample. The search must comply with the prison's LSS, be proportionate to the risk of adulteration and respect the prisoner's privacy as far as possible. An order to squat (male prisoners only) will be unlawful unless it is based on a reasonable suspicion that an item is being concealed in the anal or genital area. The prisoner will then be required to wash their hands and fingernails, prior to providing a sample of at least 35 millilitres, although if there is genuine difficulty in providing that amount a sample of 30 millilitres may be accepted. However, if a doctor or nurse has concluded that there is a medical reason for the prisoner being unable to provide sufficient volume it would be unlawful to continue to request a sample.

While providing a urine sample the prisoner should be observed indirectly. If the prisoner is required to provide the sample in the direct view of the officer (even in circumstances where there is a reasonable suspicion that the sample will be interfered with), this will constitute a breach of the prisoner's rights under ECHR Article 3 (PSO 3601, paragraph 6.26). Women prisoners may be given additional privacy whilst providing a sample, eg a cubicle with the door ajar or with a half door, although prisoners suspected of tampering or proved to have tampered with a sample in the past may be given little or no privacy (PSO 3601, paragraph 6.33).

If the prisoner is unable to provide a sample immediately, they may be confined to a cell or a room for up to 5 hours, if they need more time. Every hour the prisoner should be given approximately one-third of a pint of water. Food need only be provided if the prisoner is confined during mealtime. After 2 or 3 hours the prisoner should be offered access to a member of the healthcare team. A prisoner should not be denied access to a toilet to defecate while in confinement even if it means that they will empty their bladder at the same time. Nor should the prisoner be denied the opportunity to have a social visit.

C20 **Work and Pay**

C20.1 **Key Document**

KD PSO 4460

Rule 31(1) of the Prison Rules provides that convicted prisoners are required to work for a maximum of 10 hours per day. Remand prisoners cannot be compelled to work but may do so if the opportunity is available. Young offenders must be engaged in a programme of activities which may include work (YOI Rules, rule 37(1)). It is a disciplinary offence under the Prison Rules, rule 51(21) for a prisoner who is required to work to either fail to work properly or to refuse to work altogether.

Governors (and Directors in private prisons) are responsible for managing their own local pay schemes and rates. The scheme must:

- reflect Prison Service priorities;
- support and encourage constructive participation in regime activities;
- not provide disincentives to participation in constructive activities which are part of a prisoner's sentence/training plan or learning plan, intended to reduce the risk of re-offending;
- comply with the parameters of PSO 4460 and the IEP policies;
- reward good performance and penalize poor performance;
- be fair, open, balanced and affordable (PSO 4460, paragraph 1.2).

The statutory minimum wage does not apply to prisoners working inside prison. The minimum employed rate of £4 per week should be paid to all prisoners that are employed in work, or engaged in induction, education, training or offender behaviour programmes. Piecework (paid according to the quantity and quality produced) schemes may include rates of pay less than the minimum employed rate as long as workers have the opportunity to earn up to the minimum £4 per week. Governors must set standard rates of pay for each job or other purposeful activity completed to a satisfactory standard in a full working week which is defined as 10 morning, afternoon or evening sessions or 5 nights. The standard rate cannot be less than the minimum employed rate. In addition the Governor or Director can establish a higher rate of pay scheme for certain jobs. Eligibility for these 'higher rate' jobs usually form part of the key earnable privileges under the IEP Scheme. As part of the local scheme the Governor is required to include a system for making deductions of earnings for poor performance or attendance.

C20 Work and Pay

Unemployed prisoners (defined as those who are willing to work but for whom appropriate work cannot be found or prisoners who are unable to work) and those on short-term sickness (less than 4 weeks) will be paid at the rate of £2.50 per week. The long-term sick, retired prisoners, those on maternity leave and prisoners caring for their children full-time in Mother and Baby Units will be paid £3.25 per week. The hospital rate is £4.35 per week or 60p per day, although the governor has the discretion to authorize payment at a higher rate.

As prisoners are not in a contractual relationship with the prison most of the Health and Safety Act 1974 does not apply, however prisons are liable to inspection by the Health and Safety Executive (see Standing Order 6A(15)). Any negligence claim for injuries suffered while at work in the prison would have to be brought under common law.

Prisoners who work outside the prison are entitled to be paid the statutory minimum wage or above, and must not be treated less favourably than other workers in comparable jobs.

C21 **Healthcare**

C21.1 **Key Documents**

KD   PSO 3100

PSO 3630

PSO 3550

The Governor is responsible for ensuring that the healthcare performance standards are met (PSO 3100, paragraph 2.1). Inadequate provision and poor quality healthcare are often the source of prisoner complaints.

C21.2 **Right to Treatment and Consent**

All prisoners should be assessed within 24 hours of reception and if no immediate health issues are identified they should be offered a general health assessment within a week. There should be further medical assessments before discharge or transfer. Rule 20(1) of the Prison Rules provides that prisoners also have the right to see a doctor, nurse or other health professional. Such requests must be recorded and actioned promptly. If a request for treatment is refused, ECHR Article 3 rights (right to be free from torture, degrading and inhuman treatment) may be engaged especially if the prisoner is suffering from a serious illness or medical condition. Remand prisoners have the right to be treated by a doctor or dentist of their choice provided they have the means to cover any fees that may be incurred, and convicted prisoners have the right to be examined by a doctor of their choice if it is relevant to legal proceedings to which the prisoner is a party (Prison Rules, rule 20(5) and (6)).

Clinical decisions such as whether the prisoner should be treated in the prison or whether they should be transferred to an outside hospital must be made by the healthcare professionals. Clearly, this creates tension between competing aims as prisoners have to be escorted to and from outpatient appointments and 'bedwatch' (constant supervision by prison staff) presents particular difficulties, especially in relation to Category A prisoners. The provision of healthcare will vary from prison to prison depending on patient numbers, security risk and the availability of clinical facilities. Options include having visiting specialists attend the prison 'hospital', arranging for waiting time to take place at the prison and telemedicine (remote video consultations between health care professionals and patients). When a prisoner is transferred between prisons, to outside NHS hospitals or into the community their healthcare needs should be assessed and information passed on to ensure continuity of care. If the prisoner has a clinically urgent appointment it may not be appropriate for them to be transferred to an establishment in another area, although in exceptional circumstances security reasons may justify a transfer.

Adult prisoners and young offenders aged 16–17 have the same rights as members of the general public to refuse medical treatment even if such treatment is in their best interests, provided they have sufficient understanding to make an informed choice. Anorexia nervosa is treated differently as it is considered to be a mental illness (see **C21.3.1**), and feeding is considered to be part of the treatment programme. Children under the age of 16 may be competent to consent or refuse treatment depending on their level of understanding and intelligence. However, treatment can be administered without consent, if the prisoner is temporarily incompetent, the treatment is urgent and is in the prisoners best interest (see *Re F (Mental Patient: Sterilisation)* [1990] 2 AC 1).

C21.3 Specific Problems

Prisoners should be referred to an appropriate healthcare professional or a specialist team if at any time concern is raised about the following:

- immediate physical health problems;
- immediate mental health problems;
- significant drug or alcohol problems;
- risk of suicide and/or self harm.

C21.3.1 *Mental health problems*

The initial health assessments are rather basic and depend on accurate self-reporting by the prisoner. As a consequence many prisoners with health problems slip through the net, particularly those with mental health issues, and those that are identified often experience significant delay before they are assessed by a mental health specialist. Early intervention is crucial because of the known link between prisoners with mental health problems and suicide (see **C21.3.3**).

There are provisions under the Mental Health Act (MHA) 1983 (as amended by MHA 2007) for prisoners to be transferred to a psychiatric hospital. Remand prisoners may be transferred to hospital under section 35 or 36 for a report on their mental condition and convicted prisoners may be made subject to a section 37 hospital order as a direct alternative to punishment by imprisonment. Prisoners detained under section 37 may be discharged at any time and may appeal to the Mental Health Review Tribunal (MHRT) after 6 months. If the MHRT decides that the person is no longer suffering from symptoms of mental disorder they must be discharged, even if the risk of relapse is high. Therefore prisoners who are thought to pose a significant risk to the public if released are likely to be made subject to a section 41 restriction (Crown Court only) order in addition to a section 37 hospital order as this gives the Secretary of State a range of powers. These include the power to determine if and when the person should be released, whether any licence conditions should be imposed eg psychiatric care in the community or a return to custody if the person is no longer suffering from a mental disorder. Persons detained under a section 41 order may appeal to the MHRT. While serving a custodial sentence a prisoner can be transferred to hospital for treatment against their will if necessary under section 47.

Prisoners with severe mental health problems may be referred to the specialist units at Frankland, Whitemoor or the secure hospitals—Ashworth, Broadmoor and Rampton. Most referrals are from high security prisons. Prisoners who are considered likely to commit an offence that could cause serious physical or psychological harm from which a victim would find it very difficult to recover, are eligible but as places are limited only psychopaths and prisoners with the most severe personality disorder are likely to be offered a place. There must be a link between the disorder and the risk of violent offending.

C21.3.2 *Drug problems*

The Prison Service has adopted a two-pronged approach to tackle this ever increasing problem. Prisoners found to be in possession of illicit substances or who fail a drug test will be charged with a disciplinary offence and face the possibility of additional days the reasoning being that this will act as a deterrent; and in line with Department of Health guidelines the Prison Service has a drugs strategy which aims to identify, assess and treat substance misusers in recognition that drug use is a public health issue.

The Prison Service aims to meet the non-clinical needs of prisoners with substance misuse through CARATS (counselling, assessment, referral, advice and throughcare) which is available in all prisons, and is an integral part of the drugs strategy. CARATS provide a link between the prisoner and other multi-disciplinary services both inside and outside of the prison. Policy guidance on CARATS can be found in PSO 3630. In addition to the Department of Health guidelines PSO 3550 sets out Prison Service policy on clinical services on offer to substance mis-users in the prison system, which includes detoxification programmes, methadone maintenance and control of withdrawal symptoms.

C21.3.3 *Suicide*

Prison Service policy on suicide and self-harm prevention can be found in PSI 64/2011 Governors and Directors in private prisons must ensure that they have a local suicide prevention strategy, which must include a suicide prevention co-ordinator and a Safer Custody Team that meets regularly. An ACCT (Assessment, Care in Custody, Teamwork) plan should be opened for any prisoner identified as being at risk. Once opened a care plan must be devised which must be reviewed regularly. As part of the care plan the prisoner should be placed in appropriate accommodation which may be a double cell with a cell mate (although care should be taken to avoid a cell mate who is also at risk of suicide—see PSI 09/2011), a constant supervision cell, a safer cell, cell with CCTV, open wards or dormitory.

Except in exceptional circumstances at risk prisoners should not be placed in segregation units. Isolation is known to increase the risk of suicide, and if the prisoner is found guilty of an offence during an adjudication hearing, cellular confinement should be avoided for the same reasons. Any decision to segregate an 'at risk' prisoner must be authorized by the Governor or his deputy, and a mental health assessment must take place within 24 hours.

C22 **The Prisons and Probation Ombudsman**

C22.1 **Key Document**

KD PSI 58/2010

The Prisons and Probation Ombudsman investigates complaints by individual prisoners (in practice, this includes legal representatives acting on their behalf) who remain dissatisfied after exhausting the prison's internal complaints procedure, and will consider an investigation if the prisoner has not received a response to an internal complaint after 6 weeks. Complaints must be made in writing, but there is no prescribed format. Prisoners have a right to confidential access to the Ombudsman, and it is not for prison staff to determine whether there is any merit in the prisoner's decision to take the complaint further.

The Ombudsman can investigate any decision taken by Prison Service staff or agents, other people working in prisons and members of the IMB. However, the clinical judgement of doctors is not within the Ombudsman's remit, nor are the policy decisions of ministers or decisions which are outside the responsibility of the Prison Service (PSI 58/2010, paragraph 4.3).

A complaint to the Ombudsman should normally be submitted in writing within 3 months of exhausting the internal complaints procedure. Complaints raised more than 12 months after the date of the events will not usually be considered, unless the delay was caused by the Prison Service. However, the Ombudsman has discretion to consider late complaints if there is good reason for the delay or if the complaint raises matters of such concern that the normal time limit ought not to apply (PSI 58/2010, paragraph 4.6). Outgoing letters to the Ombudsman should be placed in a sealed envelope and marked 'Confidential Access'. If the address on the envelope is correct, staff may only open the letter (in the presence of the prisoner) if there is a reasonable belief that the enclosure is illicit. Incoming mail should be clearly marked 'confidential' and should not be opened unless there is doubt about its origins. If there is doubt the letter should be passed to the Governor unopened, and enquiries should then be made. If the letter needs to be opened this should be done in the presence of the prisoner (PSI 58/2010, paragraph 4.9).

The Ombudsman will have access to all relevant information (including information which would not be disclosed to the prisoner ie security reports), prison staff and prisoners. However, consent will be required to access the prisoner's medical records and staff personnel records. All staff will be expected to co-operate with the investigation.

C22.2 Fast Track Solutions

The Ombudsman has discretion to seek a fast track local solution if:

- the complaint is eligible for investigation within the Ombudsman's terms of reference;
- it is anticipated that the complaint will be upheld;
- all aspects of the complaint can be resolved as a result of fast track resolution;
- the original decision was taken locally on a non-reserved subject;
- there will be no wider implications beyond the individual prisoner;
- any financial settlement does not exceed the Governor's delegated authority;
- the complaint does not imply the prospect of disciplinary action against staff;
- there is no expectation that the complaint will generate media interest.

Typically, minor property losses and categorization or home detention curfew decisions are settled this way. The prisoner and the Governor or NOMS would have to agree to resolve the complaint by fast track resolution. Once the settlement has been agreed the Ombudsman will write to both parties to confirm the agreement. Where further action is required the Governor must act promptly and confirm when this has been done (PSI 58/2010, paragraph 6.6).

C22.3 Full Investigation

If local resolution is not appropriate, following a full investigation the Ombudsman will prepare a draft report which will be sent to the BCU or the DHS, which should within 7 days, alert the Ombudsman to any factual inaccuracies or sensitive material that should not be disclosed.

If the draft is acknowledged but no comments received a copy of the draft report will be sent to the prisoner. Staff will not be identified by name in the report, however they may be identifiable. If a member of staff has been criticized in the report and is identifiable NOMS will be given a further 7 days to co-ordinate a response.

Following receipt of representations (if any) the final report will be sent to NOMS and the prisoner. The final report may reject the complaint or uphold it in full or in part. If the complaint is upheld the Ombudsman will make a recommendation eg a formal apology, a review of policy or an ex gratia payment for lost property. In certain circumstances a recommendation can be made even if the complaint is rejected. NOMS should respond to the recommendation within 4 weeks. If the recommendation is accepted the Ombudsman must be notified of the action that has been taken (PSI 58/2010, paragraph 5.19).

Judicial Review proceedings should be considered if NOMS refuse to follow a recommendation.

C23 **Parliamentary Commissioner for Administration (PCA)**

C23.1 **Key Document**

KD PSI 02/2012

At any time a prisoner can write to a Member of Parliament (usually their constituency MP) requesting that their complaint be referred to the Parliamentary Commissioner for Administration (PCA). Any supporting evidence should be enclosed. The procedure is outlined in PSI 02/2012, Annex G.

The complaint must be made in writing within 12 months of occurrence of the matter that has given rise to the complaint. The MP may forward the complaint to the PCA if he or she is of the view that the complaint has some merit. If the complaint is forwarded to the PCA and it is decided that an investigation is not justified the MP will be informed and it will be their responsibility to inform the prisoner. The matter will only proceed to the investigation stage if the PCA concludes that:

(a) the complaint has merit; and
(b) there is likely to be a worthy outcome.

If the matter is worthy of investigation, and cannot be resolved by making preliminary enquiries, the PCA may commence a statutory investigation. If a complaint is upheld the PCA may make recommendations. Judicial Review proceedings should be considered if the prison refuses to follow a recommendation.

C24 **Petition to the Secretary of State**

Although there is no reference to it in the Prison Act 1952, the Prison Rules or PSIs, prisoners have the right to refer their complaint to the Secretary of State for Justice as the Minister has overall responsibility for the penal system.

In practice such petitions will be handled by civil servants.

C25 **Practical Considerations**

C25.1 **Overview**

At any stage of the complaints procedure, and on any issue, a legal representative can make written representations on behalf of a client. However, complaints that fail to meet the Sufficient Benefit Test or means test will not be funded.

Complaints about living conditions within the prison will also not normally be funded unless the prisoner has severe mental health problems, a severe learning disability or it raises serious human rights issues. If the prisoner has submitted a complaint and either received an unsatisfactory response or no response at all, an application may be submitted for Prior Approval.

Prisoners will often request Advice and Assistance because they have been on the receiving end of an adverse decision, or because they have submitted a complaint and have either received an unsatisfactory response or no response at all.

The legal representative will need to establish whether the client has already submitted a complaint. If a complaint has not been submitted and it relates to a simple or straightforward matter the client should be advised to submit a complaint on the appropriate form, and encouraged to make contact again if the response is unsatisfactory. If the complaint is serious, complex or of a sensitive nature it may be appropriate to make representations on the client's behalf even if they have not submitted a complaint, eg, a complaint about a member of staff. Each case will need to be assessed based on the individual facts.

Complaints handling must be free from unnecessary bureaucracy, and therefore written representations submitted on behalf of a client will be treated as a complaint although they fall outside the staged Requests and Complaints procedure.

Legal representatives should avoid making representations based solely on their client's version of events, unless the matter genuinely requires urgent and immediate action. Informed representations are more effective, will narrow the issues in dispute and will assist in determining whether grounds for Judicial Review arise. Consideration should be given to enclosing a statement from the client, if the factual background from their perspective is particularly relevant. In the absence of an emergency, representations to the Governor should only be made once the legal representative has obtained the following:

- copy of the relevant policy (from the Prison Service website or via the IAR under FOIA 2000);

- copy of the written reasons;
- copy of the relevant process forms, if applicable (eg segregation or re-categorization);
- copy of the documents which informed the decision (including inmate medical records);
- copy of previous relevant complaints;
- client's instructions.

Requests for disclosure of documents or information are handled flexibly. There is no prescribed format, and there is no need to specify whether the information is being sought under DPA 1998 or FOIA 2000 (see **A8**).

C25.2 Format and Content or Representations

There is no prescribed format for making written representations. Matters relating to the prison regime and formal processes other than those under the jurisdiction of the Parole Board should be addressed to the Governor.

There follows a non-exhaustive list of the issues that should be considered when drafting representations. Not all of these considerations will be relevant or appropriate as much will depend on the particular facts.

- Make the outcome sought clear from the outset.
- Use headings if there are multiple issues.
- Address factual errors/inconsistencies and weight.
- Enclose a statement from client if there is a significant dispute over facts.
- Refer to relevant law or policy documents.
- Comment on reports (positive and negative).
- Make final submissions.

C25.3 Response

A response should be received from the Governor or another operational manager within 7 to 10 days. Written reasons should be provided if the outcome sought is being denied. A failure to provide written reasons would be grounds for Judicial Review. Any reasons that are received should be carefully scrutinized however, grounds for Judicial Review are unlikely to arise unless the Governor failed to take into account relevant matters or gave undue weight to irrelevant matters.

Part D
Formal Discipline

D1 **Overview**

D1.1 **Key Document**

KD Prison Disciplinary Procedures (PDP)

The purpose of adjudication is:

- to help maintain order, control, discipline and a safe environment by investigating offences and punishing those responsible;
- to ensure that the use of authority in the establishment is lawful, reasonable and fair.

D2 **Charging Procedure**

D2.1 **Notice of Report**

Disciplinary charges are formally laid when the prisoner is personally served with Form DIS1 (Notice of Report), which is frequently
referred to as the 'nicking sheet' or being 'put on report'. Form DIS1
should be served at least 2 hours before the adjudication to give the
prisoner time to prepare a defence (PDP, paragraph 2.2). If a charge is
serious or complex, eg fighting, assault or racially aggravated offences,
more time should be allowed.

D2.2 **Reporting Officer**

The officer who discovered the offence, witnessed the offence, or
against whom the offence was committed, should normally lay the
charge, and is referred to as the 'reporting officer'. If that officer is
unavailable another member of staff may lay the charge, in which case
that member of staff's report of the alleged incident will be hearsay
evidence (see **D12.3**). If the alleged offence is discovered by a temporary member of staff or a person on a short-term contract who is
unfamiliar with the Prison or YOI Rules, an officer on a long-term
contract should be informed who will then lay the charge. The officer's
report will be hearsay evidence and the temporary employee should
be called to provide direct evidence at the adjudication hearing (PDP,
paragraph 1.9)

See *R (on the application of Haase) v Independent Adjudicator District
Judge Nuttal* [2007] EWHC 3079 (Admin), where Burnton J, held
that ECHR Article 6 is not infringed where the prosecution case is
presented by an officer who might also be a witness.

D2.3 **Time Limit**

The charge must be laid as soon as possible and within 48 hours of the
discovery of the offence, unless there are exceptional circumstances
that justify a delay (Prison Rules, rule 53 and YOI Rules, rule 58). This
time limit should be interpreted strictly and includes weekends and
Bank Holidays. If the prisoner is transferred before the charge is laid,
the receiving prison should be provided with the Notice of Report, or
details of the alleged offence and asked to lay the charge. The original
48-hour time limit would still apply. In the absence of exceptional
circumstances laying a charge late will render it void.

Once the charge has been laid the hearing must be opened the following day, save for exceptional circumstances, unless that day is a Sunday or Bank Holiday in which case the hearing should be opened on the next working day (PDP, paragraph 2.19).

D2.4 Content

The DIS1 should give details of the charge, time, date, place, rule broken, reporting officer's evidence and details/time of hearing. The prisoner should be in no doubt as to what is being alleged, and when the hearing will take place. An information sheet explaining the hearing procedure must be given and if necessary the procedure should be explained orally. More than one offence may be alleged arising from a single incident if there is evidence to support the charges and they do not constitute over-charging or offend natural justice by being duplicitous.

D2.5 Amendments

A charge cannot be changed once Form DIS1 has been served, although non-contentious details may be amended by the adjudicator provided that this does not result in injustice or unfairness. The prisoner must be informed of any proposed alterations and be given the opportunity to make representations (PDP, paragraph 2.7).

A charge cannot be reduced at the hearing, but alternative charges may be laid in exceptional circumstances eg when it is not clear whether an offence was racially aggravated. If an alternative has not been laid, and there is insufficient evidence to support a particular charge it must be dismissed. See *R v Board of Visitors of Dartmoor Prison, ex p Smith* [1986] 2 All ER 651, where the Court of Appeal held that there was nothing in the Prison Rules that allowed an alternative charge to be laid without offending the mandatory requirement under rule 53(1) that disciplinary charges are laid as soon as possible. Therefore, during an adjudication a fresh charge can only be laid if it is laid as soon as possible and if it is still within 48 hours of the offence being committed (PDP, paragraph 2.41). In these circumstances the hearing must be re-started and a new Governor or Independent Adjudicator should hear the freshly laid charge.

D2.6 Multiple Offences

If a prisoner is charged with more than one offence arising from a single incident the alleged offences should be recorded separately but the individual offences may appear on the same Notice of Report. If the prisoner is charged with a number of offences arising from separate incidents each charge should be laid on a separate Notice of Report. Adjudications on related charges may be heard at a single combined hearing. Unrelated charges against the same prisoner may be heard in sequence by the same adjudicator unless the evidence heard in one case would mean that the adjudicator would not be *de novo* for another case.

D2.7 More Than One Accused

If more than one prisoner is charged in connection with a single incident, each prisoner must be served with an individual notice but the adjudication may be heard together. Alternatively, the adjudicator may decide to hear each case separately.

D2.8 Racially Aggravated Offences

Where there is doubt about whether an alleged assault was racially aggravated the prisoner may be charged with the non-racial charge and the racial charge in the alternative. The adjudicator will then decide at the hearing whether the racial element has been proved. If the racial element is proved the non-racial offence will be dismissed, if the racial element is not proved the adjudicator will enquire into the non-racial offence.

D2.9 Drugs Offences

Substances that are suspected of being controlled drugs will be screened. Although the screening test can only show that a substance may be a controlled drug, this is sufficient for an appropriate charge to be laid. Separate charges must be laid for all drugs that test positive. Irrefutable proof can only be established by sending the sample for full forensic analysis.

Where there has been a positive test for an opiate or amphetamine and the prisoner has been receiving prescribed medication, the Governor/Director has discretion to request a confirmation test prior to charge. Small quantities of drugs or trace evidence of drugs on spoons, foil, scales or other items, however, may not be screened as this will destroy the available evidence and prevent full forensic examination.

In circumstances where a subsequent confirmation test indicates that a different charge would be more appropriate, the original charge must be dismissed and a new charge brought within 48 hours of the results of the confirmation test being received.

There will be no need for a full analysis if the prisoner enters an unequivocal guilty plea, or if the only issue is 'possession' or 'knowledge' unless the suspected drug is Class A (opiates, amphetamines, methadone, cocaine or LSD), as non-controlled drugs such as codeine or dihydrocodeine are also opiates. If the forensic analysis confirms that the drug is codeine, the prisoner may be charged with possession of an unlawful article, unless it was prescribed for him by a doctor.

D3 **Offences**

The authority to discipline prisoners is in section 47(1) of the Prison Act 1952, and the disciplinary offences are contained in the Prison Rules 1999, rule 51 (YOI Rules, rule 50).

There are 29 disciplinary offences in total, which are exhaustive. The list of offences is reproduced here.

D3.1 **Assault**

PSI 47/2011 Prisoner Discipline Procedures

Wording of Charges

1.17 PR 51 (1), YOI R 55 (1) commits any assault
   'At (time) on (date) in (place) you assaulted (name) by punching him.'

...

1.19 Assaults may be witnessed by a member of staff, or be discovered when reported to a member of staff by the alleged victim or other witness.

1.20 An assault involves unlawful force applied to another person, and is therefore not a suitable charge when a prisoner is alleged to have harmed a prison dog. In such circumstances a charge of intentionally obstructing an officer in the execution of his duties (e.g., a dog handler using a dog to conduct a search) may be appropriate.

D3.1.1 Proof required

- The accused applied force to another person or acted in such a way that the other person feared that force would be applied.
- The use of force was unreasonable in the circumstances.

D3.2 **Racially Aggravated Assault**

PSI 47/2011 Prisoner Discipline Procedures

Wording of charges

1.18 PR 51 (1A), YOI R 55 (2) commits any racially aggravated assault
   'At (time) on (date) in (place) you assaulted (name) by punching him, whilst shouting "you black bastard".'

The adjudicator must first determine whether an assault has been committed according to the requirements at **D3.1.1**.

D3.2.1 Proof required

- The accused demonstrated hostility towards the alleged victim based on the victim's membership or presumed membership of a racial group; or
- the offence was motivated partly or wholly by the accused's hostility toward a racial group of which the victim is a member.

D3.3 Detention Against Will

PSI 47/2011 Prisoner Discipline Procedures

Wording of charges

1.23 <u>PR 51 (2), YOI R 55 (3) detains any person against his will</u>
'At (time) (or 'Between (time) and (time)') on (date) in (place) you detained (name) against his will.'

D3.3.1 Proof required

- The accused detained the victim, using force, or the threat of force or any item to restrict the victim's freedom of movement.
- The detention was against the victim's will.

D3.4 Denying Access to any Part of the Prison

PSI 47/2011 Prisoner Discipline Procedures

Wording of charges

1.24 <u>PR 51 (3), YOI R 55 (4) denies access to any part of the prison / young offender institution to any officer or any person (other than a prisoner / inmate) who is at the prison / young offender institution for the purpose of working there</u>
'At (time) (or 'Between (time) and (time)') on (date) in (place) you denied access to (part of prison / YOI) to (name), an officer of the prison / YOI (or 'a person who was at the prison / YOI for the purpose of working there') by barricading your door.'

1.25 A 'detains' charge is intended to deal with a hostage taker, but where collusion with the 'victim' is suspected a 'denies access' charge may be appropriate additionally or alternatively, where the incident also involved a refusal to allow staff to enter a cell or other part of the establishment.

D3.4.1 Proof required

- The accused denied access by construction of a barricade, other impediment or use of any other means.
- The location was part of the prison or young offenders' institution.
- The person who was denied access was an officer or anyone else other than the prisoner who was at the establishment in order to work.

D3.5 **Fights with any Person**

PSI 47/2011 Prisoner Discipline Procedures

Wording of Charges

1.26 <u>PR 51 (4), YOI R 55 (5) fights with any person</u>
'At (time) on (date) in (place) you were fighting with (name)'
1.27 A fight involves two or more persons assaulting each other by inflicting unlawful force. But the force will not be unlawful if the accused only acted in self-defence in response to an assault.

D3.5.1 **Proof required**

- The prisoners involved were inflicting unlawful force on each other.
- None were only using reasonable force in self-defence.

If during the hearing it appears to the adjudicator that one prisoner was acting in self-defence, the fight charge may be dismissed against both the accused and an assault charge laid against the aggressor. The 48-hour limit will run from the time the offence was 'discovered' during the hearing. A new adjudicator will hear the fresh charge (PDP, paragraph 1.28).

D3.6 **Intentionally Endangering Health or Personal Safety**

PSI 47/2011 Prisoner Discipline Procedures

Wording of Charges

1.29 <u>PR 51 (5), YOI R 55 (6) intentionally endangers the health or personal safety of others or, by his conduct, is reckless whether such health or personal safety is endangered</u>
'At (time) on (date) in (place) you intentionally endangered (or 'by your conduct you recklessly endangered') the health or personal safety of (name(s)) by throwing a can of corrosive fluid to the ground.'
1.30 This offence can encompass a range of actions or omissions by prisoners that are intended to cause harm to others (other than assaults or fights), or where the prisoner is careless as to whether harm may result.
1.31 This charge may be appropriate in the case of a dirty protest, in addition to a charge under PR 51 (17) / YOI R 55 (18). A prisoner found in possession of a container of (possibly) adulterated urine, probably with the intention of spoiling a MDT, could be charged under this Rule, but a charge under PR 51 (6) / YOI R 55 (7), or PR 51 (25)(a) / YOI R 55 (29)(a) may be more appropriate.

D3.6.1 **Proof required**

- There was a definite and serious risk of harm to at least one person other than the accused.

- The conduct of the accused was the cause of the danger.
- The accused intended to endanger the health or safety of another, or was reckless as to whether it would be caused.

The prisoner may be found to have been reckless if he foresaw that his behaviour could endanger someone else's health and safety, but still continued with that behaviour, even though it was unreasonable in light of the circumstances. The test is not whether a reasonable person would have foreseen the risk, only if the prisoner foresaw it. The adjudicator should take into account the prisoner's personal characteristics, including age, maturity and mental capacity when considering foresight (PDP, paragraph 2.54).

D3.7 Intentionally Obstructing an Officer

PSI 47/2011 Prisoner Discipline Procedures

Wording of charges

1.33 PR 51 (6), YOI R 55 (7) intentionally obstructs an officer in the execution of his duty, or any person (other than a prisoner / inmate) who is at the prison / young offender institution for the purpose of working there, in the performance of his work
'At (time) on (date) in (place) you intentionally obstructed (name), an officer of the prison / YOI, in the execution of his or her duty (or 'a person who was at the prison / YOI for the purpose of working there, in the performance of his or her work') by placing your foot in the door.'

1.34 This might be an appropriate charge when a prisoner adulterates an MDT sample (obstructing an officer whose duty is to conduct the MDT), as an alternative to disobeying an order to comply with the MDT process by providing an unadulterated sample.

D3.7.1 Proof required

- There was an obstruction; physical barrier or other behaviour.
- The person obstructed was an officer, or someone (other than the prisoner) who was working at the prison.
- The officer was attempting to carry out his or her duty, or the person was attempting to carry out his or her work.
- The accused intended to obstruct the officer in the execution of their duty or the other person in the performance of their work.

D3.8 Escaping or Absconding from Prison

PSI 47/2011 Prisoner Discipline Procedures

Wording of charges

1.35 PR 51 (7), YOI R 55 (8) escapes or absconds from prison / a young offender institution or from legal custody

'At (time) (or 'between (time) and (time)) on (date) in (place) you escaped / absconded from HMP / HMYOI (name) (or 'from an escort').

1.36 There is no offence in law of 'absconding' from prison, only of 'escaping' either with or without the use of force. But for adjudication purposes an escape may be defined as a prisoner leaving prison custody without lawful authority by overcoming a physical security restraint such as that provided by fences, locks, bolts and bars, a secure vehicle, or handcuffs (see paragraph 1.11 for escapes from courtrooms ('dock jumpers')). An abscond is where a prisoner leaves prison custody without lawful authority but without overcoming a physical security restraint

1.37 An escape is 'discovered' (for the purposes of charging with a disciplinary offence) when the prisoner is returned to prison custody, or when someone taken into custody is identified as an escaper. The 48 hours time limit for laying a charge begins at that point. The charge is to be laid by the establishment from which the escape / abscond occurred, so if a prisoner is returned to custody in a different establishment, that establishment must inform the former location and obtain relevant documentation as soon as possible. If the prisoner is returned to custody by the police, a disciplinary charge may still be laid. However, if the police then confirm that the prisoner is being prosecuted for the escape, the adjudicator will dismiss the charge in order to avoid double jeopardy.

D3.8.1 Proof required

- The accused was held in prison or legal custody (includes being escorted to or from a prison by a prison officer or a prison custody officer, or working on an outside party).
- A copy of the committal warrant is produced together with the details of the provisional automatic release date or conditional release date at the time of the alleged escape.
- The accused escaped or absconded. It is for the adjudicator to determine whether the alleged conduct amounts to an escape, therefore the charge should detail the alleged events and not merely state that the prisoner escaped from a named prison.
- The accused had no lawful authority to act as alleged.
- The accused intended to escape.

D3.8.2 *Defences*

- The accused was authorized by the Governor to leave the prison or the control of the officer.
- The accused genuinely believed that he or she had authority to leave the prison or control of the officer.

The reasonableness or otherwise of the belief is a matter which may affect the credibility of the accused's evidence.

An escape from a courtroom while the court is sitting is a matter for the court and no disciplinary charge should be laid in respect of such an incident.

D3.9 Failure to Comply with Condition for Temporary Release

PSI 47/2011 Prisoner Discipline Procedures

Wording of charges

1.38 PR 51 (8), YOI R 55 (9) fails to comply with any condition upon which he is / was temporarily released under rule 9 / rule 5 of these rules
'At (time) (or 'between (time) and (time)') on (date) in (place), having been temporarily released, you failed to comply with the condition that you should (quote condition)'.

1.39 This is the appropriate charge when a prisoner fails to return from ROTL (release on temporary licence) on time, or fails to comply with a restriction or requirement in the licence (e.g., not to contact a named person, or to attend an arranged appointment, etc). The prisoner cannot be charged under this rule for misbehaviour that was not specifically prohibited by a licence condition. But criminal behaviour while on licence could lead to a prosecution.

D3.9.1 Proof required

- A temporary release licence, signed by a person with authority to do so, was issued to the accused.
- The terms of the licence are clear and unambiguous.
- The accused was made aware of the terms of the licence.
- A copy of the licence (preferably the original) has been produced in evidence.
- The accused failed to comply with at least one of the conditions.
- The failure to comply cannot be justified.

D3.10 Administration of Controlled Drug

PSI 47/2011 Prisoner Discipline Procedures

Wording of charges

1.41 PR 51 (9), YOI R 55 (10) is found with any substance in his urine which demonstrates that a controlled drug has, whether in prison or while on temporary release under rule 9 / 5, been administered to him by himself or by another person (but subject to rule 52 / 56)
'Between (date) and (date) you had a substance in your urine which demonstrated that (name of controlled drug) has, whether in prison or on temporary release under Prison Rule 9 / Young Offender Institution Rule 5, been administered to you by yourself or by another person between the dates of (date) and (time and date).'

1.42 This charge should be laid following a positive result from a Mandatory Drug Test (MDT) (not a compact or voluntary drug test failure – see PSI 31/2009), with separate charges being laid for each controlled drug indicated in the test result.

D3 Offences

D3.10.1 **Proof required**

- A controlled drug was administered.
- An approved sample from the accused was tested under mandatory testing arrangements, which confirmed the presence of a controlled drug.
- There were no significant irregularities in the chain of custody procedures.
- The accused consumed the controlled drug when he or she was subject to the prison rules. The later date should be the date of collection minus the minimum waiting period for the drug which tested positive.
- The accused has not been charged previously for misusing the same drug within a period of time which might mean that the current charge could have arisen from the same act as the earlier charge.

D3.10.2 *Defences*

The following are express defences:

- The controlled drug, prior to its administration, had been in the accused's lawful possession for his or her own use or was lawfully administered to the accused by another.
- The controlled drug was administered by or to the accused in circumstances in which he or she did not know and had no reason to suspect that such a drug was being administered.
- The controlled drug was administered by or to the accused under duress or without consent in circumstances where it was not reasonable for the accused to have resisted.

The adjudicator is only required to enquire into a defence if the express defence is raised or credible evidence is presented which casts doubt on the elements of the offence. Additional defences, if raised other than by the accused, must be investigated (PDP, paragraph 2.63).

D3.11 Intoxication after Consuming Alcoholic Beverage

PSI 47/2011 Prisoner Discipline Procedures

Wording of charges

1.45 PR 51 (10), YOI R 55 (11) is intoxicated as a consequence of consuming any alcoholic beverage (but subject to rule 52A / 56A)
'At (time observed by reporting officer) you were seen to be intoxicated (briefly describe circumstances)'

1.46 This charge is appropriate when a prisoner's behaviour clearly indicates intoxication, as opposed to having drunk a small amount of alcohol.

1.47 A prisoner who returns from ROTL showing signs of intoxication may be
charged under this rule. If the licence included a requirement not to drink
alcohol while temporarily released a charge under rule 51 (8) / 55 (9) may
also be appropriate.

D3.11.1 Proof required

- The accused was intoxicated. It is enough for the adjudicator to be
  satisfied that the accused's behaviour was elated beyond self-control.
- The intoxication was wholly or partly as a consequence of consuming any alcoholic beverage. The evidence must be based on the
  observations of the reporting officer carrying out the impairment
  tests, which includes an assessment not only of the individual's balance and co-ordination, but also the ability to pay attention, follow
  simple instructions and divide his or her attention between multiple
  tasks. Indicators such as slurring of speech, unstable gait or smell
  of alcohol will be significant. The adjudicator should enquire into
  other possible causes for the reported behaviour, eg, the prisoner's
  medical condition.
- The accused consumed the alcoholic beverage.
- The presence of alcohol can be determined by a positive breath
  test, although the test alone is not sufficient in the absence of
  impairment.

D3.11.2 *Defences*

- The accused did not know and had no reason to suspect he was
  consuming alcohol.
- The accused consumed the alcohol without consent when it would
  have been unreasonable for him to have resisted.

D3.12 Knowingly Consuming an Alcoholic Beverage

PSI 47/2011 Prisoner Discipline Procedures

Wording of charges

1.49 PR 51 (11), YOI R 55 (12) consumes any alcoholic beverage whether or
not provided to him by another person (but subject to rule 52A / 56A
'At (time observed by reporting officer) you were believed to have consumed an alcoholic beverage'

1.50 This charge is appropriate when a prisoner's behaviour indicates alcohol
has been drunk, but not enough to cause intoxication justifying a charge
under rule 51 (10) / 55 (11), or when the prisoner is seen to drink something that the reporting officer believes contains alcohol (see below for
evidence that a liquid may be alcoholic).

D3 Offences

D3.12.1 Proof required

- The accused's observed behaviour was such as would lead a reasonable man to conclude that it was a consequence of consuming an alcoholic beverage. The indicators would be similar to those noted at **D3.10.1**, (although proof of intoxication is not required); or
- the reporting officer or another witness saw the accused consuming a substance believed to be an alcoholic beverage.

D3.12.2 *Defences*

- The accused did not know or have reason to suspect that he was consuming alcohol.
- The accused consumed the alcohol without consent when it would have been unreasonable for him to have resisted.

D3.13 Possession of Unauthorized Article

PSI 47/2011 Prisoner Discipline Procedures

Wording of charges

1.52 PR 51 (12) / YOI R (13) has in his possession (a) any unauthorised article; or (b) a greater quantity of any article than he is authorised to have
'At (time) (or 'between (time) and (time)) on (date) in (place) you had in your possession an unauthorised article, namely a mobile phone (or 'a greater quantity of (article) than you were authorised to have, namely (number/quantity of article)'.

D3.13.1 Proof required

- The article exists, is accurately described and is found where it is so alleged.
- The accused knew of the presence of the article and its nature which can be inferred from the circumstances ie hidden or attempt made to hide it.
- The accused exercised sole or joint control over the article. A prisoner who discards an article may still be guilty of earlier possession if there is evidence of control prior to abandonment.

D3.13.2 *Defences*

- The accused genuinely believed that the article was authorized.
- The accused believed that there were no restrictions on quantity allowed in possession.

The reasonableness or otherwise of such beliefs may affect the credibility of the accused's evidence.

D3.14 Selling or Delivering Unauthorized Article

PSI 47/2011 Prisoner Discipline Procedures

Wording of charges

1.57 PR 51 (13) / YOI R 55 (14) sells or delivers to any person any unauthorised
article
'At (time) on (date) in (place) you delivered an unauthorised article,
namely (e.g., a SIM card) to (name).'

1.58 This charge is appropriate where the article is by its nature unauthorised
(e.g. drugs), or not authorised to be in the possession of the giver. It is
not necessary to show which of the two methods of passing, selling or
delivering, was used.

D3.14.1 Proof required

- The article was sold or delivered by the accused to another person.
The other person need not be a prisoner.
- The item was unauthorized.

D3.14.2 *Defences*

- The accused genuinely believed that he or she was authorized to
dispose of the item.

The reasonableness or otherwise of the belief is a matter which may
affect the credibility of the accused's evidence.

D3.15 Selling or Delivering Items for
Personal Use

PSI 47/2011 Prisoner Discipline Procedures

Wording of charges

1.59 PR 51 (14) / YOI R 55 (15) sells or, without permission, delivers to any
person any article which he is allowed to have only for his own use
'At (time) on (date) in (place) you sold (or 'delivered without permission')
(e.g., a radio) which you were allowed to have only for your own use
to (name).'
...

1.60 This charge is appropriate where the article is permitted to be in the possession of the giver, but not to be passed on without permission.

D3.15.1 Proof required

- The item was sold or delivered to another.
- The item was allowed only for the accused's own use.
- As regards delivering, the accused did not have permission.

D3.15.2 *Defences*

- The accused genuinely believed that the item was not only for his or her own use.
- The accused had permission to deliver it.

The reasonableness or otherwise of the belief is a matter which may affect the credibility of the accused's evidence.

D3.16 Taking an Article Belonging to Another Person

PSI 47/2011 Prisoner Discipline Procedures

Wording of charges

1.61 <u>PR 51 (15) / YOI R 55 (16) takes improperly any article belonging to another person or to a prison / young offender institution</u>
'At (time) (or 'between (time) and (time)') on (date) in (place) you took improperly (article) belonging to (name of person or establishment).'

1.62 This charge is appropriate whenever a prisoner, without permission, takes anything that does not belong to him or her. If the prisoner attempts to gain control of an article, but is unsuccessful, a charge under PR 51 (25) (a) / YOI R 55 (29) (a) will be more appropriate. If a prisoner improperly obtains something other than a physical article (e.g., abuse of the PIN phone system) a charge under PR 51 (26) / YOI R 55 (23) may be appropriate.

D3.16.1 Proof required

- There was an article.
- The article belonged to another person or to a prison. In many cases the only way of proving the charge beyond a reasonable doubt will be to show who owns the article.
- The accused assumed physical control of the article. If an accused has signed for another prisoner's canteen purchases but has not yet taken possession of them he or she cannot be guilty of an offence under this paragraph. The alternative will be an attempt under Prison Rules, rule 51(25), YOI Rules, rule 55.
- The article was taken improperly ie the accused did not have permission to take it.

D3.16.2 *Defences*

- The accused genuinely believed he or she owned the article or had permission to take it.

The reasonableness or otherwise of the belief is a matter which may affect the credibility of the accused's evidence.

D3.17 Intentionally Setting Fire to Part of a Prison

PSI 47/2011 Prisoner Discipline Procedures

Wording of charges

1.63 <u>PR 51 (16) / YOI R 55 (17) intentionally or recklessly sets fire to any part of a prison / young offender institution or any other property, whether or not his own</u>
'At (time) on (date) in (place) you intentionally (or 'recklessly') set fire to (part of the prison / YOI) (or (an item of property)).'

D3.17.1 Proof required

- The accused set fire to a part of the establishment or other property: property is to be taken as meaning property of a tangible nature, whether real or personal, including money, and also including creatures which are held in ownership.
- The accused intended to set fire to the property, or was reckless as to whether this would happen.

D3.18 Destroying any Part of a Prison

PSI 47/2011 Prisoner Discipline Procedures

Wording of charges

1.65 <u>PR 51 (17) / YOI R 55 (18) destroys or damages any part of a prison / young offender institution or any other property, other than his own</u>
'At (time) on (date) in (place) you destroyed (or 'damaged') a (part of prison/YOI) (or (an item of property) belonging to HMP / YOI (name of establishment) (or 'belonging to (name of person)')

1.66 This charge may be appropriate in the case of a dirty protest, in addition to a charge under PR 51 (5) / YOI 55 (6).

D3.18.1 Proof required

- Part of an establishment or other property was destroyed or damaged.
- The property did not belong to the accused.
- There was no lawful authority or excuse to damage the property.
- The article was damaged by the accused and that guilt is not determined solely on the basis of being in possession of a damaged article or in occupation of a damaged cell.

D3.18.2 *Defences*

- The accused genuinely believed that he owned the property or was entitled to damage it.

The reasonableness or otherwise of such a belief is matter which may affect the credibility of the accused.

D3.19 Causing Racially Aggravated Damage to any Part of a Prison

PSI 47/2011 Prisoner Discipline Procedures

Wording of charges

1.67 PR 51 (17A) / YOI R 55 (19) causes racially aggravated damage to, or destruction of, any part of a prison / young offender institution or any other property, other than his own

'At (time) on (date) in (place) you damaged (or 'destroyed") a (part of prison/YOI) (or (an item of property) belonging to HMP / YOI (name of establishment) (or 'belonging to (name of person)') while demonstrating (or 'motivated, partly or wholly, by') hostility towards a member or members of a racial group.'

D3.19.1 Proof required

- Part of the establishment or other property was destroyed or damaged.
- The destruction or damage was racially aggravated. At the time, or immediately before or after committing the offence, the accused demonstrates towards the victim hostility based on the victim's membership (or presumed membership) of a racial group. The offence is motivated wholly or partly by hostility towards members of a racial group based on the victim's membership of that group.
- The property did not belong to the accused.
- The article was damaged by the accused and that guilt is not determined solely on the basis of being in possession of a damaged article.
- There was no lawful excuse for damaging or destroying the property.

D3.19.2 *Defence*

- The accused genuinely believed that he owned the property or was entitled to damage it.

The reasonableness or otherwise of the belief is a matter which may affect the credibility of the accused's evidence.

D3.20 Unauthorized Presence/Absence

PSI 47/2011 Prisoner Discipline Procedures

Wording of charges

1.70 PR 51 (18) /YOI R 55 (20) absents himself from any place (where) he is required to be or is present at any place where he is not authorised to be

> 'At (time) on (date) you were absent from (place) where you were required to be (or 'you were in (place) where you were not authorised to be')'.
>
> 1.71 This charge can apply to incidents within the establishment, or outside where the prisoner is escorted, or briefly goes outside an open prison, with the intention of returning shortly (e.g., visiting a nearby shop). But if the prisoner has no intention of returning, PR 51 (7) / YOI 55 (8) will apply.

D3.20.1 Proof required

- The accused was required to be in a particular place or was not authorized to be in the place that he or she was found. It will be important to show that any local instructions to prisoners are passed to them and to the accused in particular or that reasonable steps have been taken to pass instructions to the accused.
- The accused was in fact absent from the place he or she was required to be or was in fact present at the place he or she was not authorized to be.
- The accused had no justification for his or her actions.

D3.20.2 *Defence*

- The accused genuinely believed that he was not required to be somewhere else or was authorised to be in the place he or she was found.

The reasonableness of such a belief is a matter which may affect the credibility of the accused's evidence.

D3.21 Showing Disrespect to an Officer or Prison Worker

PSI 47/2011 Prisoner Discipline Procedures

Wording of charges

1.72 PR 51 (19) / YOI R 55 (21) is disrespectful to any officer, or any person (other than a prisoner / an inmate) who is at the prison / young offender institution for the purpose of working there, or any person visiting a prison / young offender institution

'At (time) on (date) in (place) you were disrespectful to Officer (name) (or 'to (name), who was (reason for being at the prison, e.g., a teacher, probation officer, IMB member, visitor, etc) by (briefly describe how disrespect was demonstrated).'

D3.21.1 Proof required

- There was an act, whether spoken, written, or a physical gesture.
- The disrespect was directed towards a specific individual or group.
- The act was disrespectful in the ordinary meaning of the term.

D3 Offences

- The person the term was directed at was an officer or anyone else (other than a prisoner) who was at the prison for the purpose of working there, or a visitor to the prison.

D3.21.2 *Defences*

- The accused did not believe the act to be disrespectful, or that it was not directed at the officer, or a person working at the prison/YOI, or a visitor.

The reasonableness of such a belief is a matter which may affect the credibility of the accused's evidence.

D3.22 Threatening or Abusive Words and Behaviour

PSI 47/2011 Prisoner Discipline Procedures

Wording of charges

1.74 PR 51 (20) / YOI R 55 (22) uses threatening, abusive or insulting words or behaviour
'At (time) on (date) in (place) you used threatening (or 'abusive' or 'insulting') words or behaviour towards (name), by saying (quote words used) (or briefly describe behaviour)'

D3.22.1 Proof required

- The accused performed a specific act or adopted a general pattern of behaviour or said specific words. This need not be a single incident but may have continued over a period of time.
- The act, words, or pattern of behaviour were threatening, abusive or insulting. These words should be given their ordinary meanings taking into consideration the circumstances of the case. Annoying or rude is not sufficient.
- The adjudicator must be satisfied that a reasonable person at the scene would find the words or behaviour threatening abusive or insulting.

There is no specific rule prohibiting sexual acts between prisoners but if they are observed by someone who finds or could find their behaviour offensive a charge under this rule may be laid, particularly if the act occurred in a public or semi-public place within the establishment. However, if two prisoners sharing a cell engage in sexual activity during the night when they have a reasonable expectation of privacy a disciplinary charge is unlikely to be appropriate.

D3.23 Threatening or Abusive Racist Words and Behaviour

PSI 47/2011 Prisoner Discipline Procedures

Wording of charges

1.77 <u>PR 51 (20A) / YOI R 55 (23) uses threatening, abusive or insulting racist words or behaviour</u>
   'At (time) on (date) in (place) you used threatening (or 'abusive' or 'insulting') racist words or behaviour towards (name), by saying (quote words used) (or briefly describe behaviour)'

1.78 The difference between this and the previous charge is that the words or behaviour were motivated (partly or wholly) by hostility to a member or members of a racial group.

D3.23.1 Proof required

- The accused performed a specific act, said specific words or adopted a pattern of behaviour. This need not be a single act but may be continued over a period of time.
- The act, words, or pattern of behaviour were threatening, abusive, or insulting. These words should be given their ordinary meanings taking into consideration the circumstances of the case. Annoying or rude is not sufficient.
- The adjudicator must be satisfied that a reasonable person at the scene would find the words or behaviour threatening abusive or insulting.
- The act, words, or pattern of behaviour were racist (see **D3.2** for definition).

D3.24 Failure to Work Properly

PSI 47/2011 Prisoner Discipline Procedures

Wording of charges

1.81 <u>PR 51 (21) / YOI 55 (24) intentionally fails to work properly or, being required to work, refuses to do so</u>
   'At (time) on (date) in (place) you intentionally failed to work properly, by (briefly describe what the prisoner did or didn't do) (or, 'At (time) on (date) in (place), being required to work in (place) (or 'as a cleaner' etc) you refused to do so.'

1.82 The charge must make clear whether the prisoner did some work, but intentionally failed to do it properly, or refused to work at all.

1.83 This charge is appropriate when the prisoner refuses to work after arriving at the workplace. A refusal to go to the workplace may be charged under PR 51 (18) or (22) / YOI R 55 (20) or (25).

This charge covers two distinct offences: intentional failure to work properly and refusing to work.

D3 Offences

D3.24.1 Proof required

- The accused was lawfully required to work at the time and in the circumstances specified.
- The accused failed to work properly (measured against an identifiable standard) or refused to work either by an act or an omission (a refusal may be inferred from behaviour).

D3.24.2 *Defences*

- The accused genuinely believed that the work was adequate.
- The accused genuinely believed that he was not required to work there and then.

The reasonableness or otherwise of such a belief may affect the credibility of the accused's evidence.

D3.25 Disobeying a Lawful Order

PSI 47/2011 Prisoner Discipline Procedures

Wording of charges

1.84 PR 51 (22) / YOI R 55 (25) disobeys any lawful order
'At (time) on (date) in (place) you disobeyed a lawful order to (briefly describe what the prisoner was ordered to do, or stop doing).'

1.85 An order is lawful if it is reasonable and the member of staff giving it is authorised to do so in the execution of his or her duties.

1.86 A prisoner who adulterates a MDT sample may be charged with disobeying a lawful order to provide an unadulterated sample, or with intentionally obstructing an officer in the execution of his duty to conduct an MDT. A prisoner who refuses to provide any sample may be charged with disobeying a lawful order to comply with the MDT process (see above under PR 51 (9) / YOI R 10).

D3.25.1 Proof required

- The member of staff gave an order. An order is a clear indication by word and/or action given in the execution of his or her duty requiring a prisoner to do or refrain from doing something. The order need not be verbal, nor must it be prefaced by the words 'this is an order'.
- The order must be lawful.
- The accused did not comply with the order or did not comply within a reasonable period of time.
- The accused understood what was required of him/her.

D3.26 Failure to Comply with Rules or Regulations

PSI 47/2011 Prisoner Discipline Procedures

Wording of charges

1.87 PR 51 (23) / YOI R 55 (26) disobeys or fails to comply with any rule or regulation applying to him

'At (time) on (date) in (place) you disobeyed (or 'failed to comply') with the rule (or 'regulation') requiring you to (briefly describe what the rule or regulation required the prisoner / inmate to do (or not do).'

1.88 'Rule or regulation' can mean the requirements of the Prison or YOI Rules, or a local regulation applicable to that particular establishment or wing etc. Reasonable steps must have been taken to make prisoners aware of any local rules, such as notices on wings, information given during induction, training programmes for prisoners' jobs etc. The local rule or regulation must be lawful (see definition under PR 51 (22) / YOI R 55 (25) above).

This is the recommended charge to bring when a prisoner is alleged to have abstracted electricity by tampering with the mains supply or misused the pin-phone system.

D3.26.1 Proof required

- The rule or regulation applied to the accused.
- The accused was aware of the rule or regulation or reasonable steps had been taken to make the accused aware.
- Evidence that the accused had complied with the rule or regulation on previous occasions may be sufficient depending on the facts of the case.
- The rule or regulation was lawful.
- The accused did not comply with the rule or regulation.

D3.26.2 *Defence*

- The accused genuinely believed that the rule or regulation did not apply to them.

The reasonableness or otherwise of such a belief may affect the credibility of the accused's evidence.

D3.27 Receiving Controlled Drugs or Other Unauthorized Articles

PSI 47/2011 Prisoner Discipline Procedures

Wording of charges

1.89 PR 51 (24) / YOI R 55 (27) receives any controlled drug, or, without the consent of an officer, any other article, during the course of a visit (not being an interview such as is mentioned in rule 38 /16)

'At (time) on (date) during the course of your visit you received an article believed to be a controlled drug (or 'an article, namely (describe article), without the consent of an officer.')

1.90 'During the course of a visit' means the period from when the prisoner and visitor first meet until the visitor leaves the visits area. If the alleged article is found after the visit but not in the visits or post-visits searching area, or there is any other reason to doubt that it was received during the visit, a charge under PR 51 (12)(a) / YOI R 55 (13)(a) may be more appropriate. But CCTV evidence may support a charge under PR 51 (24) / YOI R 55 (27).

1.91 'Rule 38 /16' refers to visits from the prisoner's legal advisers.

D3.27.1 Proof required

- The accused received a controlled drug or other article.
- The article was received during the course of a visit ie from when the visitor and prisoner first meet until the visitor leaves the visits area, and immediately after a visit, including the searching area.
- The accused knew the controlled drug or article existed.
- The accused knew they did not have permission to have that article.
- The charge may still be proved if the accused states that the drug or article was received from another prison provided the adjudicator is satisfied it was received during the course of a visit.

D3.27.2 *Defence*

- The accused genuinely believed that permission had been granted to accept such an article from their visitor during the visit.

The reasonableness or otherwise of such a belief may affect the credibility of the accused's evidence.

D3.28 Displaying, Attaching, or Drawing Racist or Insulting Material

PSI 47/2011 Prisoner Discipline Procedures

Wording of charges

1.92 PR 51 (24A) / YOI R 55 (28) displays, attaches or draws on any part of a prison / young offender institution, or on any other property, threatening, abusive or insulting racist words, drawings, symbols or other material

> 'At (time) on (date) in (place) you displayed, attached or drew threatening, abusive or racist words, drawings, symbols or other material aimed towards (name of person or group), namely by writing graffiti saying (quote words written) (or 'by drawing a picture/symbol (describe image)').
> 1.93 The words etc will be racist if motivated (partly or wholly) by hostility to a member or members of a racial group.
> 1.94 There is no non-racial equivalent to this charge. If a prisoner displays, attaches or draws material which is threatening, abusive or insulting, but without the racial element, a charge under PR 51 (20) or (17) / YOI R 55 (22) or (18) may be appropriate.

There is no directly comparable non-racist charge. Consideration ought to be given to laying one or two alternative charges at the same time (Prison Rules, rule 20/YOI Rules, rule 22 or Prison Rules, rule 17/YOI Rules, rule 18).

D3.28.1 Proof required

- The accused drew, displayed, circulated or attached the material (or words) set out in the charge.
- The displayed or circulated material was threatening, abusive or insulting and racist. Annoying or rude is not sufficient.
- The adjudicator must be satisfied that a reasonable person at the scene would find the words or behaviour threatening abusive or insulting.
- The material (or words) were racist. (see **D3.23** for definition)

D3.28.2 *Defence*

- The accused genuinely believed that the behaviour was not racially insulting or abusive.

The reasonableness or otherwise of such a belief may affect the credibility of the accused's evidence.

D3.29 Attempting or Inciting Attempts to Commit Offences

PSI 47/2011 Prisoner Discipline Procedures

Wording of charges

1.95 <u>PR 51 (25) / YOI R 55 (29) (a) attempts to commit, (b) incites another prisoner / inmate to commit, or (c) assists another prisoner / inmate to commit or to attempt to commit, any of the foregoing offences</u>
1.96 The charge must specify whether (a), (b) or (c) applies, and refer to the relevant paragraph number of the 'foregoing offence'. For example:

'At (time) on (date) in (place) you attempted to escape from HMP (name of establishment) by climbing the fence (etc), contrary to Prison Rules 51 (25)(a) and 51 (7).'

Or, 'At (time) on (date) in (place) you incited (name of another prisoner) to assault (name of intended victim) by saying (quote words used), contrary to Prison Rules 51 (25)(b) and 51 (1).'

Or, 'At (time) on (date) in (place) you incited (names) to disobey a lawful order to leave the exercise yard, contrary to Prison Rules 51 (25)(b) and 51 (22).'

Or, 'At (time) on (date) in (place) you assisted (name) to construct a barricade so as to deny access to his cell, contrary to Prison Rules 51 (25) (c) and 51 (3).'

D3.29.1 Proof required

Evidence of attempting

- The accused did an act which was more than preparatory to the commission of the intended offence.
- The accused intended to commit the full offence.

Evidence of inciting

- The accused's action was communicated to other prisoner.
- The other prisoners were sufficiently near to be able to react to the incitement. In this context incitement means seeking to persuade another prisoner to commit a disciplinary offence by suggestion, threats, pressure, words or implication. It does not matter that nobody in fact attempted to commit the full offence.
- The act was capable of inciting other prisoners to commit the full offence.
- The full offence was either the subject of the incitement or the consequence of it.

Evidence of assistance

- Another prisoner committed an offence. This may include an attempt.
- The accused actively assisted in the commission of the offence, which made it easier to commit. It is not sufficient that the accused was aware of the offence and did nothing to prevent it occurring.

Defence

- As Prison Rules, rule 25(c)/YOI Rules, rule 29(c) is dependent upon the commission of another offence, it would be a defence if that other prisoner was found not guilty of the substantive offence.

D4 **Preliminary Matters**

D4.1 **Segregation**

The Governor's power to segregate prisoners until the first hearing of the charge is derived from Prison Rules, rule 53(4)/YOI Rules, rule 58(4). This should not be automatic. The power should be exercised only where there is a significant risk of collusion or intimidation relating to the alleged offence (PDP, paragraph 1.98). Any continued segregation after the first hearing can only be authorized under Prison Rules, rule 45/YOI Rules, rule 49, that is, on grounds of good order or discipline (PDP, paragraph 1.99).

D4.2 **Fitness for Hearing**

A list of all prisoners appearing before the adjudicator should be passed to the Healthcare unit in advance of the hearing to allow any mental or physical health concerns to be raised prior to the commencement of the proceedings (PDP, Annex A, paragraph 1.101). An Initial Segregation Health Screen (ISHS) may be conducted in advance of the hearing, if Healthcare staff consider that in the event of a finding of guilt the prisoner is likely to undergo cellular confinement as a punishment.

It is for the adjudicator to determine fitness to face the hearing (including instances where there is conflicting evidence), and any subsequent punishment based on information from Healthcare staff. The adjudicator should also consult with Healthcare staff if the prisoner's mental or physical health is likely to have been a relevant factor at the time of the alleged offence. If an ISHS was not conducted in advance but is required the adjudicator may either adjourn the hearing until it is completed or ensure it is done within 2 hours of imposing the punishment (PDP, Annex A, paragraph 1.101). If treatment and/or medication is administered by the Healthcare unit after the initial assessment but prior to the adjudication or during an adjournment the prisoner may need to be re-assessed prior to the hearing or resumed hearing.

If, for health reasons, the prisoner is unable to attend the adjudication, a doctor or nurse may be asked for an opinion as to how long this situation is likely to last and, in normal circumstances, a date should be arranged for a further assessment.

A record of any medical concerns, advice given, the adjudicator's decision and reasons must be detailed on form DIS3.

Prisoners with a disability, communication or language difficulty may require assistance to understand and participate in the hearing.

The adjudicator should consider what help may be of assistance and adjourn the hearing if necessary to ensure the necessary arrangements are in place (PDP, paragraph 1.103).

D4.2.1 Proof required

- Legal representatives concerned about a client's fitness to plead or face a hearing should notify the adjudicator as soon as possible and request a medical assessment.
- A doctor or nurse may report to the adjudicator even if the prisoner refuses to be assessed if it is in the public interest, following guidance in the NHS Code of Practice on confidentiality and consent.
- Any medical records submitted as evidence must be disclosed to the prisoner or his representative subject to any exemptions under the Data Protection Act (DPA) 1998.

D4.3 Self-harm

Disciplinary charges should not normally be brought for deliberate self-harm or preparatory acts in furtherance of that aim, even if they are repeated (PDP, paragraph 2.55). Exceptionally, disciplinary charges may be brought where the self-harm endangers the health or safety of others eg arson, and the prison authorities determine that the prisoner either intended to cause injury to others or was reckless as to whether injury would be caused. In the absence of exceptional circumstances the Prison Service must treat self-harm as a health issue and should not use punitive measures as a strategy for dealing with such behaviour.

D5 **Role of Adjudicators**

Adjudications are inquisitorial rather than adversarial. The adjudicator's role is to conduct an impartial inquiry into a report of alleged events and will, as appropriate, involve questioning the accused, the reporting officer and any witnesses to determine whether an offence has been committed under Prison Rules, rule 51/YOI Rules, rule 55.

Adjudicators are required to ensure that hearings are fair, lawful and just. This includes making sure that punishments are normally within locally published guidelines, are proportionate, and that no prisoner is charged or punished for any reason other than their disciplinary behaviour.

D5.1 **Authority to Adjudicate**

PSI 47/2011 Prisoner Discipline Procedures

Authority to adjudicate

1.3 Under Prison Rule 81 / YOI Rule 85 Governors may delegate the conduct of adjudications and related duties (such as considering requests for restoration of additional days) to any other officer of the prison or YOI. In practice this means delegation to any operational member of staff at managerial level (including former Principal Officers reassigned as Developing Prison Service Managers (DPSMs) - see PSI 54/2010) who have passed the relevant authorised training course, have suitable operational experience, and have been certified by the Governor as competent to carry out adjudication duties. In establishments operating a minor reports system these hearings may be delegated to trained and competent Senior Officers. In contracted prisons Directors may delegate adjudications to suitably trained and operationally experienced members of staff, senior enough to be left in charge of the establishment in the Director's absence. Minor reports may be delegated to suitably trained and operationally experienced middle managers.

1.4 Controllers of contracted prisons retain the authority to conduct adjudications, but are not expected to do so routinely.

1.5 Independent adjudicators (IAs) are District Judges or Deputy District Judges approved by the Lord Chancellor for the purpose of enquiring into charges referred to them. Their training is a matter for the Senior District Judge (Chief Magistrate) at the City of Westminster Magistrates' Court.

D6 **Jurisdiction**

D6.1 **Overview**

In *Ezeh & Connors v United Kingdom* [2002] 35 EHRR 28 the European Court of Human Rights held that where prisoners faced the possibility of additional days as a punishment, disciplinary charges were 'criminal' within the meaning of ECHR Article 6 (right to a fair trial), which opened up rights to a hearing before an independent and impartial tribunal, and legal representation. As a result of this decision the Government amended the Prison Rules to create a two-tier system (Prison Rules, rule 53(2):

- Governor-only (or Director) adjudications
- Independent adjudications (District Judge)

In addition serious criminal offences should be referred to the police for investigation.

All adjudications commence with an appearance before the Governor/ Director for contracted prisons, which must take place no later than the day after the charge has been laid, unless there are exceptional circumstances or the following day is a Sunday or public holiday (PDP, paragraph 2.19).

D6.2 **Governor-only Adjudications**

The vast majority of cases will be Governor-only adjudications.

If the case is not referred to the police or the Independent Adjudicator (see **D6.4**) the Governor will proceed with the hearing and investigation of the allegation. If, at any stage after jurisdiction has been retained, it becomes apparent that additional days may be justified the matter may still be referred to an Independent Adjudicator.

D6.3 **Referral to the Police**

Once the opening procedures have been completed the Governor should consider whether the alleged offences are serious enough to justify a referral to the police for further investigation and possible criminal prosecution (PDP, paragraph 2.18). These include alleged substantive and attempted offences of:

- Serious assault
- Rape
- Escape
- Possession of offensive weapons with intent to commit further offences

- Possession of Class A drugs with or without intent to supply
- Possession of Class B drugs with intent to supply
- Possession of large quantity of Class C drugs with intent to supply
- Criminal damage (where damage exceeds £2000) or arson
- Mass disobedience

D6.3.1 Key points

- A serious criminal allegation must be referred to the police at the request of the victim, however, in the absence of such a request the Governor or Director must decide each case on its merits.
- If the matter is referred to the police disciplinary charges under the Prison Rules should also be laid in the normal way, except for the most serious offences eg murder, prison mutiny, etc.
- The adjudication should be opened in the usual way and then adjourned, provided the Governor or Director is satisfied that there is a case to answer. The record of hearing (Form DIS3) has a specific 'tick box' to cover hearings adjourned for this purpose. The charge should not be referred to the Independent Adjudicator at this stage (see **D6.4**).
- If there is no criminal prosecution the Governor must consider whether to proceed with the disciplinary charge. If the CPS decides not to prosecute due to insufficient evidence, and the disciplinary charge is similar and relies on the same evidence as the criminal allegation, the Governor must dismiss the disciplinary charge. The disciplinary charge should also be dismissed if it would be unfair, eg, an unjustifiable delay by the CPS in reaching a charging decision.
- Whenever there is a criminal prosecution the disciplinary charge will not be proceeded with, as long as the prosecution 'present evidence in court'.

D6.4 Referral to Independent Adjudicator

If a case is referred to an independent adjudicator the hearing must be arranged within 28 days. The date of the referral counts as day 1 for the purposes of calculating the time limit.

Prisoners serving the following sentences (see PDP, Annex A, paragraph 2.149) are not eligible for additional days:

- Life sentences (including detention at Her Majesty's pleasure and custody for life)
- Imprisonment (Detained) for Public Protection (IPP)
- Detention and Training Orders
- Foreign national prisoners (FNP) held solely under immigration powers

- Civil prisoners sentenced under the Criminal Justice Act (CJA) 2003 (fine/confiscation defaulters and those held for contempt of court).

In *Smith* [2009] EWCH 109 the High Court ruled that if a prisoner is not eligible for additional days the case may still be referred to an Independent Adjudicator if the Governor determines that it is 'necessary or expedient'. It is intended that this will only apply in exceptional circumstances.

If the prisoner is eligible for additional days and the Governor considers that the offence is serious enough to justify such a punishment in the event of a finding of guilt or guilty plea the case should be referred to the Independent Adjudicator. The test to be applied is whether the offence poses 'a very serious risk to order and control of the establishment, or to the safety of those within it' (PDP, Annex A, paragraph 2.23).

D6.4.1 Key points

- Where determinate and indeterminate sentence prisoners are jointly charged both may be referred to an Independent Adjudicator (PDP, Annex A, paragraph 2.21).
- Where multiple offences are charged relating to the same prisoner and one is to be referred to the Independent Adjudicator, the remaining matters should also be referred (PDP, Annex A, paragraph 2.22).
- Prisoners who have been recalled to custody cannot be awarded additional days beyond their sentence expiry date.
- Although a finding of guilt is likely to adversely affect a lifer's prospects of parole Governor-only adjudications are not a breach of ECHR Article 6 (right to a fair trial) (*R (Tangney) v Secretary of State for the Home Department* [2005] EWCA Civ 1009).

Each case must be considered on its own merits, however PDP, Annex A, paragraph 2.23 offers the following guidance:

PSI 47/2011 Prisoner Discipline Procedures

Referral to an independent adjudicator

2.23 Serious assaults should always be referred, e.g. those where the injuries include broken bones, broken skin, or serious bruising, and

- those where the assault was pre-planned rather than spontaneous,
- those where the alleged offender has a previous history of violence during the current period in custody,
- the victim's role within the establishment (e.g. staff), their vulnerability, and the location of the incident, will also be factors,

- o a racially motivated assault is more likely to be referred than a non-racial one.
- Offences of detaining or denying access may be referred if they go beyond simple obstruction, perhaps to conceal a more serious violent or drug related offence
- A fight charge might be appropriately referred in view of its location, the numbers involved, and the extent of any injuries
- Endangering health and safety offences might be referred if there is evidence of intent rather than recklessness, or where the risk to others was serious. Fire setting charges, irrespective of the level of damage or the prisoners' history should always be referred.
- An escape, if not prosecuted, might be referred in view of the level of physical security that was overcome by the prisoner, any injuries to other people, and any damage to property
- MDT failures or other drug-related offences should not automatically be referred, but referral may be appropriate if Class A or a large quantity of other drugs is involved, or if the establishment has a local drugs problem it wants to deter. MDT refusals and drug smuggling will normally be referred
- Referral of possession of unauthorised article cases will depend on the nature and quantity of the item(s). Lethal weapons, Class A drugs, large quantities of other drugs, or mobile phones will usually be referred. Similar criteria apply to selling or delivering, or taking improperly
- Threatening, abusive or insulting words or behaviour may be referred if racially aggravated, but not normally otherwise
- Refusal to obey lawful orders relating to MDT or searching, or other control issues, will normally be referred
- Attempts, incites or assists charges may be referred if the 'foregoing charge' would have been referred (but see paragraph 1.97 on attempted assault)

D6.5 Offences Committed at Court

PSI 47/2011 Prisoner Discipline Procedures

Laying charges

1.11 Where an offence is alleged to have taken place in a courtroom (including a room within an establishment operating at the time as a court via a video link), while the court was sitting, no charges are to be laid; it will be for the court to deal with the allegation. If an alleged offence occurs elsewhere within the court building, when the prisoner is in the custody of prison staff or escort contractors, the Rules under which a charge may be laid will be those applicable to the establishment the prisoner has been brought from (before appearing in court), or taken to (after the court appearance).

D7 **Legal Assistance**

D7.1 **Overview**

At the commencement of the hearing the Governor must enquire whether the prisoner wishes to have any additional assistance at the start of the hearing. If the prisoner expresses an interest, the Governor must explain the possibility of:

- Legal advice;
- Legal representation;
- Assistance from a friend or adviser (known as a 'McKenzie friend').

Whenever a request for legal advice, legal representation or a McKenzie friend is granted this is likely to result in the need for an adjournment (see **D10**). It is for the prisoner to make contact with the legal representative of his choice or select a McKenzie friend. If the request is refused the adjudication will normally proceed. However, unreasonable refusals will be susceptible to challenge for breach of ECHR Article 6 (right to a fair trial) if the prisoner is subsequently found guilty of the disciplinary offence.

D7.2 **Legal Advice**

Prisoners are not entitled to legal representation at Governor-only adjudications but they are entitled to legal advice as of right under the Advice and Assistance scheme. A request for legal advice should normally be granted if it is the first time the request has been made or if the prisoner has not had sufficient time to request a solicitor.

An adjudicator can refuse access to legal advice if he is satisfied that there are good grounds, ie the prisoner, having had the opportunity, has not made a genuine attempt to instruct a solicitor and has made the request to delay the proceedings.

D7.3 **Legal Representation and McKenzie Friends**

The right to legal representation will automatically be granted if the matter is to be heard before an Independent Adjudicator.

A prisoner will rarely be granted permission to be legally represented at Governor-only adjudications but will be entitled to legal advice (see **D7.2**). However in considering requests for legal representation or a McKenzie friend (relative, friend, fellow prisoner or solicitor acting in a personal capacity) the Governor should take into account amongst other considerations the six factors identified by the

Divisional Court in *R v Secretary of State for the Home Department, ex p Tarrant* [1984] 1 All ER 799.

PSI 47/2011 Prisoner Discipline Procedures

Tarrant Principles

2.10 ...

When a request has been made, adjudicators (governors) will consider each of the following criteria and record their reasons for either refusing or allowing representation or a friend:

- The seriousness of the charge and the potential penalty

  Adjudicators should use their own judgment and knowledge of the local punishment guidelines to decide how serious a charge and potential penalty are. A penalty at or near the maximum will not necessarily mean that representation must be granted. Prisoners sometimes claim that any finding of guilt at adjudication is necessarily serious as it will influence a future Parole Board decision on release or progress to a lower category prison, but this is hypothetical. Adjudicators should only consider the seriousness of the charge and potential punishment resulting from the current adjudication, and should disregard any possible effect on the Parole Board, who will, in any case, base their decision on a range of risk factors, not just on one adjudication.

- Whether any points of law are likely to arise

  This means unusual or particularly difficult questions of legal interpretation, such as the exact definition of an offence within the Prison or YOI Rules, or the effects of a recent court judgment, not merely that a solicitor may refer to the relevant Rule. In such cases, which are likely to be rare, a qualified legal representative may be more suitable than a McKenzie friend.

- The capacity of particular prisoners to present their own case

  Prisoners who are unable to follow the proceedings or to present a written or oral defence due to language or learning difficulties, and particularly those who may have mental health problems, may need help from a friend or representative. Adjudicators will base their decision on the individual circumstances of each case (assuming they have not already decided that the prisoner is unfit to continue with the adjudication because of mental health problems – see paragraph 1.102 above)

- Procedural difficulties

  This relates to any special difficulties prisoners might have in presenting their case, such as in questioning expert or other witnesses. The circumstances in each case will vary, but where questioning witnesses is at issue a qualified legal representative will be preferable to a McKenzie friend, who may only advise, not question.

- The need for reasonable speed

  Adjudicators should balance the inevitable delay while a legal representative prepares a case, including consulting the accused prisoner and interviewing potential witnesses, with the overriding necessity to ensure natural justice. A McKenzie friend may take less time to prepare, but there is still likely to be some delay.

- The need for fairness
  If one prisoner among a group jointly charged in connection with the same incident is granted legal representation or a McKenzie friend, the others in the group may need to be treated the same. If a prisoner is granted help for one charge, the same help should be given for other charges against that prisoner arising from the same incident.

This is not an exhaustive list. The Governor is entitled to take into account any other relevant factors (including for McKenzie friends whether the proposed person is suitable) and reach a decision on the merits of each individual case.

D8 **Disclosure**

D8.1 **Legal Representation**

If the prisoner is entitled to legal representation as of right or has been granted legal representation for a Governor-only adjudication, the request for copies of the adjudication papers should be addressed to the segregation unit. The papers should be provided at no cost.

D8.2 **Legal Advice**

If the prisoner is only entitled to legal advice the papers will not normally be sent to the solicitor directly. The policy is for prisoners to request the papers and pass them on during a legal visit or post them at their own expense.

D8.3 **Checklist**

Requests should be made for the following, as appropriate:

- Notice of Report (DIS1)
- record of adjudication hearing (DIS3)
- copies of all the statements of evidence;
- wing/conduct reports (DIS6);
- medical records;
- access to video evidence;
- any other relevant document;
- site visit to the location of the alleged incident;
- names and numbers of prisoners who may be potential witnesses;
- names of members of staff who may be potential witnesses;
- local punishment guidelines.

Requests can only be refused if there are compelling reasons, eg if disclosure is likely to present a real risk to the author or persons named in the document, or where the information requested falls into one of the exemptions under DPA 1998.

D9 **Pre-hearing Preparation**

D9.1 `Key Points`

- Legal representatives contacted by a prisoner requesting representation at a forthcoming adjudication should in the first instance double-check with the prison whether the hearing is before the Governor or an Independent Adjudicator.
- If there is sufficient time a legal visit should be booked to obtain the client's instructions and a separate visit booked to interview any potential prisoner witness, if appropriate.
- It is good practice to notify the prison in writing at least 24 hours in advance of the hearing to let them know the name of the firm and the legal adviser that will be attending. However, attendance on the day without prior notice will not usually be a bar to entry (especially in local prisons) as long as the legal representative can provide suitable identification. If in doubt the legal representative should check, especially if the prison is at distance, or is a high security establishment.
- A legal visit should not be booked for the hearing date. There will be an opportunity to have a private consultation with the client prior to the hearing, although the facilities vary from prison to prison.

D9.2 Checklist

Legal representatives should take appropriate steps in preparation for an Independent Adjudication hearing, if there is sufficient time. It is important to take whatever steps are possible within the timescale, and then apply for an adjournment if necessary either orally or in writing. Not all of the following steps will be necessary or appropriate as much will depend on the circumstances of the particular case and local arrangements.

- Request disclosure (see **D8.3**);
- Check whether the charge was laid in time and has been or will be opened within 28 days;
- Consider the evidence. Is it strong? Hearsay evidence only? Circumstantial?
- Arrange legal visit: explain what needs to be proved. Advise on strength of evidence, plea, credit and sentence;
- Obtain proof of evidence and comments on the evidence in contested matters;
- Obtain background statement (including previous findings of guilt at disciplinary hearings during current sentence);

- Make arrangements to view any video evidence;
- Make arrangements to interview any witnesses;
- Instruct expert to conduct independent analysis in drugs cases (see **D9.3**);
- Notify the prison (segregation unit) in writing of the legal representative that will be attending the hearing 24 hours in advance.

D9.3 **Drugs Offences**

Prisoners are entitled to have any disputed Mandatory Drug Test (MDT) analysed by an independent laboratory before any disciplinary hearing is determined.

D9.3.1 Key points

- The Prison Service does not maintain an 'approved list', although the prison may be able to provide a list of laboratories known to have expertise in testing urine samples for controlled drugs. Solicitors are not restricted to this list and can select any laboratory to carry out the independent analysis. It will be the solicitor's responsibility to check that the laboratory has the requisite expertise.
- In drafting instructions to the laboratory legal representatives should be aware that there will often be more scope to undermine the prison service report by challenging the integrity of the process rather than the result itself.
- In exceptional circumstances a request can be made for the laboratory scientist instructed by the prison to be called to give evidence. Such an application will only be granted if the legal representative is able to persuade the Independent Adjudicator that it would be unreasonable to rely solely on the written report (see *R v Secretary of State for the Home Department ex p Wynter* [1998] 10 Admin LR 597). However, in contrast to other forms of hearsay evidence, the vast majority of forensic reports can be admitted in evidence without undermining the fairness of the proceedings.

D9.4 **Checklist**

- Provide written evidence of intent to arrange an independent analysis within 14 days of the first adjournment of the adjudication for that purpose.
- Find a laboratory willing to perform the analysis and arrange payment for it.
- Write to the adjudicator requesting release of the sample once an independent laboratory has agreed to do the work within 4 weeks

of the first adjournment for that purpose (you can also request the data pack which contains basic information about the testing of the sample).

- Ensure that the sample is independently analysed within 2 weeks of receipt of the confirmation from the adjudicator or MDT co-ordinator that the sample has been authorized for release.
- When the independent analysis has been completed, advise the adjudicator whether the report will be produced in evidence at the adjudication.
- Inform the adjudicator if there are any delays which will mean that the timescale will not be met, and give reasons for the delay.

D10 **Adjournments**

All hearings, whether Governor-only or Independent Adjudications may be adjourned for many different reasons, including the absence of the reporting officer, a key witness or insufficient time to arrange a legal visit to provide legal advice.

D10.1 Key Points

- Adjournment applications relating to Governor-only adjudications will normally be made in writing. However, for hearings before an Independent Adjudicator, consideration will have to be given to whether to make the application in writing or attend to make the application in person.
- Adjournments granted for legal advice will usually be very short, ie 7 days, which may restrict the legal representative to offering telephone advice only. To advise fully a request for a 14-day adjournment or a further adjournment (if the original adjournment was short) may be necessary.
- Much will depend on the circumstances of the case. If it is known in advance that an Independent Adjudication will be ineffective, and the 'fault' does not lie with the legal representative or the client, consideration should be given to saving time and costs by making a written application, eg where there has been a delay in the prison releasing a drug sample for independent analysis. However, if the merits of an adjournment are not clear or if there are important submissions to be made it will be more appropriate for the adjournment application to be made in person.

D10 Adjournments

- Quite often the reason behind the request for an adjournment can be resolved on the day. For example, it may be possible for prisoner or staff witnesses to attend the segregation unit. Therefore, in appropriate cases legal representatives should attend ready and willing to make progress, if the opportunity presents itself.
- If the application for an adjournment is refused and the prisoner is subsequently found guilty of the disciplinary offence, ECHR Article 6 may have been infringed, as this right includes the right to access facilities and to adequately prepare a defence.

D11 **Conduct of Adjudications**

D11.1 **Physical Arrangements**

Adjudication hearings are often held in a private room in the segregation unit. See *R (Bannatyne) v Secretary of State for the Home Department* [2004] EWHC 1921 (Admin) where it was held that there was no requirement under ECHR Article 6 for prison disciplinary proceedings to be heard in public. The adjudicator must ensure that the general atmosphere is as relaxed as possible. Although adjudications are less formal than criminal proceedings, they should be sufficiently formal to avoid diminishing the importance of the hearing (PDP, Annex A, paragraph 2.1). A prisoner must be escorted by at least 2 officers (who must take no part in the proceedings) for hearings before an Independent Adjudicator. At Governor-only adjudications it is for the Governor (or Director) to assess whether escorting officers are necessary. All parties should be seated if possible, and will remain seated when giving evidence.

D11.1.1 Key points

- The accused prisoner and escort should enter the hearing room ahead of the reporting officer and witnesses, and leave the room after the reporting officer and witnesses, to avoid any suggestion that information may have been given to the adjudicator when the prisoner was not present.
- Only one witness should be in the room at a time, except when the reporting officer wishes to question a witness (when they will necessarily both be in the room at the same time).
- There must be no opportunity for witnesses who have already given evidence to discuss the case with witnesses who are waiting to give evidence.

D11.2 **Opening the Case**

PSI 47/2011 Prisoner Discipline Procedures

Hearing procedures - preliminaries

2.7 The adjudicator will confirm that the charge has been properly laid in accord with the Prison or YOI Rules, and that time limits in relation to laying the charge and opening the hearing have been met. If an error is discovered in the adjudication paperwork the adjudicator will decide whether it would result in any unfairness or injustice to the accused prisoner to continue with the hearing. The prisoner should be informed of any errors and offered an opportunity to make representations as to why it might be unfair or unjust to continue with the hearing. Minor errors are likely to be insignificant, but more serious errors may lead to the charge not being proceeded with – see paragraphs 2.40 and 2.62.

If the prisoner is present the adjudicator should go through the following steps (either directly or through his legal representative):

PSI 47/2011 Prisoner Discipline Procedures

Hearing procedures - preliminaries

2.8 ...

- Confirm the accused prisoner's identity
- Read out the charge, and confirm that the charge as recorded on the DIS1 is identical to that on the DIS3
- Confirm that the prisoner understands the meaning of the charge and, if not, explain it
- Confirm that the prisoner generally understands the adjudication procedure
- Ask whether the prisoner wants to obtain legal advice before proceeding further, and if so, what steps have been taken to contact an adviser. If the prisoner requests more time to obtain legal advice the adjudicator should adjourn the hearing to allow this (it is for the adjudicator to decide how long the adjournment should be for, but two weeks will normally be enough)
- Confirm that the prisoner received the notice of report at least two hours before the opening of the hearing, unless the hearing is being resumed after a previous adjournment and the prisoner confirms that less than two hours has been enough time to prepare for the hearing
- Confirm that any written witness statements already provided for the hearing have been copied to the prisoner and any legal representative (if there is one, at this stage)
- Confirm that the prisoner has had sufficient time to prepare a defence. If not, ask the prisoner how much more time will be needed and consider adjourning as necessary
- Ask whether the prisoner has prepared a written statement, and if so, ensure that it is attached to the record of hearing. The statement will be read out when the prisoner comes to give evidence, or at the mitigation stage
- In IA cases prisoners are entitled to legal representation if they wish, and an adjournment should normally be granted to allow time to arrange this. In cases heard by governors, any request for legal representation or a McKenzie friend (see paragraph 2.10) should be considered under the 'Tarrant Principles' laid down by the Divisional Court in 1984 – see paragraphs 2.10-11. If the governor agrees to allow legal representation a suitable adjournment should be granted to arrange this
- If the prisoner does not want legal advice or representation, or when this has been obtained (or representation refused) and the adjourned hearing is resumed, the adjudicator should ask whether the prisoner pleas guilty or not guilty to the charge. If the prisoner equivocates or refuses to plea a not guilty plea should be recorded

- Ask whether the prisoner wishes to call any witnesses, and if so note their names and briefly outline the nature of the evidence they are expected to give (see paragraphs 2.30 and 2.37 on whether witnesses will be called)

D11.3 Proceeding in Absence

PSI 47/2011 Prisoner Discipline Procedures

Hearings in prisoner's absence

2.3 If a prisoner refuses to attend a hearing, or the adjudicator refuses to allow attendance, for example, on the grounds of disruptive behaviour or an ongoing dirty protest, the prisoner should be warned that the hearing will proceed in his or her absence. If during the course of the hearing the adjudicator is satisfied that the prisoner has ceased to be disruptive, has expressed a wish to attend or is in a suitable condition to attend then attendance will be allowed. The prisoner will be informed of the outcome at the end of the hearing.

2.4 If a prisoner is unable to attend a hearing through illness or court appearances, the adjudicator may open the hearing and adjourn it until the prisoner is available. Healthcare may be asked to advise when the prisoner is likely to be fit enough to attend, and the adjudicator should take this into account when deciding whether it would be fair to continue (natural justice).

D11.4 Impartiality

The adjudicator must ensure that the hearing is fair and unbiased. The test as expressed in *R v Liverpool Justices, ex p Topping* [1983] 1 All ER 490 is as follows:

Is there an appearance of bias?: that would depend upon whether a reasonable and fair minded person attending the hearing with knowledge of all of the relevant facts would reasonably think it would be impossible for the accused to have a fair hearing.

The adjudicator must reach a fair decision based on relevant evidence presented at the hearing and must be '*de novo*', ie he must have had no direct role in the incident that led to the alleged offence, and must disregard any prior knowledge of the prisoner and/or the prisoners previous disciplinary record, as far as reasonably possible.

D11.4.1 Key points

- There must be no prior knowledge of the evidence against the prisoner.
- There must be no knowledge of any information that might be perceived as leading to bias for or against any of the parties.

- If the adjudicator is unable to conduct the hearing *de novo* it must be adjourned and arrangements made for another adjudicator to hear the case.
- The hearing may be adjourned on the adjudicator's own volition or as a result of concerns raised by the prisoner or his legal representative.

In *R v Board of Visitors, ex p Lewis* [1986] 1 All ER 272, Woolf J held that although an individual member of the Parole Board had gained background knowledge of a particular prisoner whilst carrying out administrative duties this did not necessarily disqualify him from sitting as a member of a disciplinary board concerning that prisoner.

In the conjoined appeals of *R (on the application of Al-Hasan & Carroll) v Secretary of State for the Home Department* [2005] 1 WLR 688 the House of Lords held that as the deputy Governor had been present when the prison Governor had ordered the prisoners to squat, there was an appearance of bias when the same deputy Governor ruled on the legality of the order at a subsequent disciplinary hearing.

D12 **Evidence**

D12.1 **Witnesses**

PSI 47/2011 Prisoner Discipline Procedures

Hearing procedures – witnesses

2.29 The adjudicator should hear the evidence of the reporting officer, and ask whether the accused prisoner wishes to question the officer about that evidence. The adjudicator may also ask questions. If the prisoner wishes to question a reporting officer who is not present, or not available via a video link, the hearing is to be adjourned until the officer is available. If the prisoner does not wish to question a reporting officer who is not present the officer's written evidence in the notice of report may be accepted.

2.30 Other witnesses may be called in support of the charge, if the adjudicator agrees their evidence is relevant, and may be questioned by the prisoner, adjudicator or reporting officer. Written evidence may be accepted in the absence of the witness as above if the prisoner has no questions.

...

2.32 Prison staff may be required to appear as witnesses and give evidence as part of their duties. Prisoner witnesses may be required to attend the hearing (without any loss of pay), but cannot be compelled to give evidence. Other people may be invited to attend, but cannot be compelled to do so. Any request for the attendance of an MDT laboratory scientist must be referred to Security Group at NOMS HQ. In respect of MDT, adjudicators should exercise caution in seeking the advice of medical professionals such as prison doctors, nurses and pharmacists, or manufacturers of medication. Whilst such professionals will be qualified and knowledgeable concerning the effect of various substances on the human body, and can comment on the type, amount and frequency of a medication prescribed to a prisoner, they often do not have specific knowledge concerning the compounds present or absent in urine when such substances are consumed. They are even less likely to have specific knowledge on the methodologies and techniques used by the MDT laboratory to identify these compounds. It follows that if scientific advice is needed, it should usually first be sought from the MDT laboratory. Adjudicators should establish the level of specific expertise held by those witnesses offering scientific evidence to MDT hearings, and attach weight to their evidence accordingly.

2.33 Questioning of witnesses must be relevant to the current charge, and the adjudicator should intervene if questions stray into other irrelevant areas or are abusive. Adjudicators should assist accused prisoners who have difficulty in framing relevant questions, and ask their own questions as necessary to clarify any points. Adjudicators must use their own judgment about whether to accept evidence where there may have been collusion between witnesses, or coercion to give or retract statements.

D12 Evidence

See *R v Board of Visitors HMP Blundeston, ex p Fox Taylor* [1982] 1 All ER 646, where it was held that an adjudication would be rendered unfair if the prison authorities are aware of a witness who could assist the prisoner in his or her defence and fail to disclose that information.

D12.2 Physical Evidence

PSI 47/2011 Prisoner Discipline Procedures

Hearing procedures – witnesses

2.31 Physical evidence such as items allegedly found during a search etc, MDT reports, photographs or CCTV recordings may be introduced, and should be described on the record of hearing.

...

See *R (O'Neil) v Independent Adjudicator and Secretary of State for Justice* [2008] EWHC 1371 (Admin) where Mitting J, held that although retention of the physical evidence was an important safeguard, it did not necessarily follow that where such evidence was not retained and so could not be produced, no reliance could be placed on it. In such circumstances the adjudicator is required to assess the reason for the absence of the physical evidence and decide whether there would be any injustice in the light of the totality of the evidence.

D12.3 Hearsay Evidence

PSI 47/2011 Prisoner Discipline Procedures

Hearsay evidence

2.34 First hand evidence from someone who was present when the alleged incident took place is preferable to hearsay, where a witness reports what has been heard from someone else, but such evidence may be accepted provided this is fair to the accused prisoner. See paragraph 1.9 on evidence from temporary staff. However, where a prisoner has told someone about an incident (hearsay), but refuses to give first hand evidence at the hearing, this may cast doubt on their credibility. If the accused prisoner pleads not guilty and wishes to dispute the hearsay evidence, the adjudicator must assess whether, in the absence of a first hand witness, it would be fair to accept the evidence. If not, it must be disregarded. It would not be safe to find the prisoner guilty solely on the basis of disputed hearsay evidence.

2.35 MDT confirmation test result reports are acceptable as evidence, even though the laboratory scientist who performed the test is not present at the hearing.

See *R v Governor of HMP Swaleside ex p Wynter* [1998] 10 Admin LR 597, where it was held that the hearsay rule does not need to be strictly applied to expert scientific evidence.

D12.4 Circumstantial Evidence

PSI 47/2011 Prisoner Discipline Procedures

Circumstantial evidence

2.36 Circumstantial evidence (i.e., indirect evidence that an accused prisoner may have committed an offence) may be taken into account, but is unlikely to be sufficient to prove a charge on its own. For example, if a reporting officer gives evidence that something was undamaged when checked and it was then found to be damaged shortly after the accused prisoner was seen going to the area, this would support, but not necessarily prove, a charge of causing damage, if the prisoner was not actually seen to damage the article. The adjudicator would still need to be satisfied that all the evidence taken together proved the charge beyond reasonable doubt to find the prisoner guilty.

D12.5 Prisoner's Defence

PSI 47/2011 Prisoner Discipline Procedures

Prisoner's defence

2.37 The adjudicator should invite the accused prisoner to offer a defence to the charge, whether by a written or oral statement, and to explain his or her actions or comment on the evidence. (See paragraph 2.108 for mitigation after a charge is proved.) If the prisoner wishes to call witnesses the adjudicator should ask for an outline of the evidence they are expected to give. Witnesses on behalf of the prisoner should normally be allowed to give evidence, unless the adjudicator considers the evidence unlikely to be relevant, or that it will only confirm what has already been established as true. Prisoners should not be allowed to prolong proceedings unnecessarily by calling an excessive number of witnesses. If the adjudicator decides to refuse to allow a witness to be called the reasons for this must be fully recorded on the record of hearing, and must be on proper grounds, not merely administrative convenience or because the adjudicator already believes the accused prisoner is guilty.

D12.6 Charge 'Not Proceeded With'

PSI 47/2011 Prisoner Discipline Procedures

Charges not proceeded with

2.40 If the hearing has reached a stage where it is not possible to reach a conclusion, or where further delay would be unfair on the grounds of natural justice, the adjudicator may decide that it should not proceed further. Reasons for such a decision, which must be recorded, might include:
  • The release of the accused prisoner, or a vital prisoner witness (e.g., the victim of an alleged assault, or a prisoner jointly charged with fighting with the accused prisoner)

- The non-attendance of another material witness (e.g., a member of the public), either because they refuse to attend, or because attendance has been disallowed for security reasons
- The accused prisoner is mentally or physically unfit to attend, and is unlikely to be fit within a time when it would be fair to proceed
- The notice of report is significantly flawed, and there is no time to issue a revised version within 48 hours of the discovery of the offence
- The notice of report was not issued within 48 hours of the discovery of the offence, or the hearing was opened later than the day, or next working day, after the charge was laid, (or in IA cases, the hearing was not opened within 28 days of referral), and there were no exceptional circumstances
- The hearing has been adjourned for more than six weeks, and the adjudicator is not satisfied that it would nevertheless be fair to continue
- The adjudicator has confirmed that the prisoner is being prosecuted for the offence that is the subject of the adjudication

D12.7 Further Offences

PSI 47/2011 Prisoner Discipline Procedures

Evidence of further offences

2.41 If evidence given during the hearing indicates that further offences may have been committed, either by the accused prisoner or another prisoner, charges may be laid in respect of those offences within 48 hours of their discovery. If, during the hearing, it appears that the current charge cannot be sustained but a different offence may have been committed, the original charge may be either dismissed or not proceeded with, and new charges laid, again within 48 hours of the discovery of those offences (e.g. if a fight charge is replaced with an assault charge).

D12.8 Allegations Against Members of Staff

PSI 47/2011 Prisoner Discipline Procedures

Allegations against staff

2.42 If allegations against a member of staff are made before, or during a hearing, the adjudicator should consider whether the accusations are relevant to the current charge. If they are not relevant the person making them should be advised to make a written statement outside the adjudication, and the accusations may be investigated separately. The hearing may then proceed as normal. If the accusations are or may be relevant to the adjudication the adjudicator should either investigate them during the course of the hearing, through questioning the accused prisoner and witnesses, or, if this is not practical, adjourn for a separate, full investigation. Any evidence that comes to light as a result of this investigation must either be taken into account during the resumed adjudication and made available to the prisoner, or, if it is not presented as evidence at the hearing, the adjudicator must take no account of it in connection with the adjudication. Adjudicators who become aware of any findings of the investigation that are not presented as evidence may decide that they are no longer de novo, and hand the case over to a different adjudicator.

D12.9 Standard of Proof

Adjudications operate to the same standard of proof as criminal proceedings. Therefore a prisoner can only be found guilty of an offence if proved beyond a reasonable doubt: *R v Secretary of State for the Home Department, ex p Tarrant* [1985] 1QB 25.

Although the standard of proof is beyond a reasonable doubt it was observed in the *Tarrant* case that adjudicators are 'the masters of their own procedure' and as such the strict rules of evidence do not necessarily apply.

When all the evidence has been heard the adjudicator should invite submissions before considering the question of guilt. The adjudicator can only find the offence proved if all the elements of the offence are present, and they have been proved beyond reasonable doubt. If the charge is found proved the decision should be announced and recorded on DIS3 (record of hearing). A finding of guilt must be supported by reasons, which must also be recorded in DIS3.

D12.10 Mitigation

The prisoner or his or her legal representative should be given the opportunity to put forward mitigation, following a finding of guilt, in support of any reasons that may justify a more lenient punishment than the guidelines as set out in the local or Independent Adjudicator guidelines.

The prisoner may wish to call witnesses to support the mitigation. The adjudicator has discretion to refuse to hear a witness but that discretion must be exercised reasonably, in good faith and on proper grounds. The adjudicator will then consider DIS6 (conduct report), or an oral report outlining the clients behaviour during his current period of imprisonment and DIS5 (adjudication report) on his disciplinary record.

D13 **Punishments**

D13.1 **Overview**

The punishments imposed must be justified, proportionate and consistent. Governors or Directors may impose any punishment except additional days, which can only be imposed by an Independent Adjudicator.

Factors the adjudicator will take into account when determining the level of punishment include:

PSI 47/2011 Prisoner Discipline Procedures

Punishments

2.110 The adjudicator will then consider appropriate punishment(s), adjourning if necessary, and taking account, among other things, of:
  - the circumstances and seriousness of the offence, and its effect on the victim (if any)
  - the likely impact on the prisoner (including any health or welfare impact), the prisoner's age, behaviour in custody, and remaining time to release
  - the type of establishment and the effect of the offence on local discipline and good order, and the need to deter further similar offences by the prisoner and others
  - any guilty plea, ensuring that the prisoner was not pressured into this plea, and that the decision is based on evidence, not just the plea

D13.2 **Individual Punishments**

PSI 47/2011 Prisoner Discipline Procedures

Individual punishments

2.118 Caution PR 55 (1) (a) and (2) / YOI R 60 (1) (a) and (3)
  A caution will be appropriate when a warning to the prisoner seems sufficient to recognise the offence and discourage its repetition. It may not be suspended, or combined with any other punishment for the same charge, including activation of a suspended punishment.
2.119 Forfeiture for a period not exceeding 42 / 21 days of any of the privileges under rule 8 / 6 – PR 55 (1)(b) / YOI R 60 (1)(b)
  This means loss of privileges granted under the local Incentives and Earned Privileges scheme, (or the YJB's Rewards and Sanctions). Adjudicators must specify on the record of hearing which privileges the prisoner is to forfeit, and for how long. The maximum period of forfeiture is 42 days for adults or 21 days for young offenders.
2.120 If the forfeited privileges include a higher rate of pay or access to private cash (e.g. to buy items from the prison shop), and the establishment operates a computer based pay or shop purchasing system, the

punishment should be applied as soon as the system allows. Otherwise it should be applied as soon as it is imposed.

2.121 This punishment does not allow prisoners to forfeit anything that must be provided or allowed under the Prison / YOI Rules (i.e., things that are 'statutory' rather than a privilege). Prisoners should be allowed to buy postage stamps and PIN phone credits, and to make calls to maintain family contact or contact legal advisers, unless the offence was linked to abuse of the phone system. Access to the gym under PR 29 /YOI R 41 should not be forfeited, although additional access under IEP may be lost. In-cell televisions may be forfeited, but not normally radios, newspapers, magazines, notebooks, attendance at education, or religious activities. Possession of tobacco and smoking are privileges under Prison Rules 8 and 25 (2), and may be forfeited. Prisoners aged under 18 are not allowed to smoke at all (PSI 9/2007).

2.122 Any review of a prisoner's IEP privilege level must be dealt with separately from the adjudication procedure. An adjudicator may not downgrade a prisoner's IEP level as an adjudication punishment. (Note – legal advice has confirmed that an IEP review following a separate adjudication punishment is not double jeopardy.)

2.123 <u>Exclusion from associated work for a period not exceeding 21 days PR 55 (1) (c)</u>

This punishment only applies to adults. It is different to forfeiture of the IEP privilege of time out of cell for association under the previous rule. Prisoners serving this punishment remain on normal location, but may not do any work in association with other prisoners. They should not lose any other privileges (unless a separate punishment under the previous rule has also been imposed), other than those incompatible with the punishment under this rule.

2.124 <u>Removal for a period not exceeding 21 days from any particular activity or activities of the young offender institution, other than education, training courses, work and physical education in accordance with rules 37, 38, 39, 40 and 41 – YOI R 60 (1) (c)</u>

This punishment only applies to young offenders. The rule itself explains what activities prisoners will continue to take part in. They may be removed from any activity not excluded by the rule.

2.125 Adjudicators should ensure that combining punishments of forfeiture of privileges and exclusion from associated work or activities does not amount to cellular confinement by another name. The combined punishment should be differentiated from CC by being served on normal location rather than in segregation, and should not exceed the CC maximums of 21 or ten days.

2.126 <u>Extra work outside the normal working week for a period not exceeding 21 days and for not more than two hours on any day – YOI R 60 (1) (d)</u>

Another punishment only applicable to young offenders, which again explains itself. The extra work should be carried out a normal pace.

2.127 <u>Stoppage of or deduction from earnings for a period not exceeding 84 / 42 days PR 55 (10 (d) / YOI R 60 (1) (e)</u>

The adjudicator will specify the percentage of earnings to be lost, up to 100% (less the cost of postage stamps and PIN phone credits, as above), and the number of days this is to continue – maximum 84 days for adults, 42 days for young offenders. The pay to be lost includes gross prison earnings during the period of the punishment (normal pay and performance related or piece rate earnings) but excludes bonuses for exceptional or additional work. The stoppage or deduction should be based on the amount the prisoner actually earned during the period of punishment and not based on average earnings.

2.128 If the establishment uses a computer based pay calculation system the stoppage or deduction should be applied as soon as the system allows. Otherwise it should be applied as soon as the punishment is imposed.

2.129 There is no power under the Prison or YOI Rules to fine a prisoner, nor to deduct the cost of repairing any damage the prisoner may have caused, and the punishment must not be expressed in these terms. (The cost of damage may only be recovered, if at all, through a court order).

2.130 <u>Cellular confinement for a period not exceeding 21 days PR 55 (1) (e) and (3).</u>

2.131 <u>In the case of an offence against discipline committed by an inmate who was aged 18 or over at the time of commission of the offence, other than an inmate who is serving the period of detention and training under a detention and training order pursuant to section 100 of the Powers of Criminal Courts (Sentencing) Act 2000, confinement to a cell or room for a period not exceeding ten days – YOI R 60 (1) (f) and (2)</u> The Prison Rule means an adult prisoner may be given cellular confinement for up to 21 days for a single offence, or consecutive punishments adding up to 21 days for a number of offences arising from a single incident. The YO Rule means that if the inmate was 18 or above at the time of the offence, and is not serving a DTO, a punishment of cellular confinement or confinement to a room for up to ten days for a single offence or consecutive punishments adding up to ten days for a number of offences arising from a single incident may be given.

2.132 If an adult prisoner is serving the maximum punishment of 21 days cellular confinement and is then found guilty of a further offence, another punishment of up to seven days CC may be imposed, bringing the total up to 28 days. If, during this period, the prisoner is found guilty of a third offence, up to another seven days may be imposed, bringing the total up to 35 days.

2.133 In the case of a young offender serving the maximum ten days for a first offence, who is then found guilty of a second and third offence, up to three more days CC may be imposed for each offence, bringing the totals up to 13 then 16 days.

2.134 On each occasion adjudicators should consider whether further cellular confinement will be an effective punishment, and whether an alternative punishment might be more appropriate, particularly if the prisoner is vulnerable. For the fourth or any subsequent offences the adjudicator will consider alternative punishments as it is not possible to impose further CC while the punishment is still being served.

2.135 If a prisoner appears to be committing offences with the intention of remaining in cellular confinement so as to avoid returning to normal location, the aim should be to address whatever problems the prisoner may have on the wing, rather than continually imposing punishment.

2.136 Whenever the adjudicator is considering imposing a punishment of cellular confinement, including a suspended punishment, arrangements are to be made for a doctor or registered nurse to complete an Initial Segregation Health Screen, or else arrangements will be made for this within two hours of imposing the punishment (see PR 58 / YOI R 61). Further guidance on the segregation process, the ISHS, and on the monitoring of prisoners in CC is in PSO 1700. The adjudicator must take account of any medical advice that CC would not be an appropriate punishment for the prisoner on this occasion (e.g., because the prisoner is vulnerable and liable to self-harm), and should either consider a different punishment, or note on the record of hearing the reasons for deciding nevertheless to impose CC. A further ISHS must be completed if it is decided to activate a suspended punishment of CC (since the change of circumstances may affect a vulnerable prisoner differently to the initial suspended punishment).

2.137 Cellular confinement may be served in an ordinary cell set aside for the purpose, not necessarily in the segregation unit. A bed and bedding, a table, and a chair or stool must be provided and must not be removed as a punishment. There must be access to sanitary facilities at all times. Other furnishings and fittings may be provided at the Governor's or Director's discretion.

2.138 In the case of young offenders any cell or room used for this punishment must be certified as suitable for the purpose - see YOI R 61 (2).

2.139 Prisoners serving cellular confinement will be allowed all normal privileges other than those incompatible with the punishment (unless a separate, concurrent punishment of forfeiture of privileges has also been imposed). Compatible privileges will usually include a reasonable number of personal possessions, books, cell hobbies and activities, entering public competitions, and wearing own clothes and footwear where already allowed. Use of private cash and purchases from the prison shop will also be compatible where deliveries are made direct to the prisoner. Prisoners will continue to be able to correspond, exercise, attend religious services, make applications to the Governor, probation officer, chaplain and IMB, and have access to a phone, unless their attitude or behaviour makes it impractical or undesirable to remove them from the cell. Visits should take place separately from other prisoners.

2.140 Prisoners in cellular confinement must be observed according to the requirements set out in PSO 1700, and the healthcare unit and chaplain must be notified daily of prisoners in CC.

2.141 The day cellular confinement is imposed counts as the first day of punishment, and the prisoner may be returned to normal location at any time during the last day (i.e. the first and last days need not be whole days).

2.142 In the case of a prisoner otherwise entitled to them, forfeiture for any period of the right, under rule 43 (1), to have the articles there mentioned PR 55 (1) (g)
This punishment only applies to unconvicted prisoners who, under PR 43 (1) may pay to be supplied with, and keep in possession, books, newspapers, writing materials, and other means of occupation, other than any that the IMB or Governor object to. They may be punished by forfeiting these items for any period the adjudicator may decide.

2.143 <u>Removal from his wing or living unit for a period of 28 / 21 days PR 55 (1) (h) / YOI R 60 (1) (g)</u>

Removal from wing or unit means that the prisoner or young offender (including people under 18) is relocated to other accommodation within the establishment (i.e., away from friends and familiar surroundings), but otherwise continues to participate, as far as possible, in normal regime activities, in association with other prisoners or inmates. The prisoner should not normally lose any privileges, unless a separate punishment of forfeiture of privileges has been imposed.

2.144 The maximum periods for this punishment are 28 days for adults and 21 days for young offenders, but under 18s are only likely to merit the maximum exceptionally.

2.145 Removal from wing should not normally be served in a segregation unit, but if, exceptionally, no other accommodation is available the normal segregation procedures, including completion of an Initial Segregation Health Screen, must be followed.

D13.3 Young People

PSI 47/2011 Prisoner Discipline Procedures

Young persons held under the Prison Rules, and adult females held under the YOI Rules

2.146 A young person who commits a disciplinary offence while held on remand (unconvicted, or convicted but not yet sentenced) will be charged under Prison Rule 51 (same as an adult), but if found guilty will be punished under PR 57, i.e. the maximum numbers of days of punishments will be the same as those in YOI R 60.

2.147 An adult (aged 21 or over) female inmate held in a YOI who commits a disciplinary offence will be charged under YOI R 55, but if found guilty will be punished under YOI R 65, i.e. the maximum number of days of punishments will be the same as those in PR 55.

D13.4 Additional Days

Prisoners are only liable to additional days if they are serving determinate sentences (PDP, Annex A, paragraph 2.148). Extended sentence prisoners are also liable to additional days (PSO 6650, paragraph 11.5.1).

Independent Adjudicators can impose all of the punishments listed at **D13.2**, and in addition have the power to award up to 42 additional days for both adult prisoners and young offenders. Punishments for 2 or more offences arising out of the same incident should normally be concurrent and must not exceed 42 days in total. If consecutive sentences are imposed the adjudicator must ensure that the overall punishment is reasonable and proportionate. A punishment of additional days cannot extend a prisoner's period in custody beyond the SED (sentence expiry date).

Prisoners and young offenders on remand may receive prospective additional days which will become substantive if a determinate sentence is subsequently imposed. The prospective additional days will lapse if an indeterminate sentence is imposed or if the prisoner is found not guilty at trial (PDP, Annex A, paragraph 2.153).

D13.5 Independent Adjudicator's Punishment Guidelines 2008

PRISON ADJUDICATIONS

Independent Adjudicator's Punishment Guidelines

1. Adjudicators should first decide the starting point for the punishment. This starting point will normally be within the guideline range. The starting point suggested is for a prisoner (i) with no previous findings of guilt on adjudications and (ii) following a not guilty plea.
2. The starting point should be increased to reflect any aggravating features of the offence itself and of the offender (such as previous findings of guilt) to ascertain the provisional punishment.
3. The starting point may exceed the range if the aggravating features justify this in which case the Adjudicator should make the appropriate entry on the punishment sheet.
4. The provisional punishment should then be adjusted to reflect any personal mitigating factors.
5. Having thus ascertained the provisional punishment that takes into account all aggravating and mitigating factors the punishment should then be reduced by a third to reflect a discount for a TIMELY plea of guilty if that has been entered.
6. Punishment may be suspended for a period not exceeding six months.

[Note: These Guidelines only apply to added days. Independent Adjudicators may award any other punishment(s) available by virtue of Rule 55 (1) instead of or (with the exception of a caution) in addition to, added days but must, if additional punishment is imposed, bear in mind proportionality.]

Rule 51 Para.	Disciplinary Offence		Starting Point (Days)	Range of Added Days
1.	Commits any Assault:			
	(a) Upon staff:	Push	8	5 – 15
		Deliberate blow	28	21 – 42
		Spitting	28	21 – 42
		Weapon used	32	28 – 42
		Sustained attack	32	28 – 42
	(b) Upon inmate:	Push	5	3 – 10
		Deliberate blow	16	10 – 30
		Weapon used	32	28 – 42
		Sustained attack	32	28 – 42

D13 Punishments

1A.	Racially aggravated assault – add to above days	+ 7	+ 7
2.	Detains any person against his will.	28	21 – 42
3.	Denies access to any part of the prison to any officer or other person (other than a prisoner) who is at the prison for the purpose of working there. [Dependent on duration]	20	10 – 42
4.	Fights with any person. [If sustained treat as a sustained attack as in '1' above]	14	7 – 28
5.	Intentionally endangers the health or personal safety of others or, by his conduct, is reckless whether such health or personal safety is endangered. Intentional: Reckless:	 32 20	 28 – 42 14 – 35
6.	Intentionally obstructs an officer in the execution of his duty, or any person (other than a prisoner) who is at the prison for the purpose of working there, in the performance of his work.	14	6 – 30
7.	Escapes or absconds from any prison or legal custody. Escapes: Absconds:	 32 22	 28 – 42 14 – 42
8.	Fails to comply with any conditions upon which he is temporarily released under Rule 9.	16	10 – 30
9.	Administers a controlled drug to himself or fails to prevent the administration of a controlled drug to him by another. Class A: Class B/C: Non-prescribed medication:	 32 12 12	 28 – 42 7 – 21 7 – 21
10.	Is intoxicated as a consequence of knowingly consuming any alcoholic beverage.	20	14 – 30
11.	Knowingly consumes any alcoholic beverage other than that provided to him pursuant to a written order under Rule 25(1).	15	10 – 30

12.	Has in his possession: (a) any unauthorised articles, or (b) a greater quantity of any articles that he is authorised to have.		
	Weapons:	32	28 – 42
	Class A drugs:	32	28 – 42
	Class B/C drugs:	12	7 – 21
	Item to cheat MDT:	32	28 – 42
	Camera 'phone:	38	35 – 42
	Mobile 'phone and/or accessory:	32	28 – 42
	Alcohol:	22	14 – 42
	Other item:	13	5 – 30
13.	Sells or delivers to any unauthorised person any unauthorised article.	18	10 – 35
14.	Sells or, without permission, delivers to any person any article which he is allowed to have only for his own use.	10	6 – 21
15.	Takes improperly any article belonging to another person or to a prisoner.	18	10 – 35
16.	Intentionally or recklessly sets fire to any part of a prison or any other property, whether or not his own.		
	Intentionally:	32	30 – 42
	Recklessly:	20	14 – 35
17.	Destroys or damages any part of a prison or any other property, other than his own.		
	Intentionally:	28	21 – 42
	Recklessly:	2	7 – 21
17A.	Destroys or damages any part of a prison or any other property, other than his own, when racially aggravated. Add to above days:	+ 7	+ 7
18.	Absents himself from any place he is required to be or is present in any place where he is not authorised to be.	16	10 – 42
19.	Is disrespectful to any officer or other person (other than a prisoner) who is at the prison for the purpose of working there, or any person visiting a prison.	10	6 – 21
20.	Uses threatening, abusive or insulting words or behaviour.	14	5 – 30
20A.	Uses threatening, abusive or insulting racist words or behaviour. Add to above days:	+ 7	+ 7
21.	Intentionally fails to work properly or, being required to work, refuses to do so.	10	5 – 21

22.	Disobeys any lawful order:		
	MDT:	32	28 – 42
	Other:	16	10 – 30
23.	Disobeys or fails to comply with any rule or regulation applying to him	6	3 – 14
24.	Receives any controlled drug, or without the consent of an officer, any other article during the course of a visit (not being an interview such as is mentioned in Rule 38).	32	28 – 42
24A.	Displays, attacks or draws on any part of a prison or on any other property, threatening, abusive or insulting racist words, drawings, symbols or other material.	22	15 – 36

D13.6 Suspended Punishments

Any punishment other than a caution can be suspended for up to 6 months. A suspended punishment can be activated by the commission of a further disciplinary offence during the suspension period. Only an Independent Adjudicator can activate suspended additional days. Irrespective of any punishment for the new offence the adjudicator can:

- activate the suspension in full;
- activate the suspension in part (the remaining period will lapse);
- extend the suspension period by up to 6 months;
- take no action (PDP, Annex A, paragraph 2.114).

D13.7 Interrupted or Delayed Punishments

PSI 47/2011 Prisoner Discipline Procedures

Interrupted or delayed punishments

2.165 A period spent in hospital or prison healthcare will count as part of a punishment period, even if the punishment is not applicable in that location (e.g., loss of privileges may not be enforceable if access to TV is available in the hospital). Attendance at court or organised work will also count towards the punishment period. If a punishment is interrupted while the prisoner is on bail or unlawfully at large, the balance of the punishment, other than cellular confinement, should be served when the prisoner returns to custody in connection with the same legal proceedings. If a period of cellular confinement is interrupted the remainder of it will lapse. If a punishment is delayed or interrupted for other reasons the adjudicator should assess whether to enforce it (e.g., if the prisoner has become too ill to undergo the punishment etc). If a prisoner is released part-way through a disciplinary punishment, the punishment lapses and cannot be restarted if the prisoner later returns to custody on new criminal charges (including cases where a prisoner's current sentence ends but he or she remains in custody on remand for other offences. Technically the prisoner has been released from the current sentence).

D14 **Minor Reports**

Remand prisoners under 21 in local prisons and young offenders in YOIs may be charged with certain minor report offences. Minor Reports allow for swift punishment of lesser offences. The hearing (which may be conducted by senior officers) should normally take place within 48 hours. The normal Prison/YOI Rules and safeguards apply.

If the charge is proved, the punishments are limited to:

- a caution;
- loss of specified privileges (up to 3 days);
- loss of earnings (up to 3 days);
- extra work for no more than 2 hours a day (up to 3 days) (PDP, Annex A, paragraph 2.163).

D15 Remission and Review

The procedure for reviews and remission of punishments will depend on whether the adjudication was before a Governor or an Independent Adjudicator.

D15.1 Governor-only Adjudications

Prisoners may request an informal review of a Governor-only adjudication on the grounds of unfairness or error. If the Governor accepts that the adjudication was significantly flawed the punishment may be remitted or the finding of guilt set aside. A Governor or Director may also terminate or mitigate any partially served punishment, other than additional days, on medical advice or where the punishment has had the desired effect and is unlikely to be repeated (PDP, Annex A, paragraph 3.3).

Formal reviews are initiated on submission of form DIS8 within 6 weeks of the final adjudication hearing. Legal representatives should ensure that they have copies of the relevant documents (DIS1, DIS3, DIS5 and DIS6) prior to submitting form DIS8 to the Governor. The time limit is unlikely to be extended save for exceptional circumstances. In any event, it will be necessary to act quickly if the punishment is being served. Upon receipt of DIS8, the Governor will forward the form, together with the other relevant documents to the Briefing and Casework Unit (BCU). Prisoners serving a punishment of cellular confinement will be fast-tracked. The BCU will consider the request and make a recommendation to the Deputy Director of Custody (DDC) or Director of High Security (DHS). The DDC and DHS has the power to:

- uphold the adjudicators decision;
- quash any finding of guilt;
- terminate a punishment;
- mitigate a punishment.

If the prisoner remains dissatisfied an appeal may be submitted to the Prisons and Probation Ombudsman, or Judicial Review proceedings may be initiated, if grounds exist.

D15.2 Independent Adjudications

There is no power within the Prison/YOI Rules for a finding of guilt by an Independent Adjudicator to be quashed. However, punishments may be reduced in two ways.

D15.2.1 *Reviews under Prison Rules, rule 55/YOI Rules, rule 60B*

Legal representatives can assist prisoners in making an application for a review. The request setting out the reasons should be made in a letter or on form IA4 to the Governor within 14 days of the final adjudication hearing. Legal representatives should obtain all the relevant adjudication documents (DIS1, DIS3, DIS5 and DIS6) prior to submitting the request for a review. The Governor will forward the adjudication papers to the Chief Magistrate's Office for consideration by a nominated District Judge. As the time limit is interpreted very strictly, an application for an extension should be made directly to the Chief Magistrate's Office, within the original time limit if it is not possible to make meaningful representations in time.

Prisoners who are soon to be released, those serving a punishment of cellular confinement or a suspended punishment of cellular confinement will be fast-tracked. Having reviewed the punishment within 14 days of receipt (or sooner if fast-tracked) the District Judge may:

- uphold the punishment;
- reduce the number of additional days;
- substitute a less severe punishment;
- quash the punishment entirely.

D15.2.2 *Remission of additional days*

Prisoners who have been given additional days can apply for them to be remitted if, for 6 months (4 months for young offenders) from the date of the offence, there have been no further findings of guilt. No more than 50 per cent of the additional days can be remitted for each offence. A further application can be submitted 6 (or 4) months after the previous application provided that there have been no further findings of guilt and less than the 50 per cent maximum had been remitted on the previous occasion. The application should be made on from DIS9. Wing staff will then complete the rest of the form detailing the offences which led to the additional days, the prisoner's behaviour since the punishment was imposed, and previous applications for remission. Other members of staff, including staff from another prison if the prisoner spent at least half of the qualifying period in another establishment should also be consulted. Reports should be fair and unbiased. Negative comments should be substantiated, and positive comments should be evidenced. Previous criminal history is irrelevant (PDP, Annex A, paragraph 3.25).

Applications for remission on the grounds of good behaviour must be considered by the Governor within a month. The Governor must allow representations to be made orally if requested. If a meeting takes place the officer who completed the report should be present (if practicable).

In reaching a decision the Governor must take into account:

- whether time has been used constructively, by taking advantage of opportunities for work, education, PE and other activities;
- whether there has been a genuine change of attitude;
- whether, bearing in mind the nature of the original offence, remission is appropriate to reward a constructive approach and significant change in attitude (PDP, Annex A, paragraph 3.28).

The prisoner may be informed immediately if appearing before the Governor. In any event the decision must be confirmed in writing with reasons on form DIS9 within 7 days. The form must confirm the prisoner's earliest release date.

D15.3 Judicial Review

Findings of guilt by an Independent Adjudicator can only be challenged if there are grounds for Judicial Review. In *Deputy Governor of Parkhurst Prison ex p Leech* [1988] 1 AC 533, the House of Lords confirmed that Governor-only adjudications can also be directly challenged in the High Court.

Circumstances which may give rise to grounds for Judicial Review include:

PSI 47/2011 Prisoner Discipline Procedures

Judicial review

3.15 Judicial reviews are generally based on one or more of the following grounds:

- Ultra vires – the adjudicator acted outside the powers given to him or her by the Prison / YOI Rules
- Breach of the rules of natural justice – the adjudication was unfair because the adjudicator was biased, or the accused prisoner did not have an opportunity to present a case ('audi alteram partem' – hear the other side)
- Legitimate expectation – the adjudication was not conducted in the way, or the prisoner was not treated, as the prisoner was entitled to expect
- Inadequate reasons – the adjudicator did not give proper reasons for the decision(s)
- Fettering discretion – the adjudicator did not exercise discretion fairly, or did not have an open mind about the circumstances of the case
- Unreasonableness – the adjudicator's decision was irrational - no authority properly directing itself on the law and acting reasonably could have reached such a decision (e.g., relevant issues were ignored or irrelevant ones given weight, the wrong test was applied in reaching a finding, or a punishment was indefensibly severe)
- Breach of a right under the European Convention on Human Rights – usually Article 6 (right to a fair trial) – mostly raised in IA cases

---

Part E
Informal Discipline

E1 **Overview**

Discipline is maintained informally through the use of the following procedures:

- Segregation under the Prison/YOI Rules;
- Transfers to other prisons/units;
- Re-categorization;
- Re-grading under the Incentives and Earned Privileges (IEP) Scheme.

These procedures are more likely to form the basis of complaints than formal adjudications as they have none of the safeguards of the formal scheme and as the courts have consistently demonstrated a reluctance to involve themselves in the management decisions of prisons, Governors/Directors are free to exercise their discretion with few constraints.

E2 Segregation under Prison Rules, rule 45/YOI Rules, rule 49

E2.1 Key Document

KD PSO 1700

Prisoners may be removed from normal location to a segregation unit under this rule for reasons of good order or discipline, or for their own protection. These units are sometimes known as 'Separation and Care'.

E2.2 Good Order or Discipline (GOod)

Prisoners may be separated for reasons of GOod where there are reasonable grounds for believing that the prisoner is likely to be so disruptive or cause disruption that keeping the prisoner in normal location is unsafe. Examples of behaviour that may justify segregation include internal possession of drugs with intent to supply, failure to co-operate with anti-bullying strategies, evidence of a planned or imminent breach of security and 'dirty protests' (prisoner defecates or urinates without using sanitary facilities provided).

E2.2.1 Key points

- The decision to segregate must be reasonable and appropriate.
- Operational managers/Directors should consideration alternative methods such as transfer to another wing or prison, or close supervision on normal location.
- Segregation must be for as short a period as possible.
- Prisoners may be segregated as a direct alternative to laying a formal disciplinary charge. This has been held to be lawful—see *R v Secretary of State for the Home Department, ex p Hague* [1992] 1 AC 58.

E2.3 Own Protection

Prisoners should only be segregated in their own interest when there are good and sufficient reasons for believing that it is necessary to ensure the prisoner's safety and well-being. These prisoners, usually informants and sex offenders, are normally accommodated in Vulnerable Prisoners Units (VPUs).

E2.3.1 Key points

- Segregation in the prisoner's own interest usually applies when there is a risk of assault.

- It is not necessary for the prisoner to have already been assaulted, or made a request to be segregated.
- The prisoner may request segregation but this may be refused following an investigation by the Governor/Director.
- Prisoners may be segregated on initial reception or at any time during their period in custody.
- In exceptional circumstances segregation may be appropriate for reasons other than fear or assault eg mental health concerns.
- Where a prisoner is reluctant to be segregated in their own interest, segregation may be justified on the grounds of maintaining GOod.

E2.4 Young Offenders

PSO 1700 applies equally to young offenders. Although there are no separate policies relating to segregation there are additional welfare considerations the prison authorities are required to take into account. These include the Children Act 1989 which equally applies to young offenders aged under 18 in prison establishments, as confirmed by Munby J in *R (on the application of the Howard League) v Secretary of State for the Home Department* [2003] 1 FLR 484.

Young offenders placed in segregation should be given the opportunity to make representations: see *R (on the application of SP) v Secretary of State for the Home Department* [2004] EWHC 1418 where emphasis was placed on the importance of the welfare of the child in light of the *Howard League* case.

There are separate Rules for young offenders accommodated in Secure Training Centres (STCs). There are significant differences between the Secure Training Centre Rules 1998 (as amended) and the YOI Rules, particularly with regards to the use of force. Rule 38 of the STC Rules permits young offenders (referred to in the Rules as 'trainees') to be restrained where necessary for the purposes of GOod. This Rule is wider than the equivalent Prison and YOI Rules, and has raised particular concerns as restraint in STCs include the use of controversial 'distraction' techniques (specific holds which involve inflicting pain as a distraction to the thumb, ribs or nose). This technique will be particularly susceptible to Judicial Review.

E2.5 Procedure

The initial authorization by the operational manager/Director cannot exceed 72 hours. The prisoner must be informed of the reasons for segregation (orally and in writing), the date of the first review, and the regime pending the first review.

Healthcare must be informed within 30 minutes of the prisoner being placed on the unit and an initial segregation safety screen must be completed within 2 hours to establish whether continued segregation may be inappropriate on medical grounds. In the event that no registered doctor or nurse is on duty, the prisoner must be observed every 30 minutes, or 5 times an hour at irregular intervals if the prisoner is on an open ACCT (Assessment, Care in Custody, Teamwork—suicide or self-harm watch) until the safety screen can be completed.

The Independent Monitoring Board (IMB) must be notified within 24 hours.

E2.5.1 Key points

- Due to the purpose of segregation there will often be a need to conduct a full search of the prisoner but this must not be routine; it must be part of an immediate risk assessment.
- Governors are required to ensure that the regime in segregation units is comparable with prisoners on normal location, although in reality prisoners in segregation will spend most of their time confined to their cells.
- Juveniles must be assessed to identify which activities they can participate in with others.
- Prisoners in segregation should remain on the same IEP level unless a Review Board has taken place and decided otherwise.
- Prisoners on an open ACCT should only be placed in segregation in exceptional circumstances where they are a risk to others, no other suitable location is appropriate, and all other options have been tried or are considered inappropriate.
- A Segregation Review Board, chaired by an operational manager, acting on behalf of the Secretary of State must convene within 72 hours of segregation. The Board must include a healthcare representative, and may also include a segregation personal officer, chaplain and psychologist.
- The Board must consider the initial reasons for segregation, and any mental health or self-harm concerns. The prisoner will normally be present for part of the review and the IMB will be encouraged to have a member present as an observer.
- If the Board decides that segregation should continue subsequent reviews must take place at least every 14 days.
- Targets should be set and incentives offered for improved behaviour such as TV, gym and mini-association periods. The targets should be reasonable, specific and time bound.
- An IMB member with serious concerns about the initial or continued segregation should raise the matter in the first instance with the Governor, who should respond within 48 hours.

E2.6 Segregation No Longer Required?

If the Board decides that detention in the segregation unit is no longer appropriate the following options will be available:

* return to normal location;
* phased return to normal location (if the prisoner has been in segregation for more than a month);
* transfer to a High Supervision Unit;
* transfer to another prison/VPU.

E2.7 Practical Considerations

E2.7.1 *Written representations*

* In contrast to young offenders, adult prisoners do not have the right to make representations (see *R (on the application of SP) v Secretary of State for the Home Department* [2004] EWHC 1418, however, there is nothing to prevent legal representatives from making representations (subject to funding restrictions) to the Governor on behalf of a client.
* The relevant documentation should be obtained. If the prisoner is still in segregation by the time the documents are received proper consideration can be given to the merits of making representations.
* In most cases there will be little scope to challenge the factual basis of the decision; procedural errors however may raise grounds for Judicial Review.
* Even if it is not appropriate to make written representations, the prisoner may still submit a formal complaint through the Requests and Complaints procedure, if they have not already done so.

E2.7.2 *Judicial Review*

* The reasons given for initial segregation and any continued segregation are susceptible to Judicial Review; however, few will give rise to grounds, as truly exceptional circumstances would have to exist which the Governor had failed to take into account.
* Claims for Judicial Review based on procedural errors have a greater chance of success, eg, a failure to properly record the reasons for segregation, or to convene a Segregation Review Board within 72 hours.
* In theory prisoners retain access to the basic regime such as telephones, visits and canteen. In reality out of cell time will be limited, and therefore the opportunity to make specific requests will also be limited.
* Although it is not possible to bring an action for breach of the Prison Rules as they are regulatory only (see *R v Secretary of State for the Home Department Prison, ex p Hague* [1992] 1 AC 58), the House

of Lords in the *Hague* case recognized that if conditions become so intolerable that the prisoner suffers loss, injury or damage there would be grounds for Judicial Review as well as substantive civil actions. However, it may be difficult to establish a direct causal link between the prison conditions and the physical or mental injury.

- Segregation in special accommodation, which often includes sensory deprivation and the requirement to wear paper clothing, may be humiliating but the confinement would probably have to be for a prolonged period if Article 3 rights (freedom from inhuman or degrading treatment) are to be engaged.

E3 **Transfer to Other Prisons/Units**

E3.1 **Key Documents**

KD PSI 42/2012

PSO 1700

PSO 1810

PSO 1600

E3.2 **Close Supervision Centre (CSC)—Rule 46**

Although in theory segregation can continue indefinitely, a male adult prisoner segregated for a significant period is likely to be transferred to a Close Supervision Centre (CSC) at Wakefield, Whitemoor or Woodhill under Rule 46.

The specialist CSC units provide accommodation, management and treatment for prisoners who are assessed as posing the most significant risk to others, or good order within the establishment.

Referrals may be accepted from within or outside the high security estate, based on the following criteria:

PSI 42/2012 Close Supervision Referral Manual

Referral Criteria

- Demonstrating repeated or escalating violence towards others;
- Carried out, or orchestrated, a single serious or significant act of violence or disorder, e.g. hostage taking, murder, attempted murder, serious assault, concerted indiscipline etc;
- Causing significant day-to-day management difficulties by undermining the good order of the establishment i.e. through bullying, coercion, intimidation, threats, regime disruption and subversive activity. Involvement in such activities may not always be overt but be supported by significant intelligence indicating that individual's involvement;
- Seriously threatening and/or intimidating behaviour, directed at staff and/or prisoners;
- A long history of disciplinary offences indicative of persistent problematic behaviour;
- Repeated periods of segregation under Prison Rule 45 - Good Order or Discipline;
- A continuous period of segregation exceeding six months (3 months for non high security prisons) due to refractory behaviour;
- Failure to respond to attempts to manage his risk and behaviour using existing processes, or under the MCBS (high security estate only), and his risk to others or the safe operation of an establishment is deemed to be significant.

There are four stages to the CSC referral process: (1) referral for assessment; (2) assessment; (3) case conference; and (4) decision.

Prisoners or their legal representatives may make representations regarding placement in the CSC system following disclosure of the referral or recall paperwork or when the case is to be re-considered by the management committee.

E3.3 Special Accommodation— Prison Rules, Rule 48/YOI Rules, Rule 51

Policy guidance on the use of special cells can be found in PSO 1700. These are often known as 'strip cells'.

Duty Governors/Directors may order violent prisoners to be confined in special cells for up to 24 hours. In practice the decision is likely to be made in an emergency by prison officers, and subsequently approved by the duty Governor or officer in charge of the prison at the time.

There will be special cells in segregation units and elsewhere in the prison, such as Healthcare. Prisoners are usually stripped of their normal clothing and made to wear a paper suit before being placed in a special cell; however this practice will only be justified if the prisoner is at risk of causing life threatening harm to himself or others. The 'special accommodation' will either be a small designated cell with a raised wooden platform in place of a bed, which prisoners refer to as 'the box', or a normal cell with the bedding and furniture removed. Cardboard furniture may be placed in the cell, although this should not be routine as it is likely to result in the prisoner remaining in the cell for a longer period.

E3.3.1 Key points

- In contrast to segregation under Rule 45, confinement to a special cell cannot be used as a pre-emptive measure; the prisoner must be acting in a 'refractory or violent' manner.
- If a prisoner is removed from normal location to a special cell merely in anticipation of violent behaviour that action would be unlawful, and any force used would constitute an assault.
- Once a prisoner has been placed in a special cell Healthcare must be notified immediately, and the prisoner must be assessed by either a doctor or a nurse as soon as possible.
- The prisoner must be assessed at regular intervals (no more than an hour apart) and the detention in special accommodation must be reviewed within 24 hours, by a Review Panel.

- A member of the IMB should also attend the review to ensure that the proper procedure has been followed and that a reasonable decision has been reached, although this is not mandatory.
- Further reviews must take place every 24 hours thereafter.

E3.4 Transfer of Difficult and Disruptive Prisoners

Prisons are required to have a Local Security Strategy (LSS) to deal with difficult and disruptive prisoners. The LSS is part of the National Security Framework (NSF). The overall aim is to encourage the prisoner to behave appropriately within the holding prison. Published guidance on the transfer of difficult and disruptive prisoners is limited. However, PSO 1810 confirms that the LSS requires the Governor and the Area Manager to agree a strategy which may include:

- positive dialogue;
- use of the IEP Scheme;
- anti-bullying systems;
- internal relocation;
- adjudication awards;
- segregation;
- in-area transfer on a permanent basis;
- out of area transfers on a permanent basis (PSO 1810, paragraph 8).

Persistent non-compliance or violent behaviour is likely to result in a transfer. The prisoner should be given the opportunity to co-operate with the transfer, but if he or she refuses the Governor/Director must consider whether there is a valid reason for the refusal before making arrangements to remove the prisoner by force, if necessary.

Minimum levels of force may be used for the minimum length of time. Guidance on the use of force can be found in PSO 1600 and the policy on use of restraints is in PSO 1700.

E3.5 Practical Considerations

E3.5.1 *Written representations*

- There is no right to be allocated to a particular prison. Nor can a prisoner dictate the timing of a transfer. If a prisoner refuses to co-operate with a transfer he or she may be segregated pending a decision by the Governor, assuming the prisoner has already been removed from normal location. It is unlikely to be in the prisoner's best interests to be forcibly removed.
- Once a decision to transfer has been made it is extremely unlikely to be overturned, especially as alternative resolutions should already have been considered by this stage. However, in appropriate cases

written representations (subject to funding restrictions) may be faxed to the Governor. For example, exceptional circumstances may exist which were not taken into account when the original decision was made.

- If the prisoner is reluctant to be transferred because family members or his sole visitor would find it difficult to attend the new prison written confirmation of this should be obtained. If the difficulty is based on medical reasons the legal representative should obtain a report from the visitor's doctor.
- Although the legal representative will often be notified too late to prevent transfer, written representations can form the basis for a transfer application at the new prison.

E3.5.2 *Judicial Review*

- The reasons given justifying the transfer are susceptible to Judicial Review but will rarely offer scope for challenge. There is likely to be more scope for challenge if the procedure as set out in the LSS was not followed or if it was followed inflexibly without due regard for exceptional circumstances.
- The LSS on transfers can be obtained under the Freedom of Information Act 2000, by writing to the information access representative at the prison.

E4 **Re-categorization**

E4.1 **Key Documents**

KD   PSI 08/2013

       PSI 39/2011

       PSI 40/2011

       PSI 41/2011

Prisoners must be categorized according to the likelihood that they will escape and the risk they will pose to the public if an escape were successful. However, some prisoners, due to their behaviour, are given a higher category than would otherwise be expected so that they can be transferred to a prison with appropriate levels of supervision.

The re-categorization process must still be followed even if the transfer needs to be effected at short notice.

A prisoner can be re-categorized at any stage and in particular where the Governor takes the view that because of the prisoner's conduct there is a threat to maintaining GOod or where the re-categorization criteria in the relevant PSI apply.

E4.2 **Practical Considerations**

E4.2.1 *Written representations*

- In the disciplinary context re-categorizations often take place in an emergency.
- Post-tariff life sentence prisoners should be given the opportunity to submit representations either when re-categorization is being considered or as soon as reasonably practicable thereafter: See *Hirst v Secretary of State for the Home Department* [2001] EWCA CIV 378.
- Although other prisoners will not be invited to make representations, legal representatives can submit representations (subject to funding restrictions) on their client's behalf, if appropriate.
- A complaint through the Requests and Complaints procedure is the main and often the only means to challenge an adverse categorization decision. If the complaint is based on a factual dispute a separate form should be submitted for each error.
- A copy of the re-categorization form (RC1), and copies of the other documents that informed the decision can be obtained from the prison via the information access representative (IAR) with the written consent of the prisoner.

E4.2.2 *Judicial Review*

A claim for Judicial Review ought to be considered if the prison:

- fails to give reasons;
- provides inadequate reasons;
- applies the policy inflexibly;
- fails to follow the proper procedure.

E5 Incentives and Earned Privileges (IEP) Scheme

E5.1 Key Documents

KD PSI 11/2011

PSI 08/2012

It has been held that the Incentives and Earned Privileges (IEP) Scheme merely reflects the consequences of poor behaviour: *R (on the application of Potter) v Secretary of State for the Home Department* [2001] EWHC Admin 1401. However, although the scheme is not considered by the Prison Service or the courts to be punitive, many prisoners see it as another form of informal discipline.

Prison Rules, Rule 8/YOI Rules, Rule 6 provides that all prisons and Young Offender Institutions are required to have a system of incentives and privileges. The National Policy Framework for IEP Schemes is contained in PSI 11/2011. The national aims are:

- to encourage responsible behaviour;
- to encourage effort and achievement in work and other constructive activities;
- to encourage sentenced prisoners to engage in OASys and sentence planning and benefit from activities designed to reduce re-offending;
- to create a more disciplined, better controlled and safer environment for prisoners and staff (PSI 11/2011, paragraph 1.3).

The separate Rewards and Sanctions scheme for young people (under 18) can be found in PSI 08/2012.

E5.2 Privilege Levels

Prisons must operate a three-tier scheme which allows prisoners to earn privileges according to their behaviour and performance:

- *Basic.* Prisoners continue to participate in normal regime activities such as work, education and treatment programmes. They receive the minimum entitlements to visits, letters, phone calls and canteen, etc.
- *Standard.* All prisoners on reception are placed on this level. In addition to the basic facilities prisoners on standard level will be allowed more frequent visits, more time for association and access to an in-cell TV. They may also be eligible for higher rates of pay, increased private cash allowance and access to 'better jobs'.

- *Enhanced.* In addition to the basic and standard level privileges prisoners are likely to receive more visits, more private cash, longer association and priority for higher rates of pay, subject to resources. Some prisons have an additional 'super enhanced' tier.

E5.3 Key Earnable Privileges

Although there is a national framework, each prison will have its own local scheme. This enables the prison to tailor incentives to address specific problems, which should be sufficiently attractive to encourage prisoners to progress to the next level. Where the privilege is available it should be included in the local scheme. Additional privileges may be included, such as enhanced canteen facilities, access to the gym and mail order facilities.

There are 6 key earnable privileges:

1. *Access to private cash.* Prisoners are allowed to spend their prison earnings, and supplement this with private cash which was in their possession on reception or sent in via family or friends by postal order. Further guidance is in PSO 4465 (Prisoners' Financial Affairs), and mandatory IEP cash limits can be found in PSI 30/2008.
2. *Extra and/or improved visits.* The minimum statutory visits as set out in Prison Rules, Rule 35(2)(b)/YOI Rules, Rule 10(1)(b) may be supplemented by extra 'privilege visits' as part of the IEP scheme. See also PSI 16/2011.
3. *Higher rates of pay.* The Prison Service policy on prisoners' pay and the minimum rates are contained in PSO 4460. Governors have discretion to set local pay rates above the minimum; however, the rates should not be set at such a level that the prisoner has little incentive to participate in sentence plans aimed at reducing the risk of re-offending. Prisoners on the standard or enhanced level are eligible for higher rates of pay, although enhanced prisoners will be given priority.
4. *In-cell TV.* Standard and enhanced level prisoners will be eligible for access to in-cell TV.
5. *Wearing own clothes.* Civil and remand prisoners (other than Escape List prisoners) may wear their own clothes. As part of the IEP Scheme standard and enhanced level prisoners may also be permitted to wear their own clothes.
6. *Time out of cell.* Association time (other than work, education, offender behaviour programmes or religious services) will vary from prison to prison. Standard and enhanced level prisoners should be allowed extra time out of their cells subject to there being scope to increase the basic allowance, and availability of activities and supervisory staff (PSI 11/2011, paragraphs 3.7–3.12).

E5.4 Management of IEP Schemes

Governors must ensure that the scheme is fair and consistent. The scheme is usually overseen by an IEP Board, which may sit at the same time as a Sentence Planning Board.

Consistent good behaviour and performance as specified in the local scheme should result in advancement. The factors to be taken into account will include:

- approach to the sentence and willingness to use the time in prison constructively;
- institutional behaviour;
- attitude to people outside prison including the victim, family and others (PSI 11/2011, paragraph 2.5.2).

A pattern of deteriorating behaviour or performance may result in a demotion to a lower level. If a one-off incident is sufficiently serious, eg, assault, this may also result in a downgrade following an urgent review (PSI 11/2011, paragraph 2.5.4).

E5.4.1 Key points

- Governors may temporarily suspend privileges for operational reasons eg security, the location of the prisoner, or deployment of staff (PSI 11/2011, paragraph 4.8).
- Prisoners should be given written warnings if their behaviour or performance causes concern (PSI 11/2011, paragraph 2.3.3).
- An initial decision to downgrade a prisoner to the basic level should be reviewed within 7 days and thereafter at least monthly for adults and at least every 14 days for young offenders (PSI 11/2011, paragraph 4.3).
- Prisoners on standard level can apply for enhanced status after 3 months and thereafter at 3-monthly intervals (PSI 11/2011, paragraph 4.4).
- Standard prisoners who do not apply and enhanced prisoners should be reviewed annually or earlier if there is an overall change in behaviour (PSI 11/2011, paragraph 4.4).
- IEP assessments should take account of prisoners' progress in achieving OASys sentence planning objectives (PSI 11/2011, paragraph 4.5).
- Prisoners must be able to make representations in advance of the review. Reasons must be given explaining why the prisoner has failed to meet the criteria, and why any representations by the prisoner or his or her legal representative have been rejected (PSI 11/2011, paragraph 2.5.5).
- Loss of privileges following a finding of guilt at a disciplinary hearing is separate from the IEP Scheme and should not automatically result in a downgrade (PSI 11/2011, paragraph 4.10).

E5.5 Special Groups of Prisoners

- *Prisoners in denial of their offence.* Prisoners should not be refused an upgrade simply because they deny their offence. It is the prisoner's approach to their sentence and willingness to use their time in custody constructively to reduce re-offending which should determine the appropriate privilege level (PSI 11/2011, paragraph 4.6).

- *Retention of privilege on transfer.* When a prisoner is transferred P-NOMIS (the centralized computer system) will automatically default a prisoner's privilege level to standard regardless of their previous status. Staff should check previous history (preferably within 2 weeks of transfer), to ensure the prisoner has been placed on the appropriate privilege level. Prisoners can only receive what is available at their current location, but as far as possible establishments should liaise with each other to try to avoid significant differences and to ensure consistency at each level (PSI 11/2011, paragraphs 4.12–4.13).

- *Immigration and remand prisoners.* Unconvicted prisoners must be included in the IEP Scheme. Although they are not required to work or take part in activities they should be encouraged to do so. Where prisoners do take part in work or activities their performance and behaviour will be taken into account when considering whether to move them from standard to enhanced and vice versa. However, moves from standard to basic must be based on behaviour alone (PSI 11/2011, paragraph 4.14).

- *Foreign national prisoners.* Foreign national prisoners whose friends and family are outside the UK, should be given extra and more flexibly timed opportunities to make phone calls (including long distance calls) as an alternative to visits (PSI 11/2011, paragraph 4.17).

- *Prisoners with particular needs.* Governors should ensure that the local scheme does not penalize behaviour which is a direct consequence of a disability, specific need or age (PSI 11/2011, paragraph 4.18).

E5.6 Practical Considerations

E5.6.1 *Written representations*

Prisoners who are dissatisfied with an IEP decision should be encouraged to submit a complaint. In appropriate cases written representations (subject to funding restrictions) in support of the complaint should be submitted to the Governor.

In order to make representations, a copy of the local IEP policy, the reasons for the adverse decision and a copy of the prisoner's formal complaint (if any) should be obtained by writing to the IAR at the prison.

E5.6.2 *Judicial Review*

IEP decisions are unlikely to give rise to grounds for Judicial Review for two main reasons:

(a) there is no direct impact on liberty; and

(b) the courts are reluctant to supervise administrative functions.

In *R (on the application of Potter) v Secretary of State for the Home Department* [2001] EWHC Admin 1041 the court held that the policy of denying enhanced status to prisoners who refused to attend a sex offender treatment programme did not engage ECHR Article 6 (right to a fair trial) as 'enhanced status is an administrative matter relating to additional privileges to which there is no entitlement'. However, if a prisoner has been complying with the criteria relating to a particular privilege, withdrawal of that privilege may give rise to a Judicial Review claim on the grounds that he had a legitimate expectation.

Part F
Release and Parole

F1 **Introduction**

Determinate sentences are sentences that have been imposed for a fixed term. Within a few weeks of the sentence hearing the maximum length of the prisoner's sentence will be confirmed in writing, and the date they will become eligible for early release or parole.

Indeterminate sentences are very different. There is no automatic right to be released. The term 'lifer' is used to refer to all prisoners serving indeterminate sentences including those serving sentences for the protection of the public. The lifer will be required to serve a punitive period known as the minimum term (or tariff) before becoming eligible for parole on licence, which is the preventative period. Life licensees are at risk of being recalled to prison at any time.

There are three main ways in which prisoners may be released from prison:

- Release on Temporary Licence;
- Automatic Statutory Release;
- Discretionary Release on Parole.

F2 Overview—Release on Temporary Licence (ROTL)

F2.1 Key Documents

KD PSO 6300

PSO 3601

PSO 3620

PSI 21/2012

PSI 08/2012

ROTL enables prisoners to participate in activities outside the prison, in preparation for resettlement. It is a privilege which the prisoner must apply for, and not a right. Rule 9(3) of the Prison Rules (YOI Rules, rule 5) provides an exhaustive list of the circumstances when a prisoner may be released on temporary licence.

The policy on temporary release can be found in PSO 6300, as amended by PSI 21/2012. There are four types of temporary release, which apply to young offenders, male and female prisoners:

- resettlement day release;
- resettlement overnight release;
- childcare resettlement;
- special purpose.

The Governor must publish a protocol for all staff outlining how temporary release will be administered locally, which must be reviewed annually. A guidance leaflet for prisoners must also be published (PSO 6300, paragraph 1.1).

F2.2 Excluded Prisoners

Category B prisoners are not eligible for resettlement day release or resettlement overnight release. Those excluded from Release on Temporary Licence altogether include:

- Category A prisoners;
- prisoners on the escape list;
- prisoners subject to extradition proceedings;
- remand/unsentenced prisoners;
- sentenced prisoners remanded for further charges or sentencing.
- Prisoners held on behalf of the International Criminal Tribunal for the Former Yugoslavia (ICTY), the Special Court for Sierra Leone (SCSL) or the International Criminal Court (ICC).

F2.3 Risk Assessment

Prisoners aged 18 or over in the adult estate, will be assessed using OASys (the computer-based offender assessment and sentence management system). The equivalent risk assessment for offenders under 18 is known as ASSET. If an up-to-date OASys report is not available the risk assessment will be based on the prisoner's criminal history, behaviour in custody, a report from the home probation officer, information from the police, any views expressed by the victim, previous ROTL and any specific areas of concern, eg, drug or alcohol misuse.

Prisoners being considered for ROTL will be subject to a mandatory drug test (MDT). Save for exceptional circumstances, any approval for ROTL will be cancelled if the prisoner provides a sample that tests positive for drugs. The MDT procedure is detailed in PSO 3601. A positive voluntary drug test (VDT) will be taken into account when considering suitability for ROTL but must not replace the MDT as the principal method of drug testing. The VDT procedure is detailed in PSO 3620.

F2.4 Decision Making

The Secretary of State for Justice's power to authorize temporary release is normally delegated to the Governor. However, the decision must be considered by a Board if:

- the prisoner has not had previous ROTL;
- the application is for resettlement overnight release;
- there has been a significant change in circumstances;
- six months have elapsed since the last board meeting; or
- the application is for a different type of ROTL than the one previously granted (PSO 6300, Appendix A, paragraph 29).

The application will be considered by the Sentence Planning Board if the prisoner is subject to the sentence planning process or a ROTL Board. The ROTL Board must consist of a governor grade manager, prison officer who knows the prisoner well, a seconded probation officer, lifer liaison officer (if appropriate) and one other person with knowledge of the prisoner eg education staff (PSO 6300, Appendix A, paragraph 43).

The Board may:

- refuse to grant ROTL;
- recommend ROTL subject to approval by the Governor; or
- request further information (eg from the police, probation or immigration) and re-convene at a later date.

On receipt of the Board's recommendation, ROTL must be authorized by the Governor (or nominated operational manager). The following non-exhaustive factors may be taken into account:

- The nature of the offence
- The nature of the activity for which the release is proposed
- The proportion of the custodial period served
- The number of times the prisoner has been, or is likely to be released
- Whether the release could reasonably be expected to have a dispro-
  portionate impact on victims
- The presence of any court restraining orders
- The OASys risk of harm (if applicable)
- MAPPA level (if applicable) (PSO 6300, paragraph 1.5)

The Governor must be satisfied that the temporary release of the
prisoner would not be likely to undermine public confidence in the
administration of justice (PSO 6300, paragraph 1.5.1).

Reasons must be given in writing for any decision to refuse an ROTL
application, which must include the relevant factors that were taken
into account and the weight attached to those factors (PSO 6300,
Appendix A, paragraph 38). If the application is made in an emergency there may be no time to convene a Board and the decision will
be made by the Governor.

F2.5 Revocation

Temporary licence may be revoked at any time for good reason, even
if the conditions of release have not been broken. A prisoner arrested
by the police on suspicion of a criminal offence will be recalled, and
a disciplinary charge is likely to be laid on return to prison pending
the outcome of the police investigation (PSO 6300, paragraph 7.2.2).
A prisoner will also be recalled for non-criminal conduct which
amounts to a breach of the temporary licence conditions, and a disciplinary charge is likely to follow. Prosecution through the courts
will not necessarily bar disciplinary proceedings for other breaches of
licence (PSO 6300, paragraph 7.2.5).

F2.6 Failure to Return to Prison

The failure to return to prison after the expiry of a period of temporary
licence is likely to result in disciplinary charge under the Prison Rules,
rule 51(8) or YOI Rules, rule 55(9). The failure cannot form the basis
for an offence of escape from lawful custody. See *R v Montgomery*
[2007] EWCA Crim 2157.

F2.7 **Lifers**

Lifers (which includes all prisoners serving indeterminate sentences) are eligible for the 4 categories of temporary release. However, they must not be considered for release until transfer to open conditions has been approved by the Secretary of State and in general until the transfer has actually taken place. Where it is known that transfer will be delayed for practical (as opposed to risk related) reasons, the prisoner may exceptionally be considered for ROTL from closed conditions. Where ROTL is being considered from closed conditions the prisoner must undergo a period of supervised activity outside the prison before any unsupervised release.

Open conditions do not exist in the under 18 estate. PSI 08/2012 sets out the procedure for Governors to consider when assessing a young person's eligibility and suitability for ROTL.

ROTL decisions relating to lifers who have not been given a provisional release date must be referred to the Area Manager (PSO 6300, Appendix A, paragraph 37). The Governor must decide the frequency and duration of any release taking into account the potential sensitivities associated with the ROTL of lifers. In particular the impact on victims must be considered. Victims participating in the victim contact scheme must be given a reasonable opportunity to make representations about the conditions to be attached to any temporary release.

As with all prisoners, the temporary release licence may be revoked at any time if the prisoner is deemed to present a risk to public safety.

F2.8 **Guideline**

PSO 6300 Release on Temporary Licence
Eligibility

Type of ROTL	Proportion of period generally to be served between the date of approval for transfer to open conditions and the provisional date of the next parole hearing before ROTL may be considered
Special Purpose Licence (SPL) or (day) Childcare Resettlement Licence (CRL)	Nil. May be considered shortly after approval
Supervised activities outside the prison boundary	Quarter
Resettlement Day Release (RDR), (except for paid work)	Half
Resettlement Overnight Release (ROR) or RDR for paid work or overnight CRL	Two thirds

F3 **Resettlement Day Release (RDR)**

Prisoners who apply for resettlement day release (RDR) can be considered for the following activities:

- reparative community work/unpaid employment;
- life and work skills training/education;
- maintaining family ties;
- housing;
- probation interviews;
- job searches and interviews;
- paid employment (resettlement estate only);
- driving lessons (resettlement estate only);
- car maintenance (resettlement estate only);
- opening bank accounts (PSO 6300, paragraph 2.1).

F3.1 **Eligibility**

Prisoners who are not excluded will be eligible for RDR either 24 months before their release date or at the halfway point of the custodial period (not sentence) less half the relevant remand time, whichever is the later (PSO 6300, paragraph 2.1.4).

Prisoners assessed as suitable for home detention curfew (HDC) before they become eligible for release on RDR, may be considered for one period of RDR before their HDC release date to undertake pre-arranged interviews for work or college, if there is time. This is subject to the normal risk assessment (PSO 6300, paragraph 2.1.8).

Prisoners recalled by the Secretary of State following conditional release are not excluded, and will be eligible for RDR immediately subject to the usual risk assessment (PSO 6300, paragraph 2.1.9).

F3.2 **Frequency and Duration**

The frequency and duration of any release on RDR must be determined by the Governor. Good practice suggests that both should be gradually increased in line with the prisoner's sentence plan and personal development (PSO 6300, paragraph 2.1.10).

Category C prisoners should normally be re-categorized to Category D and transferred to open conditions prior to release on RDR. However, there may be occasions when it is appropriate for the prisoner to remain in closed conditions eg to access a course which will not be readily available in another prison (PSO 6300, paragraph 2.1.11).

F4 Resettlement Overnight Release (ROR)

Overnight release may be authorized to enable the prisoner to re-establish links with family and the local community. The temporary release is often used to facilitate interviews for work, training or accommodation (PSO 6300, paragraph 2.2). It may also be authorized to allow young offenders take part in courses run by the Prince's Trust. During the period of release the prisoner will reside at their release address, or an approved hostel.

F4.1 Eligibility

Prisoners who are not excluded will be eligible for ROR 24 months before their release date or at the halfway point of the custodial term (not sentence) less half the relevant remand time, whichever is the later, provided they pass the risk assessment (PSO 6300, paragraph 2.2.1).

F4.2 Frequency and Duration

F4.2.1 *Open conditions and resettlement*

Prisoners approved for open conditions are not necessarily suitable for ROR. Those with a parole eligibility date (PED) can apply for a maximum of one period of ROR every 4 weeks in the 6 months before the PED. Prisoners successful at their first parole can apply for one further period of ROR before release, if time allows. Prisoners unsuccessful at their first parole review must undergo a further risk assessment. Provided that the risk assessment is favourable the prisoner may apply for a maximum of one period of ROR every 4 weeks.

Prisoners who have withdrawn from the parole process may be considered for ROR 3 months after PED. They may apply for a maximum of 4 periods in the first year following PED and a maximum of 8 periods in the subsequent 12 months. The Governor must decide the appropriate frequency.

Prisoners serving 12 months and over who do not have a PED may apply for ROR no more than once in every 4 weeks after their ROR eligibility date.

F4.2.2 *Closed conditions*

Category D prisoners in closed conditions should be considered for ROR under the same arrangements as prisoners in open conditions.

F4 Resettlement Overnight Release (ROR)

Category C prisoners serving 12 months and over who do not have a PED may apply for ROR up to a maximum of 2 periods in the last 6 months before the conditional release date (CRD). Category C prisoners with a PED may apply for ROR once in the 3 months prior to PED. If they complete this period successfully they should be considered for re-categorization and transfer to open conditions.

Category C prisoners with a PED who are unsuccessful on a period of ROTL before the PED, are not re-categorized to Category D or withdraw from the parole process, may make an application for one period of ROR but will not be eligible until 3 months before any subsequent parole review.

Category C prisoners successful at their first parole review may apply for one period of ROR before release, if time allows. Category C prisoners unsuccessful at the first parole review must undergo a further risk assessment and any risks identified must be addressed before any further temporary release can take place. Providing the risk assessment is favourable they can apply for a maximum of 3 periods of ROR after the PED once every 8 weeks.

F4.2.3 *Recall prisoners—open conditions/resettlement*

If the Parole Board recommends re-release at a later date, ROR may be taken once every 4 weeks. Prisoners recommended for re-release at the sentence and licence expiry date (SLED) or licence expiry date (LED) will be eligible for ROR 24 months before the re-release date and may take ROR once every 4 weeks. Where the Parole Board recommends a further review date that date will be taken to be the PED and the policy applicable to such prisoners (see **F4.2.2**) will apply.

F4.2.4 *Recall prisoners—closed conditions*

If the Parole Board recommends re-release at a later date, ROR may be taken twice in the last 6 months. Prisoners recommended for re-release at the SLED or LED will be eligible for ROR twice in the last 6 months. Where the Parole Board recommends a further review date that date will be taken to be the PED and the policy applicable to such prisoners (see **F4.2.2**) will apply.

F4.2.5 *Duration*

The Governor must decide the appropriate duration of any period of ROR, which will not normally exceed 4 nights.

F5 Childcare Resettlement Licence (CRL)

Prisoners may be considered for overnight Childcare Resettlement Licence (CRL) if they had sole responsibility for a child under 16 prior to sentence to supplement visits and family event days at the prison.

The prisoner must satisfy the Governor that they were the sole carer of the child prior to their imprisonment and would continue to be the sole carer if they were not in prison (PSO 6300, paragraph 2.5.2). Once it has been established that the prisoner has lawful access to the child, and that CRL will not place the child at risk, the best interests of the child must be taken into account.

Governors must balance the interests of the child with the duty to maintain public confidence (PSO 6300, paragraph 2.5.6). Governors must also take into account the impact on any identifiable victims and allow a reasonable opportunity for representations to be made about the conditions if temporary release is authorized. All cases must be considered on their merits (*R (MP) v Secretary of State for Justice* [2012] EWHC 214). See also *R (on the application of X) v Secretary of State for the Home Department* [2005] EWHC 1616, where Bean J held that although the Board's refusal to grant further periods of ROTL did interfere with the prisoners ECHR Article 8 rights, the interference was justified in the circumstances of this case. The prisoner did not want her children to know she was in prison, and it was her decision to refuse visits from them which resulted in the prolonged separation.

F5.1 Frequency and Duration

CRL may be taken no more than once every 2 months and the maximum duration of each period must not exceed 3 nights away from the prison (PSO 6300, paragraph 2.5.7).

F6 Special Purpose Licence (SPL)

SPL allows for short temporary release in the event of exceptional personal circumstances. The usual risk assessments must take place even though these requests will often be made at short notice. All prisoners (except excluded prisoners) are eligible to apply at any stage of their sentence.

Grounds for SPL are:

- *Compassionate.* Temporary release will normally be granted to allow a prisoner to attend the funeral of a close relative or to visit a close relative who is terminally ill. Governors must be able to consider applications at very short notice as funerals are sometimes held within 24 hours for cultural or religious reasons. If a terminally ill relative is able to communicate, they must confirm that they wish to see the prisoner. The definition of 'close relative' is wide. It includes spouse, partners (heterosexual or homosexual) who had been living together as if they were married immediately before the imprisonment, parents, siblings and fiancés/fiancées. Step relationships and prisoners *in loco parentis* or a person who has been *in loco parentis* to the prisoner are also included. The Governor has discretion to accept any other close family relationship, and any other exceptional circumstances.
- *Medical.* Prisoners may be permitted to attend out-patient or in-patent appointments on SPL.
- *Marriage of the prisoner.* All prisoners have the right to get married in prison if they wish. Prisoners wanting to get married outside the prison should apply for temporary release on SPL. If granted, the period of release will only cover travel to the venue and the ceremony. Policy guidance on the marriage of prisoners is in PSO 4450.
- *Inter-prison transfers.* Prisoners transferring from closed conditions to open conditions or between open prisons may be granted temporary licence for that purpose, provide that they pass the risk assessment and that public confidence would not be undermined (PSO 6300, paragraph 2.7.7).
- *Court, tribunal or inquiry proceedings.* Prisoners may apply for SPL to attend civil proceedings, as an alternative to being produced on a Production Order. Prisoners must be required to attend or attendance must be in their best interests and pass a risk assessment. If the risk assessment is not passed the prisoner will be produced under escort (PSO 6300, paragraph 2.7.8).
- *Conferences with legal advisers.* Exceptionally a prisoner may be permitted to attend a meeting with his legal advisors outside the prison,

eg, if for the purposes of civil proceedings a large number of parties need to be gathered in one place (PSO 6300, paragraph 2.7.9).

• *Helping the police with their enquiries.* SPL can be used as an alternative to a police production. Policy on police productions is contained in PSO 1801 (PSO 6300, paragraph 2.7).

F6.1 Frequency and Duration

An SPL must only be issued in response to a specific event or set of circumstances that would not usually require release on a regular basis, eg, structured resettlement activities.

The duration of any temporary release on an SPL should normally be of no more than the few hours needed to achieve the stated purpose, taking into account reasonable travelling. However, the Governor may allow a licence to cover overnight absences for a maximum of 4 nights in a calendar month, and in exceptional circumstances may agree to grant a back-to-back licence.

There is no maximum duration of SPL where a prisoner is receiving in-patient treatment in hospital.

F7 **Temporary Release for Juveniles**

F7.1 **Key Document**

KD PSI 08/2012

Juveniles may apply for temporary release under the following licences:

- Resettlement Day Release (RDR)
- Resettlement Overnight Release (ROR)
- Special Purpose Licence (SPL)
- Childcare Resettlement Licence (CRL)

The Governor must develop and publish a local protocol defining the eligibility criteria and the range of appropriate activities. Temporary release must form an integral part of the training/sentence plan and provision should be linked to education, future training and employment opportunities, maintaining positive personal relationships and general resettlement.

The Governor must ensure that a thorough risk assessment is completed for all applicants, which must include ASSET and progress against the training/sentence plan objectives.

F7.2 **Eligibility**

All juveniles can apply for an SPL at any stage of their sentence. There is no minimum eligibility period. CRL, RDR and ROR eligibility applies to juveniles in the same way it applies to adults.

F7.3 **Frequency and Duration**

The Governor must decide on an appropriate duration for each SPL, allowing enough time for the purpose to be achieved. Exceptionally Governors may grant up to 4 nights' absence for compassionate grounds. There is no maximum duration for in-patient care.

The training plan and individual licences must define the frequency and duration of each period of resettlement leave. The prisoners must have a programme of activities phased in over a period of time with decreasing amounts of staff supervision outlined within the training plan. Governors may wish to develop a scheme of accompanied temporary release, which allows a member of staff to provide care and support during the absence. However, the responsibility for complying with the licence conditions remains with the prisoner at all times.

F8 **Prisoners Requiring Special Consideration**

F8.1 **Key Documents**

KD	PSO 6300
	PSI 21/2012

- *Civil prisoners and fine defaulters.* Such prisoners qualify for ROTL provided that they have been committed to prison for a sufficiently long period.
- *Prisoners in contempt of court.* May not be granted temporary release except with the permission of the clerk to the court.
- *Prisoners detained in default of a confiscation order or fine.* Such prisoners qualify provided that they have been committed to prison for a sufficiently long period. Where the prisoner has been ordered to serve a time in default which is to run consecutive to term of imprisonment the ROTL eligibility date should be calculated on the overall custodial period. The usual risk assessments must be conducted taking into account the risk of absconding in light of impending proceedings or unpaid confiscation orders.
- *Appellants.* Governors must take into account the need to produce prisoners for the appeal hearing where it has been determined by the court that their attendance is required.
- *Foreign national prisoners.* Prisoners detained solely under the Immigration Act 1971 must not be granted ROTL under the Prison/YOI Rules, although such prisoners may be released on compassionate grounds. However, prisoners in custody serving a prison sentence may apply for ROTL. Each case must be assessed on its merits taking into account the paramount importance of protection of the public. Where the prisoner's nationality is unclear this is an additional factor to be taken into account. Where there is a court recommendation for deportation, the prisoner has been served with a Notice of Intention to Deport or a deportation order is in force, the opinion of the Criminal Cases Directorate must be sought, but the final decision is at the discretion of the Governor.

F9 Challenging Refusals to Grant ROTL

Most of the time a legal representative will be contacted by a client who wants to challenge a refusal to grant ROTL, but occasionally advice may be sought in advance. If the decision has already been made written representations can be made to the Governor requesting a review, and the decision itself will be susceptible to Judicial Review.

F9.1 Written Representations

If an unsuccessful application for temporary release has been made, written reasons can be obtained (by writing to the Governor), and all information upon which the decision was based via the prisons information access representative (IAR). The prison may be happy to release the information on an ad hoc basis, if not, a formal application will have to be made to the DACU under the Data Protection Act (DPA) 1998, which will require a £10 cheque or postal order. The client's signed authority should be enclosed.

The following should be requested as appropriate:

- copy of OASys report;
- list of previous convictions;
- adjudications (during current term of imprisonment);
- home probation officers report;
- police report;
- report on the victims' views;
- reports on any previous ROTL;
- any other matters that were taken into consideration (eg drug or alcohol issues);
- written reasons.

Information can only be withheld for the following reasons:

- in the interests of national security;
- for the prevention of disorder or crime (including information relevant to prison security);
- for the protection of a third party who may be put at risk if the information is disclosed;
- on medical or psychiatric grounds;
- where the victim is the source of the information, and disclosure without their consent would breach a duty of confidence, or would prejudice the future supply of such information (PSO 6300, paragraph 6.1).

Information must not be withheld automatically. If disclosure is refused for any of the reasons just listed, legal representatives should enquire whether consideration has been given to providing a summary or an edited form of the document to protect the identity of the source (PSO 6300, paragraph 6.1.2). If the legal representative remains unhappy with the disclosure a complaint can be made to the Information Commissioner. Prisoners acting in person should make a complaint through the Requests and Complaints procedure in the first instance.

Once the legal representative is in receipt of the reasons and the information which informed the decision, detailed instructions should be obtained in preparation for submitting written representations to the Governor, if appropriate. However, it is unlikely that the decision will be overturned, in the absence of relevant information which was not taken into account at the time the original decision was made.

F9.2 Judicial Review

Although it may not be appropriate to make written representations the reasons should be carefully scrutinized as they may raise grounds for Judicial Review. A failure to give reasons will be susceptible to Judicial Review. It will be more difficult however, to base a claim for Judicial Review on the reasons themselves unless they demonstrate that irrelevant factors were taken into account or insufficient consideration was given to significant factors in the client's favour.

F10 Statutory Overview— Determinate Sentences

F10.1 Key Document

KD PSI 13/2013

Following implementation of the Legal Aid Sentencing and Punishment of Offenders (LASPO) Act 2012 the statutory provisions that govern the release of prisoners serving determinate sentences are now all set out within the Criminal Justice Act (CJA) 2003 and associated schedules, as amended.

Although prisoners currently serving sentences imposed under the Criminal Justice Act 1991 or 1967 (as amended by the Crime and Disorder Act 1998, the Powers of Court (Sentencing) Act 2000 and the Criminal Justice and Immigration Act 2008) continue to be released in accordance with those arrangements the provisions are now contained in CJA 2003.

As well as simplifying and consolidating the release provisions, LASPO 2012 abolished the sentence of Imprisonment for Public Protection (IPP), and the Extended Sentence for Public Protection (EPP) replacing them with a new Extended Determinate Sentence (EDS). LASPO 2012 also introduced a new automatic life sentence.

F10.2 Key Points

- All standard determinate sentences imposed on or after 3 December 2012 are subject to automatic release at the halfway point of the sentence and remain on licence until the end of the sentence irrespective of the date of the offence.
- Sentences of less than 12 months imposed on or after 3 December 2012 are no longer single termed. Concurrent sentences of less than 12 months run parallel to one another with unconditional release at the latest halfway point of all the sentences. Release is at the halfway point of the aggregate and is unconditional when the aggregate is less than 12 months and on licence until the sentence and licence expiry date when the aggregate is more than 12 months.
- The Prison Service has the responsibility of crediting remand time to sentences imposed on or after 3 December 2012. The Prison Service is also able to correct court directed remand time for sentences imposed on or after 3 December 2012.

- All remand time whether court directed or automatically calculated by the Prison Service is applied to the overall release date of concurrent sentences imposed prior to 3 December 2012 irrespective of the Act under which the sentence was imposed.
- The 3-month notice of supervision requirement for young adult offenders only applies to the initial release from the custodial period of a Detention and Training Order or section 91 sentences of less than 12 months.
- Release under the new EDS for prisoners convicted on or after 3 December 2012 will either be subject to parole or automatic release at the two-thirds point of the custodial term, depending on the length of the sentence and/or whether the extended sentence was imposed for a Schedule 15B offence.
- The Secretary of State can exercise executive power to re-release all recalled prisoners. Fixed term recall restrictions are removed and may be varied to a standard recall in light of new information. Parole Board decisions on EPP prisoners become a 'direction' rather than a 'recommendation' (LASPO, section 115).
- All young offenders under 21 sentenced to less than 12 months will be released with 3 months' supervision, and punishment for breach will be by court summons rather than recall (LASPO, section 115).
- Parole Board approval is no longer required for release on compassionate grounds of EPP prisoners, as their decisions are now 'directions' (LASPO, section 116).

F10.3 Summary

PSI 13/2013 Sentence Calculation – Determinate Sentenced Prisoners

2.3 Summary of CJA 2003 Sentences Types and their Release Arrangements

2.3.1 The following table provides a summary of the different types of CJA 2003 determinate sentences and the release arrangements to which they are subject.

Type of Sentence	Date Sentence Imposed	Date Offence Committed	Release Dates	Comments
SDS Less than 12 months	Any Date of Sentence	Any Date of Offence	ARD	Automatic Release at ½ way point.
			SED	Release is unconditional.

SDS 12 months or more	Sentenced On or After 03/12/2012	Any Date of Offence	CRD	Automatic Release at ½ way point.
			SLED	On licence to end of sentence.
SDS 12 months or more	Sentenced Prior to 03/12/2012	On or After 04/04/05	CRD	Automatic Release at ½ way point.
			SLED	On licence to end of sentence.
SDS 12 months but less than 4 years	Sentenced Prior to 03/12/2012	Prior to 04/04/05	CRD	Automatic Release at ½ way point.
			LED	On licence to ¾ point.
			SED	End of sentence
SDS 4 years or more Offence NOT in Schedule 15	Sentenced Prior to 03/12/2012	Prior to 04/04/05	CRD	Automatic Release at ½ way point.
			SLED	On licence to end of sentence.
SDS 4 years or more Offence in Schedule 15	Sentenced Prior to 03/12/2012	Prior to 04/04/05	PED	Eligible for discretionary release by the Parole Board at ½ way point.
			NPD	Automatic Release at ⅔ point.
			LED	On licence to ¾ point
			SED	End of sentence
Extended Determinate Sentence Section 226A or 226B Where custodial period is **both** less than 10 years AND is NOT for a Schedule 15B offence	Convicted and Sentenced On or After 03/12/2012	Any Date of Offence	CRD	Automatic Release at ⅔ point of custodial period.
			SLED	On licence to end of sentence.

Extended Determinate Sentence Section 226A or 226B Where custodial period is 10 years or more **OR** is for a Schedule 15B offence	Convicted and Sentenced On or After 03/12/2012	Any Date of Offence	PED	Eligible for discretionary release by the Parole Board at ⅔ point of custodial period.
			CRD	Automatic Release at end of custodial period.
			SLED	On licence to end of sentence.
Extended Sentence Section 227 or 228	Sentenced On or After 14/07/08 Convicted before 03/12/12	On or After 04/04/05	CRD	Automatic Release at ½ way point of custodial period.
			SLED	On licence to end of sentence.
Extended Sentence Section 227 or 228	Sentenced Prior to 14/07/08	On or After 04/04/05	PED	Eligible for discretionary release by the Parole Board at ½ way point of custodial period.
			CRD	Automatic Release at end of custodial period.
			SLED	On licence to end of sentence.
Extended Sentence Section 85 Where custodial period is less than 12 months	Convicted prior to 03/12/12	Prior to 04/04/05	CRD	Automatic Release at ½ way point of custodial period.
			LED	On licence to end of custodial period + extension period.
			SED	End of sentence

Extended Sentence Section 85 Where custodial period is 12 months but less than 4 years	Convicted prior to 03/12/12	Prior to 04/04/05	CRD	Automatic Release at ½ way point of custodial period.
			LED	On licence to ¾ point of custodial period + extension period.
			SED	End of sentence
Extended Sentence Section 85 Where custodial period is 4 years or more.	Convicted prior to 03/12/12	Prior to 04/04/05	PED	Eligible for discretionary release by the Parole Board at ½ way point of custodial period.
			NPD	Automatic Release at ⅔ point of custodial period.
			LED	On licence to ¾ point of custodial period + extension period.
			SED	End of sentence
Extended Licence Section 86 or 44 12months but less than 4 years	Convicted prior to 03/12/12	Prior to 30/09/98	CRD	Automatic Release at ½ way point of sentence.
			LED/SED	On licence to end of sentence.
Extended Licence Section 86 or 44 4 years or more	Convicted prior to 03/12/12	Prior to 30/09/98	PED	Eligible for discretionary release by the Parole Board at ½ way point of sentence.
			NPD	Automatic Release at ⅔ point of sentence.
			LED/SED	On licence to end of sentence.

F10.4 Other Sentences

In addition to these release arrangements there will be an ever decreasing number of prisoners within the prison population who were sentenced prior to 3 December 2012 and returned to prison by order of the court or sentenced prior to 1 October 1992, known as 'existing prisoners'.

F11 **Remand Time**

F11.1 **Key Document**

`KD` PSI 13/2013

A 'relevant period' of remand time, tagged bail or police detention will reduce the custodial term by a specific number of days. The licence start date will be brought forward, but the length of the licence period itself will remain the same.

Where the remand days exceed the number of days in the custodial part of the sentence the exact number of days will be credited to clear the custodial period. Although the uncredited days cannot reduce the licence period they can be used to offset any further period in custody following a return to custody or licence recall.

The 'relevant period' for the purposes of reducing the custodial part of the sentence is:

(a) Any period of tagged bail directed to count towards the sentence.
(b) Any period during which the offender was remanded in custody by a court in connection to any proceedings relating to that sentence or offence, or a substituted sentence or offence.
(c) Any period during which the offender was in police detention in connection with the offence for which sentence was passed provided the sentence was imposed before 3 December 2012 for offences committed prior to 4 April 2005.

F11.2 **Key Points**

- A remand in custody includes a remand into police custody, and a remand into the care of the local authority.
- A 'relevant period' can only be credited once to an overall sentence.
- Any remand time that has been served at the same time as another sentence of imprisonment, a term for contempt, a term in default or a recall to custody will not count as a 'relevant period'.
- Any remand time served at the same time as a period of detention under the Immigration Act 1971 will count as a 'relevant period'.
- Any remand time served prior to the imposition of a Community Order, a Conditional Discharge or a Suspended Sentence will only count as a 'relevant period' if the court re-sentences the prisoner to a term of imprisonment as a result of a breach.

F11.3 Remand in Custody (CJA 2003, section 240ZA)

The Prison Service is responsible for crediting any relevant remand time where the sentence was imposed on or after 3 December 2012.

If the sentence was imposed prior to 3 December 2012 for offences committed on or after 4 April 2005 it was for the court to direct the number of days to be credited towards the sentence.

Time spent in police custody at the investigation stage will only be credited to prisoners sentenced before 3 December 2012, for offences committed prior to 4 April 2005. The dates have to be confirmed by the police (PSI 13/2013, paragraph 4.3.4). Any part of a day spent in police detention will count as a whole day for the purposes of sentence calculation.

Attendance at the police station as a 'volunteer' does not constitute police detention and will not count.

F11.4 Remand on Bail (CJA 2003, section 240A)

Periods spent on bail whilst subject to an electronically monitored curfew for at least 9 hours per day, count as time served on remand, if directed by the court. The number of days to count must be specifically directed, subject to a maximum of half the number of days spent on tagged bail, and can be directed to count towards any sentence imposed after 3 November 2008, irrespective of the date of the offence. The Prison Service staff cannot alter the number of days on the Order of Imprisonment PSI 13/2013, paragraph 4.4.5). Prisoners who disagree with the number of days credited should pursue the matter with the court.

F11.5 Court Errors

If the court directed more days to count than the prisoner's entitlement, the direction on the warrant stands and must be taken into account when calculating the sentence. If the court directed fewer days than the prisoner's entitlement the prison must apply the correct number of days to the sentence calculation. However, if the court imposed the sentence before 3 December 2012 for an offence committed after 4 April 2005, and exercised their discretion to specifically state that remand time should not count towards the sentence, the court's intention will be honoured and the time will not be credited (PSI 13/2013, paragraph 4.3.3).

📖 *Blackstone's Criminal Practice 2014* **E2.8–E2.10**

F12 Additional Days Awarded (ADA)

F12.1 Key Document

<kbd>KD</kbd> PSI 13/2013

Prisoners or young offenders found guilty of a breach of the Prison/ YOI Rules may be ordered to serve additional days. ADAs will be added to all release dates except the SED or SLED and cannot extend the release date or licence expiry date beyond the end of the sentence.

F12.2 Key Points

- For single sentences imposed on or after 3 December 2012 and any sentences of 12 months or more imposed before 3 December 2012 for offences committed on or after 4 April 2005, ADAs may only be applied to the conditional release date (CRD)/automatic release date (ARD)/PED.
- Sentences imposed prior to 3 December 2012 for offences committed before 4 April 2005 and sentences of less than 12 months imposed prior to 3 December 2012, will form a single term and ADAs will be applied to the ARD/CRD/PED/NPD/LED.
- ADAs during any concurrent sentences that do not form a single term will defer the overall effective ARD/CRD/NPD/PED.
- Where single terms are consecutive to one another, the sentences are aggregated. Any ADAs during the custodial periods of any part of the aggregate will defer the effective ARD/CRD/NPD/PED.

F12.3 Prospective Additional Days Awarded (PADAs)

Remand prisoners may be awarded PADAs, which will only be added if they subsequently receive a custodial sentence.

Prior to 3 December 2012 for offences committed on or after 4 April 2005, the courts had the authority to direct how much remand was to be applied to the sentence, if any. PADAs during a period of remand where the court decided not to allow any remand time to count will still be applied to the sentence (PSI 13/2013, paragraph 9.9.2).

Where a prisoner is deemed to have served his sentence while on remand, the sentence will be calculated without remand time being applied. The number of PADAs will then be added to the number of days until the release date to find the total number of days in the custodial period. The remand time is then deducted to clear that number of days (PSI 13/2013, paragraph 9.9.3).

F12.4 ADAs and Licence Recall

ADAs during a fixed term recall will defer the re-release date but cannot extend beyond the SED/SLED. ADAs during the period of revocation but before the Parole Board has made a recommendation must be brought to their attention. The Parole Board can take the ADAs into account in determining whether or not to recommend re-release. If the Parole Board has taken the ADAs into account which has affected the re-release date, the Prison Service must not extend that re-release date by the ADAs. If the Parole Board has not taken the ADAs into account the Prison Service must extend the re-release date that has been set by any relevant ADAs. This will extend all dates except the SED/SLED (PSI 13/2013, paragraph 9.10.3).

Only ADAs during the revoked licence period may be remitted as previous ADAs will already have been served (PSI 13/2013, paragraph 9.11.1).

F12.5 ADAs and Home Detention Curfew

Where a prisoner has been recalled for breaching the HDC conditions the prison will apply any ADAs (imposed during the recall period) and defer all re-release dates except the SED/SLED in the usual way (PSI 13/2013, paragraph 9.10.5).

F13 **Sentence Calculation**

F13.1 **Key Document**

KD PSI 13/2013

Release and sentence calculation are interlinked.

F13.2 **Basic Principles**

- Concurrent sentences run from the date imposed.
- Consecutive sentences run from the end of the previous sentence.
- Release dates must be calculated in days.
- Remand time cannot be applied twice.
- Sentences expressed in months are calendar months.
- Sentences expressed in years are calendar years.
- Release dates falling on weekends or Bank Holidays will be brought forward to the preceding weekday.

F13.3 **Procedure**

The documents required to calculate the sentence imposed by the court, are as follows:

(i)   Order of imprisonment (F5035/F5044—Crown Court or Warrant of Commitment—Magistrate's Court);
(ii)   Trial record sheet (F5089/Court Record);
(iii) Indictment (F5088);
(iv)   Details of prospective additional days;
(v)   Remand warrants;
(vi)   Police custody records;
(vii) Back records (PSI 13/2013, paragraph 3.1.1).

Governors have a duty to ensure that release dates for prisoners serving determinate sentences are calculated accurately and in accordance with the law. The prisoner must be informed of the release dates in writing within a day and no later than 5 working days of the calculation. If missing documentation prevents a final calculation, the calculation should be marked 'provisional' and recalculated as soon as the missing data becomes available. Provisional calculations must not credit remand time, tagged bail time or police custody time until all of the relevant information is available (PSI 13/2013, paragraph 3.2.1).

The original calculation should be re-checked 14 days before a prisoner's anticipated release (PSI 13/2013, paragraph 3.4.3). Records should be reviewed to ascertain whether the calculation needs to be amended in the light of additional days, periods when the prisoner was unlawfully at large or lodged warrants/fines. A final review should take place 2 days before release by an officer other than the one that did the 14-day check (PSI 13/2013, paragraph 3.4.4).

All calculations must be re-checked by a second member of staff, who must initial the calculation sheet as verification.

F14 **Automatic Release Schemes**

F14.1 **Key Document**

KD   PSI 13/2013

Release dates are all governed by CJA 2003, as amended by LASPO 2012. However, the relevant scheme is determined by the date of sentence, and in some cases the date of the offence and the length of the sentence.

Determinate sentences fall into one of the following 4 categories:

(1) Sentences imposed on or after 3 December 2012;
(2) Sentences imposed before 3 December 2012 but on or after 1 October 1992 for offences committed on or after 4 April 2005;
(3) Sentences imposed before 3 December 2012 but on or after 1 October 1992 for offences committed before 4 April 2005;
(4) Sentences imposed before 1 October 1992.

F14.2 **Sentences Imposed On or After 3 December 2012**

F14.2.1 *General principles*

- Police custody does not count towards sentence.
- Periods on bail subject to a qualifying curfew condition and electronic tagging may count towards sentence.
- Concurrent release dates are calculated separately.
- Prisoners are released on licence at the halfway point.
- Licence continues to sentence expiry date.
- Additional days on standard determinate sentences extend the conditional release date (CRD) only.

F14.2.2 *Standard determinate sentence (SDS)*

Sentences imposed on or after 3 December 2012 are standard determinate sentences (SDSs). Prisoners who are not eligible or have not applied for HDC will be released at the halfway point. An SDS of less than 12 months has an automatic release date (ARD) at the halfway point and unconditional release until the sentence expiry date (SED). An SDS of more than 12 months has a conditional release date (CRD) at the halfway point and release on licence until the end of the sentence and licence expiry date (SLED). Release can only be delayed if additional days have been awarded.

Figure 1 Standard Determinate Sentenced Prisoners

F14.2.3 *Concurrent sentences*

When concurrent sentences are passed at the same time the longest sentence will determine the release date (PSI 13/2013, paragraph 5.5.1). When concurrent sentences are passed on different occasions, each concurrent sentence must be calculated separately. If all the sentences are less than 12 months release will be automatic at the latest halfway point and unconditional until the latest SED (PSI 13/2013, paragraph 5.5.3). If all the sentences are more than 12 months the last CRD will be the date the prisoner will be released on licence until the latest SLED (PSI 13/2013, paragraph 5.5.4).

A period of temporary release does not break one sentence from another. HDC will, however, break the sentence (PSI 13/2013, paragraph 5.5.5).

F14.2.4 *Consecutive sentences*

Sentences ordered to be served consecutively are aggregated for the purposes of calculating release dates. The total number of days is the SLED and the halfway point is the CRD (PSI 13/2013, paragraph 5.6.1).

Where all the sentences are less than 12 months and when aggregated the length of the aggregate is still less than 12 months, release is unconditional at the halfway point of the aggregate. Therefore the aggregate has an ARD and an SED (PSI 13/2013, paragraph 5.6.2). However, where the sentences of less than 12 months form an aggregate of 12 months or more, release at the halfway point of the aggregate is on licence to the end of the aggregate. Therefore, the aggregate has a CRD and a SLED (PSI 13/2013, paragraph 5.6.3).

Sentences are aggregated whether imposed on the same occasion or on different occasions, provided the prisoner has not been released from the custodial part of the earlier sentence before the consecutive sentence is passed (PSI 13/2013, paragraph 5.6.4).

F14.2.5 *Extended Determinate Sentence (EDS)*

Section 124 LASPO created the EDS by inserting a new section 226A into CJA 2003, and Schedule 18 inserted a new Schedule 15B.

An EDS will be imposed on an offender who is:

- over 18;
- convicted of a specified offence on or after 3 December 2012 (regardless of when the offence was committed);
- presents a significant risk to the public of serious harm from further specified offences;
- is not suitable for a life sentence; and either
  - (i) has a previous conviction for a Schedule 15B offence, or
  - (ii) the custodial term would be at least 4 years.

The extension period imposed must not exceed 5 years in respect of a violent offence, and 8 years in respect of a sexual offence. EDSs of less than 10 years and non-Schedule 15B offences will be released automatically at the two-thirds point.

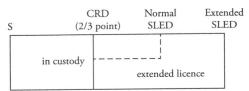

Figure 2 Extended Determinate Sentence (less than 10 years and non-Schedule 15B offence)

F14.3 Sentences Imposed Before 3 December 2012 (Offence On or After 4 April 2005)

Such sentences are treated in the same way as standard determinate sentences (SDSs) imposed on or after 3 December 2012 (see **F14.2.2**). Concurrent sentences run parallel to each other and consecutive sentences are aggregated (PSI 13/2013, paragraph 5.7.1).

F14.4 Sentences Imposed Before 3 December 2012 (Offence Before 4 April 2005)

F14.4.1 *General principles*

- Prisoners are defined as 'short term' (serving less than 4 years) or 'long term' (serving 4 years or more).
- Remand time is calculated by the prison.
- Police detention counts towards remand time.

F14.4.2 *Automatic unconditional release (AUR)*

Short-term prisoners serving less than 3 months must be released automatically at the halfway point, known as the automatic release date (ARD). Prisoners serving 3 months or more but less than 12 months may be eligible for HDC. If not released early under HDC the prisoner will be released at the halfway point, ie the ARD. Additional days will extend the ARD. There is no licence period, and there is no longer an 'at risk' period (PSI 13/2013, paragraph 5.7.2).

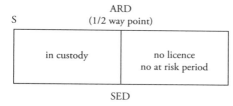

Figure 3 Automatic Unconditional Release

F14.4.3 *Automatic conditional release (ACR)*

• Prisoners sentenced to 12 months or more but less than 4 years for offences committed prior to 4 April 2005.

Such prisoners must be released automatically at the halfway point (CRD), and will remain on licence until the three-quarter point—the licence expiry date (LED). If the licence is breached, the prisoner may be recalled to prison. These prisoners are no longer 'at risk' of being returned to custody if they commit an imprisonable offence between the date of release and the SED (PSI 13/2013, paragraph 5.7.3). Additional days will extend the CRD and LED. Most ACR prisoners will be eligible for HDC.

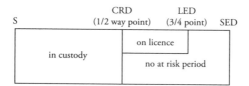

Figure 4 Automatic Conditional Release (12 months or more but less than 4 years)

F14.4.4 *'Conversion' cases*

Since 9 June 2008 prisoners sentenced to 4 years or more for non-violent and non-sexual offences have been released automatically at the halfway point (CRD), and remain on licence until the end of the sentence known as the sentence and licence expiry date (SLED) (PSI 13/2013, paragraph 5.7.2). Therefore the release of these prisoners is in line with SDSs (see Figure 1). Release can only be delayed if additional days have been awarded.

F14.4.5 *'Old style' Extended Sentence for Public Protection (EPP)*

An EPP prisoner sentenced on or after 14 July 2008, and convicted before 3 December 2012, for offences committed on or after 4 April 2005, will be released automatically at the halfway point of the custodial term and will be on licence until the end of the custodial term plus the period of the extended licence.

A section 85 EPP prisoner sentenced for offences committed before 4 April 2005 who was subject to CJA 1991 (now CJA 2003, Schedule 20B), will be released automatically at the halfway point where the sentence is less than 4 years. The prisoner will remain on licence until the three-quarter point of the custodial term plus the extension period. The final quarter of the custodial term is at the end of the extension period. However, the prisoner is no longer 'at risk'.

These sentences are no longer available.

F14.5 Sentences Imposed Before 1 October 1992

Prisoners sentenced to imprisonment before CJA 1991 came into force are known as 'existing prisoners'. There are special provisions in CJA 2003, Schedule 20B, Part 3 for the few 'existing prisoners' that remain.

Automatic release of an 'existing prisoner' is unconditional at the two-thirds point of the sentence (NPD) with eligibility for consideration for parole at the later of either the one-third point of the sentence or 6 months from date of sentence (PED). Release on parole would be on a licence expiring at the two-thirds point.

F15 **Juveniles and Young Offenders**

F15.1 **Key Document**

KD PSI 13/2013

For young offenders there are currently 5 possible determinate sentences the court may impose:

- Detention in a Young Offenders Institution (offenders aged 18 but under 21)
- Detention under section 91 of the PCC(S)A 2000 for certain 'grave offences' (offenders aged under 18)
- Detention and Training Order (offenders under 18)
- Detention for offenders aged 14–17 under Schedule 5A, paragraph 14(1) the Policing and Crime Act 2009, for breach of a gang injunction (PSI 39/2012, paragraph 14.1.2)
- Extended Determinate Sentence.

The framework for calculation of release dates for young offenders is the same as it is for adults. Release dates are determined by the length of the sentence and when they were imposed. Remand time will count towards sentence in the normal way.

F15.1 **DYOI and Detention under PCC(S)A 2000, section 91**

For offenders serving a term of less than 12 months, release will be at the halfway point of the term imposed but, unlike adults who are released unconditionally, release in these cases is on a 3-month supervision notice under section 256B of the CJA 2003. Offenders serving 12 months or more will be released at the halfway point on licence until the relevant LED/SLED.

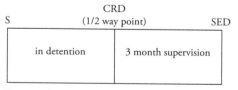

Figure 5 Detention (less than 12 months)

A failure to comply with a supervision order may result in either a fine or a period of detention up to a maximum of 30 days under section 256C of the CJA 2003. An offender imprisoned for a period of detention of up to 30 days will serve the term in full before being re-released. Release will be on anything extant of the original 3-month supervision notice.

A new sentence imposed concurrently to a section 256C breach will run parallel and release will take place on the latest release date. A new sentence imposed consecutively to a section 256C breach will be calculated separately from the breach term and will commence on the day after the breach term has been served in full.

F15.2 Detention and Training Orders (DTOs)

A DTO, like a sentence of imprisonment, normally begins on the date it was imposed by the court. It is divided into a period of detention and training and a period of supervision. The release date of the offender will normally be the halfway point of the term of the DTO. When calculating the release dates the Prison Service does not credit remand/tagged bail time. The court should have taken any such time that is relevant to the DTO into account when determining its length.

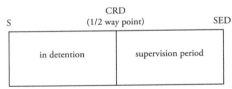

Figure 6 Detention and Training Order

F15.2.1 *Multiple DTOs*

Offenders may receive more than one DTO. Concurrent and consecutive DTOs must be treated as a single term for the purpose of calculating release dates if:

(a) they were made on the same date, or
(b) where they were made on different dates, the offender has not been released at any time during the period beginning with the first and ending with last sentence date.

Where concurrent and overlapping DTOs are imposed, the length of the single term is determined by the date of sentence of the first DTO to the latest end date of the DTOs. DTOs to be served consecutively are, for the purpose of the calculation of release dates, added together and treated as a single term equal to the combined total of the DTOs. This also applies to DTOs imposed by different courts on different days, providing the offender has not been released at any time before the second DTO was imposed and the warrant or court order clearly indicates that the DTOs are to be served consecutively.

F15.2.2 *Early and late release*

The Secretary of State may bring a release date forward:

(a) if there are exceptional circumstances justifying early release on compassionate grounds; or

(b) to reflect progress in custody. The release date may be brought forward by up to one month, for DTOs of 8 months or more but less than 18 months, and by up to 2 months, for DTOs of 18 months or more.

The Secretary of State may make an application for a release date to be deferred by order of a youth court:

(a) by up to one month for DTOs of 8 months or more but less than 18 months;

(b) by up to 2 months for DTOs of 18 months or more.

F15.2.3 *Interaction with DYOIs*

DTOs and DYOIs are never treated as a single term. They are never ordered to run concurrently or consecutively to one another, as they are structured differently and have different release provisions. However, in practice they may take effect concurrently or consecutively if they both take effect at the same time. When either the period of supervision under the DTO or the sentence expiry date of the sentence of DYOI is reached, the offender ceases to be 'subject concurrently' to both.

If an offender serving a DTO in custody becomes concurrently subject to a DYOI, the DYOI is treated as beginning on the day it is passed and runs parallel to the DTO. Release cannot take place until the latest release date produced by the two terms. If an offender serving a DTO becomes consecutively subject to a DYOI, the DYOI will begin on the day after the day the offender would otherwise have been released from the DTO.

Where a DYOI is imposed on an offender who has previously received a DTO, any remand or tagged bail time taken into account by the court in determining the duration of the DTO must be disregarded for the purpose of determining the amount of remand or tagged bail time relevant to the DYOI.

If an offender has been released from the custodial part of the DTO the DYOI must commence on the day it is passed by the court unless the offender is subject to a period of detention imposed for breach of a DTO in which case the DYOI may take effect in the ways described above in relation to an offender who is still serving a DTO in custody.

Where an offender is concurrently subject to both a DTO and a DYOI, for the purpose of determining release dates or recall or re-detention, the offender is treated as subject only to the sentence imposed on the later occasion. This is subject to the proviso that release cannot take place until the offender has reached both release dates.

The imposition of a later sentence of DYOI does not mean that the previous DTO ceases to have effect. It is possible for an offender subject to a DTO to be given a DYOI and, after having completed that sentence, to be required to complete any outstanding supervision period of the DTO. It is also possible for a court to impose a DTO and a DYOI on the same date. On release the offender will be released on the required licences relevant to both the DTO and the DYOI at the point of release.

F15.2.4 *Interaction with PCC(S)A 2000, section 91 and extended sentences*

In such cases, the section 91 or extended sentence and the DTO will be calculated separately. Concurrent terms will run parallel to one another and consecutive terms will start on the day after the release of the term to be served first.

F15.3 Breach of Supervision

LASPO provides that on or after 3 December 2012, breaches of a DTO can be punished even after the term of the DTO has finished. The court retains the power to impose a period of detention for breach of a DTO and creates a new power to impose a further period of supervision instead of custody for the breach. The maximum period of supervision or detention will be 3 months or the period beginning with the date of the failure to comply with the requirement and ending with the last day of the term of the DTO, whichever is the shorter.

Where the court imposes a period of detention or supervision for breach, it takes immediate effect and can run concurrently with the DTO's supervision period. For repeated breaches, the court can impose further periods of supervision (or detention or a fine) and this may continue until the young person completes the order.

F15.4 Re-offending During the DTO (PCC(S)A 2000, section 105)

If an offender commits an imprisonable offence during the supervision period of a DTO the court may order his detention for a period up to the length of the number of days between the date on which the new offence was committed and the date the existing DTO expires. The court may order this period of detention to be served either before and be followed by, or be served concurrently with, any sentence imposed for the new offence. The period of re-detention must be served in full. Therefore, any sentence imposed for the new offence is not combined with the period of re-detention to form a single term. A concurrent DTO or sentence of DYOI will have its own release dates and will run parallel to the section 105 period. A consecutive DTO or sentence of DYOI will begin on the day after the last day of the section 105 period.

F15.5 Breach of a Gang Injunction

Offenders may be made subject to an injunction to prevent gang-related violence. Offenders aged 14–17 who breach the terms of the injunction, may be ordered by the court to serve a period of detention of up to 3 months. The term imposed must be served in full. There are no early release provisions.

Offenders aged 18 or over who breach a gang injunction will be dealt with under contempt procedures.

F15.6 Extended Determinate Sentence

An EDS will be imposed on an offender who is:

- under 18; and
- convicted of a specified offence on or after 3 December 2012 (regardless of when the offence was committed); and
- presents a significant risk to the public of serious harm; and
- is not suitable for detention for life sentence; and
- for whom the custodial term would be at least 4 years.

The extension period imposed must not exceed 5 years in respect of a violent offence, and 8 years in respect of a sexual offence.

F16 Unlawfully at Large (UAL)

F16.1 Key Document

KD 39/2012

F16.2 Key Points

- Any period during which a sentenced prisoner is unlawfully at large (UAL) will not count towards the sentence served unless the Secretary of State for Justice directs that it should count due to exceptional circumstances eg the prisoner was released in error (see PSI 39/2012, Appendix F for further examples).

- Where a prisoner has been deemed to be UAL as a result of being released in error, the first day UAL will be the day after the release in error took place and the last day will be the day before arrest/return to custody.

- The UAL period will extend all dates including the SED. For the purposes of calculating the UAL period the date of absence and the date of recapture will not count if the prisoner escaped or absconded prior to 21 July 2008. However, these dates do count if the escapes and absconds occurred after 21 July 2008.

- A prisoner whose licence has been revoked whilst not in custody will be deemed to be UAL. For sentence calculation purposes the first day of UAL will be the day following the revocation of licence. The last day of UAL will be the day before arrest. The same applies to revocations of temporary release licences.

- A sentenced prisoner recaptured abroad, including the Irish Republic, may on return to custody in the UK, make an application for the time spent in custody pending extradition to count as time served.

F17 Home Detention Curfew (HDC)

F17.1 Key Documents

KD PSI 43/2012

PSI 31/2003

PSI 31/2006

PSO 6700

F17.2 Provisions

HDC allows certain prisoners to be released early subject to a curfew and electronic tagging. LASPO has amended the CJA provisions to create a single statutory scheme. As of 3 December 2012 all HDC releases are governed by section 246 of the CJA 2003. The curfew requirement is imposed under section 253.

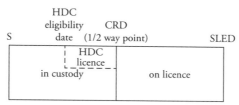

Figure 7 Home Detention Curfew

F17.3 Statutory Exceptions

The following are not eligible for HDC:

> **PSI 43/2012 The Legal Aid, Sentencing and Punishment of Offenders (LASPO) Act 2012 – Home Detention Curfew (HDC)**
>
> (i) prisoners serving a sentence for a term of 4 years or more (determined by the aggregate of the terms with consecutive sentences, and by the period from the start of the first to the end of the last term with concurrent sentences);
>
> (ii) violent and sexual offenders currently serving an extended sentence imposed under section 226A, 227 or 228 of the CJA03;
>
> (iii) prisoners currently serving a sentence for an offence under section 1 of the Prisoners (Return to Custody) Act 1995 (for failure to return to custody following a period of temporary release);
>
> (iv) prisoners currently subject to a hospital order, hospital direction or transfer direction under section 37, 45A or 47 of the Mental Health Act 1983;

(v)   prisoners currently serving a sentence imposed under paragraph 9(1)(b) or (c) or 10(1)(b) or (c) of Schedule 8 of the CJA03 in a case where the prisoner has failed to comply with a curfew requirement of a community order;

(vi)   prisoners subject to the notification requirements of Part 2 of the Sexual offences Act 2003;

(vii) prisoners currently liable to removal from the United Kingdom;

(viii) prisoners who have been released on HDC and have, at any time, been recalled to prison under section 255(1)(a) CJA03 or 38A(1) CJA91 (breach of the HDC curfew condition), unless the prisoner has successfully appealed the revocation;

(ix)   prisoners who have been released on licence under section 248 (compassionate early release from custody) during the currency of the sentence, and have been recalled to prison under section 254;

(x)   prisoners who have, at any time been returned to prison under section 40 of the Criminal Justice Act 1991 or section 116 of the Powers of the Criminal Courts (Sentencing) Act 2000; and

(xi)   prisoners who have less than 14 days remaining between the date of sentence and the date on which the prisoner will have served the requisite custodial period.

Prisoners on remand for other offences should not normally be assessed for HDC. However, the Governor has discretion to initiate assessment in exceptional circumstances, eg, if it is likely that the prisoner will become eligible and still be in a position to be subject to a curfew for at least 14 days.

F17.4 Presumed Unsuitable

Amid concerns that public confidence was being undermined, PSI 31/2003 was issued introducing the policy that certain prisoners should be 'presumed unsuitable' for release on HDC. A prisoner presumed unsuitable may only be released on HDC in exceptional circumstances. Prisoners who fall into this category should be given the opportunity to make representations which will be considered by the Governor, however if the prisoner has any history of committing sexual offences the decision will be made by the HDC policy team based in NOMS. The level of risk the prisoner poses is precluded from ever amounting to exceptional circumstances, in and of itself, no matter how low. There will therefore be very few cases that meet the criteria and as 'a rule of thumb such cases will stand out' (PSI 31/2003, paragraph 33).

PSI 43/2012, Annex B lists current examples of offences for which prisoners will be 'presumed unsuitable'.

PSI 43/2012 The Legal Aid, Sentencing and Punishment of Offenders (LASPO) Act 2012 – Home Detention Curfew (HDC) Annex B

Offence Category	Examples:
Homicide	Manslaughter
	Attempted Murder
	Making Threats to kill
	Conspiring or soliciting etc to commit murder
	Causing Death by Reckless/Dangerous Driving
	Causing Death by careless driving when under the influence of drink or drugs
	Aggravated vehicle taking resulting in death
Explosives	Causing GBH by explosion
	Attempting/Causing an explosion with intent
	Placing explosives with intent
	Making explosives
	Possession of explosives with intent to endanger life
Terrorism	**Anti-Terrorism, Crime and Security Act 2001:** Use of nuclear weapons
	Assisting or inducing certain weapons
	Use of noxious substances or things to cause harm and intimidate
	Terrorism Act 2000: Membership of proscribed organisation
	Money laundering, fund raising etc
	Weapons training
	Directing a terrorist organisation
	Possession of articles for terrorist purposes
	Collection of information for terrorist purposes Inciting another person to commit an act of terrorism outside the UK
	Committing terrorist related offences outside the UK by a UK national/resident
	Prevention of Terrorism Act 2005: Breaches of control orders under section 9(1) and (2) (But **not** breaches under s9(3))
	Terrorism Act 2006: Encouragement of terrorism
	Dissemination of terrorist publications
	Preparation of terrorist acts
	Training for terrorism Attendance at a place used for terrorist training

	Making and possession of devices or materials
	Misuse of devices or material and misuse and damage of facilities
	Terrorist threats relating to devices, materials or facilities
Possession of offensive weapons	Possession of an offensive weapon
	Possessing a sharp bladed instrument
Possession of firearms with intent	Possession of firearms (including imitation firearms) with intent to:
	- endanger life or commit an offence
	- resist arrest
	- cause fear of violence
	Possession of a firearm whilst committing an offence
Cruelty to Children	Ill treatment or neglect
	Child abduction
	Abandoning children under 2 years
	Other offences, not elsewhere specified, where a person aged 16 years or more who has the custody, charge or care of any child or young person under 16 years wilfully assaults or causes unnecessary suffering (ie this may include those convicted of, for example, ABH or GBH instead of child cruelty)
Offences aggravated on the grounds of race, religion or sexual orientation	Racially or religiously aggravated offences under the Crime and Disorder Act 1998 – sections 29 to 32:
	- malicious wounding or GBH
	- ABH
	- common assault
	- criminal damage
	- intentional harassment, alarm or distress
	- harassment
	- causing fear of violence
	Incitement to racial hatred offences under sections 18–23 of The Public Order Act 1986; and Incitement to hatred on the grounds of religion or sexual orientation offences under section 29B to 29G of the Public Order Act 1986
	- use of words or behaviour or display of written material
	- publishing or distributing written material
	- public performance of play
	- distributing, showing or playing a recording
	- broadcasting material
	- possessing material

F17.5 Minimum Periods

The HDC date must be calculated at the same time as the statutory release date, and the prisoner must be informed of both at the same time. The minimum sentence is 12 weeks, and prisoners must not be released on HDC until they have served at least 28 days (PSI 43/2012, paragraph 2.3).

F17.5.1 *Multiple offences*

A prisoner is presumed unsuitable for HDC if any sentence forming part of the overall custodial term currently being served relates to a presumed unsuitable offence. Where one of the sentences is statutorily excluded from HDC, the prisoner will be ineligible in relation to that sentence and will be presumed unsuitable whilst serving the other sentences. Prisoners sentenced under CJA 1991 will be statutorily excluded for the single term (PSI 43/2012, paragraph 2.5).

F17.5.2 *No separate penalty*

Where a prisoner has been convicted of a 'presumed unsuitable' offence but the court disposal is recorded as 'no separate penalty', this should not be treated as serving a sentence of imprisonment for the purposes of considering HDC. Any prisoner who has been advised that they are presumed unsuitable for HDC solely because of such a disposal may now be considered for HDC under the normal assessment process. The behaviour leading to the conviction will be taken into account in that process alongside other relevant factors (PSI 43/2012, paragraph 2.9).

F17.6 Procedure

The ICA forms (used for categorization) are used as a checklist to ensure that all the relevant documents are collated, in particular previous convictions, disciplinary offences, reports on any offender behaviour programmes completed and home circumstances assessment. Sentence planning assessments and reviews if available, will be taken into account and all prisoners who have a realistic prospect of being released on HDC should be encouraged to find suitable accommodation if they are of no fixed abode, or unable to return to their previous address for whatever reason. The Probation Service may be able to assist the prisoner in finding a bail hostel place, housing association or local authority housing depending on the circumstances.

The risk assessment process should commence 10 weeks before the HDC eligibility date, unless the prisoner is ineligible, and should not normally be commenced if there would be insufficient time to

F17 Home Detention Curfew (HDC)

complete the assessment and allow for at least 14 days on curfew. Category A prisoners are not excluded from HDC, although as they have already been assessed as posing a serious risk to the public, they will only be considered if they apply and if there are exceptional circumstances which merit initiating a risk assessment (PSI 31/2003, paragraph 2.5.1).

There are two assessment procedures:

1. *Standard suitability assessment.* All eligible prisoners must undergo the standard assessment which is based on custodial records, reports from the prison and a report from the home probation officer (PSO 6700, paragraph 5.3.2). Any prisoner wanting to be considered for HDC must complete form HDC2 giving details of the proposed release address and any other residents. If the prisoner does not want to be considered for HDC this should be confirmed in writing on the form. Part 2 of the form, which requires up-to-date information on the prisoner's suitability for HDC, will be completed by a member of staff who has regular contact with the prisoner. The form and the core documents will then be considered by the custody-based supervisor who will assess whether there are any issues that the prison staff or community-based offender manager should be invited to comment on, and Healthcare may be consulted if there are mental health concerns. The process may be fast-tracked (no report from the home probation officer) if it is clear the prisoner is unsuitable for HDC and the report would not add to the assessment, although the prisoner must still be considered under the enhanced assessment (PSO 6700, paragraph 5.9.4). If at this stage it appears that the prisoner is suitable or may be suitable form HDC3 will be sent to the home probation officer for the area the prisoner intends to reside, to comment on the suitability of the release address having sought the views of the victim (if any) and other residence (if appropriate). Once HDC3 has been received the seconded probation officer will review the documents and confirm on form HDC1 that the prisoner is suitable for HDC. Unless there are clear grounds to require an enhanced assessment the HDC1 is then forwarded to the Governor to confirm suitability and authorize release.

2. *Enhanced assessment.* An enhanced assessment will be required if the prisoner:
   - is serving over one year and does not have a successful record of temporary release during their current sentence; or
   - scored as high risk on the risk predictor scores for violent or sex offences or for risk of re-imprisonment; or
   - is judged in the suitability assessment to require further consideration (PSO 6700, paragraph 5.3.3).

Enhanced assessments are considered by a board which must include the Governor or an operational manager, a custody-based offender supervisor (or member of the throughcare team) and if possible a member of staff officer who has had regular contact with the prisoner.

F17.7 Release

If release is authorized form HDC7 must be faxed to the tagging contractor, the Probation Service, the National Identity Service at Scotland Yard and the community-based offender supervisor officer 14 days prior to release (PSO 6700, paragraph 8.1.1). The prisoner will be released on licence, if he consents to the conditions, including the cost of the electricity used by the monitoring device, which is nominal. If the prisoner does not own the phone line consent from the owner must be obtained, otherwise a new phone line will be installed by the contractor. The curfew period must be at least 9 hours, but in practice will usually be 12 hours. Prior to setting the curfew condition the Governor may take into account any recommendations from the community-based offender supervisor, eg, to take account of night work, childcare arrangements and hospital appointments (PSO 6700, paragraph 6.2.5).

Release on HDC can only be refused where there is:

- an unacceptable risk to the victim or members of the public; or
- a pattern of offending which indicates a likelihood of re-offending during the HDC period; or
- a likelihood of failure to comply with the conditions of curfew; or
- lack of a suitable address; or
- shortness of the potential curfew ie less than 14 days (PSO 6700, paragraph 5.13.3).

If HDC is refused the prisoner will be informed on form HDC6.

F18 **Challenging HDC Refusals**

Prisoners must be notified of HDC decisions as soon as possible. In the event of a refusal the prisoner must be provided with reasons, and informed of their right to appeal through the complaints procedure. See *R (Whiston) v Secretary of State for Justice* [2012] EWCA Civ 1374 where the court held that revocation of the decision to release on HDC did not breach Article 5(4) as it did not break the link between sentence and detention. See also *R (Francis) v Secretary of State for Justice and Secretary of State for the Home Department* [2012] EWCA Civ 1200 and *R (Serrano) v Secretary of State for Justice and Secretary of State for the Home Department* [2012] EWHC 3216 for prisoners who face deportation but are not liable to removal.

The prisoner can also complain about the curfew conditions, however, signing the licence will be taken as acceptance of the conditions and a withdrawal of the right to appeal. Legal representatives should request a copy of the written reasons by writing to the Governor and can obtain copies of the information that was taken into account during the risk assessment via the IAR. The prisoner is entitled to know if any information has been withheld, which will only be justified if it is necessary on one of the following grounds:

- the interests of national security;
- the prevention of crime or disorder, including information relevant to prison security;
- the protection of information which may put a third party at risk;
- medical or psychiatric grounds where the mental and/or physical health of the prisoner could be impaired (PSO 6700, paragraph 7.6).

The information must not be withheld automatically, and cannot normally be withheld on the basis of concerns raised by a third party eg the victim or a local resident, without giving the prisoner the opportunity to respond (PSO 6700, paragraph 7.5). The Governor must give proper consideration to whether the information can be disclosed in a summarized or edited form to protect the identity of a source.

Prisoners acting in person should make a complaint under the Requests and Complaints procedure if they remain dissatisfied after consideration of the reasons, and in appropriate cases legal representatives should submit written representations to the Governor. Complaints related to release are given priority. If possible the appeal should be considered by an operational manager of a higher grade than the manager that made the original decision, who must consider the matter afresh and address all of the points raised in the representations. If the original decision is upheld reasons must be given, and if based on the same reasons, these should be expanded and clarified. If the response is unsatisfactory a complaint can be made to the Prisons and Probation Ombudsman.

A failure to give reasons will be susceptible to Judicial Review. The reasoning itself may also be susceptible if, eg, irrelevant non risk factors were taken into account, or if insufficient weight was given to factors in the client's favour.

F19 **Challenging Sentence Calculation**

Sentence calculation can be very complicated. If the prisoner disputes the accuracy of a sentence calculation the legal representative will need to establish whether:

- prison staff have made a mistake;
- the client has misunderstood the principles; or
- the calculation is accurate but based on erroneous information.

Mistakes by prison staff are not uncommon, but neither are misunderstandings by prisoners. Legal representatives will need a copy of the disputed calculation, which can be obtained from the prison via the IAR with a signed authority, or directly from the client. Consideration will also need to be given to the guidelines in PSI 39/2012, especially if the sentence is not straightforward.

In cases where the mistake is based on an error in a document that has been relied on, (eg the court warrant) legal representatives should ensure that the mistake is rectified. If any additional documents are required (eg adjudication record confirming number of additional days awarded) these can be obtained by making an informal request.

Written representations should be addressed to the Governor. Prisoners acting in person should appeal though the Complaints procedure. If the matter remains unresolved a complaint may be submitted to the Prisons and Probation Ombudsman. However, pursuing an internal complaint will be inappropriate if the calculation dispute is likely to affect the prisoners release date. In those circumstances Judicial Review will be the only effective remedy.

F20 **Parole—Determinate Sentences**

The Parole Board has authority under powers delegated by the Secretary of State to direct the release of the following determinate prisoners:

- Extended Determinate Sentences (EDSs) where the custodial period is 10 years or more;
- 'old style' extended sentences;
- DCR sentences—4 years or more for sexual or violent offences committed before 4 April 2005;
- recalled on licence.

All parole decisions relating to determinate and extended sentence prisoners will initially be considered by a paper panel. The panel will decide whether the case can be determined on the papers or whether to refer the case to an oral hearing (see **F24.3** and **F32.4**).

F20.1 **Extended Determinate Sentence**

LASPO, section 124 created the EDS by inserting a new section 226A into CJA 2003, and Schedule 18 inserted a new Schedule 15B.

An EDS will be imposed on an offender who is:

- over 18; and
- convicted of a specified offence on or after 3 December 2012 (regardless of when the offence was committed); and
- presents a significant risk to the public of serious harm from further specified offences; and
- is not suitable for a life sentence; and either
    (i) has a previous conviction for a Schedule 15B offence or
    (ii) the custodial term would be at least 4 years.

The extension period imposed must not exceed 5 years in respect of a violent offence, and 8 years in respect of a sexual offence. Any EDS where the custodial period is 10 years or more or where the EDS was imposed for a Schedule 15B offence will be referred to the Parole Board for consideration of early release at the two-thirds point.

The prisoner will be eligible for parole two-thirds of the way through the custodial term, known as the Parole Eligibility Date (PED). The Parole Board may recommend release at any time between the PED and the CRD also known as the custodial end date (CED). The prisoner will be released automatically at the CRD. Additional days will extend the CRD and PED only. Release will then be on licence until the extended SLED. Prisoners subject to extended sentences are not eligible for HDC.

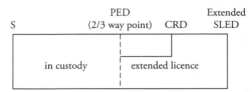

Figure 8 Extended Determinate Sentence (10 years or more for a Schedule 15B offence)

F20.2 'Old Style' Extended Sentence for Public Protection

EPP prisoners sentenced before 14 July 2008 are eligible for release on parole at the halfway point (PED) of the custodial term. The Parole Board may recommend release at any time between the halfway point of the custodial part of the sentence and the CRD at the end of the custodial period. If parole is not granted the prisoner will be released at the CRD, and will be on licence until the extended SLED.

A section 85 EPP prisoner sentenced to 4 years or more will be released between the halfway point (PED) and the two-thirds point (NPD) at the discretion of the Parole Board. The prisoner will remain on licence until the three-quarter point of the custodial term plus the extension period.

F20.3 Discretionary Conditional Release (DCR)— Violent and Sexual Offences

Under CJA 2003 (as amended), Discretionary Conditional Release applies to:

- prisoners sentenced to 4 years or more on or after 1 October 1992 in respect of sexual or violent offences committed prior to 4 April 2005
- prisoners who received multiple sentences for sexual or violent offences committed on or after 4 April 2005, each less than 12 months with a combined length of 4 years or more.

DCR prisoners serving 4 years or more have a PED at the halfway point and a non parole date (NPD) at the two-thirds point. If not released early on parole, DCR prisoners will be released automatically at NPD. Prisoners released on their NPD are released on licence under supervision until the three-quarter point which is the licence expiry date (LED). The prisoner is liable to recall for breach of licence conditions. Additional days will extend the PED, the LED and the NPD.

F21 Parole—Indeterminate Sentence Prisoners (ISPs)

F21.1 Key Document

KD PSO 4700 Indeterminate Sentence Manual

There are various types of life sentences but for the purposes of sentence management indeterminate sentence prisoners are classed as lifers. ISPs have no automatic right to be released. They must serve a minimum term before becoming eligible for release (unless released on compassionate grounds). Release is determined by the Parole Board who must be satisfied that the prisoner does not pose an unacceptable risk.

Risk factors identified by OASys will trigger referrals to offender behaviour programmes. These programmes are important as the Parole Board rely on the reports as an objective measure of risk.

F21.2 Life Sentences

- *Mandatory Life imprisonment.* Adults convicted of murder and aged 21 or over when the offence was committed automatically receive a mandatory life sentence (Murder (Abolition of Death Penalty) Act 1965). Since 18 December 2003 minimum terms for murder are set by the sentencing judge. Transitional arrangements are in place for mandatory lifers who, prior to that date, had their minimum term set by the Home Secretary.
- *Discretionary life sentence.* This sentence was imposed for offenders aged 21 or over for offences such as attempted murder, manslaughter, arson and serious sexual assaults under section 90 of the PCC(S)A 2000, and is now imposed for offenders aged 18 or over where the maximum sentence is life imprisonment and the offender meets the dangerousness criteria in section 225 of the CJA 2003.
- *Custody for life.* On conviction for murder offenders aged 18 or over but under 21 on the date of conviction will automatically be sentenced to 'custody for life' which is the equivalent of a mandatory sentence for adults over 21 (PCC(S)A 2000, section 93). Prior to CJA 2003 this sentence was imposed as a discretionary life sentence for offences other than murder where the offender met the dangerousness criteria, and is now imposed as a discretionary life sentence for offences other than murder where the offender is aged 18 or over at conviction and found to be dangerous under section 225 of the CJA 2003.

- *Detention at Her Majesty's Pleasure.* On conviction for murder persons aged 10 or over but under 18 when the offence was committed, will be detained at 'Her Majesty's Pleasure'.

- *Detention for life.* Prior to CJA 2003 this was imposed as a discretionary life sentence for offenders aged 10 or over but under 18 convicted of an offence other than murder for which a discretionary life sentence could be imposed for offenders aged 21. It is now imposed on offenders aged under 18 who are convicted of a serious offence and meet the dangerous criteria in section 226 of the CJA 2003.

- *New automatic life sentence.* LASPO inserted this sentence into CJA 2003 for offenders over 18 who are convicted of an offence in the new Schedule 15B on or after 3 December 2012, which would otherwise warrant a custodial period of 10 years or more and has a previous Schedule 15B conviction with 10-year determinate or 5-year indeterminate sentence.

- *Imprisonment for Public Protection (IPP).* The IPP was replaced by the new Extended Determinate Sentence. There will be significant numbers of IPP prisoners in the prison population for some time. Dangerous offenders (convicted of specified violent or sexual offences) committed before 3 December 2012 were imprisoned for an indeterminate period if the court considered that there was a significant risk of further specified offences being committed which would cause serious harm to the public. An IPP sentence could only be imposed if the case did not meet the criteria for a discretionary life sentence (section 224(2) of the CJA 2003).

- *Detention for Public Protection (DPP).* The DPP applied in the same circumstances as the IPP for offenders under 18.

- *'Old style' automatic lifers.* The automatic life sentence was replaced by the IPP. Prior to CJA 2003, in the absence of exceptional circumstances, automatic life sentence were imposed on offenders aged 18 or over convicted of a second violent or sexual offence on the basis that they pose a danger to the public. Although this sentence is no longer available there will be a significant number of automatic lifers in the prison population for some time to come.

Blackstone's Criminal Practice 2014 **E3** and **E4**

F22 Test for Release

F22.1 Initial Release

LASPO introduced a new test for release for determinate sentenced prisoners, and the power to direct release (rather than recommend it). The test came into force on 3 December 2012, and applies to all determinate prisoners at first release (EDS, DCR, 'old style' extended sentences, and 1967 'existing prisoners'). The test is as follows: 'The Parole Board must not give a direction [for release]...unless the Board is satisfied that it is no longer necessary for the protection of the public for the prisoner to be confined.' The identification and management of risk is therefore the sole consideration, rather than balancing the risk of any type of offending with the benefits of release.

The test is the same as the statutory test for the release of indeterminate sentenced prisoners (section 28(6)(b) of the Crime (Sentences) Act 1997). (See Guidance to Parole Board Members at **F32.4**.)

F22.1.1 *Type of offending*

There is currently no direct case law on the type of further offending the Parole Board should protect the public from in relation to determinate sentenced prisoners. However, see *R v (Foley) v Parole Board and Secretary of State for Justice* [2012] EWHC 2184. Parole Board guidance advises panels to interpret the test to protect the public from the commission of violent or sexual offences. The risk need not be of serious violent or sexual offending.

Indeterminate sentenced prisoners may be released if the risk they pose is no more than minimal. In the *Foley* case the court expressed doubt that applying a more stringent release test for determinate sentenced prisoners could be objectively justified.

F22.2 Licence Recall

Although LASPO is silent on the test for release of recalled determinate sentenced prisoners, Parole Board guidance advises panels to apply the same public protection test as described earlier, and in addition, states that they may decline to re-release where the breach indicates that effective supervision on licence can no longer be maintained. Panels may apply a balance of probabilities, but of paramount importance is the risk to the public of further offences during the licence period.

F22 Test for Release

In considering re-release of extended sentence prisoners following recall, the Parole Board must direct release unless:

- it is satisfied that there exists a risk that the offender will commit offences of the type for which he or she was sentenced (ie violent or sexual offences). The risk need not be of serious offending or to life and limb; or
- the licence has broken down to the point that effective supervision is no longer possible.

In relation to lifers the Parole Board is required to be satisfied about risk before directing release. In light of the potential unfairness, given the presumption applied in favour of extended sentence prisoners, the Parole Board have advised panel members to make a positive finding of risk in lifer cases if possible. (See Guidance to Parole Board members at **F32.4**.)

LASPO inserted new sections into CJA 2003, giving the Parole Board the power to direct release following recall rather than recommend it.

F23 **Move to Open Conditions**

It is Parole Board policy that the majority of lifers will be released from open conditions. Before considering release from closed conditions, panels should consider the full policy in Annex I, Oral Hearings Guide 2012.

The parole review framework must be flexible enough to take into account exceptional circumstances. Positive recommendations will not be enough in and of themselves but see *R (on the application of Guittard) v Secretary of State for Justice* [2009] EWHC 2951 where the court found that the Secretary of State had acted unlawfully in failing to consider the transfer of IPP prisoners to open conditions outside of a parole review. Indeterminate sentenced prisoners may seek a 'Guittard Direction' if their circumstances are sufficiently exceptional or compelling.

PSO 6010 Generic Parole Process

2.2.1 Indeterminate sentenced prisoners will normally only be transferred from closed to open conditions when a positive Parole Board recommendation has been accepted by the respective Case Managers in the PPCS on behalf of the Secretary of State. The process is as follows:

- The Parole Board, having considered the prisoner's dossier containing all relevant reports, makes a recommendation for transfer to open conditions.
- The respective PPCS Case Manager considers the Parole Board's recommendation and decides (on behalf of the Secretary of State) whether to accept or reject that recommendation, taking into account the Secretary of State's Directions to the Parole Board (see Annex 1), and will issue reasons for their decision. Where the Case Manager is minded to reject such a recommendation, Ministerial approval will be sought.
- The OMU Manager (or equivalent) *must* then arrange for the prisoner to be informed of the Parole Board's recommendation and reasons, including their advice on outstanding risk areas that need further exploration.
- The OMU Manager (or equivalent) *must* inform the prisoner of the Secretary of State's decision and reasons for accepting or rejecting the Parole Board recommendation.
- Where the Parole Board has recommended a transfer to open conditions and this has been agreed by PPCS the Governor *must* e-mail the recommendation to Population Management Section (PMS), using the appropriate inter-prison escort booking form. PMS will then arrange the transfer.
- For indeterminate sentenced prisoners who are not recommended for open conditions, any requirement for the allocation and arrangements for the transfer of prisoners in the closed prison estate e.g. high Security, Category B and Category C, remains a matter for the holding establishments.

F24 ISP Parole Procedure

F24.1 Key Documents

KD PSO 4700 Indeterminate Sentence Manual

PSO 6010 Generic Parole Process

Parole Board Rules 2011

The Parole Board for England and Wales—Practice Guidance for Oral Hearings

The Parole Board for England and Wales—Oral Hearings Guide 2012

F24.2 Pre-tariff Review

The Parole Board Rules (PBR) 2004 do not apply to the first Parole Board review, as the pre-tariff review has developed as a matter of policy. The purpose of the first review is to consider whether the ISP has made sufficient progress to merit transfer to open conditions. The process will usually begin 3 years before the minimum term expires but can be shortened depending on the tariff expiry date. Pre-tariff reviews do not normally take place for prisoners with a tariff of less than 3 years (PSO 6010, paragraph 2.1.1).

Pre-tariff reviews do not engage ECHR Article 5 rights (right to liberty and security) as the review is not concerned with the issue of liberty, and therefore there is no right to an oral hearing. However, since 2007 the Parole Board policy is to consider all pre-tariff reviews on the papers initially, and refer to an oral hearing any case where the decision would be a recommendation for transfer to open conditions. The pre-tariff review should be brought forward for ISPs who have progressed to Category C conditions 4 and a half years before tariff expiry. To increase the prisoner's chances of release at tariff expiry, it is open to the prison to identify suitable cases and recommend the advancement of the pre-tariff review date to the Public Protection Casework Section (PPCS) Case Manager.

Where the Parole Board does not recommend open conditions at the pre-tariff review, a further pre-tariff review on the papers may be considered in exceptional circumstances. This may arise where there is time for the prisoner to make further progress and allow for a meaningful period in open conditions prior to the tariff expiry review (PSO 6010, paragraph 2.1.3). There is no automatic right to a further pre-tariff review.

If the Parole Board recommends that the prisoner remains in closed conditions, (referred to as a 'knock-back'), the PPCS will confirm the reasons in writing, including the risk factors that need to be addressed, and the date of the next review which will normally be at tariff expiry (PSO 6010, paragraph 2.1.5).

F24.3 The Review Process Overview

PSO 6010 Generic Parole Process

1.2.1 The GPP process sets out the key milestones that are required to be achieved at various stages through the process. The role of PPCS Case Managers is to oversee the system targets and Case Administration Officers in establishments, or those responsible for the parole process, must input data onto PPUD on the worksheets for the areas that their establishment is responsible for.

1.2.2 The process set out below highlights the key milestones and required action by relevant parties in the process.

1st Stage	CASE ADMINISTRATION	
Week	Actions	Responsibility
Wk 26	PPUD creates review	PPCS
	PPUD informs PPCS/PB/Prison to commence review	PPCS
	PB issues notification of target hearing period (Post-Tariff only) and letter to prisoner	PB
	Prison request all relevant reports	Prison
	PPCS commence skeleton Dossier	PPCS
Wk 22	Deadline – PPCS send skeleton dossier to prison	PPCS
Wk 21	Deadline for receipt of skeleton dossier	Prison
	Deadline for prisoner response to PB, including name of legal representative and Offender Manager	Prison
Wk 18	Relevant reports received	Prison
	Prison compiles/paginates dossier	Prison
	Prison issues dossier to prisoner + reps/disclosure form	Prison
	Deadline – Prison sends dossier to PB/PPCS/Solicitor	Prison
Wk 17	PB assess dossier – return if incomplete	PB
Wk 16	Deadline – for return of all returned dossiers	Prison

F24 ISP Parole Procedure

Wk 14	Deadline – Prisoner to submit representations – personal/legal	Prison
	PB copies dossier to ICM member	PB
Wk 13	ICM issues Standard Directions on outstanding dossiers	PB
Wk 12	PB consider Pre- and Post-Tariff dossiers on papers	PB
	Pre-tariff – PB issues negative recommendation or refers dossier to oral hearing and issues ICM Directions	PB
	Post-tariff – PB issues negative decision or ICM Directions for Oral hearing (If negative decision issued, prisoner has 28 days to accept or challenge decision)	PB
Wk 10	Prison confirms all ICM Directions complied with	Prison
	PPCS confirms all ICM Directions complied with	PPCS
	PB lists case for oral hearing	PB
Wk 08	PB issue oral hearing exact date notification	PB
	PB identifies panel members	PB
	PB confirms hearing date to all parties	PB
	Deadline for any challenge to negative decision issued at week 12 to be forwarded to PB by prison/legal representative	Prison
	Secretary of States view to be provided (where appropriate)	PPCS
Wk 06	PB copies dossier to members	PB
	Chair issues further Directions (if required) and rules on applications for non-disclosure, victim and witness attendance	PB
Wk 04	Prison confirms all outstanding Directions complied with	Prison
	PPCS confirms all outstanding Directions complied with	PPCS
	PB issues Timetable for oral hearing to all parties	PB

Wk 0	End of 1st stage	
2nd Stage	**CALENDAR MONTH FOR LISTING ORAL HEARING (THIS WILL ALWAYS BE THE 1st OF THE MONTH)**	
	PB Oral Hearing taking place during this calendar month	PB
3rd Stage	**POST ORAL HEARING**	
	Deadline for receipt of PB decision (2 weeks following oral hearing)	PB
Process end date	Release at tariff expiry/Consideration of transfer to open conditions/setting new review date	PPCS

1.3 Week 26 – Commencement of parole process

1.3.1 The prompt commencement of the process by establishments is imperative so that the review commences on time, and the whole system targets can be met.

1.3.2 On week 26 PPUD informs PPCS/establishments to commence review by identifying the beginning of the review via a 'to do' list. Case Administration Officers must ensure that they are aware of review commencement and must request relevant reports. The target date for completion of the reports is 8 Weeks from commencement of review. The list of relevant reports must be agreed with the Offender Manager for IPPs or the Prison Service Designated Staff Member (PSDSM) for Lifers following the Sentence Plan Review (SPR) meeting and should take account of any directions made by the previous Parole Board panel. The Parole Board will also issue a notification of review commencement in cases of tariff-expired Lifer's/IPP's at week 26. At the same time, the nominated PPCS Case Manager commences the skeleton dossier preparation.

1.3.3 Offender Managers, Offender Supervisors and Prison Service Designated Staff must be alert to cases where psychological and psychiatric input may be necessary and ensure that the relevant reports are commissioned from the experts at the earliest opportunity, or to establish from the experts whether such reports are necessary. Failure to commission expert reports may lead to delays in the parole process at a later stage.

1.4 Week 21 – Skeleton dossier disclosure

1.4.1 This is the target date for receipt by establishments of the skeleton dossier, which is completed by the PPCS Case Manager. This skeleton dossier must contain, where available:
- An Index Sheet
- The note formally referring the case to the Parole Board for consideration

- The pro-forma case summary (other than in IPP cases where the prisoner has spent less than 8 years in custody) containing the basic details of the case including the period of time the prisoner has served in custody, his or her current location, the dates of remand, sentence and length of tariff, and brief details of the Index Offence
- Offence related papers. These must include (where they exist) the summary of offence prepared by PPCS (including reference to sources relied upon), transcript of the trial judge's sentencing remarks, the pre and post trial sentence reports prepared by qualified probation staff, a current list of previous convictions as recorded on the Police National Computer (i.e. within the last 12 months but more recent if convictions within the last 12 months) and any other relevant papers such as psychiatric or psychological reports prepared for trial and/ or sentencing, information on any appeals lodged and Trial Judge's report to Home Secretary (for lifers sentence before 18.12.03).
- A record of adjudications since remand in custody/sentencing extracted from IIS including establishment, offence, date of hearing, result (proven or dismissed) and punishment. A summary of reports of progress in prison including Therapeutic Community and Dangerous and Severe Personality Disorder (DSPD) Unit reports
- Reports from any offending behaviour courses completed in custody
- Previous Parole Board decision if a subsequent review

1.4.2 It is also the deadline for the prison to forward the prisoner's reply form indicating how s/he wishes to proceed with their review. They have two options:
- proceed to oral hearing
- consider case on papers

A prisoner cannot decide to opt out of the process. At the same time, they should also advise details of their legal representative and Offender Manager in the space provided on the form.

1.5 Week 18 – Disclosure of completed dossier

1.5.1 This is the deadline for receipt of all reports by Case Administration Officers, who must collate and paginate the dossier using the skeleton dossier and reports provided by those report writers necessary and as described in paragraph 1.5.4 & 1.5.5.

1.5.2 Governors must ensure that procedures are in place to check that dossiers contain the mandatory reports prior to sending to the Parole Board. This should be confirmed by Governors signing off the dossier to confirm that all required reports have been completed to the required standards and ensuring that they include assessments by suitably competent staff, who will generally be those who have independently accredited risk assessment and management expertise, for example a qualified probation officer or forensic psychologist. The dossier must include contributions from a range of staff as effective risk assessment is based on a multi-disciplinary approach drawing on evidence from a range of sources This is a key consideration for Offender Managers (in IPP cases) and PSDSMs (in Lifer cases) in determining what reports should be included in a parole dossier.

1.5.3 Case Administration Officers must disclose completed dossier to the Parole Board, PPCS, and the prisoner. If the prisoner's legal representative requests a copy of the dossier this must be provided.

1.5.4 The aim of Governors must be ensure that staff writing reports for the parole process possess the necessary skills and training to undertake that work. Staff must be appropriately trained and skilled in accordance with paragraph 1.5.5.

1.5.5 Establishments must add the following reports in respect of Lifer cases (see 1.5.5 for IPP) which are mandatory for establishments to obtain before disclosing to the Parole Board:

- Home Probation Officer's report (PAROM1) completed by a qualified probation officer, countersigned by line manager to meet quality standards identified by NSMART (the Probation Service system for monitoring standards)

- Prison Service Designated Staff Member's (PSDSM) report (SPR K). This report will only normally be completed if the Offender Supervisor is not sufficiently qualified or experienced. If the SPR K is required to be completed it must be undertaken by the PSDSM who is responsible for the assessment, sentence planning and reviews of progress of the prisoner and assesses if there have been any changes to the risk and status of the prisoner. The PSDSM report presents a risk assessment which includes attitudes to offence, victim information, and an assessment of any risks presented by the prisoner during his time in custody. The PSDSM must state in their report their level of experience and length of time working with lifers. The PSDSM must also state their qualifications and training courses attended which relate to working with life sentenced prisoners. Where the report writer is not a qualified probation officer, they should ideally have, as a minimum, successfully completed the Introduction to Risk Assessment and Management (IRAM) and Management of Indeterminate Sentences and Risk (MISaR) training courses or equivalent (e.g. Life in the 21st Century) to demonstrate their knowledge and skills in risk assessment and management and have some previous experience of working with life sentence prisoners. This is not a mandatory requirement but Governors should plan for it to be so by April 2010. The PSDSM must confirm in the SPR K whether an Offender Supervisor has been allocated to the lifer concerned and if so, that an SPR C is included in the dossier before submission. If there is no Offender Supervisor allocated to the lifer, the PSDSM must address the additional issues which would other wise have been covered by the Offender Supervisor [sections in the SPR C on Behaviour in Prison and Response to Sentence Plan]. In these cases, the PSDSM must confirm that they have liaised directly with the Offender Manager and the personal officer or other wing staff who can comment first hand on the behaviour of the lifer

- Offender Supervisor's (OS) report (SPR C). In Lifer cases if there is a separate Offender Supervisor also working with the prisoner then a SPR C must be included in the dossier. This must be confirmed by the PSDSM in their report. The OS has information and views relevant to the decision on release or about transfer to open conditions. The OS must also state their qualifications and training courses attended which relate to working with life sentenced prisoners The OS should as a minimum have attended the IRAM training course. All OS staff should also eventually have attended the MISaR course

- Relevant Key Worker's reports (SPR D) to include where relevant reports from the following staff CARAT worker, interventions and activity supervisors, offending behaviour programmes staff, therapeutic community, DSPD staff, personal officer or wing staff
- The **full** OASys report reviewed within the last 12 months of the target month for the review hearing and countersigned by OASys supervisor

1.5.6 Establishments must add the following reports in respect of IPP (see 1.5.4 for Lifer) cases, which are governed by the Offender Management model Phase III (OM3), and are mandatory for establishments to obtain prior to disclosing to the Parole Board:

- Offender Manager's overview report (PAROM1) (see comments above)
- Offender Supervisor report (SPR C). The OS has information and views relevant to suitability for release or transfer to open conditions. The OS must state their qualifications and training courses attended which relate to working with life sentenced prisoners. The OS should as a minimum have attended the IRAM and the MISaR courses or their equivalent e.g. Life in the 21st Century The report prepared by OS in IPP cases must comment on the risks the prisoner may pose if released into the community .
- Relevant Key Workers reports (SPR D) (see comments above)
- The **full** OASys report (see comments above)

1.5.7 Dossiers which do not include all mandatory documents will be rejected by the Parole Board. A dossier will only be recorded on PPUD as received by the Board once it is accepted as complete.

1.5.8 Other reports may be added to either lifer or IPP dossiers if the author has had relevant contact with the prisoner or if requested by the Offender Manager (for IPPs) or PSDSM (for lifers), Parole Board or PPCS:

- Psychologist (SPR E)
- Healthcare (SPR F)
- Psychiatrist (SPR G)
- Security (SPR H)
- Prisoner's comments (SPR J).

These reports may also be requested as a direction from the Parole Board at the directions stage (week 14).

Templates explaining what should be included under each heading in all the above reports, both the mandatory and discretionary reports, are set out in the Implementation Manual Phase III Offender Management and Indeterminate Sentence Prisoners published in November 2007 and which came into operation from 7th January 2008.

1.5.9 Reports from psychologists are only usually required in cases where there have been substantive psychological input or significant personality issues.

1.5.10 Psychiatric reports are only usually required where there are mental health issues on which to report.

1.5.11 In some cases, it may be that the Multi-Agency Public Protection Panel (MAPPP) plans should inform parole decisions. Where this information is not immediately available via the PAROM1 report, an executive summary of the MAPPP meeting relating to the prisoner *must* be included in the dossier following consultation with the information owner.

1.5.12 Mandatory report writers *must* have access to independent accounts of the prisoner's index and previous offences when completing their reports i.e. judge's sentencing remarks, CPS document. This is available in skeleton dossiers and confidential summary dossiers, which from the 7th January 2008 has been replaced by Source Sentence Planning Documents. PAROM1 writers must have access to MAPPA and VISOR information where it exists.

1.5.13 If some documents e.g. judge's sentencing remarks cannot be provided, this should be clearly indicated in the dossier by PPCS so that ICM assessors and panel chairs do not make unnecessary directions. Dossier logs should include such information.

1.5.14 Offender Managers (for IPP cases) and PSDSMs (for Lifer cases) must, in deciding what reports should be included in a parole dossier, discuss this with staff working with the prisoner during the Sentence Plan Review meeting as required within the Offender Management Phase III Implementation Manual and must ensure that at least one report is prepared by an individual with independently accredited risk assessment expertise e.g. a qualified probation officer (PAROM1) or forensic psychologist (SPR E).

1.5.15 Governors must ensure that:
- Parole dossiers are stored securely with controlled access
- Prisoners have ready access to their parole dossier as frequently as the facilities and resources of the prison allow
- copies of the prisoners dossiers available to his or her legal representative on request.

1.5.16 In deciding how prisoners have access to their dossiers, the OMU Manager (or equivalent) should bear in mind the possible effect on the prisoner and the establishment should the contents of the dossier become widely known. Particular care should be taken in those cases where there are vivid accounts of the offence, the cases are notorious, or those relating to sexual offences. Establishments may consider it more prudent to allow the prisoner access to the dossier only at times when the prisoner is locked in his or her cell, for example at lunchtime or overnight.

1.6 Week 17 – Parole Board rejection of incomplete dossiers

1.6.1 Parole Board will 'reject' any dossier that is missing mandatory reports as specified above or if reports do not fulfil the minimum standards (set out in Annex 2). If this occurs the target for completion of dossier will have been missed by establishments.
The establishment must provide the missing reports by week 14.

1.7 Week 14 – Administration of completed dossiers and Parole Board Directions

1.7.1 This is the deadline for receipt of prisoner representations. As soon as the prisoner's representations have been received they must be paginated by the Case Administration Officers and forwarded to the Parole Board and PPCS.

1.7.2 Case Administration Officers must ensure that the 'rejected' dossiers are completed by this week. Although the dossier completion target has been missed the receipt of a completed dossier will allow for the end-to-end target to continue to be met. (Note that any reports added at this time must be disclosed.)

1.7.3 The Parole Board Intensive Case Management process (ICM) commences.

1.8 Week 12 – Parole Board paper hearing and referral to oral hearing

1.8.1 Parole Board considers the case 'on the papers' and a negative decision (decision not to release) may be made and issued by the Board at this stage in the process. If a negative decision is not issued following the consideration "on the papers" the case will be referred to an oral hearing.

1.8.2 Directions may be issued by the Parole Board at this stage. These Directions may be split into two sections. Section 1 Directions must be complied with before a case can be allocated an exact date for the hearing. Section 2 Directions (e.g. addendum reports and updates) must be complied with at least 4 weeks before the exact hearing date. Directions should clearly specify the information or question pertaining to assessment of risk which the Parole Board panel will need in order to make a decision. The PPCS Case Manager will request that the Offender Management Unit within the establishment to identify who is the appropriate (ie qualified) person to provide information requested and to ensure that the information or report is submitted within the agreed timescale. Directions should provide reasonable timeframes to allow NOMS staff to provide the necessary information.

1.8.3 PPCS Case Managers are responsible for overseeing the compliance with Parole Board directions. They will liaise with Case Administration Officers and the relevant probation staff, to ensure that directions issued by the Parole Board are complied with in the timescales set. Case administration officers must work with the PPCS Case Managers to ensure that directions are complied with.

1.8.4 Only when Section 1 directions have been complied with, will cases be listed for hearing by the Parole Board. The deadlines for compliance with directions will often be short but PPCS Case Managers and Governors must endeavour to comply with directions within the timescales that are set. Where a Parole Board direction issued by the Parole Board cannot be delivered within the required timescale or where the information is either not available or would incur disproportionate cost, the Governor must alert the PPCS Case Manager who will consider whether to appeal or seek a variation of the direction/s under the Parole Board Rules.

1.8.5 PPCS Case Managers will be responsible for submitting all appeal variation requests in response to Parole Board directions. They will also be responsible for applying, where appropriate, to have information withheld from the prisoner.

1.9 Week 10 – Parole Board decision and completion of directions

1.9.1 The Parole Board decision arising from considering the case "on the papers" will be received by PPCS and the establishment by Week 10. This is also the target date for completion of any Section 1 directions required prior to the case being listed for an oral hearing. The Parole Board will only refer the case to be listed for an oral hearing if all these directions are complied with.

1.9.2 Case Administration Officers may also be requested by the PPCS Case Manager to arrange for the attendance of witnesses to the oral hearing. A witness may only attend if so directed by the Parole Board. In any case where a witness refuses to attend the PPCS Case Manager must be advised immediately. It may be necessary to obtain a witness summons. Where a witness summons is required; the obtaining of such will be undertaken by the PPCS Case Manager. The expectation is that NOMS staff directed to give evidence at a Parole Board hearing will comply.

1.10 Week 8 – Notification of oral hearing date from Parole Board

1.10.1 The Parole Board notifies PPCS, the establishment, prisoner and legal representative of the oral hearing date. Establishments must book suitable accommodation, as well as organise the escorting of visitors, prisoners and other arrangements relevant to the oral hearing. Further information on the requirements of establishments for oral hearings can be obtained from the Parole Board Case Managers allocated to establishments.

1.10.2 Case Administration Officers must notify any witnesses directed by the Board of their requirement to attend the proposed oral hearing.

1.10.3 Week 8 is also the target date for disclosure of Secretary of State's view where one is to be provided. In cases where PPCS provide no view the Parole Board must be notified accordingly by the PPCS Case Manager.

1.10.4 In cases where a negative decision has been issued by the Parole Board and the prisoner appeals that decision; the case will revert back to Week 12 for the purposes of the parole process. If no challenge is made to the Parole Board decision, then the notification of the Parole Board will be confirmed

1.11 Week 6 – Panel Chair Directions

1.11.1 The dossier is copied to panel members by the Parole Board secretariat. The chair of the panel may issue further directions (such as updates or addendum reports and calling additional witnesses). Witnesses warned to attend at the ICM stage will be confirmed or stood down by the Chair. Again the PPCS Case Manager will liaise with the Case Administration Officer to ensure that the directions are complied with and any changes are fully communicated to those affected.

1.11.2 Where a person wishes to attend an oral hearing as an observer, an application should be made, through the PPCS Case Manager to the

Parole Board in writing who can agree to any such request, subject to the prisoner's agreement.

1.11.3 The attendance of witnesses at an oral hearing is a matter for the Parole Board to determine and each party to the hearing must apply in writing to the Parole Board (copied to the other party) for leave to call witnesses. In many cases the Parole Board will have already identified relevant witnesses, usually at the ICM stage, details of which will be placed on PPUD by the Parole Board Secretariat.

1.12 Week 4 – Timetable for oral hearing

1.12.1 Any Directions in Section 2 of the ICM Directions form must have been complied with by this stage.

1.12.2 The Parole Board issues the timetable for oral hearing to the PPCS, establishment, prisoner, and prisoners' legal representative (if known).

1.12.3 Where establishments have been notified of oral hearing listing times that are unrealistic the Parole Board Case Managers must be notified immediately and asked to amend the timetable accordingly. Many establishments are able to cater for oral hearings continuing during lock up periods and these should continue where appropriate and agreed by Governors.

1.13 Week 0 – Start of calendar month listing period and oral hearing

1.13.1 This is the 1st day of the calendar month listing period in which the oral hearing is to be held.

1.13.2 In cases where no Secretary of State's view is provided by PPCS, no representative of the Secretary of State is required from establishments. However relevant staff may still be called to an oral hearing to give evidence as a witness.

1.13.3 In some cases where a Secretary of State's view is provided the representative of the Secretary of State will be an advocate from PPCS and the PPCS Case Manager will alert the prison and the Parole Board in advance of the hearing where an advocate plans to attend. In those cases where an advocate has not been allocated the Governor (or their designated competent person) must represent the Secretary of State's view. In private prisons the representative of the Secretary of State must be the Controller or Deputy Controller; it cannot be delegated.

1.13.4 In cases where PPCS have provided a Secretary of State's view that does not accord with the views of the designated representative of the Secretary of State from the establishment and there is no advocate available to attend the hearing and present the case, the Governor *must* nominate another member of staff to present the case. Where the designated member of staff view does accord with the Secretary of State's view provided by PPCS, then that person may perform a dual role by giving personal witness evidence and representing the view provided. The representative of the Secretary of State does not have the authority to change the Secretary of State's "official" view. The relevant PPCS Case Manager should be consulted where any concerns or doubts about the Secretary of State's view arise in advance of the hearing, or exceptionally during the hearing.

1.14 Receipt of Parole Board decision (2 weeks from date of oral hearing)

1.14.1 This is the deadline for receipt of the Parole Board decision following the oral hearing. Release preparation is commenced by PPCS Case Managers if release is directed.

1.14.2 PPCS Case Managers will also commence consideration of Parole Board recommendations that the prisoner be transferred to open conditions (where appropriate).

1.15 Parole process end date

1.15.1 This is the review process end date. *The prisoner must be released at tariff expiry, if directed by the Parole Board.* (Only if the release is subject to certain public safety conditions that are awaited can the prisoner be held beyond tariff date and the implementation of the conditions must be reviewed on a daily basis by PPCS Case Managers)

1.15.2 Where no recommendation for transfer to open conditions, or a direction for release is made, PPCS Case Managers will set the next review date.

F24.4 Further Reviews

The purpose of second and subsequent reviews is to assess the lifer's suitability for release and therefore ECHR Article 5 and the right to an oral hearing are engaged. In *R (on the application of Spence) v Secretary of State for the Home Department)* [2003] EWCA Civ 732), the Court of Appeal rejected the argument that the timings of reviews should be considered by a court-like body on the grounds that Judicial Review provided adequate protection from arbitrary and unfair decisions. All decisions on the timing of subsequent reviews must be determined on their individual merits by PPCS case managers on behalf of the Secretary of State.

Lifers are entitled to a Parole Board review at least every 2 years. The 2-year gap between reviews should be viewed as the maximum period as there will often be grounds to consider release or transfer to open conditions much sooner, eg, where the prisoner has addressed very specific issues which were the only concern at the last review. In *Hirst v United Kingdom* [2001] Crim LR 919 the court held that there had been a breach of ECHR Article 5(4) when the Secretary of State had refused on 2 separate occasions to follow the Parole Board recommendation that Mr Hirst should be transferred to open conditions. The periods of 21 months and 2 years between reviews were not justified given the considerable progress that he had made during his sentence.

F24.5 Transfer of Prisoners During Review

PSO 6010 Generic Parole Process

2.5.1 The parole process is considerably disrupted if a prisoner is transferred during the course of a review. While it is accepted that there are exceptional compassionate, security or discipline reasons for such a move, prisoners whose applications for parole are underway should not normally be transferred before their parole dossier has been completed. Only in exceptional circumstances may prisoners be transferred. This may be appropriate, for example, where it is necessary to transfer the prisoner to complete offending behaviour work as identified through the sentence planning process. In cases where this has been necessary Governors must inform the Parole Board and PPCS of the reasons for the move.

F24.6 Mental Health Cases

PSO 6010 Generic Parole Process

2.6 Mental Health Cases

2.6.1 Prisoners may be transferred under the Mental Health Act 1983 either for assessment or as a long term transfer for as long as that prisoner is assessed as requiring it by qualified medical practitioners. Whilst time spent in a hospital counts towards the sentence for tariff purposes, in the event that a prisoner is transferred to hospital during any part of the parole review process, that review will be suspended until the remission of the prisoner to the prison setting. Governors must inform the Parole Board and the relevant PPCS Case Manager of any transfer of a prisoner to the mental health estate, and when a prisoner returns to HMPS custody ensuring that reasons for transfer and return are provided.

The Parole Board may conduct a review in respect of a patient who is still detained under the Mental Health Act 1983

- where the MHRT decides that treatment is no longer necessary but a transfer back to prison would adversely affect the patient's mental health; or
- where the MHRT decides that, had the patient been sentenced under the Mental Health Act, he or she would not be discharged under the same Act.

F24.7 The Paper Review

All second and subsequent parole reviews must first be considered by a single panel member who will decide on the basis of the dossier alone (including any written representations) whether to:

(a) refer the case to a full 3-member oral hearing; or

(b) make a provisional decision that the prisoner is unsuitable for release (PBR, rule 16).

All decisions require written reasons (PBR, rule 16(3)). If the panel decides that the status quo should be maintained the prisoner can either accept the decision, which will then become final, or request an oral hearing. Requests for oral hearings must be made to the Parole Board within 19 weeks of the case being referred to the Board (PBR, rule 17(2)), and copied to the PPCS.

If the provisional decision is in favour of release or transfer to open conditions, the case will be transferred to a 3-member panel. A direction to release the prisoner will be binding on the Secretary of State; however, a recommendation that the prisoner be transferred to open conditions is advisory only.

In advising a prisoner whether to accept an unfavourable decision, factors for and against will need to be taken into consideration. If the Parole Board does not make any positive recommendations the merits of an oral hearing will depend on the individual facts of the case. See Parole Board Guidance on oral hearings.

F24.8 Oral Hearings Referrals

F24.8.1 *Mandatory referrals*

Although there is no right to an oral hearing in the Parole Board Rules 2011, it is Parole Board policy to refer all indeterminate sentenced prisoners assessed by a single panel member as being unsuitable for release, or assessed as a likely candidate for a progressive move whether pre or post tariff to an oral hearing.

Indeterminate sentenced prisoners will also be referred for an oral hearing at their first review following recall. The prisoner may opt out of an oral hearing.

F24.8.2 *Requests*

All recalled determinate sentence prisoners, referred to the Parole Board and assessed as unsuitable for release may request an oral hearing as part of their written representations. Reasons must be provided within 19 weeks of the case being referred to the Board (PBR, rule 17(2)). They may also request an oral hearing on receipt of a negative paper decision. The Parole Board will only grant an oral hearing if, in accordance with the judgment in *R (on the application of Smith and West) v Parole Board* [2005] 1 WLR 350, it is justified in the interest of fairness.

Discretionary Conditional Release (DCR) prisoners, and extended sentence prisoners may also apply for an oral hearing in advance of the paper panel consideration of their case. There is no specific policy entitling such prisoners to apply for an oral hearing following a negative decision by a paper panel, although each case will be considered on its merits.

F24.8.3 *Guidance*

The guidance issued by the Parole Board in 2011 when the 2009 Rules were in force continues to apply.

The Parole Board For England and Wales Practice Guidance for Oral Hearings

Guidance

Life and indeterminate sentenced prisoners

Decisions on oral hearings will be taken by a Parole Board member. The member will consider this in all cases, regardless of whether the prisoner has requested an oral hearing. An oral hearing will normally be granted in two sets of circumstances:

1. Where the member considers there is a realistic prospect of release or a move to open conditions; or
2. In any case where the assessment of risk requires live evidence from the prisoner and/or witnesses.

The second circumstance would include a case where release or a progressive move is *not* a realistic outcome, but where live evidence is needed to determine the risk factors. It is envisaged that this will be a relatively rare step to take and would normally only be necessary where experts disagreed about a risk factor; for example, whether or not there was a sexual element to an offence that needed exploring. It is only intended to apply this principle where there is a dispute about whether an issue is a risk factor at all, not necessarily whether it has been addressed or not. Disputes over future handling of prisoners (the specific coursework or treatment plans for example) are not matters for the Parole Board and as such, would not generally mean that an oral hearing was required.

The second principle would be applied in cases where live evidence is needed to settle a dispute of fact **which is relevant to the Board's decision** or where the Board decides, for whatever reason, that it can only fairly assess risk and make its decision with the benefit of an oral hearing.

An oral hearing will not *normally* be granted where there is no realistic prospect of release or open conditions, but where such outcomes are requested by the prisoner, detailed reasons will be given for refusing, in particular where the prisoner is already in category C or D.

Decisions will normally be taken at the Intensive Case Management (ICM) stage. In a case where a negative decision has been issued, the prisoner has

---

the right to apply for an oral hearing. These requests will be considered by the duty ICM member. The member who gave a negative decision will not consider the oral hearing request.

Recall hearings for lifers/IPPs will go forward to an oral hearing. The presumption is that an oral hearing will take place unless the prisoner waives his right to one.

Determinate/extended sentence recall cases

All such recalled prisoners are initially considered by a paper panel. That panel can decide whether the case can be decided on the papers or whether to send the case to an oral hearing.

An oral hearing for a recall case will normally be granted in three sets of circumstances:

1. Where the prisoner disputes the circumstances of the recall **and** the facts of the recall are central to the question of risk and re-release; or
2. Where the prisoner argues that the recall incident was justified for some reason, or was not as serious as alleged **and** this affects the assessment of risk; or
3. **Any** case where the assessment of risk requires live evidence from the prisoner and/or witnesses.

Where a case is sent to oral hearing, the panel will state what the oral hearing is intended to achieve and will set out, so far as the panel is able, what evidence and/ or witnesses will need to be available. These are not formal directions, which in due course will be made by the oral hearing panel chair. But they will enable witnesses and others to be alerted as soon as possible about what the member who will hear the case is likely to require.

Where a prisoner applies for an oral hearing s/he must provide reasons supporting such an application and where such a request is refused, the panel member will provide written reasons for the decision to refuse.

F25 **Pre-Hearing Preparation**

If the review proceeds to an oral hearing the prisoner will be entitled to legal representation. In preparation for the hearing it may be necessary to consider the following.

F25.1 **Directions**

A written request for directions can be made to the Chair of the panel (copied to the PPCS) in relation to the timetable, service of documents, disclosure, withheld information, submission of evidence or attendance of witnesses (PBR, rule 10(2)). Requests often relate to missing documents or requests for more time to instruct an independent expert, but can also include applications for the Secretary of State to call a particular witness. The request should specify the direction being sought, and its relevance. In complex cases or where there is substantial dispute it may be appropriate to hold an oral directions hearing. Rule 11(2) provides that parties should be given at least 14 days' notice, but the hearing can be heard sooner by agreement. The venue will be where it is most convenient for the Chair. A representative from the PPCS will usually attend on behalf of the Secretary of State. The prisoner will not be produced. If the application is based on legal submissions a skeleton argument will often assist, and should be served in advance. Notification of the directions should be served as soon as practicable (PBR, rule 10(9)). Queries relating to the administration should be raised with the panel's case manager.

F25.2 **Witnesses**

Requests for witnesses to attend the hearing to give evidence should be made in writing to the Parole Board, and copied to the PPCS within 20 weeks of the case being listed (PBR, rule 22(1)). Most of the witnesses, including any independent experts will have written a report for the dossier. PBR, rule 22(2) provides that the request should confirm the name, address and occupation of the witness but this will only be strictly necessary if the witness is a family member or report writer whose report has not previously been disclosed. However, it will always be necessary to fully justify a request for a witness to attend the hearing, as the number of witnesses will have a bearing on both time and costs. Some witnesses may be reluctant to attend for various reasons. Although a request can be made for a direction that the witness attends the hearing, the Parole Board has no power to compel a witness. The case of *R (on the application of Brooks) v Parole Board* [2004] EWCA Civ 80 confirmed that a witness summons can be sought from the county court or High Court, although it is very unlikely to be necessary in the majority of cases. The Parole Board also has no power to exclude evidence placed before it by the Secretary of State but may attach no weight to it in appropriate circumstances— see *R (McGetrick) v Parole Board and Secretary of State for Justice* [2012] EWHC 882 where material from the Secretary of State containing allegations which were never found proved was put before the panel.

Witnesses should only be requested if they are likely to make a significant contribution to the hearing, if their evidence is contested, or if the fairness of the hearing may be affected. If the Board directs that a witness should attend the hearing, it will be the responsibility of the party who made the request to notify the witness of the date, time and venue. As hearsay evidence is admissible even if it is contested, it will often be necessary to apply for a direction that the Secretary of State (PPCS) call the source of any damaging evidence as a witness, and apply for a witness summons if necessary. The application should also seek a direction that the Secretary of State obtain and serve a witness statement and any relevant documents. See *R (Weszka) v Parole Board* [2012] EWHC 827 where police intelligence, the provenance of which was not provided, was served on the day of the hearing. As no directions had been sought as to its late submission and no assessment had been made as to its reliability, the Parole Board's decision was quashed as the hearing was procedurally unfair.

In addition to witnesses any party can apply for an observer to be present at the hearing (PBR, rule 23). A member of the prisoner's family or a close friend may attend to offer support, and (with the prisoner's permission) a trainee legal representative or other fee earner may be permitted to attend for training purposes.

F25.3 Deferrals and Adjournments

Prisoners cannot opt out of the review process. It will continue with or without the prisoner's involvement. However, a deferral can be requested if, eg, the prisoner needs time to complete an offender behaviour course that will assist the Parole Board in assessing whether risk to the public has been reduced, a material witness is unable to attend, the prisoner needs more time to obtain legal representation. Further examples include where a prisoner in open conditions has completed most of what is required and is nearing the end of a course, needs to complete a minimum number of home leaves or the release plan is not yet in place but is likely to be soon. Such requests should be made to the PPCS, and copied to the Lifer Manager.

Requests for an adjournment may be made at any time before evidence is called; however, the later the request the more persuasive the reasons will have to be, particularly as there will cost implications for the Parole Board. All requests other than those made at the hearing itself should be made in writing to the PPCS. Usually either a duty judge or the Chair (if a panel has been allocated) will consider the reasons for the request (PBR, rule 12(1)). The application is likely to be refused if the information will not be available for some time or if it is not likely to be relevant to the outcome. If the application is to be renewed at the hearing itself, the panel should be put on notice.

F25.4 The Hearing

The hearing will be held in private and will normally take place at the prisoner's holding prison (or the Parole Hub video-link facility in London) before a 3-member panel. The Chair will usually be a circuit judge (or High Court judge in the most serious cases). The other members of the panel will normally be a psychiatrist and a lay person, psychologist or criminologist. In addition to the prisoner and his legal representative there will usually be a panel administrator, the lifer manager or a representative from the PPCS on behalf of the Secretary of State, and any witnesses.

The procedural rules governing the hearing are contained in PBR, rule 25. The Chair normally opens the hearing by explaining the order of proceedings that the panel proposes to adopt. The PPCS representative will be invited to state their view on suitability for release, followed by an opening submission by the prisoner's legal representative (PBR, rule 25(2)(b)). The prisoner will be the first to give evidence. The hearing is inquisitorial rather than adversarial, although when there are factual disputes in issue a much more adversarial approach may be adopted. The hearing may be adjourned once the Parole Board has started to hear evidence if the panel needs further information that is not readily available. When the panel resumes at a later date it should consist of the same panel members. Hearsay evidence is admissible, even if contested.

Once all the evidence has been heard each party will be invited to make closing submissions. Although the Parole Board's opinion on an early review can be requested if it is anticipated that they will not direct release or recommend a transfer, any opinion expressed would not be binding on the Secretary of State. If it is clear that the Parole Board will not be able to direct immediate release, eg, because a bail hostel place or drug rehabilitation bed is not yet available the Board should be invited to adjourn the decision. The Parole Board will then be able to reconvene at a later date in the absence of the parties to consider the release package. If the hearing is not adjourned the case will be determined and will inevitably result in a 'knock-back'. An application could be made to the PPCS for an early referral back to the Parole Board once the bail hostel or rehabilitation place becomes available but there is no guarantee that they will accede to this request.

F25.5 Decisions

The decision of the panel must be confirmed to all parties in writing within 14 days of the hearing. If the Parole Board is unable to come to a unanimous decision a majority decision will be acceptable (PBR, rule 13(2)). The following options are available:

(1) Direct release, and recommend additional licence conditions, if appropriate. The Secretary of State must give effect to this decision. The PPCS will arrange for the prisoner to be released and will draw up the life licence. This should not take more than 5 working days unless it is dependant on a hostel place.

(2) Recommend a move to open conditions. This is advisory only. A senior caseworker at the PPCS will decide on behalf of the Secretary of State whether to accept this recommendation. The prisoner should be notified by the PPCS within 6 weeks.

(3) No release and no transfer to open conditions. The PPCS will notify the prisoner of when the next review will take place.

The panel must give reasons for their decision (PBR, rule 26), and the PPCS must also provide written reasons if they refuse to accept a recommendation of the Parole Board on behalf of the Secretary of State. The reasons are susceptible to Judicial Review. However, the Parole Board and the Secretary of State are not required to accept the opinions expressed by the report writers even if they are unanimous. As long as the reasoning is well considered, grounds for Judicial Review will not arise.

F26 **Practical Considerations**

F26.1 **Checklist for a Second or Subsequent Parole Review**

- Request parole dossier from the prison.
- Request any missing documents (keep disclosure under review).
- Request disclosure under DPA 1998, if applicable.
- Go through dossier with client. Obtain instructions and comments.
- Consider a deferral, if appropriate.
- Prepare and draft client's statement.
- Prepare and submit written representations, enclosing client's statement if appropriate.
- Consider provisional decision following paper sift. If unfavourable, advise client on merits of oral hearing. Consider 'sufficient benefit test'.
- Consider instruction of independent expert. If appropriate apply for extension of financial limit.
- Consider release and/or transfer issues. What is in dispute? What is agreed?
- Prepare for oral hearing. Consider witness and direction requirements. Is a deferral necessary?
- Obtain further instructions, as appropriate.
- Arrange for witnesses to attend hearing. Obtain witness summons if necessary.
- If final decision is unfavourable, consider whether grounds for Judicial Review arise.

F27 **Prisoners Maintaining Innocence**

The Probation Service and Parole Board are required to assume that a prisoner found guilty by the courts has been rightly convicted. Although there is no rule or policy which prevents prisoners who deny guilt from progressing through the system or from being released, protesting innocence may have a bearing on the assessment of risk.

Denial does not in itself indicate an increased risk but it will make it more difficult to make a proper assessment of the risk factors and therefore an assessment of the extent to which these factors have been reduced. Many deniers refuse to participate in any offender behaviour work and some refuse to undertake certain offending behaviour programmes such as the Sex Offender Treatment Programmes (SOTP) and Controlling Anger and Learning to Manage It (CALM) as they depend on the prisoner being willing to discuss their offences. Participation in the Cognitive Self Change Programme (CSCP) is at the discretion of the Treatment Manager if the prisoner denies committing the offence. However, cognitive skills programmes such as Enhanced Thinking Skills (ETS) and substance misuse programmes do not require admissions to be made.

Where innocence is maintained the risk assessment will be based on offender behaviour work the prisoner has been willing or able to participate in, police reports regarding the offence, social history information, the prisoner's performance in interview and their behaviour whilst in custody. By taking this information into account it should be possible to identify underlying risk factors which can be assessed over time to determine whether the risk has increased or decreased.

The current level of risk is the key indicator in assessing whether the prisoner should be released or made subject to a progressive move (PSO 4700, paragraph 4.14.15). See *R v Secretary of State for the Home Department, ex p Zulfikar* [1996] COD 256 and *R v Secretary of State for the Home Department, ex p Lillycrop* The Times, 13 December 1996.

F28 **Short Tariff Prisoners**

F28.1 **Key Documents**

KD PSO 4700 Indeterminate Sentence Manual

PSO 6010 Generic Parole Process

Short tariff prisoners are usually defined as those serving a minimum term of 6 years or less. Typically these will be IPP prisoners, although there will also be discretionary or even mandatory lifers serving short minimum terms. ISPs with short tariffs may need to be managed differently from ISPs with longer tariffs, to ensure the Parole Board has sufficient information to make a risk-based decision.

The essential elements of the parole process for short tariff prisoners, is as follows:

> ### PSO 4700 Indeterminate sentence manual
>
> #### 4.10 Short Tariff ISPs
>
> #### 4.10.2
> - *All ISPs should be prioritised for interventions and offending behaviour programmes according to the risk of harm they pose and length of time left till tariff expiry. In other words, and taking into account the ISP's own responsibility to address the risk of harm they present to the public and known victims, the ISP must be offered reasonable opportunity, as far as possible given the available resources, to address their risk factors in time for their Parole Board review.*
> - *Sentence planning meetings must take into account the time the ISP has until their Parole Board review when considering the tailoring and sequencing of interventions to assist the ISP to reduce their risk.*
> - It is essential the initial sentence planning meeting and any additional risk assessments are completed as quickly as possible, as the maximum time allowed may overrun the offender's Parole Board review.

F28.2 **Pre-tariff Review**

Pre-tariff reviews are not normally conducted for prisoners with a tariff of less than 3 years. If it is not feasible to conduct a pre-tariff review the review date will be set at tariff expiry. The Parole Board may also consider a transfer to open conditions at the same time.

Prisoners serving a minimum tariff of between 3 and 6 years will be reviewed as close to the halfway point as possible.

The pre-tariff review date is the parole process end date of the Generic Parole Process (PSO 6010, paragraph 2.1.1).

F28.3 Policy on Transfer to Open Conditions

PSO 4700 Indeterminate sentence manual

4.10 Short Tariff ISPs

4.10.4 **Policy on Transfer to Open Conditions for Short Tariff ISPs.** The Secretary of State's Directions to the Parole Board on mandatory lifers state that 'a period in open conditions is essential for most life sentence prisoners (lifers). It allows the testing of areas of concern in conditions nearer to those in the community than can be found in closed prisons'. The Directions do not specifically refer to other lifers or IPP, but the Parole Board's general approach has been to use the Directions as guidance for other cases.

4.10.5 Short tariff ISPs with tariffs of 30 months can be compared with determinates serving 4 to 5 years, 80% of whom are released from closed prisons. *It is, therefore, not essential for those short tariff ISPs who are likely to be released on tariff expiry, to spend a period in open conditions, but the principle as to whether a period in open conditions is necessary is a decision which must be made on a case by case basis, taking into account the presenting circumstances.*

4.10.6 Short tariff ISPs who are not released when the Parole Board first considers their case are more likely to be required to spend a period of time in open conditions prior to release. Identifying such cases is clearly important and staff in Offender Management Units have a vital role in ensuring their reports to the Parole Board reflect this.

F29 **Licence Conditions**

F29.1 **Key Document**

`KD` PSI 40/2012

F29.2 **Home Detention Curfew Licence**

There are two types of HDC licence:

1. *Stand alone HDC licence.* Prisoners serving 3 months or more but less than 12 months who are eligible for HDC will be released on an HDC licence. There are only two conditions: to observe a curfew and not to commit further offences while on licence. Once the HDC licence has expired (at the halfway point) the prisoner will not be subject to any other licence conditions but will be liable to recall for breach of licence until SLED.

2. *Combined HDC licence and standard licence.* Adult prisoners serving 12 months or more who are eligible for HDC, will be subject to the HDC licence conditions until the halfway point and will then be subject to the standard licence conditions. Young offenders will always be released on licence for at least 3 months.

F29.3 **Standard Conditions**

The 6 standard conditions are:

> ### PSI 40/2012 Licences and Licence Conditions
>
> #### Standard Conditions
> 2.3 *A licence must contain the six standard licence conditions set out below. Wording may vary slightly on some standard licences such as some Indeterminate Sentenced Prisoner (ISP, meaning a life sentenced offender or Indeterminate Sentence for Public Protection (IPP)) licences.*
> > i) *To keep in touch with your supervising officer in accordance with any instruction you may be given;*
> > ii) *If required, to receive visits from your supervising officer at your home/ place of residence (e.g. an Approved Premises);*
> > iii) *Permanently to reside at an address approved by your supervising officer and notify him/her in advance of any proposed change to address or any proposed stay (even for one night) away from that approved address;*
> > iv) *Undertake only such work (including voluntary work) approved by your supervising officer and notify him or her in advance of any proposed change;*
> > v) *Not to travel outside the United Kingdom unless otherwise directed*

> by your supervising officer (permission for which will be given in
> exceptional circumstances only) or for the purpose of complying with
> immigration/deportation;
>
> vi) To be well behaved, not to commit any offence and not to do any-
> thing which could undermine the purpose of your supervision, which
> is to protect the public, prevent you from re-offending and help you to
> re-settle successfully into the community.

F29.4 Additional Conditions

Additional licence conditions can be recommended by the Probation
Service for the following:

- prisoners sentenced to 12 months or more but less than 4 years
  under CJA 1991 (ACR prisoners);
- prisoners sentenced to 4 years or more under CJA 1991 (DCR prisoners convicted of non-violent and non-sexual offences only);
- prisoners sentenced to 12 months or more under CJA 2003.

The additional conditions listed in PSI 40/2012, Appendix A, are as
follows:

1. *Contact requirement.* Must attend appointments with a named
   medical practitioner which includes any reasonable requirement
   to undergo drug counselling.
2. *Prohibited activity requirement.* Restriction on work or other activity with persons under a specified age, and restrictions on the use of
   a computer or other electronic devise without prior approval.
3. *Residency requirement.* Must reside at named address and must not
   reside elsewhere without prior approval (standard condition only
   requires notification of a change of address).
4. *Prohibited residency requirement.* Must not reside at the same
   address as any child under a specified age without prior approval.
5. *Prohibited contact requirement.* Not to contact specified individuals
   eg the victim or children under a specified age without prior approval.
6. *Programme requirement.* Must attend any offender behaviour
   programmes as required by supervising officer or participate in a
   prolific or priority offender (PPO) project.
7. *Curfew requirement.* Observe a curfew during specified hours.
   Electronic tagging can be imposed for prisoners notified to the
   Public Protection and Courts Unit as a critical case, and prisoners
   who are MAPPA level 3.
8. *Exclusion requirement.* Not to enter a specified area, enter a specified road or enter specified places such as children's play areas,
   swimming baths or schools, etc.
9. *Supervision requirement.* Report to a police station at a specified
   time and place; provide details of possession of any vehicle or any
   developing relationship.

F29 Licence Conditions

10. *Non-association requirement.* Must not contact or associate with named individuals.
11. *Drug testing condition.* Although this is not a listed 'requirement' it can be included on a licence. It is limited to offenders identified as prolific or priority offenders convicted of specified offences committed after 4 April 2005.

The final list of conditions will be sent to the Governor who will issue the licence on behalf of the Secretary of State for prisoners subject to automatic release (PSI 40/2012, paragraph 2.9).

F29.5 Victims

PSI 40/2012 Licences and Licence Conditions

2.29 *Victims who qualify for victim contact (either as statutory victims under the Victim Scheme, or those who have been opted into the scheme by the relevant Probation Trust on a discretionary basis) have the right to make representations about licence conditions that relate to them and must be informed about relevant conditions which are included in the offender's licence under the statute of section 35 of the Domestic Violence, Crime and Victims Act 2004 (2004 Act).* The Craven Judgement (2001) has allowed for conditions to be imposed on the licence in order to prevent distress caused to the victim by a possible encounter between the victim and offender, rather than to protect them from a specific risk posed by the offender.

F29.6 Exclusion Zones

PSI 40/2012 Licences and Licence Conditions

2.30 Exclusion zones constitute an interference with the rights of offenders under article 8 of the ECHR (right to a private and family life). However, this interference can be justified if it is necessary and proportionate. Necessary means an appropriate way of interfering with the right bearing in mind the objective it is sought to achieve and proportionate means there is no less intrusive means of achieving that objective. *R (Craven) v Home Secretary* is authority that sparing the victim and the victim's family from the emotional harm that may arise from a chance meeting with the offender is an objective that can justify the interference constituted by an exclusion zone. *However, the zone and any applicable restrictions must be considered carefully and be no greater in extent or severity than is needed to minimise the risk of chance encounters whilst taking into consideration the effects on the offender's ability to visit family or friends, undertake work or carry out other legitimate activities. The interference with the article 8 rights of the offender's family must also be considered and it should be recognised that the complete eradication of any risk will often not be achievable whilst maintaining a proportionate exclusion zone.*

2.31 A 'no contact' condition or exclusion zone (see below) does not have to be restricted to the victim of the index offence. It could be the victim of a previous offence where they have been brought into the victim contact scheme on a discretionary basis, or the family of the victim of the index offence, particularly where there is evidence that the offender may target them or seek to make contact even though contact may cause distress. These conditions can even be imposed for the protection of the offender. It might also be appropriate to have a 'no contact' or exclusion zone condition for someone who is at risk of becoming a victim, or who is vulnerable to the particular risk posed to the offender. This may be particularly pertinent with offenders who have a history of domestic violence, as evidenced by previous call outs, or intelligence from children's services etc.

F29.7 Parole Board Recommendations

On the recommendation of the Parole Board only, the Probation Service can request additional licence conditions for DCR prisoners convicted of violent and sexual offences, extended sentence prisoners and recalled prisoners.

A request for recommendations will be made by the Probation Service in the report prepared for the parole dossier. If the Board directs release, the recommended conditions will be included. If the Board does not recommend release it may recommend additional conditions that should be imposed at the CRD or NPD. The recommendation will be binding for DCR prisoners and extended sentence prisoners serving less than 15 years. For prisoners serving more than 15 years the final decision will be made by the Secretary of State.

F29.8 Judicial Recommendations

Section 238 of the CJA 2003 gives the sentencing court the authority to recommend additional licence conditions when sentencing for offences committed on or after 4 April 2005. There is a presumption that the recommendation will be included in the licence. Although the recommendation must be considered it is not binding on the Secretary of State. If the circumstances have changed the Probation Service can seek prior approval from the post release section of the PPCS, to not include the recommendation. The judge will be notified and provided with reasons if the post release section confirms that the recommendation should be omitted (PSI 40/2012, paragraph 2.16). If it is accepted it must be included on the relevant licence.

F30 **Breach of Licence**

All offenders released on licence having served a determinate sentence will be liable to recall on the authority of the Secretary of State under section 254 of the CJA 2003, irrespective of whether the sentence was imposed under CJA 1991 or CJA 2003.

All prisoners sentenced to life imprisonment will be released on life licence if granted parole, which will remain in force until death. They will also be subject to supervision by the Probation Service which on application may be cancelled after at least 4 years (10 years for sex offenders), and liable to recall to prison if at any time they no longer represent an acceptable risk to the community. IPP licencees may potentially be on licence for life, but after 10 years an application may be made for the licence to be cancelled, and if granted, the offender will no longer be liable to recall. The PPCS will consult with the Parole Board before varying or cancelling any licence condition.

F30.1 **Breach of HDC Curfew Alone**

All prisoners released on HDC licence are liable to be recalled for breach of the curfew condition alone, if eg they:

- are absent from the curfew address during the specified curfew hours;
- damage or tamper with the monitoring equipment;
- withdraw consent to the monitoring arrangements;
- can no longer be electronically monitored at the specified address.

The PPCS will be contacted by the electronic monitoring contractor, and will then decide on behalf of the Secretary of State whether to recall the prisoner under the HDC recall provisions or on a standard recall (see **F32**). In deciding the type of recall the PPCS will take into account the assessment of risk of serious harm and re-offending, and the amount of time the offender has to serve between the date of recall and the conditional release date, as the decision will affect the length of time the offender will have to serve in custody before being eligible for re-release.

Once a recalled prisoner is back in custody the PPCS must be notified as soon as possible, and a dossier should be sent to the prisoner within 24 hours of notification. The prisoner will have the opportunity to make representations against the recall. A paper review will be conducted by the PPCS and the prisoner should be notified of the decision within 3 working days. If the appeal is allowed, the prisoner will be re-released on HDC. If the appeal is refused, prisoners sentenced to less than 12 months will be released at the halfway point without supervision and those sentenced to 12 months or more will be released on licence. All dates will be adjusted to take account of any time spent unlawfully at large. Prisoners recalled because their whereabouts could no longer be electronically monitored can apply to be re-released on HDC as soon as suitable alternative arrangements can be made.

F30.2 Breach of Standard and Additional Licence Conditions

Determinate sentence offenders serving 12 months or more who have been released on licence will be liable to recall at any time during the licence period and will remain on licence until the sentence expiry date. The Probation Service must notify the PPCS if an offender is not complying with the conditions of his licence, or otherwise poses a risk of harm or a risk of re-offending. However, the final decision on recall will be made by staff in the PPCS on behalf of the Secretary of State. Once an offender has been recalled, re-release will be determined by one of three options: (i) fixed term recall, (ii) standard recall or (iii) emergency recall.

All offenders who are recalled to prison must be informed of the reasons for their recall and their right to make representations to the Parole Board. If the Board recommends release the Secretary of State must give effect to that recommendation. However, under the new provisions not all recalled prisoners will automatically be referred to the Parole Board for consideration for release. Referral will depend on the type of recall and whether the Secretary of State has exercised an executive power to release.

F30.3 Summary of Changes to Release and Recall Made by the LASPO Act 2012

PSI 30/2012 Annex A

Subject	Summary of Change	Old provision	New provision
Remand time	Now calculated and applied administratively by prisons and no longer directed by courts.	s240 CJA 2003.	s240ZA CJA 2003 (as inserted by s108 LASPO).
Less than 12 month sentences	Release provision now contained in CJA 2003, not the CJA 1991 (remains the same – unconditional release at ½ way point – but no longer any 'at risk' period).	s33 CJA 1991.	s243A CJA 2003 (as inserted by s111 LASPO).

Home Detention Curfew (HDC)	All HDC releases now under a single 2003 Act scheme (as amended by LASPO), rather than slightly different statutory schemes for 1991 and 2003 Act prisoners. Following categories now statutorily excluded from HDC: • Prisoners serving 4 years or more; • Those with a previous HDC breach; • Those previously returned to prison under s40 or s116.	s246 CJA 2003 and s34A CJA 1991.	s246 CJA 2003 (as amended by s112 LASPO).
Sentences imposed after 3/12/2012 for offences committed before 4/4/2005	All standard determinate sentences of 12 months or more imposed after 3 December 2012 are subject to the 2003 Act release regime (release at ½ way point, on licence to end of sentence) even where offences committed before 4 April 2005.	s33 CJA 1991.	s244 CJA 2003.
Fixed Term Recalls (FTRs)	Certain prisoners are no longer excluded from getting a FTR, namely: • Schedule 15 sexual or violent offenders; • those with a previous FTR; • those released on HDC. (Extended sentence and IPP prisoners remain excluded.)	s255B CJA 2003.	s255B CJA 2003 (amended version as substituted by s114 LASPO).
Re-release following recall	Prisoners serving extended sentences who have been recalled are no longer excluded from the power for the Secretary of State (PPCS) to re-release them back on to licence. (Indeterminate sentence prisoners (IPPs and lifers) remain excluded and may only be re-released by the Parole Board.)	s255C CJA 2003.	s255C CJA 2003 (amended version as substituted by s114 LASPO).

Supervision of Young Offenders	DYOI and s91 prisoners serving less than 12 months continue to require 3 months supervision on release, subject to the following changes: • No longer applies to prisoners serving more than 12 months who have been recalled and re-released at SED; • Supervision always runs for 3 months and no longer expires on 22nd birthday if sooner; • Breaches still taken back to court but any new term imposed for breach is served in full (rather than release at ½ way point as before).	s65 CJA 1991.	s256B and s256C CJA 2003 (as inserted by s115 LASPO).
S116 power to order 'return' to prison (1991 Act sentences only).	The s116 power in respect of prisoners serving a '1991 Act' sentence has been completely repealed, so courts can no longer order an offender to serve the outstanding part of their sentence for a new offence committed during the 'at risk' period of a 1991 Act sentence. No sentence will have an 'at risk' period any more – including those of less than 12 months which are now governed by the CJA 2003. Section 40A (3 month licences for offenders released from a s116 return of less than 12 months) is also repealed – so no new s40A licences will be issued after 3 December.	s116 Powers of Criminal Courts (Sentencing) Act 2000. s40A CJA 1991.	None.

F30 Breach of Licence

Extended Determinate Sentences (EDS) and abolition of IPP and EPP sentences.	Offenders convicted on or after 3 December for serious (Schedule 15) violent or sexual offences will no longer receive an IPP or EPP sentence (or a s85 extended sentence) but a new Extended Determinate Sentence (EDS) – or life sentence in the most serious cases.	s225, s226, s227, s228 CJA 2003. s85 Powers of Criminal Courts (Sentencing) Act 2000.	s226A, s226B CJA 2003 (as inserted by s124 LASPO). s246A (as inserted by s125 LASPO).
	EDS prisoners must serve a minimum of two-thirds of the custodial term. If less than 10 years, release is automatic at the two-thirds point.		s247 CJA 2003 will continue to apply for the release of prisoners already serving EPP sentences under s227 or s228.
	If 10 years or more, or for a Schedule 15B offence, release between two-thirds and end of the custodial term is at Parole Board discretion.		s28 Crime (Sentences) Act 1997 will continue to govern release of prisoners already serving IPP sentences imposed under s225 or s226.
	Release is on licence to end of extension period.		
	Prisoners already serving EPP or IPP sentences imposed before commencement will continue to be subject to the same release provisions as before, which have not been changed by LASPO.		

F31 **Fixed Term Recall (FTR)**

F31.1 **Key Document**

`KD` PSI 30/2012

Offenders who do not present a risk of serious harm to the public will be recalled for a fixed period of up to 28 days, and will then be re-released on licence automatically. The fixed term recall is designed to remove the offender from the environment where he is at risk of causing harm or re-offending and to give the Probation Service time to review the supervision arrangements. If necessary, the offender may be made subject to additional licence conditions on re-release. An offender will only be made subject to FTR if they are assessed as both eligible and suitable.

F31.2 **Eligibility**

All offenders who are recalled for breach of their licence conditions will be eligible for FTR except those serving an extended sentence (CJA 2003, as amended by LASPO, section 114).

F31.3 **Suitability**

Offenders who have been identified as being eligible for FTR must be assessed for suitability. An offender will only be suitable for automatic re-release if the Secretary of State is satisfied that at the end of the 28-day period he will not present an identifiable risk of serious harm to the public. Serious harm in this context means death or serious physical or psychological injury. No offender assessed as presenting a high or very high risk of serious harm will be suitable for FTR.

F31.4 **Initiating on FTR**

Recall will be initiated by the offender's Offender Manager who must identify at the outset (i) whether the offender will be eligible for FTR; (ii) the level of risk of harm to the public based on the current OASys assessment; and (iii) the likely impact 28 days in custody will have on the assessment of risk of serious harm. If the offender is eligible for FTR, the risk of harm is low or medium and would not be adversely affected by 28 days in custody (suitability criteria) the offender manager will make a formal FTR request. In appropriate cases the offender manager may recommend additional licence conditions. The request will be e-mailed to the PPCS casework team within 24 hours of the

F31 Fixed Term Recall (FTR)

decision to request recall. The PPCS on behalf of the Secretary of State will then have to decide whether to revoke the licence and recall the prisoner under a FTR, or under standard recall (see **F32**).

F31.5 Re-release under FTR

Offenders who are subject to an FTR must be re-released automatically on licence no later than 28 days, calculated from the date the offender was returned to prison, and therefore once back in custody arrangements should immediately be made for re-release. Any additional licence conditions considered necessary should be listed in the breach report, and will be added to the standard licence by the Governor prior to release.

F31.6 Parole Board Review

Prisoners that make representations against their recall before the FTR expires will be referred to the Parole Board. If the case is considered before the automatic release date and the Board recommends release the Secretary of State must give effect to that recommendation. If the case is not considered in time, or if the Parole Board do not direct release the prisoner will be released on or before the expiry of 28 days.

F31.7 Secretary of State Review

The Secretary of State has a wide discretion to release an FTR prisoner at any time before the end of the 28-day period. This power is delegated to the PPCS. In practice this discretion is only exercised in the prisoner's favour if the Offender Manager can satisfy the PPCS that early release would reduce the risk of further breaches of licence and would not increase the risk of harm to the public, eg, where the recall decision was based on the lack of suitable accommodation and a new address has been approved which forms the basis of a re-release package.

F32 **Standard Recall**

Offenders who are not eligible or suitable for FTR will be made subject to a standard recall provided the risk of serious harm is not high or imminent. All standard recall prisoners are liable to remain in custody until the end of their sentence, irrespective of whether the original licence was under CJA 1991 or CJA 2003. However, the Parole Board or the Secretary of State may direct early release if they are satisfied that continued detention is no longer necessary for the protection of the public.

F32.1 **Suitability**

Extended sentence offenders and those not deemed suitable for an FTR will be made subject to a standard recall (CJA 2003, as amended by LASPO, section 114).

F32.2 **Initiating a Standard Recall**

The offender's Offender Manager will initiate a standard recall if the criteria for an FTR have not been met. The request for recall should be e-mailed to the PPCS team within 24 hours of the decision to recall. The PPCS is required to process the request within 24 hours and the police have a target to trace and arrest the offender within 96 hours.

F32.3 **Re-release under Standard Recall**

The Offender Manager should prepare a report and submit it to the PPCS within 14 days of the prisoner's return to custody. The report must also be served on the prisoner. The report should contain a review of the assessments, any further information relevant to the offender's risk, a risk management/sentence plan and a clear recommendation on release based on the evidence and the Offender Manager's judgement on manageability in the community.

Offenders in custody on a standard recall (including extended sentence prisoners) will be released (i) at the discretion of the Secretary of State, (ii) on the recommendation of the Parole Board, or (iii) on sentence expiry.

Executive release will be dependent on the Secretary of State being satisfied that custody is no longer necessary for the protection of the public, either because the prisoner does not present a risk of serious harm or the risk of re-offending is acceptable and manageable.

If the prisoner remains in custody after 28 days their case must automatically be referred to the Parole Board. Having considered the recall decision and any representations the Parole Board will make one of the following decisions:

- direct immediate release;
- direct release at a specified future date;
- make no direction.

The CJA 2003, as amended by section 114 of the LASPO includes extended sentence prisoners in the power to direct release.

Where the Board makes no recommendation, the Secretary of State must refer the case back to the Board within 12 months of the previous determination. In addition to annual reviews by the Parole Board, the Secretary of State is obliged to regularly review the offender's case so that in appropriate cases a prisoner can be referred back to the Board early or re-released under the discretionary powers if the prisoner's circumstances have changed and the prisoner presents an acceptable risk.

There is a presumption that the prisoner will be re-released or a date will be set for future re-release unless:

- the prisoner's continued liberty presents an unacceptable risk of a further offence being committed; or
- the prisoner has failed to comply with one or more of his licence conditions; and that failure suggests that the objectives of probation supervision have been undermined.

F32.4 Guidance

Guidance to members in all cases where the Parole Board has the power to direct release is set out here:

Guidance to Members 2013

1. This document has been produced to coincide with the Secretary of State's withdrawal of his Directions, previously issued under section 239(6) of the Criminal Justice Act 2003 and section 32(6) of the Criminal Justice Act 1991. This guidance applies to all cases where the Parole Board has the power to direct release; and does not apply to recommendations for the transfer of prisoners serving indeterminate sentences to open conditions. The Secretary of State's Directions in respect of the latter remain in force.

2. It is for each panel to decide for itself how to apply this guidance in an individual case. The guidance is to be read in conjunction with the "Guidance to members on LASPO (2012)", section 28(6) of the Crime (Sentences) Act and any relevant case law.

3. In reaching a decision whether or not to direct release, panels will take account of all relevant material, both written and, if applicable, verbal. It will be for each panel to decide what weight, if any, should be attached to each piece of material.

4. In most cases a panel will consider the following, where appropriate and available, in reaching its decision:

(i)   the nature and circumstances of the index offence and any previous offences;

(ii) any information relating to the offender's personal circumstances and background;

(iii) any reports prepared for the trial and the sentencing remarks and any judgment of the Court of Appeal, House of Lords or Supreme Court in the case;

(iv) the prisoner's attitude and behaviour towards, and relationships with, others, including authority figures;

(v)   assessments resulting from programmes, courses of treatment, or other activities designed either directly or indirectly to address his offending behaviour;

(vi) any medical, psychiatric or psychological considerations where relevant to the assessment of risk;

(vii) actuarial assessments of risk;

(viii) the prisoner's behaviour during outside activities during the sentence and any such periods in the past, including periods spent on licence or bail;

(ix) in the case of an indeterminate sentenced prisoner, the time spent in custody since expiry of the tariff;

(x)   representations from a victim;

(xi) the prisoner's attitude to, and the likelihood of compliance with, conditions of release on licence;

(xii) plans for supervision on release and the suitability of the release address;

(xiii) written or verbal representations made by the prisoner and his representative;

(xiv) any other material, information or fact deemed by the panel to be relevant to the assessment of risk.

5. Each case will be treated on its merits and without discrimination on any ground.

F32.5 Emergency Recall

Offenders will be liable to an emergency recall if:

• there is current evidence of a high risk or very high risk of serious harm to the public;

• the offender is subject to MAPPA level 3 arrangements or it is a critical public protection case;

• the offender's behaviour has deteriorated to such an extent that re-offending is believed to be imminent.

The PPCS will be required to process the request for emergency recall within 2 hours with a view to the offender being traced and arrested by the police within 48 hours. Emergency recalls will often be requested through the 'out of hours' service.

In all other respects the process and re-release provisions will be the same as for standard recalls.

F32.6 **Oral Hearings**

Recalled prisoners can request an oral hearing if, following a paper review, the Board refuse to direct re-release. Reasons will have to be provided, as the Board will only grant an oral hearing if, in accordance with the judgment in *R (on the application of Smith and West) v Parole Board* [2005] 1 WLR 350, it is justified in the interest of fairness. This is not confined to disputed facts. It may be appropriate to request an oral hearing if, eg, the history and background is complicated, or if there is substantial mitigation which could be put more effectively at an oral hearing. Each application must be considered on its individual merits.

The oral hearings procedure is outlined at **F24.8.3**. The Parole Board Rules apply to oral recall hearings, but the timetable will be directed by the Chair of the panel, as the review should be conducted as soon as possible.

F33 **Challenging Adverse Parole Decisions**

There is no right of appeal against a refusal to recommend a transfer to open conditions, a refusal to accept a recommendation or a refusal to direct release. However, Parole Board decisions and those of the Secretary of State are susceptible to Judicial Review, but this is not an appeal; it is a review of the decision-making process.

Although all parole decisions are susceptible to Judicial Review, grounds are more likely to arise in the following circumstances.

F33.1 Inadequate Reasons

On receipt of the written reasons legal representatives will need to consider whether the reasoning makes sense, and whether they adequately reflect the issues and points that were raised. In particular: Do the reasons themselves demonstrate that proper consideration has been given to the points made in the client's favour? Were irrelevant matters taken into account? Was undue weight given to contested hearsay? Was undue weight given to a denial of guilt? Was the recall decision based on the commission of further offences alone?

Although the key issue will be the reasons given at the time, the Parole Board may expand on the original reasons in their affidavit, however care will have to be taken to avoid giving the impression that the decision is being justified with the benefit of hindsight.

F33.2 Delayed Review

Reviews should be tailored to the individual, and so although there is a statutory limit of not more than 2 years between reviews, this should be regarded as a maximum, as it may be appropriate for the Parole Board to conduct an earlier review if the prisoner is making significant progress—see *Hirst v United Kingdom* [2001] Crim LR 919. The prisoner was a discretionary lifer. The Panel had recommended a transfer to open conditions on 2 separate occasions but both were refused by the Home Secretary. The court held that an automatic 2-year wait between reviews particularly where there was real prospect of progress towards release amounted to a breach of ECHR Article 5 (right to liberty and security).

F34 **Release on Compassionate Grounds**

Prisoners who have not reached their ARD, CRD or PED date may apply for release on compassionate grounds. The application should be submitted to the Governor. If the Governor is in support of the application it will be forwarded to the PPCS together with medical reports, probation reports or other supporting information (PSO 6000, paragraph 12.1). The PPCS may refuse the application, or refer it to Ministers. All decisions to grant release on compassionate grounds must be made at ministerial level.

If release is approved the PPCS will issue a standard parole licence which will run until the prisoner's original licence expiry date. If any of the conditions are breached the prisoner may be recalled to prison in the usual way. However, a miraculous recovery from a terminal illness would not justify recall. Fine defaulters and those in contempt of court serving custodial penalties who are released on compassionate grounds will not be subject to any licence conditions.

The general principles are:

- the release of the prisoner should not put the safety of the public at risk;
- approval should not normally be based on facts of which the sentencing or appeal court was aware;
- the release should serve some specific purpose (PSO 6000, paragraph 12.3.1).

F34.1 Medical Reasons

In assessing applications on medical grounds the Governor must consider whether:

(a) the prisoner is suffering from a terminal illness and death is likely to occur soon; or the prisoner is bedridden or similarly incapacitated; and
(b) the risk of re-offending has passed; and
(c) there are adequate arrangements for the prisoner's care and treatment outside prison; and
(d) early release will bring some significant benefit to the prisoner or his family (PSO 6000, Appendix A).

F34.2 **Tragic Family Circumstances**

Applications based on tragic family circumstances are more difficult to assess than medical cases, and are more likely to be resolved by Release on Temporary Licence. In assessing applications based on tragic family circumstances the Governor must consider whether:

(i) the circumstances of the prisoner or the family have changed to the extent that if the prisoner has served the sentence imposed, the hardship suffered would be of exceptional severity, greater than the court could have foreseen; and

(ii) the risk of re-offending has passed; and

(iii) it can be demonstrated beyond doubt that there is a real urgent need for the prisoner's permanent presence with his family; and

(iv) early release will bring some significant benefit to the prisoner or his family, which cannot be provided by any other person or agency (PSO 6000, Appendix A).

F35 Early Removal Scheme (ERS)

F35.1 Key Document

KD PSI 59/2011

The CJA 2003 introduced the ERS for foreign national prisoners (FNPs) serving determinate sentences. Prisoners are liable to removal from the UK within the meaning of section 259 of the CJA 2003 if:

- they are liable to deportation and have been notified of a decision to deport;
- the sentencing court recommended deportation;
- leave to enter the UK has been refused;
- they are an illegal immigrant;
- they are liable to removal for overstaying, breach of conditions of leave, or obtained leave by deception.

ERS is mandatory. All determinate FNPs who are liable for removal must be considered under the scheme. However ERS is likely to be refused in the following circumstances:

- there is clear evidence that the prisoner is planning further crime, including plans to evade immigration control and return to the UK unlawfully;
- there is evidence of violence or threats of violence in prison on a number of occasions;
- the FNP has been dealing in class A drugs in custody;
- the FNP is serving a sentence for a terrorism or terrorism-related offence;
- there are other matters of similar gravity relating to public safety (PSI 59/2011, paragraph 2.8).

Prisoners serving an indeterminate sentence will be considered under the Tariff Expired Removal Scheme (see **F37**).

FNPs can only be removed early under the scheme if the UK Border Agency is able to effect their removal during the ERS period. It may not be possible to remove FNPs if they have an immigration appeal pending; are serving a consecutive sentence for contempt; are in default of payment (fine or confiscation order); or have outstanding criminal charges.

The maximum ERS period is 270 days before the halfway point (CRD, ARD, SED). Prisoners must serve a minimum period of a quarter of their sentence before being eligible for early removal.

F36 Facilitated Return Scheme (FRS)

The FRS is operated by the FRS team in the UK Border Agency's Criminal Casework Directorate. It is a voluntary scheme available to non-EEA nationals only, designed to encourage FNPs to return to their country of origin by offering financial incentives. Prisoners accepted on to the scheme must co-operate with the removal and waive their right to appeal against deportation.

Although separate from ERS the two schemes are often implemented in parallel.

F37 **Tariff Expired Removal Scheme (TERS)**

F37.1 **Key Document**

KD   PSI 18/2012

LASPO introduced TERS for FNPs serving indeterminate sentences. TERS is mandatory. All indeterminate FNPs who are liable for removal must be considered under the scheme by the PPCS. Prisoners serving a determinate sentence will be considered under the Early Removal Scheme (see **F35**).

FNPs can only be removed early if the UK Border Agency is able to effect their removal during the TERS period. FNPs may not be suitable for removal if:

- the prisoner has a confiscation order or is subject to confiscation proceedings;
- the prisoner has outstanding criminal charges;
- there is clear evidence the prisoner is planning further criminal offences, including planning to evade the immigration authorities and return to the UK unlawfully;
- the prisoner is serving a sentence for terrorism or terrorism related offences.

Although indeterminate sentence prisoners can only be released on the authority of the Parole Board, such prisoners can be released under TERS at the discretion of the Secretary of State without referral to the Parole Board (PSI 18/2012, paragraph 4.2).

F38 **Repatriation**

Foreign national prisoners (FNPs) who have been sentenced to a term of imprisonment may be transferred to their own country to serve the remainder of their sentence, under provisions in the Repatriation of Prisoners Act 1984. To be eligible for repatriation there must be an international agreement in place between the prisoner's country of origin and the UK.

Repatriation can either take place on a voluntary basis, or on a compulsory basis depending on the relevant international arrangement. Although voluntary repatriation will be considered on a case by case basis the following requirements must usually be met:

- There must be at least six months of the sentence remaining.
- The prisoner will normally be a national of the country concerned (although some countries may accept non-national residents).
- There must not be any appeals outstanding against either conviction or sentence.
- The offence for which they have been convicted must also be an offence in the country of origin.
- Both the UK Government and the Government of the other country concerned must agree to the transfer (PSI 52/2011, paragraph 2.84).

A prisoner who wants to be repatriated should make a written request to the Governor. The application can be made on the internal complaint form and should provide the following details: full name, date of birth, address in home country, passport number and date of issue. The application will be forwarded to NOMS HQ, who will consult with the Secretary of State and officials from the prisoner's home country. If repatriation is considered to be appropriate the prisoner will be transferred to their home country to serve the equivalent sentence that could have been imposed in that country. The period of time the prisoner has already served, and any remission will be taken into account.

F39 **Special Remission**

In exceptional circumstances a sentence may be reduced by Royal Prerogative of Mercy, if the sentence has been miscalculated to the detriment of the prisoner or as a reward for meritorious conduct.

F39.1 **Miscalculation of Sentence**

Immediate action must be taken to rectify calculation errors once a mistake has been identified. If the recalculation means that the prisoner has already been detained beyond his release date, discharge and supervision arrangements must be actioned promptly.

Where a recalculation, although correct, results in a release date later than the original date given to the prisoner, consideration must be given to honouring that date or maintaining the correct sentence. The distress to the prisoner will be weighed against the duty of the Prison Service to ensure that the sentence imposed by the court is implemented. The length of time the prisoner has been under the misapprehension, the extent of the release plans based on the incorrect date, and deliberate concealment of the error are all factors that may be taken into account. In practice it is likely that prisoner will have to have been persistently misled for this discretionary power to be exercised in his or her favour. The views of the sentencing court may be sought (PSI 39/2012, paragraph 13.1.5).

Where a recalculation reveals that a prisoner has been released early in error consideration must be given as to whether to instruct the police to return the prisoner to prison to serve the remainder of the sentence. In determining whether to recall the person similar considerations as just described will need to be taken into account. Where the Regional Custody Manager decides that the person should not be recalled, a Royal Prerogative will need to be sought retrospectively to validate the incorrect release.

F39.2 **Reward for Meritorious Conduct**

Meritorious conduct is not defined. It is likely to include situations where a prisoner has assisted staff who were at risk of harm or provided information to the prison authorities in truly exceptional circumstances.

Recommendations from the Governor are considered by the Regional Custody Manager through the Offender Management Public Protection Group or the Directorate of High Security Prisons depending on the location of the prisoner. If the request is granted, a Royal warrant will be issued.

Part G
Judicial Review

G1 **Overview**

G1.1 **Key Documents**

KD Civil Procedure Rules, Part 54

Practice Direction 54A—Judicial Review

During any period of custody the Governor, other operational managers, prison staff and the Parole Board will make operational, managerial or disciplinary decisions that have a direct effect on the prisoner's rights or interests. These decisions, which cut across the full spectrum of prison life, are all susceptible to Judicial Review.

Identifying Judicial Review cases will often involve difficult questions of judgement. Judicial Review is a review of the decision-making process, which has little to do with the result or the factual merits, except to the extent that it is:

- irrational (see **G4.2**);
- based on factual errors (eg wrongly recorded previous convictions);
- necessary to make a finding of 'precedent fact' ie a finding of fact that needs to be established before the court can consider whether the decision was lawful.

G1.2 **The Defendant**

The appropriate defendant will depend on who made the decision under challenge:

- *The Secretary of State for Justice* (SoS)—The SoS has general 'superintendence of prisons' and should always be named as a defendant. The SoS will be the primary defendant for decisions made by the Briefing and Casework Unit (BCU), the Director of High Security (DHS) and the Public Protection Unit (PPU).
- *Prison Governor/Director*—for decisions made on the Governor's authority such as non-Category A categorization, Governor-only adjudications and segregation.
- *Independent Adjudicator*—for independent adjudications.
- *The Parole Board*—for decisions relating to release or transfer to open conditions.
- *The Probation Service*—for decisions relating to the assessment of risk, licence conditions and supervision.

The Letter Before Claim should be sent to the specific authorized government department to ensure a prompt response. Where the claim concerns a decision by a department or body for whom the Treasury

G1 Overview

Solicitor acts (eg Ministry of Justice) and the Treasury Solicitor has already been involved in the case a copy should be sent to:

The Treasury Solicitor
One Kemble Street
London
WC2B 4TS

In all other circumstances, the letter should be sent to the address on the letter notifying the decision.

G2 **Alternative Remedy**

As Judicial Review is a remedy of last resort prisoners are required to exhaust alternative resolutions, if available, before making a claim. This usually means the prisoner should at the very least make a complaint through the Requests and Complaints procedure. However, pursuing an internal complaint will be inappropriate if the prisoner is due to be released imminently or would be released imminently if the application was successful eg a challenge to an award of additional days where the prisoner is coming towards the end of his sentence.

There can be no obligation to pursue a complaint with the Independent Monitoring Board (IMB) as it has no statutory power to overturn decisions. Recommendations made by the Prisons and Probation Ombudsman are advisory only, and as there is no appeal procedure to challenge decisions of the Parole Board, decisions made by or on behalf of the Secretary of State and findings of guilt by an Independent Adjudicator, only Judicial Review can provide a remedy.

In *R v Deputy Governor of Parkhurst Prison, ex p Leech* [1988] 1 AC 533 the House of Lords rejected the argument that the courts had no jurisdiction to judicially review the disciplinary powers of the Governor as the Secretary of State had a duty under section 4(2) of the Prison Act 1952 to ensure that all personnel comply with the Act and Prison Rules, thereby providing an effective remedy. In the later case of *R v Secretary of State for the Home Department, ex p Hague* [1992] 1 AC 58, the Home Office accepted that the courts had jurisdiction to review the Governor's management decisions, however, it was argued that prisoners should be denied relief if they had not exhausted internal avenues of complaint. This argument was also rejected by the Court of Appeal.

G3 Overlap with Civil Actions

Prisoners can pursue civil actions (in private law) against the prison authorities for:

- *negligence*—where there is was common law duty of care to the prisoner, the prison authority's action or failure to take action fell below the standard required in law and the injury caused was a reasonably foreseeable consequence of the breach.
- *assault and battery*—assault being an apprehension of imminent unlawful force, and battery the actual unlawful touching of another.
- *misfeasance in a public office*—the deliberate and dishonest abuse of power.

Breaches of the Prison Rules are only actionable if in addition to the breach there has been a 'civil wrong', which has resulted in some form of financial loss or physical injury (see *R v Secretary of State for the Home Department, ex p Hague* [1992] 1 AC 58). The Human Rights Act (HRA) 1998 incorporated most of the European Convention of Human Rights (ECHR) into domestic law, and therefore prisoners are able to challenge breaches of their fundamental human rights in Judicial Review proceedings and private law claims.

It is important to recognize that there will be occasions when the public law and the private law overlap. For example, if a prisoner is segregated under Rule 45 for fighting and restrained on the authority of the Governor in a body belt, what might have been a lawful restraint would become unlawful if the Governor fails to obtain the written authority of the IMB or Secretary of State to continue with the restraint beyond 24 hours. Releasing the prisoner temporarily so that he or she can consume food and water, and then restraining him again using force would be an assault. In these circumstances the breach of the Rules would be ancillary to the assault, and therefore rather than pursuing a declaration that the restraint was unlawful it would be more appropriate to initiate a county court claim for assault.

In addition, prisoners can make county court claims under the Race Relations Act 1976 (as amended), the Sex Discrimination Act 1977 and the Disability Discrimination Act 1995.

G4 **Grounds for Judicial Review**

In the GCHQ case (*Council of Civil Service Unions v Minister for the Civil Service* [1985] AC 374), Lord Diplock classified the main grounds for Judicial Review as illegality, irrationality and procedural impropriety. These grounds are not fixed and often overlap.

G4.1 **Illegality**

The Governor, Parole Board and Secretary of State must understand the law that governs their decision-making powers and must apply it correctly. Examples of illegality are as follows:

- *Ultra vires.* The board or official had no power to make the decision or exceeded their powers.
- *Error in law.* Misapplication of the law to the detriment of the claimant.
- *Fndamental factual error.* Leading to a failure to take into account a relevant consideration.
- *Irrelevant factors.* Should not have been but were taken into account.

G4.2 **Irrationality**

Decisions must not be unreasonable, which some prisoners may confuse with 'unfavourable'. The traditional *Wednesbury* approach (see *Associated Provincial Picture Houses Ltd v Wednesbury Corporation* [1948] 1 KB 223 CA) gave way to 'proportionality' following the implementation of the HRA. The House of Lords decision in *R v Secretary of State for the Home Department, ex p Daly* [2001] HL 26 represents a departure from the earlier approach, in that the degree of scrutiny and the extent of justification required from the state will depend on the nature of the impact on the individual and the nature of the decision.

Examples of irrationality are:

- *Inflexibly following a policy.* Individual circumstances must be taken into account.
- *Failure to give reasons.* Decisions affecting the rights or interests of prisoners require an explanation.
- *Inadequate reasons.* Reasons must be full enough to demonstrate that a reasonable decision has been reached, and must address the issues in dispute.

G4.3 Procedural Impropriety

There are three main forms of procedural impropriety:

- *Failure to follow a policy or procedure.* If a procedure is in place it must be followed.
- *Bias or impartiality.* The decision-maker should not only be unbiased but should be seen to be so.
- *Unfairness.* This involves the concept of natural justice, the requirement to provide reasons and respect for legitimate expectations.

G4.4 Human Rights

Following the implementation of the HRA, incompatibility with the ECHR became a further ground. Section 6 HRA provides that it is unlawful for a public authority to act in a way that is incompatible with an ECHR right.

Some rights are absolute eg Article 3 (right to be free from torture, inhuman or degrading treatment). There are no exceptions or limitations to this right and in the prison law context, this will usually relate to the conditions of detention. It is the cumulative effect of poor conditions that can turn a substandard regime into intolerable 'inhuman and degrading treatment'. For example, see *R v Governor of Frankland Prison, ex p Russell* [2000] EWHC Admin 365. As a result of the prisoner's refusal to wear prison clothing he was not permitted to attend the servery for his meals; instead one meal a day was brought to his cell. Lightman J held that the policy of restricting meals was unlawful as it failed to give effect to Rule 24 regarding the provision of food. However, he indicated that the result may have been the same under Article 3 as the policy was inflexible, arbitrary and failed to take into account basic health safeguards.

Other rights such as Article 5 (the right to liberty and security) are qualified rights; which may be interfered with, if they are necessary and proportionate. Article 5 has been important in establishing the right to an oral hearing in certain contexts, such as the review of detention once the minimum term has been served (see *R (on the application of Anderson) v Secretary of State for the Home Department* [2003] 1 AC 837) and when considering challenges to licence recall, which was established following the decision in *R (on the application of Smith and West) v Parole Board* [2005] HL 1 where it was held that the Parole Board had a common law duty to adopt a fair procedure when considering whether prisoners recalled to prison should be re-released, and in fulfilling that duty an oral hearing may well be required. A prisoner whose rights under Article 5 have been breached may claim damages. In *R (on the application of Hirst) v Secretary of State for the Home Department* [2005] EWHC 1480 (Admin) the court held that the review of the prisoner's recall on licence had been held up because there was a 14-day delay in serving the dossier. Without the dossier the prisoner could not submit the written representations, which triggers the oral review process, and therefore the right to a speedy hearing under Article 5(4) had been breached. The prisoner was awarded £1,500 in damages.

Article 6 (right to a fair hearing) is very similar to the common law right, both of which include the right of access to an independent and impartial tribunal. These rights were held to be engaged whenever prisoners faced the prospect of additional days at adjudication hearings (see *Ezeh and Conners v United Kingdom* [2004] 39 EHRR 1). As a result of this important decision such adjudications are referred to independent adjudicators (District Judge) and prisoners have the right to legal representation.

Article 8 rights (right to a private life) clearly include the right not to be subjected to searches that go beyond that which is reasonable and necessary: see *R v Secretary of State for the Home Department ex p Daly* [2001] 2 AC 532.

G5 **Procedure**

The procedure for making a claim for Judicial Review is set out in the Civil Procedure Rules (CPR Part 54). Claims will be heard by a judge of the Administrative Court, which is part of the Queen's Bench Division of the High Court. A key feature of the procedure is the duty of candour. Both parties have an obligation to provide a complete and accurate account of the facts, as the court will not usually hear oral examination or cross examination of witnesses. Incomplete or misleading claims may be rejected for that reason alone.

G5.1 **Letter Before Claim**

Central to the Pre-action Protocol is the requirement to serve a Letter Before Claim. The Legal Aid Agency (LAA) would normally expect a Letter Before Claim before granting Full Representation. However, the Pre-action Protocol may be dispensed with if the claim is urgent.

The Letter Before Claim should:

- clearly identify the date and details of the decision being challenged;
- provide a clear summary of the facts;
- outline the reasons for challenge;
- detail any information required and explain why it is relevant;
- provide details of any known interested party (usually the Secretary of State for the Ministry of Justice); and
- make clear the action that is being sought.

The defendant should be allowed 14 days to reply before the claim is lodged on behalf of the claimant. If the matter is urgent it may be appropriate to request a response in a shorter time, but it is always good practice to put the other side on notice. Solicitors should use the pro-forma as set out in Annex A of the Pre-action Protocol.

G5.2 **Pre-issue**

Where a claim is contested in whole or in part an assessment should be made as to whether the response weakens the claim. If the response suggests that the claim has been substantially weakened consideration should be given to abandonment. However, if the claim is to be pursued the following documents should be prepared:

- Claim Form (N461)
- Copy of the decision under challenge
- Witness statement(s)
- Authorities

- Notice of issue of public funding
- List of essential reading
- Any application for directions

If it is not possible to file all of the necessary documents with the Claim Form, a covering letter should clearly state which documents are missing together with an explanation. The defendant will be entitled to seek an extension of time for lodging the acknowledgement of service until the missing documents are received.

Consideration should be given to instructing counsel to draft the claim form, as it will form the basis for argument at the substantive hearing. The claim form should address the issues raised by the defendant in their response to the Letter Before Claim.

G5.3 Issuing Proceedings

The Claim Form (Form N461), additional documents and the fee must be filed promptly, and within 3 months of the decision being challenged. The time limit cannot be extended by agreement of the parties, but can be extended by the Administrative Court if there is good reason for the delay and it would not be detrimental to good public administration, eg, difficulties in securing public funding.

This must not be construed as a 3-month time limit, as the claim will be struck out if it has not been made promptly even if it was lodged within 3 months. If the time limit has expired the client's witness statement or a separate statement from the solicitor should explain the chronology of events, reasons for the delay and any factors relevant to the issue of prejudice to third parties or the conduct of good administration.

At least 5 paginated claimant bundles (court, defendant, counsel, client, own copy) should be prepared. The claimant must file two copies with the Administrative Court Office, and should include:

- Draft index
- Claim Form (to be sealed for service)
- Witness statements
- Exhibits
- Legislation bundle
- List of essential reading
- Notice of issue of emergency representation certificate
- Notice of issue of substantive representation certificate
- Copy of representation certificate

Once issued the claim must be served on the defendant and any other interested parties within 7 days. A Certificate of Service should be lodged in the Administrative Court office within 7 days of serving the defendant and any interested party (Form N215).

Applications which do not comply with the CPR Part 54 and the accompanying Practice Direction will only be accepted in exceptional circumstances, ie where a decision from the court is required within 14 days of lodging the application. However, an undertaking to comply with the CPR within a specified period will be required.

If the claim is not resolved during the pre-action stage the defendant is obliged to serve an acknowledgement of service within 21 days of service of the claim form. This has to be served on the claimant and the Administrative Court, and must contain a summary of the defendant's grounds for contesting the claim. Although there is no provision within the CPR for the claimant to serve a reply a brief response may be lodged. The response should be served on the defendant and any interested party.

G5.4 Permission Stage

The permission stage is designed to filter out those claims that have no prospect of success. An Administrative Court judge will consider the case on the papers. If permission is granted, the case will proceed to a full hearing, and the judge may give directions. A further fee will be payable at this stage. If the judge refuses permission the claimant has 5 working days to make an application can be made for the matter to be reconsidered at an oral hearing, if appropriate.

If at the oral hearing the judge refuses to grant permission a further appeal can be made to the Court of Appeal. At this stage it would be wise to reconsider the merits of the case in light of the indication from the High Court that the claimant does not have an arguable case. In any event a positive Advice from counsel would be required before the LAA would fund such an appeal. Assuming public funding is granted, counsel may seek to persuade the court to grant permission on conditions or limited to certain grounds only.

G5.5 Oral Hearing

If permission is granted and the defendant is contesting the claim, they must serve a response detailing their grounds for objection and any written evidence within 35 days of service of the order granting permission. Solicitors must apply for an amendment of the public funding certificate for all work up to and including trial, which will require an Advice from counsel. Consideration will also need to be given to whether the claim form needs to be amended or further witness statements obtained.

When a claim is ready to be heard the case will be placed in a warned list and all parties will be informed by letter. This letter should be sent to counsel's clerk who will liaise with the court with regards to listing. The solicitor must prepare the trial bundle, which must be paginated, indexed and include all the required documents. The trial bundle should then be sent to the defendant who should be given an opportunity to comment. It is good practice to provide a deadline. The bundle should also be sent to counsel in time for them to draft a skeleton argument which must be served not less than 21 working days before the hearing. Defendants wishing to make representations should serve a skeleton argument not less than 14 days before the hearing. Although the timeframe is often breached the courts are becoming increasingly vigilant.

The case will normally be heard by a single judge from the Administrative Court panel, who will have read the papers prior to the hearing. Counsel instructed on behalf of the claimant will introduce the case, by referring to the witness statements and addressing the court as to the law. The defendant's counsel will then present the case in response.

G6 **Remedies**

The remedies available to the court are all discretionary. Even if the court were to accept that the law had been breached the claimant has no right to a remedy. Often the case will be remitted back to the decision-maker to reconsider the decision afresh; however, this does not mean that the authority cannot make the same decision again using different or more detailed reasons.

The remedies are as follows:

- *Quashing order*. This is the most common order made by the Administrative Court, and if granted will nullify the decision, making it completely invalid. Such an order is usually made when the Parole Board or prison authority have acted outside of their powers, and will usually result in the matter being referred back to the decision-maker for reconsideration.
- *Prohibiting order*. As the name suggests this order will prevent the public authority from implementing an ultra vires decision, eg, or an act which would breach the common law principles of natural justice.
- *Declaration*. A declaration is a judgment of the court that seeks to resolve the legal position between parties by clarifying their rights or obligations. For example, if a new local policy was introduced at a particular prison which was subsequently declared unlawful, the legal position between the Governor and the prisoners would be made clear.
- *Injunction*. An injunction is an order made by the court to prevent a body or authority from acting in a particular way. In certain circumstances the court may impose an interim injunction pending the outcome of the full hearing.
- *Mandatory order*. A mandatory order requires a party to act, eg, to improve prison conditions. A failure to comply with this order would be a contempt of court.
- *Damages*. Damages are only available if the court finds that the body or authority has acted unlawfully and the claim relates to a private law claim such as negligence or a claim under HRA 1988.

The Prison Rules 1999
1999 No. 728

Original rules came into force 1st April 1999. Latest amendment came into force 1st January 2010.

ARRANGEMENT OF RULES

Part I Interpretation

GENERAL

Part II Prisoners

GENERAL

WOMEN PRISONERS

RELIGION

MEDICAL ATTENTION

Appendix 1

PHYSICAL WELFARE AND WORK

EDUCATION AND LIBRARY

COMMUNICATIONS

REMOVAL, SEARCH, RECORD AND PROPERTY

CONTROL, SUPERVISION, RESTRAINT AND DRUG TESTING

Part VI Supplemental

Schedule Explanatory Note

In exercise of the powers conferred upon me by section 47 of the Prison Act 1952, I hereby make the following Rules:

Part I Interpretation

1. Citation and commencement

These Rules may be cited as the Prison Rules 1999 and shall come into force on 1st April 1999.

2. – Interpretation

(1) In these Rules, where the context so admits, the expression –

'adjudicator' means a District Judge (Magistrates' Courts) or Deputy District Judge (Magistrates' Courts) approved by the Lord Chancellor for the purpose of inquiring into a charge which has been referred to him;

'communication' includes any written or drawn communication from a prisoner to any other person, whether intended to be transmitted by means of a postal service or not, and any communication from a prisoner to any other person transmitted by means of a telecommunications system;

'controlled drug' means any drug which is a controlled drug for the purposes of the Misuse of Drugs Act 1971;

'convicted prisoner' means, subject to the provisions of rule 7(3), a prisoner who has been convicted or found guilty of an offence or committed or attached for contempt of court or for failing to do or abstain from doing anything required to be done or left undone, and the expression 'unconvicted prisoner' shall be construed accordingly;

'fixed term prisoner' has the meaning assigned to it by section 237(1) of the Criminal Justice Act 2003;

'governor' includes an officer for the time being in charge of a prison;

'health care professional' means a person who is a member of a profession regulated by a body mentioned in section 25(3) of the National Health Service Reform and Health Care Professions Act 2002 and who is working within the prison;

'health care provider' includes any provider of health services, whether or not commissioned by an NHS body (within the meaning given by section 28(6) of the National Health Service 2006);

'information technology equipment' includes any laptop or notebook computer, desktop computer, gaming console, handheld computing device, personal organiser or any electronic device containing a computer processor and capable of connecting to the internet, and any reference to information technology equipment includes a reference to –

(a) a component part of a device of that description; or
(b) any article designed or adapted for use with any information technology equipment (including any disk, film or other separate article on which images, sounds, computer code or other information may be stored or recorded);

'intercepted material' means the contents of any communication intercepted pursuant to these Rules;

'intermittent custody order' has the meaning assigned to it by section 183 of the Criminal Justice Act 2003;

'legal adviser' means, in relation to a prisoner, his counsel or solicitor, and includes a clerk acting on behalf of his solicitor;

'officer' means an officer of a prison and, for the purposes of rule 40(2), includes a prisoner custody officer who is authorised to perform escort functions in accordance with section 89 of the Criminal Justice Act 1991;

'prison minister' means, in relation to a prison, a minister appointed to that prison under section 10 of the Prison Act 1952;

'short-term prisoner' and 'long-term prisoner' have the meanings assigned to them by section 33(5) of the Criminal Justice Act 1991, as extended by sections 43(1) and 45(1) of that Act;

'telecommunications system' means any system (including the apparatus comprised in it) which exists for the purpose of facilitating the transmission of communications by any means involving the use of electrical or electro-magnetic energy;

'the 2003 Act' means the Criminal Justice Act 2003

(2) In these Rules –
(a) a reference to an award of additional days means additional days awarded under these Rules by virtue of section 42 of the Criminal Justice Act 1991 or by virtue of section 257 of the 2003 Act.

(b) a reference to the Church of England includes a reference to the Church in Wales; and

(c) a reference to a numbered rule is, unless otherwise stated, a reference to the rule of that number in these Rules and a reference in a rule to a numbered paragraph is, unless otherwise stated, a reference to the paragraph of that number in that rule.

Part II Prisoners

GENERAL

3. Purpose of prison training and treatment

The purpose of the training and treatment of convicted prisoners shall be to encourage and assist them to lead a good and useful life.

4. Outside contacts

(1) Special attention shall be paid to the maintenance of such relationships between a prisoner and his family as are desirable in the best interests of both.

(2) A prisoner shall be encouraged and assisted to establish and maintain such relations with persons and agencies outside prison as may, in the opinion of the governor, best promote the interests of his family and his own social rehabilitation.

5. After care

From the beginning of a prisoner's sentence, consideration shall be given, in consultation with the appropriate after-care organisation, to the prisoner's future and the assistance to be given him on and after his release.

6. Maintenance of order and discipline

(1) Order and discipline shall be maintained with firmness, but with no more restriction than is required for safe custody and well ordered community life.

(2) In the control of prisoners, officers shall seek to influence them through their own example and leadership, and to enlist their willing co-operation.

(3) At all times the treatment of prisoners shall be such as to encourage their self-respect and a sense of personal responsibility, but a prisoner shall not be employed in any disciplinary capacity.

7. Classification of prisoners

(1) Prisoners shall be classified, in accordance with any directions of the Secretary of State, having regard to their age, temperament and record and with a view to maintaining good order and

facilitating training and, in the case of convicted prisoners, of furthering the purpose of their training and treatment as provided by rule 3.

(2) Unconvicted prisoners –

    (a) shall be kept out of contact with convicted prisoners as far as the governor considers it can reasonably be done, unless and to the extent that they have consented to share residential accommodation or participate in any activity with convicted prisoners; and

    (b) shall under no circumstances be required to share a cell with a convicted prisoner.

(3) Prisoners committed or attached for contempt of court, or for failing to do or abstain from doing anything required to be done or left undone:

    (a) shall be treated as a separate class for the purposes of this rule;

    (b) notwithstanding anything in this rule, may be permitted to associate with any other class of prisoners if they are willing to do so; and

    (c) shall have the same privileges as an unconvicted prisoner under rules 20(5), 23(1) and 35(1).

(4) Nothing in this rule shall require a prisoner to be deprived unduly of the society of other persons.

8. Privileges

(1) There shall be established at every prison systems of privileges approved by the Secretary of State and appropriate to the classes of prisoners there, which shall include arrangements under which money earned by prisoners in prison may be spent by them within the prison.

(2) Systems of privileges approved under paragraph (1) may include arrangements under which prisoners may be allowed time outside their cells and in association with one another, in excess of the minimum time which, subject to the other provisions of these Rules apart from this rule, is otherwise allowed to prisoners at the prison for this purpose.

(3) Systems of privileges approved under paragraph (1) may include arrangements under which privileges may be granted to prisoners only in so far as they have met, and for so long as they continue to meet, specified standards in their behaviour and their performance in work or other activities.

(4) Systems of privileges which include arrangements of the kind referred to in paragraph (3) shall include procedures to be followed in determining whether or not any of the privileges concerned shall be granted, or shall continue to be granted, to a prisoner; such procedures shall include a requirement that the

prisoner be given reasons for any decision adverse to him together with a statement of the means by which he may appeal against it.

(5) Nothing in this rule shall be taken to confer on a prisoner any entitlement to any privilege or to affect any provision in these Rules other than this rule as a result of which any privilege may be forfeited or otherwise lost or a prisoner deprived of association with other prisoners.

9. Temporary release

(1) The Secretary of State may, in accordance with the other provisions of this rule, release temporarily a prisoner to whom this rule applies.

(2) A prisoner may be released under this rule for any period or periods and subject to any conditions.

(3) A prisoner may only be released under this rule:

    (a) on compassionate grounds or for the purpose of receiving medical treatment;

    (b) to engage in employment or voluntary work;

    (c) to receive instruction or training which cannot reasonably be provided in the prison;

    (d) to enable him to participate in any proceedings before any court, tribunal or inquiry;

    (e) to enable him to consult with his legal adviser in circumstances where it is not reasonably practicable for the consultation to take place in the prison;

    (f) to assist any police officer in any enquiries;

    (g) to facilitate the prisoner's transfer between prisons;

    (h) to assist him in maintaining family ties or in his transition from prison life to freedom.

(4) A prisoner shall not be released under this rule unless the Secretary of State is satisfied that there would not be an unacceptable risk of his committing offences whilst released or otherwise failing to comply with any condition upon which he is released.

(5) The Secretary of State shall not release under this rule a prisoner serving a sentence of imprisonment if, having regard to:

    (a) the period or proportion of his sentence which the prisoner has served or, in a case where paragraph (10) does not apply to require all the sentences he is serving to be treated as a single term, the period or proportion of any such sentence he has served; and

    (b) the frequency with which the prisoner has been granted temporary release under this rule,

the Secretary of State is of the opinion that the release of the prisoner would be likely to undermine public confidence in the administration of justice.

(6) If a prisoner has been temporarily released under this rule during the relevant period and has been sentenced to imprisonment for a criminal offence committed whilst at large following that release, he shall not be released under this rule unless his release, having regard to the circumstances of this conviction, would not, in the opinion of the Secretary of State, be likely to undermine public confidence in the administration of justice.

(7) For the purposes of paragraph (6), 'the relevant period':

(a) in the case of a prisoner serving a determinate sentence of imprisonment, is the period he has served in respect of that sentence, unless, notwithstanding paragraph (10), the sentences he is serving do not fall to be treated as a single term, in which case it is the period since he was last released in relation to one of those sentences under Part II of the Criminal Justice Act 1991 ('the 1991 Act') or Chapter 6 of Part 12 of the 2003 Act;

(b) in the case of a prisoner serving an indeterminate sentence of imprisonment, is, if the prisoner has previously been released on licence under Part II of the Crime (Sentences) Act 1997 or Part II of the 1991 Act or Chapter 6 of Part 12 of the 2003 Act, the period since the date of his last recall to prison in respect of that sentence or, where the prisoner has not been so released, the period he has served in respect of that sentence; or

(c) in the case of a prisoner detained in prison for any other reason, is the period for which the prisoner has been detained for that reason; save that where a prisoner falls within two or more of sub-paragraphs (a) to (c), the 'relevant period', in the case of that prisoner, shall be determined by whichever of the applicable sub-paragraphs produces the longer period.

(8) A prisoner released under this rule may be recalled to prison at any time whether the conditions of his release have been broken or not.

(9) This rule applies to prisoners other than persons committed in custody for trial or to be sentenced or otherwise dealt with before or by any Crown Court or remanded in custody by any court.

(10) For the purposes of any reference in this rule to an inmate's sentence, consecutive terms and terms which are wholly or partly concurrent shall be treated as a single term.

(11) In this rule:

(a) any reference to a sentence of imprisonment shall be construed as including any sentence to detention or custody; and

(b) any reference to release on licence or otherwise under Part II of the 1991 Act includes any release on licence under any legislation providing for early release on licence.

Appendix 1

10. Information to prisoners

(1) Every prisoner shall be provided, as soon as possible after his reception into prison, and in any case within 24 hours, with information in writing about those provisions of these Rules and other matters which it is necessary that he should know, including earnings and privileges, and the proper means of making requests and complaints.

(2) In the case of a prisoner aged less than 18, or a prisoner aged 18 or over who cannot read or appears to have difficulty in understanding the information so provided, the governor, or an officer deputed by him, shall so explain it to him that he can understand his rights and obligations.

(3) A copy of these Rules shall be made available to any prisoner who requests it.

11. Requests and complaints

(1) A request or complaint to the governor or independent monitoring board relating to a prisoner's imprisonment shall be made orally or in writing by the prisoner.

(2) On every day the governor shall hear any requests and complaints that are made to him under paragraph (1).

(3) A written request or complaint under paragraph (1) may be made in confidence.

WOMEN PRISONERS

12. Women prisoners

(1) Women prisoners shall normally be kept separate from male prisoners.

(2) The Secretary of State may, subject to any conditions he thinks fit, permit a woman prisoner to have her baby with her in prison, and everything necessary for the baby's maintenance and care may be provided there.

RELIGION

13. Religious denomination

A prisoner shall be treated as being of the religious denomination stated in the record made in pursuance of section 10(5) of the Prison Act 1952 but the governor may, in a proper case and after due enquiry, direct that record to be amended.

14. Special duties of chaplains and prison ministers

(1) The chaplain or a prison minister of a prison shall –

(a) interview every prisoner of his denomination individually soon after the prisoner's reception into that prison and shortly before his release; and

(b) if no other arrangements are made, read the burial service at the funeral of any prisoner of his denomination who dies in that prison.

(2) The chaplain shall visit daily all prisoners belonging to the Church of England who are sick, under restraint or undergoing cellular confinement; and a prison minister shall do the same, as far as he reasonably can, for prisoners of his denomination.

(3) The chaplain shall visit any prisoner not of the Church of England who is sick, under restraint or undergoing cellular confinement, and is not regularly visited by a minister of his denomination, if the prisoner is willing.

15. Regular visits by ministers of religion

(1) The chaplain shall visit the prisoners belonging to the Church of England.

(2) A prison minister shall visit the prisoners of his denomination as regularly as he reasonably can.

(3) Where a prisoner belongs to a denomination for which no prison minister has been appointed, the governor shall do what he reasonably can, if so requested by the prisoner, to arrange for him to be visited regularly by a minister of that denomination.

16. Religious services

(1) The chaplain shall conduct Divine Service for prisoners belonging to the Church of England at least once every Sunday, Christmas Day and Good Friday, and such celebrations of Holy Communion and weekday services as may be arranged.

(2) Prison ministers shall conduct Divine Service for prisoners of their denominations at such times as may be arranged.

17. Substitute for chaplain or prison minister

(1) A person approved by the Secretary of State may act for the chaplain in his absence.

(2) A prison minister may, with the leave of the Secretary of State, appoint a substitute to act for him in his absence.

18. Sunday work

Arrangements shall be made so as not to require prisoners of the Christian religion to do any unnecessary work on Sunday, Christmas Day or Good Friday, or prisoners of other religions to do any such work on their recognised days of religious observance.

Appendix 1

19. Religious books

There shall, so far as reasonably practicable, be available for the personal use of every prisoner such religious books recognised by his denomination as are approved by the Secretary of State for use in prisons.

MEDICAL ATTENTION

20. Health services

(1) The governor must work in partnership with local health care providers to secure the provision to prisoners of access to the same quality and range of services as the general public receives from the National Health Service.

(2) Every request by a prisoner to see a health care professional shall be recorded by the officer to whom it was made and promptly communicated to a health care professional.

(3) If an unconvicted prisoner desires the attendance of a named registered medical practitioner or dentist other than one already working in the prison, and will pay any expense incurred, the governor must, if satisfied that there are reasonable grounds for the request and unless the Secretary of State otherwise directs, allow the prisoner to be visited and treated by that practitioner or dentist, in consultation with a registered medical practitioner who works in the prison.

(4) Subject to any directions given in the particular case by the Secretary of State, a registered medical practitioner selected by or on behalf of a prisoner who is a party to any legal proceedings must be afforded reasonable facilities for examining the prisoner in connection with the proceedings, and may do so out of hearing but in the sight of an officer.

(5) A prisoner may correspond, in accordance with arrangements made by the Secretary of State for the confidential handling of correspondence, with a registered medical practitioner who has treated the prisoner for a life threatening condition, and such correspondence may not be opened, read or stopped unless the governor has reasonable cause to believe its contents do not relate to the treatment of that condition.

21. Special illnesses and conditions

(1) A registered medical practitioner working within the prison shall report to the governor on the case of any prisoner whose health is likely to be injuriously affected by continued imprisonment or any conditions of imprisonment. The governor shall send the report to the Secretary of State without delay, together with his own recommendations.

22. Notification of illness or death

(1) If a prisoner dies, becomes seriously ill, sustains any severe injury or is removed to hospital on account of mental disorder, the governor shall, if he knows his or her address, at once inform the prisoner's spouse or next of kin, and also any person who the prisoner may reasonably have asked should be informed.

(2) If a prisoner dies, the governor shall give notice immediately to the coroner having jurisdiction, to the independent monitoring board and to the Secretary of State.

PHYSICAL WELFARE AND WORK

23. Clothing

(1) An unconvicted prisoner may wear clothing of his own if and in so far as it is suitable, tidy and clean, and shall be permitted to arrange for the supply to him from outside prison of sufficient clean clothing:

Provided that, subject to rule 40(3):

(a) he may be required, if and for so long as there are reasonable grounds to believe that there is a serious risk of his attempting to escape, to wear items of clothing which are distinctive by virtue of being specially marked or coloured or both; and

(b) he may be required, if and for so long as the Secretary of State is of the opinion that he would, if he escaped, be highly dangerous to the public or the police or the security of the State, to wear clothing provided under this rule.

(2) Subject to paragraph (1) above, the provisions of this rule shall apply to an unconvicted prisoner as to a convicted prisoner.

(3) A convicted prisoner shall be provided with clothing adequate for warmth and health in accordance with a scale approved by the Secretary of State.

(4) The clothing provided under this rule shall include suitable protective clothing for use at work, where this is needed.

(5) Subject to rule 40(3), a convicted prisoner shall wear clothing provided under this rule and no other, except on the directions of the Secretary of State or as a privilege under rule 8.

(6) A prisoner may be provided, where necessary, with suitable and adequate clothing on his release.

24. Food

(1) Subject to any directions of the Secretary of State, no prisoner shall be allowed, except as authorised by a health care professional to have any food other than that ordinarily provided.

Appendix 1

(2) The food provided shall be wholesome, nutritious, well prepared and served, reasonably varied and sufficient in quantity.

(3) Any person deemed by the governor to be competent, shall from time to time inspect the food both before and after it is cooked and shall report any deficiency or defect to the governor.

(4) In this rule 'food' includes drink.

25. Alcohol and tobacco

(1) No prisoner shall be allowed to have any intoxicating liquor.

(2) No prisoner shall be allowed to smoke or to have any tobacco except as a privilege under rule 8 and in accordance with any orders of the governor.

26. Sleeping accommodation

(1) No room or cell shall be used as sleeping accommodation for a prisoner unless it has been certified in the manner required by section 14 of the Prison Act 1952 in the case of a cell used for the confinement of a prisoner.

(2) A certificate given under that section or this rule shall specify the maximum number of prisoners who may sleep or be confined at one time in the room or cell to which it relates, and the number so specified shall not be exceeded without the leave of the Secretary of State.

27. Beds and bedding

Each prisoner shall be provided with a separate bed and with separate bedding adequate for warmth and health.

28. Hygiene

(1) Every prisoner shall be provided with toilet articles necessary for his health and cleanliness, which shall be replaced as necessary.

(2) Every prisoner shall be required to wash at proper times, have a hot bath or shower on reception and thereafter at least once a week.

(3) A prisoner's hair shall not be cut without his consent.

29. Physical education

(1) If circumstances reasonably permit, a prisoner aged 21 years or over shall be given the opportunity to participate in physical education for at least one hour a week.

(2) The following provisions shall apply to the extent circumstances reasonably permit to a prisoner who is under 21 years of age –

    (a) provision shall be made for the physical education of such a prisoner within the normal working week, as well as evening and weekend physical recreation; the physical education activities will be such as foster personal responsibility and the prisoner's interests and skills and encourage him to make good use of his leisure on release; and

(b) arrangements shall be made for each such prisoner who is a convicted prisoner to participate in physical education for two hours a week on average.

(3) In the case of a prisoner with a need for remedial physical activity, appropriate facilities will be provided.

30. Time in the open air

If the weather permits and subject to the need to maintain good order and discipline, a prisoner shall be given the opportunity to spend time in the open air at least once every day, for such period as may be reasonable in the circumstances.

31. Work

(1) A convicted prisoner shall be required to do useful work for not more than 10 hours a day, and arrangements shall be made to allow prisoners to work, where possible, outside the cells and in association with one another.

(2) A registered medical practitioner or registered nurse working within the prison may excuse a prisoner from work on medical grounds.

(3) No prisoner shall be set to do work of a kind not authorised by the Secretary of State.

(4) No prisoner shall work in the service of another prisoner or an officer, or for the private benefit of any person, without the authority of the Secretary of State.

(5) An unconvicted prisoner shall be permitted, if he wishes, to work as if he were a convicted prisoner.

(6) Prisoners may be paid for their work at rates approved by the Secretary of State, either generally or in relation to particular cases.

EDUCATION AND LIBRARY

32. Education

(1) Every prisoner able to profit from the education facilities provided at a prison shall be encouraged to do so.

(2) Educational classes shall be arranged at every prison and, subject to any directions of the Secretary of State, reasonable facilities shall be afforded to prisoners who wish to do so to improve their education by training by distance learning, private study and recreational classes, in their spare time.

(3) Special attention shall be paid to the education and training of prisoners with special educational needs, and if necessary they shall be taught within the hours normally allotted to work.

(4) In the case of a prisoner of compulsory school age as defined in section 8 of the Education Act 1996, arrangements shall be made for his participation in education or training courses for at least 15 hours a week within the normal working week.

33. Library

A library shall be provided in every prison and, subject to any directions of the Secretary of State, every prisoner shall be allowed to have library books and to exchange them.

COMMUNICATIONS

34. Communications generally

(1) Without prejudice to sections 6 and 19 of the Prison Act 1952 and except as provided by these Rules, a prisoner shall not be permitted to communicate with any person outside the prison, or such person with him, except with the leave of the Secretary of State or as a privilege under rule 8.

(2) Notwithstanding paragraph (1) above, and except as otherwise provided in these Rules, the Secretary of State may impose any restriction or condition, either generally or in a particular case, upon the communications to be permitted between a prisoner and other persons if he considers that the restriction or condition to be imposed –

(a) does not interfere with the convention rights of any person; or

(b)
    (i) is necessary on grounds specified in paragraph (3) below

    (ii) reliance on the grounds is compatible with the convention right to be interfered with; and

    (iii) the restriction or condition is proportionate to what is sought to be achieved.

(3) The grounds referred to in paragraph (2) above are –

(a) the interests of national security;

(b) the prevention, detection, investigation or prosecution of crime;

(c) the interests of public safety;

(d) securing or maintaining prison security or good order and discipline in prison;

(e) the protection of health or morals;

(f) the protection of the reputation of others;

(g) maintaining the authority and impartiality of the judiciary; or

(h) the protection of the rights and freedoms of any person.

(4) Subject to paragraph (2) above, the Secretary of State may require that any visit, or class of visits, shall be held in facilities which include special features restricting or preventing physical contact between a prisoner and a visitor.

(5) Every visit to a prisoner shall take place within the sight of an officer or employee of the prison authorised for the purposes of this rule by the governor (in this rule referred to as an 'authorised employee'), unless the Secretary of State otherwise directs, and for the purposes of this paragraph a visit to a prisoner shall be taken to take place within the sight of an officer or authorised employee if it can be seen by an officer or authorised employee by means of an overt closed circuit television system.

(6) Subject to rule 38, every visit to a prisoner shall take place within the hearing of an officer or authorised employee, unless the Secretary of State otherwise directs.

(7) The Secretary of State may give directions, either generally or in relation to any visit or class of visits, concerning the day and times when prisoners may be visited.

(8) In this rule –

    (a) references to communications include references to communications during visits;

    (b) references to restrictions and conditions upon communications include references to restrictions and conditions in relation to the length, duration and frequency of communications; and

    (c) references to convention rights are to the convention rights within the meaning of the Human Rights Act 1998.

35. Personal letters and visits

(1) Subject to paragraph (8), an unconvicted prisoner may send and receive as many letters and may receive as many visits as he wishes within such limits and subject to such conditions as the Secretary of State may direct, either generally or in a particular case.

(2) Subject to paragraphs (2A) and (8), a convicted prisoner shall be entitled –

    (a) to send and to receive a letter on his reception into a prison and thereafter once a week; and

    (b) to receive a visit twice in every period of four weeks, but only once in every such period if the Secretary of State so directs.

(2A) A prisoner serving a sentence of imprisonment to which an intermittent custody order relates shall be entitled to receive a visit only where the governor considers that desirable having regard to the extent to which he has been unable to meet with his friends and family in the periods during which he has been temporarily released on licence.

(3) The governor may allow a prisoner an additional letter or visit as a privilege under rule 8 or where necessary for his welfare or that of his family.

(4) The governor may allow a prisoner entitled to a visit to send and to receive a letter instead.

(5) The governor may defer the right of a prisoner to a visit until the expiration of any period of cellular confinement.

(6) The independent monitoring board may allow a prisoner an additional letter or visit in special circumstances, and may direct that a visit may extend beyond the normal duration.

(7) The Secretary of State may allow additional letters and visits in relation to any prisoner or class of prisoners.

(8) A prisoner shall not be entitled under this rule to receive a visit from:
  (a) any person, whether or not a relative or friend, during any period of time that person is the subject of a prohibition imposed under rule 73; or
  (b) any other person, other than a relative or friend, except with the leave of the Secretary of State.

(9) Any letter or visit under the succeeding provisions of these Rules shall not be counted as a letter or visit for the purposes of this rule.

35A. Interception of communications

(1) The Secretary of State may give directions to any governor concerning the interception in a prison of any communication by any prisoner or class of prisoners if the Secretary of State considers that the directions are –
  (a) necessary on grounds specified in paragraph (4) below; and
  (b) proportionate to what is sought to be achieved.

(2) Subject to any directions given by the Secretary of State, the governor may make arrangements for any communication by a prisoner or class of prisoners to be intercepted in a prison by an officer or an employee of the prison authorised by the governor for the purposes of this rule (referred to in this rule as an 'authorised employee') if he considers that the arrangements are –
  (a) necessary on grounds specified in paragraph (4) below; and
  (b) proportionate to what is sought to be achieved.

(2A) The governor may not make arrangements for interception of any communication between a prisoner and
  (a) the prisoner's legal adviser; or
  (b) any body or organisation with which the Secretary of State has made arrangements for the confidential handling of correspondence, unless the governor has reasonable cause to believe that the communication is being made with the intention of furthering a criminal purpose and unless authorised by the chief operating officer of the prison service.

(3) Any communication by a prisoner may, during the course of its transmission in a prison, be terminated by an officer or an authorised employee if he considers that to terminate the communication is –

    (a) necessary on grounds specified in paragraph (4) below; and

    (b) proportionate to what is sought to be achieved by the termination.

(4) The grounds referred to in paragraphs (1)(a), (2)(a) and (3)(a) above are –

    (a) the interests of national security;

    (b) the prevention, detection, investigation or prosecution of crime;

    (c) the interests of public safety;

    (d) securing or maintaining prison security or good order and discipline in prison;

    (e) the protection of health or morals; or

    (f) the protection of the rights and freedoms of any person.

(5) Any reference to the grounds specified in paragraph (4) above in relation to the interception of a communication by means of a telecommunications system in a prison, or the disclosure or retention of intercepted material from such a communication, shall be taken to be a reference to those grounds with the omission of sub-paragraph (f).

(6) For the purposes of this rule 'interception'–

    (a) in relation to a communication by means of a telecommunications system, means any action taken in relation to the system or its operation so as to make some or all of the contents of the communications available, while being transmitted, to a person other than the sender or intended recipient of the communication; and the contents of a communication are to be taken to be made available to a person while being transmitted where the contents of the communication, while being transmitted, are diverted or recorded so as to be available to a person subsequently; and

    (b) in relation to any written or drawn communication, includes opening, reading, examining and copying the communication.

35B. Permanent log of communications

(1) The governor may arrange for a permanent log to be kept of all communications by or to a prisoner.

(2) The log referred to in paragraph (1) above may include, in relation to a communication by means of a telecommunications system in a prison, a record of the destination, duration and cost of the communication and, in relation to any written or drawn

Appendix 1

communication, a record of the sender and addressee of the communication.

35C. Disclosure of material

The governor may not disclose to any person who is not an officer of a prison or of the Secretary of State or an employee of the prison authorised by the governor for the purposes of this rule any intercepted material, information retained pursuant to rule 35B or material obtained by means of an overt closed circuit television system used during a visit unless –

- (a) he considers that such disclosure is –
  - (i) necessary on grounds specified in rule 35A(4); and
  - (ii) proportionate to what is sought to be achieved by the disclosure; or
- (b)
  - (i) in the case of intercepted material or material obtained by means of an overt closed circuit television system used during a visit, all parties to the communication or visit consent to the disclosure; or
  - (ii) in the case of information retained pursuant to rule 35B, the prisoner to whose communication the information relates, consents to the disclosure.

35D. Retention of material

(1) The governor shall not retain any intercepted material or material obtained by means of an overt closed circuit television system used during a visit for a period longer than 3 months beginning with the day on which the material was intercepted or obtained unless he is satisfied that continued retention of it is –
  - (a) necessary on grounds specified in rule 35A(4); and
  - (b) proportionate to what is sought to be achieved by the continued retention.
(2) Where such material is retained for longer than 3 months pursuant to paragraph (1) above the governor shall review its continued retention at periodic intervals until such time as it is no longer held by the governor.
(3) The first review referred to in paragraph (2) above shall take place not more than 3 months after the decision to retain the material taken pursuant to paragraph (1) above, and subsequent reviews shall take place not more than 3 months apart thereafter.
(4) If the governor, on a review conducted pursuant to paragraph (2) above or at any other time, is not satisfied that the continued retention of the material satisfies the requirements set out in paragraph (1) above, he shall arrange for the material to be destroyed.

356

36. Police interviews

A police officer may, on production of an order issued by or on behalf of a chief officer of police, interview any prisoner willing to see him.

37. Securing release

A person detained in prison in default of finding a surety, or of payment of a sum of money, may communicate with and be visited at any reasonable time on a weekday by any relative or friend to arrange for a surety or payment in order to secure his release from prison.

38. Visits from legal advisers

(1) Where the legal adviser of a prisoner in any legal proceedings, civil or criminal, to which the prisoner is a party visits the prisoner, the legal adviser shall be afforded reasonable facilities for interviewing him in connection with those proceedings, and may do so out of hearing but in the sight of an officer.

(2) On such a visit, a prisoner's legal adviser may, subject to any directions given by the Secretary of State, interview the prisoner in connection with any other legal business out of hearing but in the sight of an officer.

39. Delivery and receipt of legally privileged material

(1) A prisoner may deliver to, or receive from, the prisoner's legal adviser and any court, either by post or during a legal visit under rule 38, any legally privileged material and such material may only be opened, read or stopped by the governor in accordance with the provisions of this rule.

(2) Material to which this rule applies may be opened if the governor has reasonable cause to believe that it contains an illicit enclosure and any such enclosures shall be dealt with in accordance with the other provision of these Rules.

(3) Material to which this rule applies may be opened, read and stopped if the governor has reasonable cause to believe its contents endanger prison security or the safety of others or are otherwise of a criminal nature.

(4) A prisoner shall be given the opportunity to be present when any material to which this rule applies is opened and shall be informed if it or any enclosure is to be read or stopped.

(5) A prisoner shall on request be provided with any writing materials necessary for the purposes of paragraph (1).

(6) In this rule, 'court' includes the European Commission of Human Rights, the European Court of Human Rights and the European Court of Justice; and 'illicit enclosure' includes any article possession of which has not been authorised in accordance with the other provisions of these Rules and any material to or from a person other than the prisoner concerned, his legal adviser or a court.

Appendix 1

REMOVAL, SEARCH, RECORD AND PROPERTY

40. Custody outside prison

(1) A person being taken to or from a prison in custody shall be exposed as little as possible to public observation, and proper care shall be taken to protect him from curiosity and insult.

(2) A prisoner required to be taken in custody anywhere outside a prison shall be kept in the custody of an officer appointed or a police officer.

(3) A prisoner required to be taken in custody to any court shall, when he appears before the court, wear his own clothing or ordinary civilian clothing provided by the governor.

41. Search

(1) Every prisoner shall be searched when taken into custody by an officer, on his reception into a prison and subsequently as the governor thinks necessary or as the Secretary of State may direct.

(2) A prisoner shall be searched in as seemly a manner as is consistent with discovering anything concealed.

(3) No prisoner shall be stripped and searched in the sight of another prisoner, or in the sight of a person of the opposite sex.

42. Record and photograph

(1) A personal record of each prisoner shall be prepared and maintained in such manner as the Secretary of State may direct.

(2) Every prisoner may be photographed on reception and subsequently, but no copy of the photograph or any other personal record shall be given to any person not authorised to receive it.

(2A) In this rule 'personal record' may include personal information and biometric records (such as fingerprints or other physical measurements).

43. Prisoners' property

(1) Subject to any directions of the Secretary of State, an unconvicted prisoner may have supplied to him at his expense and retain for his own use books, newspapers, writing materials and other means of occupation, except any that appears objectionable to the independent monitoring board or, pending consideration by them, to the governor.

(2) Anything, other than cash, which a prisoner has at a prison and which he is not allowed to retain for his own use shall be taken into the governor's custody. An inventory of a prisoner's property shall be kept, and he shall be required to sign it, after having a proper opportunity to see that it is correct.

(2A) Where a prisoner is serving a sentence of imprisonment to which an intermittent custody order relates, an inventory as referred to in paragraph (2) shall only be kept where the value of that property is estimated by the governor to be in excess of £100.

(3) Any cash which a prisoner has at a prison shall be paid into an account under the control of the governor and the prisoner shall be credited with the amount in the books of the prison.

(4) Any article belonging to a prisoner which remains unclaimed for a period of more than one year after he leaves prison, or dies, may be sold or otherwise disposed of; and the net proceeds of any sale shall be paid to the National Association for the Care and Resettlement of Offenders, for its general purposes.

(5) The governor may confiscate any unauthorised article found in the possession of a prisoner after his reception into prison, or concealed or deposited anywhere within a prison.

44. Money and articles received by post

(1) Any money or other article (other than a letter or other communication) sent to a convicted prisoner through the post office shall be dealt with in accordance with the provisions of this rule, and the prisoner shall be informed of the manner in which it is dealt with.

(2) Any cash shall, at the discretion of the governor, be –
  (a) dealt with in accordance with rule 43(3);
  (b) returned to the sender; or
  (c) in a case where the sender's name and address are not known, paid to the National Association for the Care and Resettlement of Offenders, for its general purposes:

Provided that in relation to a prisoner committed to prison in default of payment of any sum of money, the prisoner shall be informed of the receipt of the cash and, unless he objects to its being so applied, it shall be applied in or towards the satisfaction of the amount due from him.

(3) Any security for money shall, at the discretion of the governor, be –
  (a) delivered to the prisoner or placed with his property at the prison;
  (b) returned to the sender; or
  (c) encashed and the cash dealt with in accordance with paragraph (2).

(4) Any other article to which this rule applies shall, at the discretion of the governor, be –
  (a) delivered to the prisoner or placed with his property at the prison;
  (b) returned to the sender; or

   (c) in a case where the sender's name and address are not known or the article is of such a nature that it would be unreasonable to return it, sold or otherwise disposed of, and the net proceeds of any sale applied in accordance with paragraph (2).

SPECIAL CONTROL, SUPERVISION AND RESTRAINT AND DRUG TESTING

45. Removal from association

(1) Where it appears desirable, for the maintenance of good order or discipline or in his own interests, that a prisoner should not associate with other prisoners, either generally or for particular purposes, the governor may arrange for the prisoner's removal from association accordingly.

(2) A prisoner shall not be removed under this rule for a period of more than 72 hours without the authority of the Secretary of State and authority given under this paragraph shall be for a period not exceeding 14 days but it may be renewed from time to time for a like period.

(3) The governor may arrange at his discretion for a prisoner removed under this rule to resume association with other prisoners at any time, and in exercising that discretion the governor must fully consider any recommendation that the prisoner resumes association on medical grounds made by a registered medical practitioner or registered nurse working within the prison.

(4) This rule shall not apply to a prisoner the subject of a direction given under rule 46(1).

46. Close supervision centres

(1) Where it appears desirable, for the maintenance of good order or discipline or to ensure the safety of officers, prisoners or any other person, that a prisoner should not associate with other prisoners, either generally or for particular purposes, the Secretary of State may direct the prisoner's removal from association accordingly and his placement in a close supervision centre of a prison.

(2) A direction given under paragraph (1) shall be for a period not exceeding one month, but may be renewed from time to time for a like period, and shall continue to apply notwithstanding any transfer of a prisoner from one prison to another.

(3) The Secretary of State may direct that such a prisoner as aforesaid shall resume association with other prisoners, either within a close supervision centre or elsewhere.

(4) In exercising any discretion under this rule, the Secretary of State shall take account of any relevant medical considerations which are known to him.

(5) A close supervision centre is any cell or other part of a prison designated by the Secretary of State for holding prisoners who are subject to a direction given under paragraph (1).

47. Use of force

(1) An officer in dealing with a prisoner shall not use force unnecessarily and, when the application of force to a prisoner is necessary, no more force than is necessary shall be used.

(2) No officer shall act deliberately in a manner calculated to provoke a prisoner.

48. Temporary confinement

(1) The governor may order a refractory or violent prisoner to be confined temporarily in a special cell, but a prisoner shall not be so confined as a punishment, or after he has ceased to be refractory or violent.

(2) A prisoner shall not be confined in a special cell for longer than 24 hours without a direction in writing given by an officer of the Secretary of State. Such a direction shall state the grounds for the confinement and the time during which it may continue.

49. Restraints

(1) The governor may order a prisoner to be put under restraint where this is necessary to prevent the prisoner from injuring himself or others, damaging property or creating a disturbance.

(2) Notice of such an order shall be given without delay to a member of the independent monitoring board, and to a registered medical practitioner or to a registered nurse working within the prison.

(3) On receipt of the notice, the registered medical practitioner or registered nurse referred to in paragraph (2), shall inform the governor whether there are any medical reasons why the prisoner should not be put under restraint. The governor shall give effect to any recommendation which may be made under this paragraph.

(4) A prisoner shall not be kept under restraint longer than necessary, nor shall he be so kept for longer than 24 hours without a direction in writing given by an officer of the Secretary of State (not being an officer of a prison). Such a direction shall state the grounds for the restraint and the time during which it may continue.

(5) Particulars of every case of restraint under the foregoing provisions of this rule shall be forthwith recorded.

(6) Except as provided by this rule no prisoner shall be put under restraint otherwise than for safe custody during removal, or on

medical grounds by direction of a registered medical practitioner or of a registered nurse working within the prison. No prisoner shall be put under restraint as a punishment.

(7) Any means of restraint shall be of a pattern authorised by the Secretary of State, and shall be used in such manner and under such conditions as the Secretary of State may direct.

50. Compulsory testing for controlled drugs

(1) This rule applies where an officer, acting under the powers conferred by section 16A of the Prison Act 1952 (power to test prisoners for drugs), requires a prisoner to provide a sample for the purpose of ascertaining whether he has any controlled drug in his body.

(2) In this rule 'sample' means a sample of urine or any other description of sample specified in the authorisation by the governor for the purposes of section 16A of the Prison Act 1952.

(3) When requiring a prisoner to provide a sample, an officer shall, so far as is reasonably practicable, inform the prisoner:
   (a) that he is being required to provide a sample in accordance with section 16A of the Prison Act 1952; and
   (b) that a refusal to provide a sample may lead to disciplinary proceedings being brought against him.

(4) An officer shall require a prisoner to provide a fresh sample, free from any adulteration.

(5) An officer requiring a sample shall make such arrangements and give the prisoner such instructions for its provision as may be reasonably necessary in order to prevent or detect its adulteration or falsification.

(6) A prisoner who is required to provide a sample may be kept apart from other prisoners for a period not exceeding one hour to enable arrangements to be made for the provision of the sample.

(7) A prisoner who is unable to provide a sample of urine when required to do so may be kept apart from other prisoners until he has provided the required sample, save that a prisoner may not be kept apart under this paragraph for a period of more than 5 hours.

(8) A prisoner required to provide a sample of urine shall be afforded such degree of privacy for the purposes of providing the sample as may be compatible with the need to prevent or detect any adulteration or falsification of the sample; in particular a prisoner shall not be required to provide such a sample in the sight of a person of the opposite sex.

50A. Observation of prisoners by means of an overt closed circuit television system

(1) Without prejudice to his other powers to supervise the prison, prisoners and other persons in the prison, whether by use of an overt closed circuit television system or otherwise, the governor may make arrangements for any prisoner to be placed under constant observation by means of an overt closed circuit television system while the prisoner is in a cell or other place in the prison if he considers that -

  (a) such supervision is necessary for –
    (i) the health and safety of the prisoner or any other person;
    (ii) the prevention, detection, investigation or prosecution of crime; or
    (iii) securing or maintaining prison security or good order and discipline in the prison; and
  (b) it is proportionate to what is sought to be achieved.

(2) If an overt closed circuit television system is used for the purposes of this rule, the provisions of rules 35C and 35D shall apply to any material obtained.

50B. Compulsory testing for alcohol

(1) This rule applies where an officer, acting under an authorisation in force under section 16B of the Prison Act 1952 (power to test prisoners or alcohol), requires a prisoner to provide a sample for the purpose of ascertaining whether he has alcohol in his body.

(2) When requiring a prisoner to provide a sample an officer shall, so far as is reasonably practicable, inform the prisoner –
  (a) that he is being required to provide a sample in accordance with section 16B of the Prison Act 1952; and
  (b) that a refusal to provide a sample may lead to disciplinary proceedings being brought against him.

(3) An officer requiring a sample shall make such arrangements and give the prisoner such instructions for its provision as may be reasonably necessary in order to prevent or detect its adulteration or falsification.

(4) Subject to paragraph (5) a prisoner who is required to provide a sample may be kept apart from other prisoners for a period not exceeding one hour to enable arrangements to be made for the provision of the sample.

(5) A prisoner who is unable to provide a sample of urine when required to do so may be kept apart from other prisoners until he has provided the required sample, except that a prisoner may not be kept apart under this paragraph for a period of more than 5 hours.

Appendix 1

(6) A prisoner required to provide a sample of urine shall be afforded such degree of privacy for the purposes of providing the sample as may be compatible with the need to prevent or detect any adulteration or falsification of the sample; in particular a prisoner shall not be required to provide such a sample in the sight of a person of the opposite sex.

OFFENCES AGAINST DISCIPLINE

51. Offences against discipline

A prisoner is guilty of an offence against discipline if he –

(1) commits any assault;

(1A) commits any racially aggravated assault;

(2) detains any person against his will;

(3) denies access to any part of the prison to any officer or any person (other than a prisoner) who is at the prison for the purpose of working there;

(4) fights with any person;

(5) intentionally endangers the health or personal safety of others or, by his conduct, is reckless whether such health or personal safety is endangered;

(6) intentionally obstructs an officer in the execution of his duty, or any person (other than a prisoner) who is at the prison for the purpose of working there, in the performance of his work;

(7) escapes or absconds from prison or from legal custody;

(8) fails to comply with any condition upon which he is temporarily released under rule 9;

(9) is found with any substance in his urine which demonstrates that a controlled drug has, whether in prison or while on temporary release under rule 9, been administered to him by himself or by another person (but subject to rule 52);

(10) is intoxicated as a consequence of consuming any alcoholic beverage (but subject to rule 52A);

(11) consumes any alcoholic beverage whether or not provided to him by another person (but subject to rule 52A);

(12) has in his possession –
    (a) any unauthorised article, or
    (b) a greater quantity of any article than he is authorised to have;

(13) sells or delivers to any person any unauthorised article;

(14) sells or, without permission, delivers to any person any article which he is allowed to have only for his own use;

(15) takes improperly any article belonging to another person or to a prison;

(16) intentionally or recklessly sets fire to any part of a prison or any other property, whether or not his own;

(17) destroys or damages any part of a prison or any other property, other than his own;

(17A) causes racially aggravated damage to, or destruction of, any part of a prison or any other property, other than his own;

(18) absents himself from any place he is required to be or is present at any place where he is not authorised to be;

(19) is disrespectful to any officer, or any person (other than a prisoner) who is at the prison for the purpose of working there, or any person visiting a prison;

(20) uses threatening, abusive or insulting words or behaviour;

(20A) uses threatening, abusive or insulting racist words or behaviour;

(21) intentionally fails to work properly or, being required to work, refuses to do so;

(22) disobeys any lawful order;

(23) disobeys or fails to comply with any rule or regulation applying to him;

(24) receives any controlled drug, or, without the consent of an officer, any other article, during the course of a visit (not being an interview such as is mentioned in rule 38);

(24A) displays, attaches or draws on any part of a prison, or on any other property, threatening, abusive or insulting racist words, drawings, symbols or other material;

(25)

    (a) attempts to commit,

    (b) incites another prisoner to commit, or

    (c) assists another prisoner to commit or to attempt to commit, any of the foregoing offences.

51A. Interpretation of rule 51

(2) For the purposes of rule 51 words, behaviour or material are racist if they demonstrate, or are motivated (wholly or partly) by, hostility to members of a racial group (whether identifiable or not) based on their membership (or presumed membership) of a racial group, and 'membership', 'presumed', 'racial group' and 'racially aggravated' shall have the meanings assigned to them by section 28 of the Crime and Disorder Act 1998(a).

52. Defences to rule 51(9)

It shall be a defence for a prisoner charged with an offence under rule 51(9) to show that:

    (a) the controlled drug had been, prior to its administration, lawfully in his possession for his use or was administered to him in the course of a lawful supply of the drug to him by another person;

    (b) the controlled drug was administered by or to him in circumstances in which he did not know and had no reason to suspect that such a drug was being administered; or

    (c) the controlled drug was administered by or to him under duress or to him without his consent in circumstances where it was not reasonable for him to have resisted.

52A. Defences to rule 51(10) and rule 51(11)

It shall be a defence for a prisoner charged with an offence under rule 51(10) or (11) to show that –

    (a) the alcohol was consumed by him in circumstances in which he did not know and had no reason to suspect that he was consuming alcohol;

    (b) the alcohol was consumed by him without his consent in circumstances where it was not reasonable for him to have resisted.

53. Disciplinary charges

(1) Where a prisoner is to be charged with an offence against discipline, the charge shall be laid as soon as possible and, save in exceptional circumstances, within 48 hours of the discovery of the offence.

(2) Every charge shall be inquired into by the governor or, as the case may be, the adjudicator.

(3) Every charge shall be first inquired into not later, save in exceptional circumstances or in accordance with rule 55A(5), than:

    (a) where it is inquired into by the governor, the next day, not being a Sunday or public holiday, after it is laid;

    (b) where it is referred to the adjudicator under rule 53A(2), 28 days after it is so referred.

(4) A prisoner who is to be charged with an offence against discipline may be kept apart from other prisoners pending the governor's first inquiry or determination under rule 53A.

53A. Determination of mode of inquiry

(1) Before inquiring into a charge the governor shall determine whether it is so serious that additional days should be awarded for the offence, if the prisoner is found guilty.

(2) Where the governor determines:

    (a) that it is so serious, he shall:

       (i) refer the charge to the adjudicator forthwith for him to inquire into it;

      (ii) refer any other charge arising out of the same incident to the adjudicator forthwith for him to inquire into it; and

(iii) inform the prisoner who has been charged that he has done so;

(b) that it is not so serious, he shall proceed to inquire into the charge.

(3) If:

(a) at any time during an inquiry into a charge by the governor; or

(b) following such an inquiry, after the governor has found the prisoner guilty of an offence but before he has imposed a punishment for that offence, it appears to the governor that the charge is so serious that additional days should be awarded for the offence if (where sub-paragraph (a)) the prisoner is found guilty, the governor shall act in accordance with paragraph (2)(a)(i) to (iii) and the adjudicator shall first inquire into any charge referred to him under this paragraph not later than, save in exceptional circumstances, 28 days after the charge was referred.

54. Rights of prisoners charged

(1) Where a prisoner is charged with an offence against discipline, he shall be informed of the charge as soon as possible and, in any case, before the time when it is inquired into by the governor or, as the case may be, the adjudicator.

(2) At an inquiry into a charge against a prisoner he shall be given a full opportunity of hearing what is alleged against him and of presenting his own case.

(3) At an inquiry into a charge which has been referred to the adjudicator, the prisoner who has been charged shall be given the opportunity to be legally represented.

55. Governor's punishments

(1) If he finds a prisoner guilty of an offence against discipline the governor may, subject to paragraph (2) and to rule 57, impose one or more of the following punishments:

(a) caution;

(b) forfeiture for a period not exceeding 42 days of any of the privileges under rule 8;

(c) exclusion from associated work for a period not exceeding 21 days;

(d) stoppage of or deduction from earnings for a period not exceeding 84 days;

(e) cellular confinement for a period not exceeding 21 days;

(f) [...] Revoked by Prison (Amendment) Rules 2002/2116 Sch.1 para.5(c) (August 15, 2002)

    (g) in the case of a prisoner otherwise entitled to them, forfeiture for any period of the right, under rule 43(1), to have the articles there mentioned.

    (h) removal from his wing or living unit for a period of 28 days.

(2) A caution shall not be combined with any other punishment for the same charge.

(3) If a prisoner is found guilty of more than one charge arising out of an incident, punishments under this rule may be ordered to run consecutively but, in the case of a punishment of cellular confinement, the total period shall not exceed 21 days.

(4) In imposing a punishment under this rule, the governor shall take into account any guidelines that the Secretary of State may from time to time issue as to the level of punishment that should normally be imposed for a particular offence against discipline.

55A. Adjudicator's punishments

(1) If he finds a prisoner guilty of an offence against discipline the adjudicator may, subject to paragraph (2) and to rule 57, impose one or more of the following punishments:

    (a) any of the punishments mentioned in rule 55(1);

    (b) in the case of a short-term prisoner or long-term prisoner or fixed-term prisoner, an award of additional days not exceeding 42 days.

(2) A caution shall not be combined with any other punishment for the same charge.

(3) If a prisoner is found guilty of more than one charge arising out of an incident, punishments under this rule may be ordered to run consecutively but, in the case of an award of additional days, the total period added shall not exceed 42 days and, in the case of a punishment of cellular confinement, the total period shall not exceed 21 days.

(4) This rule applies to a prisoner who has been charged with having committed an offence against discipline before the date on which the rule came into force, in the same way as it applies to a prisoner who has been charged with having committed an offence against discipline on or after that date, provided the charge is referred to the adjudicator no later than 60 days after that date.

(5) Rule 53(3) shall not apply to a charge where, by virtue of paragraph (4), this rule applies to the prisoner who has been charged.

55B. Review of adjudicator's punishment

(1) A reviewer means a Senior District Judge (Chief Magistrate) approved by the Lord Chancellor for the purposes of conducting a review under this rule or any deputy of such a judge as nominated by that judge.

(2) Where a punishment is imposed by an adjudicator under rule 55A(1), a prisoner may, within 14 days of receipt of the punishment, request in writing that a reviewer conducts a review.

(3) The review must be commenced within 14 days of receipt of the request and must be conducted on the papers alone.

(4) The review must only be of the punishment imposed and must not be a review of the finding of guilt under rule 55A.

(5) On completion of the review, if it appears to the reviewer that the punishment imposed was manifestly unreasonable he may –

   (a) reduce the number of any additional days awarded;
   (b) for whatever punishment has been imposed by the adjudicator, substitute another punishment which is, in his opinion, less severe; or
   (c) quash the punishment entirely.

(6) A prisoner requesting a review shall serve any additional days awarded under rule 55A(1)(b) unless and until they are reduced.

56. Forfeiture of remission to be treated as an award of additional days

(1) In this rule, 'existing prisoner' and 'existing licensee' have the meanings assigned to them by paragraph 8(1) of Schedule 12 to the Criminal Justice Act 1991.

(2) In relation to any existing prisoner or existing licensee who has forfeited any remission of his sentence, the provisions of Part II of the Criminal Justice Act 1991 shall apply as if he had been awarded such number of additional days as equals the numbers of days of remission which he has forfeited.

57. Offences committed by young persons

(1) In the case of an offence against discipline committed by an inmate who was under the age of 21 when the offence was committed (other than an offender in relation to whom the Secretary of State has given a direction under section 13(1) of the Criminal Justice Act 1982 that he shall be treated as if he had been sentenced to imprisonment) rule 55 or, as the case may be, rule 55A shall have effect, but –

   (a) the maximum period of forfeiture of privileges under rule 8 shall be 21 days;
   (b) the maximum period of stoppage of or deduction from earnings shall be 42 days;
   (c) the maximum period of cellular confinement shall be ten days
   (d) the maximum period of removal from his cell or living unit shall be 21 days.

(2) In the case of an inmate who has been sentenced to a term of youth custody or detention in a young offender institution, and

by virtue of a direction of the Secretary of State under section 99 of the Powers of Criminal Courts (Sentencing) Act 2000, is treated as if he had been sentenced to imprisonment for that term, any punishment imposed on him for an offence against discipline before the said direction was given shall, if it has not been exhausted or remitted, continue to have effect:

(a) if imposed by a governor, as if made pursuant to rule 55;

(b) if imposed by an adjudicator, as if made pursuant to rule 55A.

58. Cellular confinement

Before deciding whether to impose a punishment of cellular confinement the governor, adjudicator or reviewer shall first enquire of a registered medical practitioner or registered nurse working within the prison, as to whether there are any medical reasons why the punishment is unsuitable and shall take this advice into account when making his decision.

59. Prospective award of additional days

(1) Subject to paragraph (2), where an offence against discipline is committed by a prisoner who is detained only on remand, additional days may be awarded by the adjudicator notwithstanding that the prisoner has not (or had not at the time of the offence) been sentenced.

(2) An award of additional days under paragraph (1) shall have effect only if the prisoner in question subsequently becomes a short-term or long-term prisoner or fixed-term prisoner whose sentence is reduced, under section 67 of the Criminal Justice Act 1967 or section 240 of the 2003 Act, by a period which includes the time when the offence against discipline was committed.

59A. Removal from a cell or living unit

Following the imposition of a punishment of removal from his cell or living unit, a prisoner shall be accommodated in a separate part of the prison under such restrictions of earnings and activities as the Secretary of State may direct.

60. Suspended punishments

(1) Subject to any directions given by the Secretary of State, the power to impose a disciplinary punishment (other than a caution) shall include power to direct that the punishment is not to take effect unless, during a period specified in the direction (not being more than six months from the date of the direction), the prisoner commits another offence against discipline and a direction is given under paragraph (2).

(2) Where a prisoner commits an offence against discipline during the period specified in a direction given under paragraph (1) the person dealing with that offence may –
  (a) direct that the suspended punishment shall take effect;
  (b) reduce the period or amount of the suspended punishment and direct that it shall take effect as so reduced;
  (c) vary the original direction by substituting for the period specified a period expiring not later than six months from the date of variation; or
  (d) give no direction with respect to the suspended punishment.
(3) Where an award of additional days has been suspended under paragraph (1) and a prisoner is charged with committing an offence against discipline during the period specified in a direction given under that paragraph, the governor shall either:
  (a) inquire into the charge and give no direction with respect to the suspended award; or
  (b) refer the charge to the adjudicator for him to inquire into it.

61. Remission and mitigation of punishments and quashing of findings of guilt

(1) Except in the case of a finding of guilt made, or a punishment imposed, by an adjudicator under rule 55A(1), the Secretary of State may quash any finding of guilt and may remit any punishment or mitigate it either by reducing it or by substituting another award which is, in his opinion, less severe.
(2) Subject to any directions given by the Secretary of State, the governor may, on the grounds of good behaviour, remit or mitigate any punishment already imposed by an adjudicator or governor.

Part III Officers of Prisons

62. General duty of officers

(1) It shall be the duty of every officer to conform to these Rules and the rules and regulations of the prison, to assist and support the governor in their maintenance and to obey his lawful instructions.
(2) An officer shall inform the governor promptly of any abuse or impropriety which comes to his knowledge.

63. Gratuities forbidden

No officer shall receive any unauthorised fee, gratuity or other consideration in connection with his office.

Appendix 1

64. Search of officers

An officer shall submit himself to be searched in the prison if the governor so directs.

Any such search shall be conducted in as seemly a manner as is consistent with discovering anything concealed.

65. Transactions with prisoners

(1) No officer shall take part in any business or pecuniary transaction with or on behalf of a prisoner without the leave of the Secretary of State.
(2) No officer shall without authority bring in or take out, or attempt to bring in or take out, or knowingly allow to be brought in or taken out, to or for a prisoner, or deposit in any place with intent that it shall come into the possession of a prisoner, any article whatsoever.

66. Contact with former prisoners

No officer shall, without the knowledge of the governor, communicate with any person whom he knows to be a former prisoner or a relative or friend of a prisoner or former prisoner.

67. Communications to the press

(1) No officer shall make, directly or indirectly, any unauthorised communication to a representative of the press or any other person concerning matters which have become known to him in the course of his duty.
(2) No officer shall, without authority, publish any matter or make any public pronouncement relating to the administration of any institution to which the Prison Act 1952 applies or to any of its inmates.

68. Code of discipline

The Secretary of State may approve a code of discipline to have effect in relation to officers, or such classes of officers as it may specify, setting out the offences against discipline, the awards which may be made in respect of them and the procedure for dealing with charges.

69. Emergencies

Where any constable or member of the armed forces of the Crown is employed by reason of any emergency to assist the governor of a prison by performing duties ordinarily performed by an officer of a prison, any reference in Part II of these Rules to such an officer (other than a governor) shall be construed as including a reference to a constable or a member of the armed forces of the Crown so employed.

Part IV Persons Having Access to a Prison

70. Prohibited articles

No person shall, without authority, convey into or throw into or deposit in a prison, or convey or throw out of a prison, or convey to a prisoner, or deposit in any place with intent that it shall come into the possession of a prisoner, any article whatever. Anything so conveyed, thrown or deposited may be confiscated by the governor.

70A. List C Articles

A List C article is any article or substance in the following list—

(a) tobacco;

(b) money;

(c) clothing;

(d) food;

(e) drink;

(f) letters;

(g) paper;

(h) books;

(i) tools;

(j) information technology equipment.

71. Control of persons and vehicles

(1) Any person or vehicle entering or leaving a prison may be stopped, examined and searched and in addition any such person may be photographed, fingerprinted or required to submit to other physical measurement.

(1A) Any such search of a person shall be carried out in as seemly a manner as is consistent with discovering anything concealed about the person or their belongings.

(2) The governor may direct the removal from a prison of any person who does not leave on being required to do so.

72. Viewing of prisons

(1) No outside person shall be permitted to view a prison unless authorised by statute or the Secretary of State.

(2) No person viewing the prison shall be permitted to take a photograph, make a sketch or communicate with a prisoner unless authorised by statute or the Secretary of State.

73. Visitors

(1) Without prejudice to any other powers to prohibit or restrict entry to prisons, or his powers under rules 34 and 35, the Secretary of State may prohibit visits by a person to a prison or to a prisoner in a prison for such periods of time as he considers necessary if the Secretary of State considers that such a prohibition is –
   (a) necessary on grounds specified in rule 35A(4); and
   (b) is proportionate to what is sought to be achieved by the prohibition.

(2) Paragraph (1) shall not apply in relation to any visit to a prison or prisoner by a member of the independent monitoring board of the prison, or justice of the peace, or to prevent any visit by a legal adviser for the purposes of an interview under rule 38 or visit allowed by the board of visitors under rule 35(6).

Part V Independent Monitoring Board

74. Disqualification for membership

Any person, directly or indirectly interested in any contract for the supply of goods or services to a prison, shall not be a member of the independent monitoring board for that prison and any member who becomes so interested in such a contract shall vacate office as a member.

75. Independent monitoring board

(1) A member of the board of visitors for a prison appointed by the Secretary of State under section 6(2) of the Prison Act 1952 shall subject to paragraphs (3) and (4) hold office for three years, or such lesser period as the Secretary of State may appoint.

(2) A member –
   (a) appointed for the first time to the independent monitoring board for a particular prison; or
   (b) reappointed to the board following a gap of a year or more in his membership of it,

   shall, during the period of 12 months following the date on which he is so appointed or (as the case may be) reappointed, undertake such training as may reasonably be required by the Secretary of State.

(3) The Secretary of State may terminate the appointment of a member if he is satisfied that –
   (a) he has failed satisfactorily to perform his duties;
   (b) he has failed to undertake training he has been required to undertake under paragraph (2), by the end of the period specified in that paragraph;

(c) he is by reason of physical or mental illness, or for any other reason, incapable of carrying out his duties;

(d) he has been convicted of such a criminal offence, or his conduct has been such, that it is not in the Secretary of State's opinion fitting that he should remain a member; or

(e) there is, or appears to be or could appear to be, any conflict of interest between the member performing his duties as a member and any interest of that member, whether personal, financial or otherwise.

(4) Where the Secretary of State:

(a) has reason to suspect that a member of the independent monitoring board for a prison may have so conducted himself that his appointment may be liable to be terminated under paragraph (3)(a) or (d); and

(b) is of the opinion that the suspected conduct is of such a serious nature that the member cannot be permitted to continue to perform his functions as a member of the board pending the completion of the Secretary of State's investigations into the matter and any decision as to whether the member's appointment should be terminated, he may suspend the member from office for such period or periods as he may reasonably require in order to complete his investigations and determine whether or not the appointment of the member should be so terminated; and a member so suspended shall not, during the period of his suspension, be regarded as being a member of the board, other than for the purposes of this paragraph and paragraphs (1) and (3).

(5) A board shall have a chairman and a vice chairman who shall be members of the board.

(6) The Secretary of State shall –

(a) upon the constitution of a board for the first time, appoint a chairman and a vice chairman to hold office for a period not exceeding twelve months;

(b) thereafter appoint, before the date of the first meeting of the board in any year of office of the board, a chairman and vice chairman for that year, having first consulted the board; and

(c) promptly fill, after first having consulted the board, any casual vacancy in the office of chairman or vice chairman.

(7) The Secretary of State may terminate the appointment of a member as chairman or vice chairman of the board if he is satisfied that the member has –

(a) failed satisfactorily to perform his functions as chairman (or as the case may be) vice chairman;

(b) has grossly misconducted himself while performing those functions.

76. Proceedings of boards

(1) The independent monitoring board for a prison shall meet at the prison once a month or, if they resolve for reasons specified in the resolution that less frequent meetings are sufficient, not fewer than eight times in twelve months.

(2) The board may fix a quorum of not fewer than three members for proceedings.

(3) The board shall keep minutes of their proceedings.

(4) The proceedings of the board shall not be invalidated by any vacancy in the membership or any defect in the appointment of a member.

77. General duties of boards

(1) The independent monitoring board for a prison shall satisfy themselves as to the state of the prison premises, the administration of the prison and the treatment of the prisoners.

(2) The board shall inquire into and report upon any matter into which the Secretary of State asks them to inquire.

(3) The board shall direct the attention of the governor to any matter which calls for his attention, and shall report to the Secretary of State any matter which they consider it expedient to report.

(4) The board shall inform the Secretary of State immediately of any abuse which comes to their knowledge.

(5) Before exercising any power under these Rules the board and any member of the board shall consult the governor in relation to any matter which may affect discipline.

78. Particular duties

(1) The independent monitoring board for a prison and any member of the board shall hear any complaint or request which a prisoner wishes to make to them or him.

(2) The board shall arrange for the food of the prisoners to be inspected by a member of the board at frequent intervals.

(3) The board shall inquire into any report made to them, whether or not by a member of the board, that a prisoner's health, mental or physical, is likely to be injuriously affected by any conditions of his imprisonment.

79. Members visiting prisons

(1) The members of the independent monitoring board for a prison shall visit the prison frequently, and the board shall arrange a rota whereby at least one of its members visits the prison between meetings of the board.

(2) A member of the board shall have access at any time to every part of the prison and to every prisoner, and he may interview any prisoner out of the sight and hearing of officers.

(3) A member of the board shall have access to the records of the prison, except that members of the board shall not have access to any records held for the purposes of or relating to conduct authorised in accordance with Part 2 of the Regulation of Investigatory Powers Act 2000.

80. Annual report

(1) The independent monitoring board for a prison shall, in accordance with paragraphs (2) and (3) below, from time to time make a report to the Secretary of State concerning the state of the prison and its administration, including in it any advice and suggestions they consider appropriate.

(2) The board shall comply with any directions given to them from time to time by the Secretary of State as to the following matters:
    (a) the period to be covered by a report under paragraph (1);
    (b) the frequency with which such a report is to be made; and
    (c) the length of time from the end of the period covered by such a report within which it is to be made; either in respect of a particular report or generally; providing that no directions may be issued under this paragraph if they would have the effect of requiring a board to make or deliver a report less frequently than once in every 12 months.

(3) Subject to any directions given to them under paragraph (2), the board shall, under paragraph (1), make an annual report to the Secretary of State as soon as reasonably possible after 31st December each year, which shall cover the period of 12 months ending on that date or, in the case of a board constituted for the first time during that period, such part of that period during which the board has been in existence.

Part VI Supplemental

81. Delegation by governor

The governor of a prison may, with the leave of the Secretary of State, delegate any of his powers and duties under these Rules to another officer of that prison.

82. Contracted out prisons

(1) Where the Secretary of State has entered into a contract for the running of a prison under section 84 of the Criminal Justice Act 1991 ('the 1991 Act') these Rules shall have effect in relation to that prison with the following modifications –

    (a) references to an officer in the Rules shall include references to a prisoner custody officer certified as such under section 89(1) of the 1991 Act and performing custodial duties;

    (b) references to a governor in the Rules shall include references to a director approved by the Secretary of State for the purposes of section 85(1)(a) of the 1991 Act except –

        (i) in rule 81 the reference to a governor shall include a reference to a controller appointed by the Secretary of State under section 85(1)(b) of the 1991 Act; and

        (ii) in rules 62(1), 66 and 77 where references to a governor shall include references to the director and the controller;

        (iii) in rules 45, 48, 49, 53, 53A, 54, 55, 57, 60 and 61 where references to a governor shall include a reference to the director or the controller;

    (c) rule 68 shall not apply in relation to a prisoner custody officer certified as such under section 89(1) of the 1991 Act and performing custodial duties.

(1A) The director of a prison may, with the leave of the Secretary of State, delegate any of his powers and duties under rules 45, 48, 49, 53, 53A, 55, 57, 60 and 61 to another officer of that prison.

83. Contracted out parts of prisons

Where the Secretary of State has entered into a contract for the running of part of a prison under section 84(1) of the Criminal Justice Act 1991, that part and the remaining part shall each be treated for the purposes of Parts II to IV and Part VI of these Rules as if they were separate prisons.

84. Contracted out functions at directly managed prisons

(1) Where the Secretary of State has entered into a contract under section 88A(1) of the Criminal Justice Act 1991 ('the 1991 Act') for any functions at a directly managed prison to be performed by prisoner custody officers who are authorised to perform custodial duties under section 89(1) of the 1991 Act, references to an officer in these Rules shall, subject to paragraph (2), include references to a prisoner custody officer who is so authorised and who is performing contracted out functions for the purposes of, or for purposes connected with, the prison.

(2) Paragraph (1) shall not apply to references to an officer in rule 68.

(3) In this rule, 'directly managed prison' has the meaning assigned to it by section 88A(5) of the 1991 Act.

85. Revocations and savings

(1) Subject to paragraphs (2) and (3) below, the Rules specified in the Schedule to these Rules are hereby revoked.

(2) Without prejudice to the Interpretation Act 1978, where a prisoner committed an offence against discipline contrary to rule 47 of the Prison Rules 1964 prior to the coming into force of these Rules, those rules shall continue to have effect to permit the prisoner to be charged with such an offence, disciplinary proceedings in relation to such an offence to be continued, and the governor to impose punishment for such an offence.

(3) Without prejudice to the Interpretation Act 1978, any award of additional days or other punishment or suspended punishment for an offence against discipline awarded or imposed under any provision of the rules revoked by this rule, or those rules as saved by paragraph (2), or treated by any such provision as having been awarded or imposed under the rules revoked by this rule, shall have effect as if awarded or imposed under the corresponding provision of these Rules.

Jack Straw
One of Her Majesty's Principal Secretaries of State
Home Office

10th March 1999

Appendix 2

The Young Offender Institution Rules 2000
SI 2000 No. 3371

Original rules came into force 1st April 2001. Latest amendment came into force 1st January 2010.

ARRANGEMENT OF RULES

Part III Officers of Young Offender Institutions

Part IV Persons Having Access to a Young Offender Institution

Part V Independent Monitoring Board

Part VI Supplemental

Schedule: Revocations Explanatory Note

In pursuance of section 47 of the Prison Act 1952 I hereby make the following Rules:

Part I Preliminary

1. Citation and commencement

(a) These Rules may be cited as the Young Offender Institution Rules 2000 and shall come into force on 1st April 2001.

(b) The Rules set out in the Schedule to this Order are hereby revoked.

2. Interpretation

(1) In these Rules, where the context so admits, the expression –

'adjudicator' means a District Judge (Magistrates' Courts) or Deputy District Judge (Magistrates' Courts) approved by the Lord Chancellor for the purpose of inquiring into a charge which has been referred to him;

'communication' includes any written or drawn communication from an inmate to any other person, whether intended to be transmitted by means of a postal service or not, and any communication from an inmate to any other person transmitted by means of a telecommunications system;

'compulsory school age' has the same meaning as in the Education Act 1996;

'controlled drug' means any drug which is a controlled drug for the purposes of the Misuse of Drugs Act 1971;

'fixed-term prisoner' has the meaning assigned to it by section 237(1) of the Criminal Justice Act 2003;

'governor' includes an officer for the time being in charge of a young offender institution;

'health care professional' means a person who is a member of a profession regulated by a body mentioned in section 25(3) of the National Health Service Reform and Health Care Professions Act 2002 and who is working within the young offender institution;

Appendix 2

'health care provider' includes any provider of health services, whether or not commissioned by an NHS body (within the meaning given by section 28(6) of the National Health Service 2006);

'information technology equipment' includes any laptop or notebook computer, desktop computer, gaming console, handheld computing device, personal organiser or any electronic device containing a computer processor and capable of connecting to the internet, and any reference to information technology equipment includes a reference to –

  (a) a component part of a device of that description; or
  (b) any article designed or adapted for use with any information technology equipment (including any disk, film or other separate article on which images, sounds, computer code or other information may be stored or recorded);

'inmate' means a person who is required to be detained in a young offender institution;

'intercepted material' means the contents of any communication intercepted pursuant to these Rules;

'legal adviser' means, in relation to an inmate, his counsel or solicitor, and includes a clerk acting on behalf of his solicitor;

'minister appointed to a young offender institution' means a minister so appointed under section 10 of the Prison Act 1952;

'officer' means an officer of a young offender institution;

'short-term prisoner' and 'long-term prisoner' have the meanings assigned to them by section 33(5) of the Criminal Justice Act 1991, as extended by sections 43(1) and 45(1) of that Act;

'telecommunications system' means any system (including the apparatus comprised in it) which exists for the purpose of facilitating the transmission of communications by any means involving the use of electrical or electro-magnetic energy;

'the 2003 Act' means the Criminal Justice Act 2003.

(2) In these Rules a reference to –

  (a) an award of additional days means additional days awarded under these Rules by virtue of section 42 of the Criminal Justice Act 1991 or by virtue of section 257 of the 2003 Act;
  (b) the Church of England includes a reference to the Church of Wales; and
  (c) a reference to a numbered rule is, unless otherwise stated, a reference to the rule of that number in these Rules and a reference to a numbered paragraph is in a rule, unless otherwise stated, a reference to the paragraph of that number in that rule.

Part II Inmates

GENERAL

3. Aims and general principles of young offender institutions

(1) The aim of a young offender institution shall be to help offenders to prepare for their return to the outside community.

(2) The aim mentioned in paragraph (1) shall be achieved, in particular, by -

    (a) providing a programme of activities, including education, training and work designed to assist offenders to acquire or develop personal responsibility, self-discipline, physical fitness, interests and skills and to obtain suitable employment after release;

    (b) fostering links between the offender and the outside community; and

    (c) co-operating with the services responsible for the offender's supervision after release.

4. Classification of inmates

Inmates may be classified, in accordance with any directions of the Secretary of State, taking into account their ages, characters and circumstances.

RELEASE

5. Temporary release

(1) The Secretary of State may, in accordance with the other provisions of this rule, release temporarily an inmate to whom this rule applies.

(2) An inmate may be released under this rule for any period or periods and subject to any conditions.

(3) An inmate may only be released under this rule:

    (a) on compassionate grounds or for the purpose of receiving medical treatment;

    (b) to engage in employment or voluntary work;

    (c) to receive instruction or training which cannot reasonably be provided in the young offender institution;

    (d) to enable him to participate in any proceedings before any court, tribunal or inquiry;

    (e) to enable him to consult with his legal adviser in circumstances where it is not reasonably practicable for the consultation to take place in the young offender institution;

    (f) to assist any police officer in any enquiries;

    (g) to facilitate the inmate's transfer between the young offender institution and another penal establishment;

(h) to assist him in maintaining family ties or in his transition from life in the young offender institution to freedom; or

(4) An inmate shall not be released under this rule unless the Secretary of State is satisfied that there would not be an unacceptable risk of his committing offences whilst released or otherwise of his failing to comply with any condition upon which he is released.

(5) Where at any time an offender is subject concurrently:

  (a) to a detention and training order; and

  (b) to a sentence of detention in a young offender institution, he shall be treated for the purposes of paragraphs (6) and (7) as if he were subject only to the one of them that was imposed on the later occasion.

(6) The Secretary of State shall not release under this rule an inmate if, having regard to:

  (a) the period or proportion of his sentence which the inmate has served or, in a case where paragraph (10) does not apply to require all the sentences he is serving to be treated as a single term, the period or proportion of any such sentence he has served; and

  (b) the frequency with which the inmate has been granted temporary release under this rule, the Secretary of State is of the opinion that the release of the inmate would be likely to undermine public confidence in the administration of justice.

(7) If an inmate has been temporarily released under this rule during the relevant period and has been sentenced to any period of detention, custody or imprisonment for a criminal offence committed whilst at large following that release, he shall not be released under this rule unless his release, having regard to the circumstances of his conviction, would not, in the opinion of the Secretary of State, be likely to undermine public confidence in the administration of justice; and for this purpose the 'relevant period':

  (a) in the case of an inmate serving a determinate sentence of imprisonment, detention or custody, is the period he has served in respect of that sentence, unless, notwithstanding paragraph (10), the sentences he is serving do not fall to be treated as a single term, in which case it is the period since he was last released in relation to one of those sentences under Part II of the Criminal Justice Act 1991 ('the 1991 Act') or section 100 of the Powers of the Criminal Courts (Sentencing) Act 2000 ('the 2000 Act') or Chapter 6 of Part 12 of the 2003 Act; or

  (b) in the case of an inmate serving an indeterminate sentence of imprisonment, detention or custody, is, if the inmate has previously been released on licence under Part II of the 1991

Act or Part II of the Crime (Sentences) Act 1997 or Chapter 6 of Part 12 of the 2003 Act, the period since the date of his last recall to a penal establishment in respect of that sentence or, where the inmate has not been so released, the period he has served in respect of that sentence, save that where an inmate falls within both of sub-paragraphs (a) and (b) above, the 'relevant period', in the case of that inmate, shall be determined by whichever of the applicable sub-paragraphs that produces the longer period.

(8) An inmate released under this rule may be recalled at any time whether the conditions of his release have been broken or not.

(9) This rule applies to inmates other than persons committed in custody for trial or to be sentenced or otherwise dealt with before or by the Crown Court or remanded in custody by any court.

(10) For the purposes of any reference in this rule to an inmate's sentence, consecutive terms and terms which are wholly or partly concurrent shall be treated as a single term.

(11) In this rule, any reference to release on licence under Part II of the 1991 Act includes any release on licence under any earlier legislation providing for early release on licence.

CONDITIONS

6. Privileges

(1) There shall be established at every young offender institution systems of privileges approved by the Secretary of State and appropriate to the classes of inmates thereof and their ages, characters and circumstances, which shall include arrangements under which money earned by inmates may be spent by them within the young offender institution.

(2) Systems of privileges approved under paragraph (1) may include arrangements under which inmates may be allowed time outside the cells and in association with one another, in excess of the minimum time which, subject to the other provisions of these Rules apart from this rule, is otherwise allowed to inmates at the young offender institution for this purpose.

(3) Systems of privileges approved under paragraph (1) may include arrangements under which privileges may be granted to inmates only in so far as they have met, and for so long as they continue to meet, specified standards in their behaviour and their performance in work or other activities.

(4) Systems of privileges which include arrangements of the kind referred to in paragraph (3) shall include procedures to be followed in determining whether or not any of the privileges concerned shall be granted, or shall continue to be granted, to an

inmate; such procedures shall include a requirement that the inmate be given reasons for any decision adverse to him together with a statement of the means by which he may appeal against it.

(5) Nothing in this rule shall be taken to confer on an inmate any entitlement to any privilege or to affect any provision in these Rules other than this rule as a result of which any privilege may be forfeited or otherwise lost or an inmate deprived of association with other inmates.

7. Information to inmates

(1) Every inmate shall be provided, as soon as possible after his reception into the young offender institution, and in any case within 24 hours, with information in writing about those provisions of these Rules and other matters which it is necessary that he should know, including earnings and privileges, and the proper method of making requests and complaints.

(2) In the case of an inmate aged under 18, or an inmate aged 18 or over who cannot read or appears to have difficulty in understanding the information so provided, the governor, or an officer deputed by him, shall so explain it to him that he can understand his rights and obligations.

(3) A copy of these Rules shall be made available to any inmate who requests it.

8. Requests and complaints

(1) A request or complaint to the governor or independent monitoring board relating to an inmate's detention shall be made orally or in writing by that inmate.

(2) On every day the governor shall hear any oral requests and complaints that are made to him under paragraph (1).

(3) A written request or complaint under paragraph (1) may be made in confidence.

9. Communications generally

(1) Without prejudice to sections 6 and 19 of the Prison Act 1952 and except as provided by these Rules, an inmate shall not be permitted to communicate with any person outside the young offender institution, or such person with him, except with the leave of the Secretary of State or as a privilege under rule 7.

(2) Notwithstanding paragraph (1), and except as otherwise provided in these Rules, the Secretary of State may impose any restriction or condition, either generally or in a particular case, upon the communications to be permitted between an inmate and other persons if he considers that the restriction or condition to be imposed—

    (a) does not interfere with the Convention rights of any person; or

    (b) is necessary on grounds specified in paragraph (3) below, provided that:

        (i) reliance on the grounds is compatible with the Convention right to be interfered with; and

        (ii) the restriction or condition is proportionate to what is sought to be achieved.

(3) The grounds referred to in paragraph (2) are –

    (a) the interests of national security;

    (b) the prevention, detection, investigation or prosecution of crime;

    (c) the interests of public safety;

    (d) securing or maintaining security or good order and discipline in the young offender institution;

    (e) the protection of health or morals;

    (f) the protection of the reputation of others;

    (g) maintaining the authority and impartiality of the judiciary; or

    (h) the protection of the rights and freedoms of any person.

(4) Subject to paragraph (2), the Secretary of State may require that any visit, or class of visits, shall be held in facilities which include special features restricting or preventing physical contact between an inmate and a visitor.

(5) Every visit to an inmate shall take place within the sight of an officer or employee of the young offender institution authorised for the purposes of this rule by the governor (in this rule referred to as an 'authorised employee'), unless the Secretary of State otherwise directs, and for the purposes of this paragraph a visit to an inmate shall be taken to take place within the sight of an officer or authorised employee if it can be seen by an officer or authorised employee by means of an overt closed circuit television system.

(6) Subject to rule 13, every visit to an inmate shall take place within the hearing of an officer or authorised employee, unless the Secretary of State otherwise directs.

(7) The Secretary of State may give directions, either generally or in relation to any visit or class of visits, concerning the day and times when inmates may be visited.

(8) In this rule –

    (a) references to communications include references to communications during visits;

    (b) references to restrictions and conditions upon communications include references to restrictions and conditions in relation to the length, duration and frequency of communications; and

    (c) references to Convention rights are to the Convention rights within the meaning of the Human Rights Act 1998.

10. Personal letters and visits

(1) Subject to paragraph (7) an inmate shall be entitled –
    (a) to send and to receive a letter on his reception into a young offender institution and thereafter once a week; and
    (b) to receive a visit twice in every period of four weeks, but only once in every such period if the Secretary of State so directs.

(2) The governor may allow an inmate an additional letter or visit as a privilege under rule 6 or when necessary for his welfare or that of his family.

(3) The governor may allow an inmate entitled to a visit to send and to receive a letter instead.

(4) The governor may defer the right of an inmate to a visit until the expiration of any period of confinement to a cell or room.

(5) The independent monitoring board may allow an inmate an additional letter or visit in special circumstances, and may direct that a visit may extend beyond the normal duration.

(6) The Secretary of State may allow additional letters and visits in relation to any inmate or class of inmates.

(7) An inmate shall not be entitled under this rule to receive a visit from –
    (a) any person, whether or not a relative or friend, during any period of time that person is the subject of a prohibition imposed under rule 77; or
    (b) any other person, other than a relative or friend, except with the leave of the Secretary of State.

(8) Any letter or visit under the succeeding provisions of these Rules shall not be counted as a letter or visit for the purposes of this rule.

11. Interception of communications

(1) The Secretary of State may give directions to any governor concerning the interception in a young offender institution of any communication by any inmate or class of inmates if the Secretary of State considers that the directions are –
    (a) necessary on grounds specified in paragraph (4); and
    (b) proportionate to what is sought to be achieved.

(2) Subject to any directions given by the Secretary of State, the governor may make arrangements for any communication by an inmate or class of inmates to be intercepted in a young offender institution by an officer or an employee of the young offender institution authorised by the governor for the purposes of this rule (referred to in this rule as an 'authorised employee') if he considers that the arrangements are –

    (a) necessary on grounds specified in paragraph (4); and

    (b) proportionate to what is sought to be achieved.

(2A) The governor may not make arrangements for interception of any communication between an inmate and

    (a) the inmate's legal adviser; or

    (b) any body or organisation with which the Secretary of State has made arrangements for the confidential handling of correspondence,

unless the governor has reasonable cause to believe that the communication is being made with the intention of furthering a criminal purpose and unless authorised by the chief operating officer of the prison service

(3) Any communication by an inmate may, during the course of its transmission in a young offender institution, be terminated by an officer or an authorised employee if he considers that to terminate the communication is –

    (a) necessary on grounds specified in paragraph (4); and

    (b) proportionate to what is sought to be achieved by the termination.

(4) The grounds referred to in paragraphs (1)(a), (2)(a) and (3)(a) are –

    (a) the interests of national security;

    (b) the prevention, detection, investigation or prosecution of crime;

    (c) the interests of public safety;

    (d) securing or maintaining security or good order and discipline in the young offender institution;

    (e) the protection of health or morals; or

    (f) the protection of the rights and freedoms of any person.

(5) Any reference to the grounds specified in paragraph (4) in relation to the interception of a communication by means of a telecommunications system in a young offender institution, or the disclosure or retention of intercepted material from such a communication, shall be taken to be a reference to those grounds with the omission of sub-paragraph (f).

(6) For the purposes of this rule 'interception' –

    (a) in relation to a communication by means of a telecommunications system, means any action taken in relation to the system or its operation so as to make some or all of the contents of the communications available, while being transmitted, to a person other than the sender or intended recipient of the communication; and the contents of a communication are to be taken to be made available to a person while being transmitted where the contents of the communication, while being transmitted, are diverted or recorded so as to be available to a person subsequently; and

(b) in relation to any written or drawn communication, includes opening, reading, examining and copying the communication.

12. Permanent log of communications

(1) The governor may arrange for a permanent log to be kept of all communications by or to an inmate.

(2) The log referred to in paragraph (1) may include, in relation to a communication by means of a telecommunications system in a young offender institution, a record of the destination, duration and cost of the communication and, in relation to any written or drawn communication, a record of the sender and addressee of the communication.

13. Disclosure of material

(1) The governor may not disclose to any person who is not an officer of a young offender institution or of the Secretary of State or an employee of the young offender institution authorised by the governor for the purposes of this rule any intercepted material, information retained pursuant to rule 12 or material obtained by means of an overt closed circuit television system used during a visit unless –

(a) he considers that such disclosure is –
   (i) necessary on grounds specified in rule 11(4); and
   (ii) in the same way as in para 54(1)(a), proportionate to what is sought to be achieved by the disclosure;

(b) in the case of intercepted material or material obtained by means of an overt closed circuit television system used during a visit, all parties to the communication or visit consent to the disclosure; or

(c) in the case of information retained pursuant to rule 12, the inmate to whose communication the information relates, consents to the disclosure.

14. Retention of material

(1) The governor shall not retain any intercepted material or material obtained by means of an overt closed circuit television system used during a visit for a period longer than 3 months beginning with the day on which the material was intercepted or obtained unless he is satisfied that continued retention of it is –

(a) necessary on grounds specified in rule 11(4); and

(b) proportionate to what is sought to be achieved by the continued retention.

(2) Where such material is retained for longer than three months pursuant to paragraph (1) the governor shall review its continued retention at periodic intervals until such time as it is no longer held by the governor.

(3) The first review referred to in paragraph (2) shall take place not more than three months after the decision to retain the material taken pursuant to paragraph (1) and subsequent reviews shall take place not more than three months apart thereafter.

(4) If the governor, on a review conducted pursuant to paragraph (2) or at any other time, is not satisfied that the continued retention of the material satisfies the requirements set out in paragraph (1), he shall arrange for the material to be destroyed.

15. Police interviews

A police officer may, on production of an order issued by or on behalf of a chief officer of police, interview any inmate willing to see him.

16. Visits from legal advisers

(1) Where the legal adviser of an inmate in any legal proceedings, civil or criminal, to which the inmate is a party visits the inmate, the legal adviser shall be afforded reasonable facilities for interviewing him in connection with those proceedings, and may do so out of hearing of an officer.

(2) On such a visit an inmate's legal adviser may, with the leave of the Secretary of State, interview the inmate in connection with any other legal business.

17. Delivery and receipt of legally privileged material

(1) An inmate may deliver to, or receive from, the inmate's legal adviser and any court, either by post or during a legal visit under rule 16, any legally privileged material and such material may only be opened, read or stopped by the governor in accordance with the provisions of this rule.

(2) Material to which this rule applies may be opened if the governor has reasonable cause to believe that it contains an illicit enclosure and any such enclosure shall be dealt with in accordance with the other provisions of these Rules.

(3) Material to which this rule applies may be opened, read and stopped if the governor has reasonable cause to believe its contents endanger prison or young offender institution security or the safety of others or are otherwise of a criminal nature.

(4) An inmate shall be given the opportunity to be present when any material to which this rule applies is opened and shall be informed if it or any enclosure is to be read or stopped.

(5) An inmate shall on request be provided with any writing materials necessary for the purposes of paragraph (1).

(6) In this rule, 'court' includes the European Court of Human Rights and the European Court of Justice; and 'illicit enclosure' includes any article possession of which has not been authorised in accordance with the other provisions of these Rules and any material to or from a person other than the inmate concerned, his legal adviser or a court.

18. Securing release of defaulters

An inmate detained in a young offender institution in default of payment of a fine or any other sum of money may communicate with, and be visited at any reasonable time on a weekday by, any relative or friend for payment in order to secure his release.

19. Clothing

(1) An inmate shall be provided with clothing adequate for warmth and health in accordance with a scale approved by the Secretary of State.

(2) The clothing provided under this rule shall include suitable protective clothing for use at work, where this is needed.

(3) Subject to the provisions of rule 45(3), an inmate shall wear clothing provided under this rule and no other, except on the directions of the Secretary of State or as a privilege under rule 6.

(4) An inmate shall where necessary be provided with suitable and adequate clothing on his release.

20. Food

(1) Subject to any directions of the Secretary of State, no inmate shall be allowed, except as authorised by a health care professional working within the young offender institution, to have any food other than that ordinarily provided.

(2) The food provided shall be wholesome, nutritious, well prepared and served, reasonably varied and sufficient in quantity.

(3) Any person deemed by the governor to be competent, shall from time to time inspect the food both before and after it is cooked, and shall report any deficiency or defect to the governor.

(4) In this rule, 'food' includes drink.

21. Alcohol and tobacco

(1) No inmate shall be allowed to have any intoxicating liquor.

(2) No inmate shall be allowed to smoke or to have any tobacco except in accordance with any directions of the Secretary of State.

22. Sleeping accommodation

(1) No room or cell shall be used as sleeping accommodation for an inmate unless it has been certified by an officer of the Secretary of State (not being an officer of a young offender institution) that its size, lighting, heating, ventilation and fittings are adequate for health, and that it allows the inmate to communicate at any time with an officer.

(2) A certificate given under this rule shall specify the maximum number of inmates who may sleep in the room or cell at one time, and the number so specified shall not be exceeded without the leave of the Secretary of State.

23. Beds and bedding

Each inmate shall be provided with a separate bed and with separate bedding adequate for warmth and health.

24. Hygiene

(1) Every inmate shall be provided with toilet articles necessary for his health and cleanliness, which shall be replaced as necessary.

(2) Every inmate shall be required to wash at proper times, have a hot bath or shower on reception and thereafter at least once a week.

(3) An inmate's hair shall not be cut without his consent.

25. Female inmates

The Secretary of State may, subject to any conditions he thinks fit, permit a female inmate to have her baby with her in a young offender institution, and everything necessary for the baby's maintenance and care may be provided there.

26. Library books

A library shall be provided in every young offender institution and, subject to any directions of the Secretary of State, every inmate shall be allowed to have library books and to exchange them.

MEDICAL ATTENTION

27. Health services

(1) The governor must work in partnership with local health care providers to secure the provision to inmates in the young offender institution of access to the same quality and range of services as the general public receives from the National Health Service.

(2) Every request by an inmate to see a health care professional shall be recorded by the officer to whom it was made and promptly communicated to a health care professional.

(3) If an unconvicted inmate desires the attendance of a named registered medical practitioner or dentist other than one already working in the young offender institution, and will pay any expense incurred, the governor must, if satisfied that there are reasonable grounds for the request and unless the Secretary of State otherwise directs, allow the inmate to be visited and treated by that practitioner or dentist, in consultation with a registered medical practitioner who works in that institution.

(4) Subject to any directions given in the particular case by the Secretary of State, a registered medical practitioner selected by or on behalf of an inmate who is a party to any legal proceedings must be afforded reasonable facilities for examining the inmate in connection with the proceedings, and may do so out of hearing but in the sight of an officer.

(5) An inmate may correspond, in accordance with arrangements made by the Secretary of State for the confidential handling of correspondence, with a registered medical practitioner who has treated the inmate for a life threatening condition, and such correspondence may not be opened, read or stopped unless the governor has reasonable cause to believe its contents do not relate to the treatment of that condition.

28. Special illnesses and conditions

(1) A registered medical practitioner working within the young offender institution shall report to the governor on the case of any inmate whose health is likely to be injuriously affected by continued detention or any conditions of detention. The governor shall send the report to the Secretary of State without delay, together with his own recommendations.

29. Notification of illness or death

(1) If an inmate dies, or becomes seriously ill, sustains any severe injury or is removed to hospital on account of mental disorder, the governor shall, if he knows his or her address, at once inform the inmate's spouse or next of kin, and also any person who the inmate may reasonably have asked should be informed.

(2) If an inmate dies, the governor shall give notice immediately to the coroner having jurisdiction, to the independent monitoring board and to the Secretary of State.

RELIGION

30. Religious denomination

An inmate shall be treated as being of the religious denomination stated in the record made in pursuance of section 10(5) of the Prison Act 1952, but the governor may, in a proper case after due inquiry, direct that record to be amended.

31. Special duties of chaplains and appointed ministers

(1) The chaplain or a minister appointed to a young offender institution shall –
   (a) interview every inmate of his denomination individually as soon as he reasonably can after the inmate's reception into that institution and shortly before his release; and
   (b) if no other arrangements are made, read the burial service at the funeral of any inmate of his denomination who dies in that institution.
(2) The chaplain shall visit daily all inmates belonging to the Church of England who are sick, under restraint or confined to a room or cell; and a minister appointed to a young offender institution shall do the same, as far as he reasonably can, for inmates of his own denomination.
(3) If the inmate is willing, the chaplain shall visit any inmate not of the Church of England who is sick, under restraint or confined to a room or cell, and is not regularly visited by a minister of his own denomination.

32. Regular visits by ministers of religion, etc

(1) The chaplain shall visit regularly the inmates belonging to the Church of England.
(2) A minister appointed to a young offender institution shall visit the inmates of his denomination as regularly as he reasonably can.
(3) The governor shall, if so requested by an inmate belonging to a denomination for which no minister has been appointed to a young offender institution do what he reasonably can to arrange for that inmate to be visited regularly by a minister of that denomination.
(4) Every request by an inmate to see the chaplain or a minister appointed to a young offender institution shall be promptly passed on to the chaplain or minister.

33. Religious services

(1) The chaplain shall conduct Divine Service for inmates belonging to the Church of England at least once every Sunday,

Christmas Day and Good Friday, and such celebrations of Holy Communion and weekday services as may be arranged.

(2) A minister appointed to a young offender institution shall conduct Divine Service for inmates of his denomination at such times as may be arranged.

34. Substitute for chaplain or appointed minister

(1) A person approved by the Secretary of State may act for the chaplain in his absence.

(2) A minister appointed to a young offender institution may, with the leave of the Secretary of State, appoint a substitute to act for him in his absence.

35. Sunday work

Arrangements shall be made so as not to require inmates to do any unnecessary work on Sunday, Christmas Day or Good Friday nor inmates of religions other than the Christian religion to do any unnecessary work on their recognised days of religious observance (as in alternative, but not in addition, to those days).

36. Religious books

There shall, so far as reasonably practicable, be available for the personal use of every inmate such religious books recognised by his denomination as are approved by the Secretary of State for use in young offender institutions.

OCCUPATION AND LINKS WITH THE COMMUNITY

37. Regime activities

(1) An inmate shall be occupied in a programme of activities provided in accordance with rule 3 which shall include education, training courses, work and physical education.

(2) In all such activities regard shall be paid in individual assessment and personal development.

(3) A registered medical practitioner working within the young offender institution may excuse an inmate from work or any other activity on medical grounds.

(4) An inmate may be required to participate in regime activities for no longer than the relevant period in a day, 'the relevant period' for this purpose being –

    (a) on a day in which an hour or more of physical education is provided for the inmate, 11 hours;

    (b) on a day in which no such education is provided for the inmate, ten hours; or

(c) on a day in which a period of less than an hour of such education is provided for the inmate, the sum of ten hours and the period of such education provided,

provided that he may not be required to participate in any one regime activity for more than eight hours in a day.

(5) Inmates may be paid for their work or participation in other activities at rates approved by the Secretary of State, either generally or in relation to particular cases.

38. Education

(1) Provision shall be made at a young offender institution for the education of inmates by means of programmes of class teaching or private study within the normal working week and, so far as practicable, programmes of evening and weekend educational classes or private study. The educational activities shall, so far as practicable, be such as will foster personal responsibility and an inmate's interests and skills and help him to prepare for his return to the community.

(2) In the case of an inmate of compulsory school age, arrangements shall be made for his participation in education or training courses for at least 15 hours a week within the normal working week.

(3) In the case of an inmate aged 17 or over who has special educational needs, arrangements shall be made for education appropriate to his needs, if necessary within the normal working week.

(4) In the case of a female inmate aged 21 or over who is serving a sentence of imprisonment or who has been committed to prison for default and who is detained in a young offender institution instead of a prison, reasonable facilities shall be afforded if she wishes to improve her education, by class teaching or private study.

39. Training courses

(1) Provision shall be made at a young offender institution for the training of inmates by means of training courses, in accordance with directions of the Secretary of State.

(2) Training courses shall be such as will foster personal responsibility and an inmate's interests and skills and improve his prospects of finding suitable employment after release.

(3) Training courses shall, so far as practicable, be such as to enable inmates to acquire suitable qualifications.

40. Work

(1) Work shall, so far as practicable, be such as will foster personal responsibility and an inmate's interests and skills and help him to prepare for his return to the community.

Appendix 2

(2) No inmate shall be set to do work of a kind not authorised by the Secretary of State.

41. Physical education

(1) Provision shall be made at a young offender institution for the physical education of inmates within the normal working week, as well as evening and weekend physical recreation. The physical education activities shall be such as will foster personal responsibility and an inmate's interests and skills and encourage him to make good use of his leisure on release.

(2) Arrangements shall be made for each inmate, other than one to whom paragraph (3) and (5) applies, to participate in physical education for at least two hours a week on average or, in the case of inmates detained in such institutions or parts of institutions as the Secretary of State may direct, for at least 1 hour each weekday on average, but outside the hours allotted to education under rule 38(2) in the case of an inmate of compulsory school age.

(3) If circumstances reasonably permit, a female inmate aged 21 years or over shall be given the opportunity to participate in physical education for at least one hour a week.

(4) In the case of an inmate with a need for remedial physical activity, appropriate facilities shall be provided.

(5) If the weather permits and subject to the need to maintain good order and discipline, a female inmate aged 21 years or over shall be given the opportunity to spend time in the open air at least once every day, for such period as may be reasonable in the circumstances.

42. Outside contacts

(1) The governor shall encourage links between the young offender institution and the community by taking steps to establish and maintain relations with suitable persons and agencies outside the institution.

(2) The governor shall ensure that special attention is paid to the maintenance of such relations between an inmate and his family as seem desirable in the best interests of both.

(3) Subject to any directions of the Secretary of State, an inmate shall be encouraged, as far as practicable, to participate in activities outside the young offender institution which will be of benefit to the community or of benefit to the inmate in helping him to prepare for his return to the community.

43. After-care

(1) From the beginning of his sentence, consideration shall be given, in consultation with the appropriate supervising service, to an

inmate's future and the help to be given to him in preparation for and after his return to the community.

(2) Every inmate who is liable to supervision after release shall be given a careful explanation of his liability and the requirements to which he will be subject while under supervision.

DISCIPLINE AND CONTROL

44. Maintenance of order and discipline

(1) Order and discipline shall be maintained, but with no more restriction than is required in the interests of security and well-ordered community life.

(2) Notwithstanding paragraph (1), regimes may be established at young offender institutions under which stricter order and discipline are maintained and which emphasise strict standards of dress, appearance and conduct; provided that no inmate shall be required to participate in such a regime unless he has been first assessed as being suitable for it and no inmate shall be required to continue with such a regime if at any time it appears that he is no longer suitable for it.

(3) For the purposes of paragraph (2), whether an inmate is suitable for a stricter regime is to be assessed by reference to whether he is sufficiently fit in mind and body to undertake it and whether, in the opinion of the Secretary of State, experience of the regime will further his rehabilitation.

(4) In the control of inmates, officers shall seek to influence them through their own example and leadership, and to enlist their willing co-operation.

45. Custody outside a young offender institution

(1) A person being taken to or from a young offender institution in custody shall be exposed as little as possible to public observation and proper care shall be taken to protect him from curiosity and insult.

(2) An inmate required to be taken in custody anywhere outside a young offender institution shall be kept in the custody of an officer appointed under section 3 of the Prison Act 1952 or of a police officer.

(3) An inmate required to be taken in custody to any court shall, when he appears before the court, wear his own clothing or ordinary civilian clothing provided by the governor.

46. Search

(1) Every inmate shall be searched when taken into custody by an officer, on his reception into a young offender institution and

subsequently as the governor thinks necessary or as the Secretary of State may direct.

(2) An inmate shall be searched in as seemly a manner as is consistent with discovering anything concealed.

(3) No inmate shall be stripped and searched in the sight of another inmate or in the sight of a person of the opposite sex.

47. Record and photograph

(1) A personal record of each inmate shall be prepared and maintained in such manner as the Secretary of State may direct, but no part of the record shall be disclosed to any person not authorised to receive it.

(2) Every inmate may be photographed on reception and subsequently, but no copy of the photograph or any other personal record shall be given to any person not authorised to receive it.

(2A) In this rule 'personal record' may include personal information and biometric records (such as fingerprints or other physical measurements).

48. Inmates' property

(1) Anything, other than cash, which an inmate has at a young offender institution and which he is not allowed to retain for his own use shall be taken into the governor's custody.

(2) Any case which an inmate has at a young offender institution shall be paid into an account under the control of the governor and the inmate shall be credited with the amount in the books of the institution.

(3) Any article belonging to an inmate which remains unclaimed for a period of more than 1 year after he is released, or dies, may be sold or otherwise disposed of; and the net proceeds of any sale shall be paid to the National Association for the Care and Resettlement of Offenders, for its general purposes.

(4) The governor may confiscate any unauthorised article found in the possession of an inmate after his reception into a young offender institution, or concealed or deposited within a young offender institution.

49. Removal from association

(1) Where it appears desirable, for the maintenance of good order or discipline or in his own interests, that an inmate should not associate with other inmates, either generally or for particular purposes, the governor may arrange for the inmate's removal from association accordingly.

(2) An inmate shall not be removed under this rule for a period of more than 72 hours without the authority of the Secretary of State and authority given under this paragraph shall be for a period not exceeding 14 days but it may be renewed from time to time for a like period.

(3) The governor may arrange at his discretion for an inmate removed under this rule to resume association with other inmates at any time, and in exercising that discretion the governor must fully consider any recommendation that the inmate resumes association on medical grounds made by a registered medical practitioner or registered nurse working within the young offender institution.

50. Use of force

(1) An officer in dealing with an inmate shall not use force unnecessarily and, when the application of force to an inmate is necessary, no more force than is necessary shall be used.

(2) No officer shall act deliberately in a manner calculated to provoke an inmate.

51. Temporary confinement

(1) The governor may order an inmate who is refractory or violent to be confined temporarily in a special cell or room, but an inmate shall not be so confined as a punishment, or after he has ceased to be refractory or violent.

(2) A cell or room shall not be used for the purpose of this rule unless it has been certified by an officer of the Secretary of State (not being an officer of a young offender institution) that it is suitable for the purpose, that its size, lighting, heating, ventilation and fittings are adequate for health, and that it allows the inmate to communicate at any time with an officer.

(3) In relation to any young offender institution, section 14(6) of the Prison Act 1952 shall have effect so as to enable the provision of special rooms instead of special cells for the temporary confinement of refractory or violent inmates.

(4) An inmate shall not be confined under this rule for longer than 24 hours without a direction in writing given by an officer of the Secretary of State.

52. Restraints

(1) The governor may order an inmate to be put under restraint where this is necessary to prevent the inmate from injuring himself or others, damaging property or creating a disturbance.

(2) The governor may not order an inmate aged under 17 to be put under restraint, except that he may order such an inmate be placed in handcuffs where this is necessary to prevent the inmate from injuring himself or others, damaging property or creating a disturbance.

(3) Notice of such an order shall be given without delay to a member of the independent monitoring board and to a registered medical practitioner or registered nurse working within the young offender institution.

(4) On receipt of the notice, the registered medical practitioner or registered nurse referred to in paragraph (3), shall inform the governor whether there are any reasons why the inmate should not be put under restraint. The governor shall give effect to any recommendation which may be made under this paragraph.

(5) An inmate shall not be kept under restraint longer than necessary, nor shall he be so kept for longer than 24 hours without a direction in writing given by an officer of the Secretary of State (not being an officer of a young offender institution). Such a direction shall state the grounds for the restraint and the time during which it may continue.

(6) Particulars of every case of restraint under the foregoing provisions of this rule shall be forthwith recorded.

(7) Except as provided by this rule no inmate shall be put under restraint otherwise than for safe custody during removal, or on medical grounds by direction of a registered medical practitioner or registered nurse working within the young offender institution. No inmate shall be put under restraint as a punishment.

(8) Any means of restraint shall be of a pattern authorised by the Secretary of State, and shall be used in such manner and under such conditions as the Secretary of State may direct.

53. Compulsory Testing for controlled drugs

(1) This rule applies where an officer, acting under the powers conferred by section 16A of the Prison Act 1952 (power to test inmates for drugs), requires an inmate to provide a sample for the purposes of ascertaining whether he has any controlled drug in his body.

(2) In this rule 'sample' means a sample of urine or any other description of sample specified in the authorisation by the governor for the purposes of section 16A.

(3) When requiring an inmate to provide a sample, an officer shall, so far as is reasonably practicable, inform the inmate:

    (a) that he is being required to provide a sample in accordance with section 16A of the Prison Act 1952; and

(b) that a refusal to provide a sample may lead to disciplinary proceedings being brought against him.

(4) An officer shall require an inmate to provide a fresh sample, free from any adulteration.

(5) An officer requiring a sample shall make such arrangements and give the inmate such instructions for its provision as may be reasonably necessary in order to prevent or detect its adulteration or falsification.

(6) An inmate who is required to provide a sample may be kept apart from other inmates for a period not exceeding one hour to enable arrangements to be made for the provision of the sample.

(7) An inmate who is unable to provide a sample of urine when required to do so may be kept apart from other inmates until he has provided the required sample, save that an inmate may not be kept apart under this paragraph for a period of more than 5 hours.

(8) An inmate required to provide a sample of urine shall be afforded such degree of privacy for the purposes of providing the sample as may be compatible with the need to prevent or detect any adulteration or falsification of the sample; in particular an inmate shall not be required to provide such a sample in the sight of a person of the opposite sex.

54. Supervision of inmates by means of an overt closed circuit television system

(1) Without prejudice to his powers to make arrangements for the supervision of inmates in his custody, the governor may make arrangements for any inmate to be placed under constant supervision by means of an overt closed circuit television system placed in a cell, dormitory or other place in the young offender institution if he considers that –
  (a) such supervision is necessary for –
     (i) the health and safety of the inmate or any other person;
     (ii) the prevention, detection or prosecution of crime; or
     (iii) securing or maintaining security or good order and discipline in the young offender institution; and
  (b) it is proportionate to what is sought to be achieved.

(2) If an overt closed circuit television system is used for the purposes of this rule, the provisions of rules 13 and 14 shall apply to any material obtained.

54A. Compulsory testing for alcohol

(1) This rule applies where an officer, acting under an authorisation in force under section 16B of the Prison Act 1952 (power to test

prisoners for alcohol), requires an inmate to provide a sample for the purpose of ascertaining whether he has alcohol in his body.

(2) When requiring an inmate to provide a sample an officer shall, so far as is reasonably practicable, inform the inmate –
   (a) that he is being required to provide a sample in accordance with section 16B of the Prison Act 1952; and
   (b) that a refusal to provide a sample may lead to disciplinary proceedings being brought against him.

(3) An officer requiring a sample shall make such arrangements and give the inmate such instructions for its provision as may be reasonably necessary in order to prevent or detect its adulteration or falsification.

(4) Subject to paragraph (5) an inmate who is required to provide a sample may be kept apart from other inmates for a period not exceeding one hour to enable arrangements to be made for the provision of the sample.

(5) An inmate who is unable to provide a sample of urine when required to do so may be kept apart from other inmates until he has provided the required sample, except that an inmate may not be kept apart under this paragraph for a period of more than 5 hours.

(6) An inmate required to provide a sample of urine shall be afforded such degree of privacy for the purposes of providing the sample as may be compatible with the need to prevent or detect any adulteration or falsification of the sample; in particular an inmate shall not be required to provide such a sample in the sight of a person of the opposite sex.

55. Offences against discipline

An inmate is guilty of an offence against discipline if he –

(1) commits any assault;
(2) commits any racially aggravated assault;
(3) detains any person against his will;
(4) denies access to any part of the young offender institution to any officer or any person (other than an inmate) who is at the young offender institution for the purpose of working there;
(5) fights with any person;
(6) intentionally endangers the health or personal safety of others or, by his conduct, is reckless whether such health or personal safety is endangered;
(7) intentionally obstructs an officer in the execution of his duty, or any person (other than an inmate) who is at the young offender institution for the purpose of working there, in the performance of his work;

(8) escapes or absconds from a young offender institution or from legal custody;

(9) fails to comply with any condition upon which he was temporarily released under rule 5 of these rules;

(10) is found with any substance in his urine which demonstrates that a controlled drug has, whether in prison or while on temporary release under rule 5, been administered to him by himself or by another person (but subject to rule 56);

(11) is intoxicated as a consequence of consuming any alcoholic beverage (but subject to rule 56A);

(12) consumes any alcoholic beverage whether or not provided to him by another person (but subject to rule 56A);

(13) has in his possession –
  (a) any unauthorised article, or
  (b) a greater quantity of any article than he is authorised to have;

(14) sells or delivers to any person any unauthorised article;

(15) sells or, without permission, delivers to any person any article which he is allowed to have only for his own use;

(16) takes improperly any article belonging to another person or to a young offender institution;

(17) intentionally or recklessly sets fire to any part of a young offender institution or any other property, whether or not his own;

(18) destroys or damages any part of a young offender institution or any other property other than his own;

(19) causes racially aggravated damage to, or destruction of, any part of a young offender institution or any other property, other than his own;

(20) absents himself from any place where he is required to be or is present at any place where he is not authorised to be;

(21) is disrespectful to any officer, or any person (other than an inmate) who is at the young offender institution for the purpose of working there, or any person visiting a young offender institution;

(22) uses threatening, abusive or insulting words or behaviour;

(23) uses threatening, abusive or insulting racist words or behaviour;

(24) intentionally fails to work properly or, being required to work, refuses to do so;

(25) disobeys any lawful order;

(26) disobeys or fails to comply with any rule or regulation applying to him;

(27) receives any controlled drug or, without the consent of an officer, any other article, during the course of a visit (not being an interview such as is mentioned in rule 16);

(28) displays, attaches or draws on any part of a young offender institution, or on any other property, threatening, abusive, or insulting racist words, drawings, symbols or other material;

(29)
    (a) attempts to commit,
    (b) incites another inmate to commit, or
    (c) assists another inmate to commit or to attempt to commit,
    any of the foregoing offences.

56. Defences to rule 55(10)

It shall be a defence for an inmate charged with an offence under rule 55(10) to show that –

(a) the controlled drug had been, prior to its administration, lawfully in his possession for his use or was administered to him in the course of a lawful supply of the drug to him by another person;

(b) the controlled drug was administered by or to him in circumstances in which he did not know and had no reason to suspect that such a drug was being administered; or

(c) the controlled drug was administered by or to him under duress or to him without his consent in circumstances where it was not reasonable for him to have resisted.

56A. Defences to rule 55(11) and rule 55(12)

It shall be a defence for an inmate charged with an offence under rule 55(11) or (12) to show that –

(a) the alcohol was consumed by him in circumstances in which he did not know and had no reason to suspect that he was consuming alcohol; or

(b) the alcohol was consumed by him without his consent in circumstances where it was not reasonable for him to have resisted.

57. Interpretation of rule 55

For the purposes of rule 55 words, behaviour or material shall be racist if they demonstrate or are motivated (wholly or partly) by hostility to members of a racial group (whether identifiable or not) based on their membership (or presumed membership) of a racial group, and 'membership', 'presumed', 'racial group' and 'racially aggravated', shall have the meanings assigned to them by section 28 of the Crime and Disorder Act 1998.

58. Disciplinary charges

(1) Where an inmate is to be charged with an offence against discipline, the charge shall be laid as soon as possible and, save in exceptional circumstances, within 48 hours of the discovery of the offence.

(2) Every charge shall be inquired into by the governor or, as the case may be, the adjudicator.

(3) Every charge shall be first inquired into not later, save in exceptional circumstances or in accordance with rule 60A(5) or rule 65(4), than:

    (a) where it is inquired into by the governor, the next day, not being a Sunday or public holiday, after it is laid;

    (b) where it is referred to the adjudicator under rule 58A(2), 28 days after it is so referred.

(4) An inmate who is to be charged with an offence against discipline may be kept apart from other inmates pending the governor's first inquiry or determination under rule 58A.

58A. Determination of mode of inquiry

(1) Before inquiring into a charge the governor shall determine whether it is so serious that additional days should be awarded for the offence, if the inmate is found guilty.

(2) Where the governor determines:

    (a) that it is so serious, he shall:

        (i) refer the charge to the adjudicator forthwith for him to inquire into it;

        (ii) refer any other charge arising out of the same incident to the adjudicator forthwith for him to inquire into it; and

        (iii) inform the inmate who has been charged that he has done so;

    (b) that it is not so serious, he shall proceed to inquire into the charge.

(3) If:

    (a) at any time during an inquiry into a charge by the governor; or

    (b) following such an inquiry, after the governor has found the inmate guilty of an offence but before he has imposed a punishment for that offence,

it appears to the governor that the charge is so serious that additional days should be awarded for the offence if (where sub-paragraph (a) applies) the inmate is found guilty, the governor shall act in accordance with paragraph (2)(a)(i) to (iii) and the adjudicator shall first inquire into any charge referred to him under this paragraph not later than, save in exceptional circumstances, 28 days after the charge was referred.

59. Rights of inmates charged

(1) Where an inmate is charged with an offence against discipline, he shall be informed of the charge as soon as possible and, in any case, before the time when it is inquired into by the governor or, as the case may be, the adjudicator.

(2) At an inquiry into charge against an inmate he shall be given a opportunity of hearing what is alleged against him and of presenting his own case.

(3) At an inquiry into a charge which has been referred to the adjudicator, the inmate who has been charged shall be given the opportunity to be legally represented.

60. Governor's punishments

(1) If he finds an inmate guilty of an offence against discipline the governor may, subject to paragraph (3) and rule 65 impose one or more of the following punishments:

    (a) caution;

    (b) forfeiture for a period not exceeding 21 days of any of the privileges under rule 6;

    (c) removal for a period not exceeding 21 days from any particular activity or activities of the young offender institution, other than education, training courses, work and physical education in accordance with rules 37, 38, 39, 40 and 41;

    (d) extra work outside the normal working week for a period not exceeding 21 days and for not more than two hours on any day;

    (e) stoppage of or deduction from earnings for a period not exceeding 42 days;

    (f) in the case of an offence against discipline committed by an inmate who was aged 18 or over at the time of commission of the offence, other than an inmate who is serving the period of detention and training under a detention and training order pursuant to section 100 of the Powers of Criminal Courts (Sentencing) Act 2000, confinement to a cell or room for a period not exceeding ten days;

    (g) removal from his wing or living unit for a period not exceeding 21 days;

(2) If an inmate is found guilty of more than one charge arising out of an incident punishments under this rule may be ordered to run consecutively, but, in the case of a punishment of cellular confinement the total period shall not exceed ten days.

(3) A caution shall not be combined with any other punishment for the same charge.

(4) In imposing a punishment under this rule, the governor shall take into account any guidelines that the Secretary of State may from time to time issue as to the level of punishment that should normally be imposed for a particular offence against discipline.

60A. Adjudicator's punishments

(1) If he finds a inmate guilty of an offence against discipline the adjudicator may, subject to paragraph (2) and to rule 65, impose one or more of the following punishments:

(a) any of the punishments mentioned in rule 60(1);

(b) in the case of an inmate who is a short-term prisoner or long-term prisoner or fixed-term prisoner, an award of additional days not exceeding 42 days.

(2) A caution shall not be combined with any other punishment for the same charge.

(3) If an inmate is found guilty of more than one charge arising out of an incident, punishments under this rule may be ordered to run consecutively but, in the case of an award of additional days, the total period added shall not exceed 42 days and, in the case of a punishment of cellular confinement, the total period shall not exceed ten days.

(4) This rule applies to an inmate who has been charged with having committed an offence against discipline before the date on which the rule came into force, in the same way as it applies to an inmate who has been charged with having committed an offence against discipline on or after that date, provided the charge is referred to the adjudicator no later than 60 days after that date.

(5) Rule 58(3) shall not apply to a charge where, by virtue of paragraph (4), this rule applies to the inmate who has been charged.

60B. Review of adjudicator's punishment

(1) A reviewer means a Senior District Judge (Chief Magistrate) approved by the Lord Chancellor for the purposes of conducting a review under this rule or any deputy of such a judge as nominated by that judge.

(2) Where a punishment is imposed by an adjudicator under rule 60A(1) or rule 65(1A) an inmate may, within 14 days of receipt of the punishment, request in writing that a reviewer conducts a review.

(3) The review must be commenced within 14 days of receipt of the request and must be conducted on the papers alone.

(4) The review must only be of the punishment imposed and must not be a review of the finding of guilt.

(5) On completion of the review, if it appears to the reviewer that the punishment imposed was manifestly unreasonable, he may –

(a) reduce the number of any additional days awarded;

(b) for whatever punishment has been imposed by the adjudicator, substitute another punishment which is, in his opinion, less severe; or

(c) quash the punishment entirely.

(6) An inmate requesting a review shall serve any additional days awarded under rule 60A(1)(b) or 65(1A)(b) unless and until they are reduced.

61. Confinement to a cell or room

(1) Before deciding whether to impose a punishment of confinement to a cell or room, the governor, adjudicator or reviewer shall first enquire of a registered medical practitioner or registered nurse working within the young offender institution, as to whether there are any medical reasons why the punishment is unsuitable and shall take this into account when making his decision.

(2) No cell or room shall be used as a detention cell or room for the purpose of a punishment of confinement to a cell or room unless it has been certified by an officer of the Secretary of State (not being an officer of a young offender institution) that it is suitable for the purpose; that its size, lighting, heating, ventilation and fittings are adequate for health; and that it allows the inmate to communicate at any time with an officer.

62. Removal from wing or living unit

Following the imposition of a punishment of removal from his wing or living unit, an inmate shall be accommodated in a separate part of the young offender institution under such restrictions of earnings and activities as the Secretary of State may direct.

63. Suspended punishments

(1) Subject to any directions of the Secretary of State, the power to impose a disciplinary punishment (other than a caution) shall include a power to direct that the punishment is not to take effect unless, during a period specified in the direction (not being more than six months from the date of the direction), the inmate commits another offence against discipline and a direction is given under paragraph (2).

(2) Where an inmate commits an offence against discipline during the period specified in a direction given under paragraph (1), the person dealing with that offence may –
   (a) direct that the suspended punishment shall take effect; or
   (b) reduce the period or amount of the suspended punishment and direct that it shall take effect as so reduced; or
   (c) vary the original direction by substituting for the period specified therein a period expiring not later than six months from the date of variation; or
   (d) give no direction with respect to the suspended punishment.

(3) Where an award of additional days has been suspended under paragraph (1) and an inmate is charged with committing an offence against discipline during the period specified in a direction given under that paragraph, the governor shall either:

    (a) inquire into the charge and give no direction with respect to the suspended award; or

    (b) refer the charge to the adjudicator for him to inquire into it.

64. Remission and mitigation of punishments and quashing of findings of guilt

(1) Except in the case of a finding of guilt made, or a punishment imposed, by an adjudicator under rule 60A(1)(b) or rule 65(1A)(b) the Secretary of State may quash any findings of guilt and may remit a disciplinary punishment or mitigate it either by reducing it or by substituting a punishment which is, in his opinion, less severe.

(2) Subject to any directions given by the Secretary of State, the governor may, on the grounds of good behaviour, remit or mitigate any punishment already imposed by an adjudicator, or governor.

65. Adult female inmates: disciplinary punishments

(1) In the case of a female inmate aged 21 years or over, rule 60 shall not apply, but the governor may, if he finds the inmate guilty of an offence against discipline, impose one or more of the following punishments:

    (a) caution;

    (b) forfeiture for a period not exceeding 42 days of any of the privileges under rule 6;

    (c) removal for a period not exceeding 21 days from any particular activity or activities of the young offender institution, other than education, training courses, work and physical education in accordance with rules 37, 38, 39, 40 and 41;

    (d) stoppage of or deduction from earnings for a period not exceeding 84 days;

    (e) confinement to a cell or room for a period not exceeding 21 days;

(1A) In the case of a female inmate aged 21 years or over, where a charge has been referred to the adjudicator, rule 60A shall not apply, but the adjudicator may if he finds the inmate guilty of an offence against discipline, impose one or more of the following punishments:

    (a) any of the punishments mentioned in paragraph (1);

    (b) in the case of an inmate who is a short-term or long-term prisoner or fixed-term prisoner, an award of additional days not exceeding 42 days.

(2) If an inmate is found guilty of more than one charge arising out of an incident, punishments under this rule may be ordered to run consecutively, but in the case of an award of additional days, the total period added shall not exceed 42 days.

(3) Paragraph (1A) applies to an inmate who has been charged with having committed an offence against discipline before the date on which that paragraph came into force, in the same was as it applies to an inmate who has been charged with having committed an offence against discipline on or after that date, provided the charge is referred to the adjudicator no later than 60 days after that date.

(4) Rule 58(3) shall not apply to a charge where, by virtue of paragraph (3), paragraph (1A) applies to the inmate who has been charged.

66. Forfeiture of remission to be treated as an award of additional days

(1) In this rule, 'existing prisoner' and 'existing licensee' have the meanings assigned to them by paragraph 8(1) of Schedule 12 to the Criminal Justice Act 1991.

(2) In relation to any existing prisoner or existing licensee who has forfeited any remission of his sentence, the provisions of Part II of the Criminal Justice Act 1991 shall apply as if he had been awarded such number of additional days as equals the number of days of remission which he has forfeited.

Part III Officers of Young Offender Institutions

67. General duty of officers

(1) It shall be the duty of every officer to conform to these Rules and the rules and regulations of the young offender institution, to assist and support the governor in their maintenance and to obey his lawful instructions.

(2) An officer shall inform the governor promptly of any abuse or impropriety which comes to his knowledge.

68. Gratuities forbidden

No officer shall receive any unauthorised fee, gratuity or other consideration in connection with his office.

69. Search of officers

An officer shall submit himself to be searched in a young offender institution if the governor so directs. Any such search shall be conducted in as seemly a manner as is consistent with discovering anything concealed.

70. Transactions with inmates
(1) No officer shall take part in any business or pecuniary transaction with or on behalf of an inmate without the leave of the Secretary of State.
(2) No officer shall, without authority, bring in or take out, or attempt to bring in or take out, or knowingly allow to be brought in or taken out, to or for an inmate, or deposit in any place with intent that it shall come into the possession of an inmate, any article whatsoever.

71. Contact with former inmates, etc
No officer shall, without the knowledge of the governor, communicate with any person who he knows to be a former inmate or a relative or friend of an inmate or former inmate.

72. Communications to the press, etc
(1) No officer shall make, directly or indirectly, any unauthorised communication to a representative of the press or any other person concerning matters which have become known to him in the course of his duty.
(2) No officer shall, without authority, publish any matter or make any public pronouncement relating to the administration of any institution to which the Prison Act 1952 applies or to any of its inmates.

73. Code of discipline
The Secretary of State may approve a code of discipline to have effect in relation to officers, or such classes of officers as it may specify, setting out the offences against discipline, the awards which may be made in respect of them and the procedure for dealing with charges.

Part IV Persons Having Access to a Young Offender Institution

74. Prohibited articles
No person shall, without authority, convey into or throw into or deposit in a young offender institution, or convey to an inmate, or deposit in any place with intent that it shall come into the possession of an inmate, any article whatsoever. Anything so conveyed, thrown or deposited may be confiscated by the governor.

Appendix 2

74A. List C Articles

A List C article is any article or substance in the following list –

(a) tobacco;
(b) money;
(c) clothing;
(d) food;
(e) drink;
(f) letters;
(g) paper;
(h) books;
(i) tools;
(j) information technology equipment.

75. Control of persons and vehicles

(1) Any person or vehicle entering or leaving a young offender institution may be stopped, examined and searched and in addition any such person may be photographed, fingerprinted or required to submit to other physical measurement;

(1A) Any such search of a person shall be carried out in as seemly a manner as is consistent with discovering anything concealed about the person or their belongings

(2) The governor may direct the removal from a young offender institution of any person who does not leave on being required to do so.

76. Viewing of young offender institutions

(1) No outside person shall be permitted to view a young offender institution unless authorised by statute or the Secretary of State.

(2) No person viewing a young offender institution shall be permitted to take a photograph, make a sketch or communicate with an inmate unless authorised by statute or the Secretary of State.

77. Visitors

(1) Without prejudice to any other powers to prohibit or restrict entry to young offender institutions, or his powers under rules 9 and 10, the Secretary of State may prohibit visits by a person to a young offender institution or to an inmate in a young offender institution for such periods of time as he considers necessary if the governor considers that such a prohibition is –
   (a) necessary on grounds specified in rule 11(4); and
   (b) is proportionate to what is sought to be achieved by the prohibition.

(2) Paragraph (1) shall not apply in relation to any visit to a young offender institution or inmate by a member of the independent monitoring board of the young offender institution, or justice of the peace, or to prevent any visit by a legal adviser for the purposes of an interview under rule 16 or visit allowed by the independent monitoring board under rule 10(5).

Part V Independent Monitoring Board

78. Disqualification for membership

Any person directly or indirectly interested in any contract for the supply of goods or services to a young offender institution shall not be a member of the independent monitoring board for that institution and any member who becomes so interested in such a contract shall vacate office as a member.

79. Appointment

(1) A member of the independent monitoring board for a young offender institution appointed by the Secretary of State under section 6(2) of the Prison Act 1952 shall subject to paragraphs (3) and (4) hold office for three years or such shorter period as the Secretary of State may appoint.

(2) A member –

    (a) appointed for the first time to the independent monitoring board for a particular young offender institution; or

    (b) re-appointed to the board following a gap of a year or more in his membership of it,

shall, during the period of 12 months following the date on which he is so appointed or (as the case may be) re-appointed, undertake such training as may reasonably be required by the Secretary of State.

(3) The Secretary of State may terminate the appointment of a member if satisfied that –

    (a) he has failed satisfactorily to perform his duties;

    (b) he has failed to undertake training he has been required to undertake under paragraph (2), by the end of the period specified in that paragraph;

    (c) he is by reason of physical or mental illness, or for any other reason, incapable of carrying out his duties;

    (d) he has been convicted of such a criminal offence, or his conduct has been such, that it is not in the Secretary of State's opinion fitting that he should remain a member; or

    (e) there is, or appears to be, or could appear to be, any conflict of interest between the member performing his duties as a member and any interest of that member, whether personal, financial or otherwise.

(4) Where the Secretary of State:

    (a) has reason to suspect that a member of the independent monitoring board for a young offender institution may have so conducted himself that his appointment may be liable to be terminated under paragraph (3)(a) or (d); and

    (b) is of the opinion that the suspected conduct is of such a serious nature that the member cannot be permitted to continue to perform his functions as a member of the board pending the completion of the Secretary of State's investigations into the matter and any decision as to whether the member's appointment should be terminated,

he may suspend the member from office for such period or periods as he may reasonably require in order to complete his investigations and determine whether or not the appointment of the member should be so terminated; and a member so suspended shall not, during the period of the suspension, be regarded as being a member of the board, other than for the purposes of this paragraph and paragraphs (1) and (2).

(5) A board shall have a chairman and a vice chairman, who shall be members of the board.

(6) The Secretary of State shall –

    (a) upon the constitution of a board for the first time, appoint a chairman and a vice chairman to hold office for a period not exceeding 12 months;

    (b) thereafter appoint, before the date of the first meeting of the board in any year of office of the board, a chairman and a vice chairman for that year, having first consulted the board; and

    (c) promptly fill, after having first consulted the board, any casual vacancy in the office of chairman or vice chairman.

(7) The Secretary of State may terminate the appointment of a member as chairman or vice chairman of the board if he is satisfied that the member has –

    (a) failed satisfactorily to perform his functions as chairman or (as the case may be) vice-chairman; or

    (b) has grossly misconducted himself whilst performing those functions.

80. Proceedings of boards

(1) The independent monitoring board for a young offender institution shall meet at the institution at least once a month.

(2) The board may fix a quorum of not fewer than three members for proceedings.

(3) The board shall keep minutes of their proceedings.

(4) The proceedings of the board shall not be invalidated by any vacancy in the membership or any defect in the appointment of a member.

81. General duties of boards

(1) The independent monitoring board for a young offender institution shall satisfy themselves as to the state of the premises, the administration of the institution and the treatment of the inmates.

(2) The board shall inquire into and report upon any matter into which the Secretary of State asks them to inquire.

(3) The board shall direct the attention of the governor to any matter which calls for his attention, and shall report to the Secretary of State any matters which they consider it expedient to report.

(4) The board shall inform the Secretary of State immediately of any abuse which comes to their knowledge.

(5) Before exercising any power under these Rules, the board and any member of the board shall consult the governor in relation to any matter which may affect discipline.

82. Particular duties

(1) The independent monitoring board for a young offender institution and any member of the board shall hear any complaint or request which an inmate wishes to make to them or him.

(2) The board shall arrange for the food of the inmates to be inspected by a member of the board at frequent intervals.

(3) The board shall inquire into any report made to them, whether or not by a member of the board, that an inmate's health, mental or physical, is likely to be injuriously affected by any conditions of his detention.

83. Members visiting young offender institutions

(1) The members of the independent monitoring board for a young offender institution shall visit the institution frequently, and the board shall arrange a rota for the purpose.

(2) A member of the board shall have access at any time to every part of the institution and to every inmate, and he may interview any inmate out of the sight and hearing of officers.

(3) A member of the board shall have access to the records of the prison, except that members of the board shall not have access to any records held for the purposes of or relating to conduct authorised in accordance with Part 2 of the Regulation of Investigatory Powers Act 2000.

Appendix 2

84. Annual report

(1) The independent monitoring board for a young offender institution shall, in accordance with paragraphs (2) and (3), from time to time make a report to the Secretary of State concerning the state of the institution and its administration, including in it any advice and suggestions they consider appropriate.

(2) The board shall comply with any directions given to them from time to time by the Secretary of State as to the following matters –
   (a) the period to be covered by a report under paragraph (1);
   (b) the frequency with which such a report is to be made; and
   (c) the length of time from the end of the period covered by such a report within which it is to be made,

either in respect of a particular report or generally; provided that no directions may be issued under this paragraph if they would have the effect of requiring a board to make or deliver a report less frequently than once in every 12 months.

(3) Subject to any directions given to them under paragraph (2), the board shall, under paragraph (1), make an annual report to the Secretary of State as soon as reasonably possible after 31st December each year, which shall cover the period of 12 months ending on that date or, in the case of a board constituted for the first time during that period, such part of that period during which the board has been in existence.

Part VI Supplemental

85. Delegation by governor

The governor of a young offender institution may, with the leave of the Secretary of State, delegate any of his powers and duties under these Rules to another officer of that institution.

86. Contracted out young offender institutions

(1) Where the Secretary of State has entered into a contract for the running of a young offender institution under section 84 of the Criminal Justice Act 1991 (in this rule 'the 1991 Act') these Rules shall have effect in relation to that young offender institution with the following modifications –
   (a) references to an officer shall include references to a prisoner custody officer certified as such under section 89(1) of the 1991 Act;
   (b) references to a governor shall include references to a director approved by the Secretary of State for the purposes of section 85(1)(a) of the 1991 Act except –

    (i) in rule 85 the reference to a governor shall include a reference to a controller appointed by the Secretary of State under section 85(1)(b) of the 1991 Act; and

    (ii) in rules 67(1), 71 and 81 where references to a governor shall include references to a director and a controller;

    (iii) in rules 49, 51, 52, 58, 58A, 60, 63, 64 and 65 where references to a governor shall include a reference to the director or the controller;

  (c) rule 73 shall not apply in relation to a prisoner custody officer certified as such under section 89(1) of the 1991 Act and performing custodial duties.

(1A) The director of a prison may, with the leave of the Secretary of State, delegate any of his powers and duties under rules 49, 51, 52, 58, 58A, 60, 63, 64 and 65 to another officer of that prison.

87. Contracted out parts of young offender institutions

Where the Secretary of State has entered into a contract for the running of part of a young offender institution under section 84(1) of the Criminal Justice Act 1991, that part and the remaining part shall each be treated for the purposes of Parts I to IV and Part VI of these Rules as if they were separate young offender institutions.

88. Contracted out functions at directly managed young offender institutions

(1) Where the Secretary of State has entered into a contract under section 88A(1) of the Criminal Justice Act 1991 for any functions at a directly managed young offender institution to be performed by prisoner custody officers who are authorised to perform custodial duties under section 89(1) of that Act, references to an officer in these Rules shall, subject to paragraph (2), include references to a prisoner custody officer who is so authorised and who is performing contracted out functions for the purposes of, or for purposes connected with, the young offender institution.

(2) Paragraph (1) shall not apply to references to an officer in rule 73.

(3) In this rule 'directly managed young offender institution' means a young offender institution which is not a contracted out young offender institution.

89. Revocations and savings

(1) Subject to paragraphs (2) and (3), the Rules specified in the Schedule to these Rules are hereby revoked.

(2) Without prejudice to the Interpretation Act 1978 ('the 1978 Act'), where an inmate committed an offence against discipline contrary to rule 50 of the Young Offender Institution Rules 1988

('the 1988 Rules') prior to the coming into force of these Rules, the 1988 Rules shall continue to have effect to permit the prisoner to be charged with such an offence, disciplinary proceedings in relation to such an offence to be continued, and the governor to impose punishment for such an offence.

(3) Without prejudice to the 1978 Act, any award of additional days or other punishment or suspended punishment for an offence against discipline awarded or imposed under any provision of the Rules revoked by this rule, or the 1988 Rules as saved by paragraph (2), or treated by any such provision as having been awarded or imposed under the Rules revoked by this rule, shall have effect as if awarded or imposed under the corresponding provision of these Rules.

Jack Straw
One of Her Majesty's Principal Secretaries of State
Home Office

21st December 2000

The Parole Board Rules 2011
SI 2011 No. 2947

Made 8th December 2011
Laid before Parliament 12th December 2011
Coming into force 3rd January 2012

Contents

Part 1 Introduction

Part 2 General

Part 3 Proceedings without a hearing relating to the initial release of a prisoner serving an indeterminate sentence

Part 4 Proceedings with a hearing

The Secretary of State, in exercise of the powers conferred by section 239(5) of the Criminal Justice Act 2003[1], makes the following Rules.

Part 1 Introduction

Title, commencement, revocation and transition

1.—(1) These Rules may be cited as the Parole Board Rules 2011 and shall come into force on 3rd January 2012.

(2) The Parole Board Rules 2004[2] are revoked.

(3) The revocation of the Parole Board Rules 2004 does not affect anything done under those rules before 3rd January 2012.

Interpretation

2. In these Rules:

'Board' means the Parole Board, continued by section 239(1) of the Criminal Justice Act 2003;

---

[1] 2003 c.44.

[2] The Parole Board Rules 2004 were made under section 32(5) of the Criminal Justice Act 1991 (c.53) and were not made by statutory instrument. Section 32(5) of the Criminal Justice Act 1991 was repealed by sections 303(a) and 332 and Part 7 of Schedule 37 of the Criminal Justice Act 2003 and its provisions were re-enacted in section 239(5) of that Act. The Parole Board Rules 2004 were amended by the Parole Board (Amendment) Rules 2009 (S.I. 2009/408).

'Chairman' means the chairman of the Board appointed under paragraph 2 of Schedule 19 to the Criminal Justice Act 2003;

'Chair' means a chairman of a panel appointed under rule 5(3);

'Determinate sentence' means a sentence of imprisonment other than an indeterminate sentence;

'Indeterminate sentence' means a sentence of imprisonment listed under section 34(2) of the Crime (Sentences) Act 1997[3];

'Panel' means a panel appointed in accordance with rule 5(1) or (2);

'Oral panel' means a panel which determines a case or matter at a hearing;

'Party' means a prisoner or the Secretary of State;

'Prison' includes a young offender institution or any other institution where a prisoner is or has been detained; and

'Single member' means a member of the Board who has been appointed to constitute a panel in accordance with rule 5(1).

Application

3.—(1) These Rules apply where the Secretary of State refers a case to the Board relating to the release or recall of a prisoner.

(2) Rule 7(3) applies only where the Secretary of State refers a case to the Board relating to the initial release of a prisoner serving an indeterminate sentence.

(3) Part 3 of these Rules applies only where the Secretary of State refers a case to the Board relating to the release of a prisoner serving an indeterminate sentence.

(4) A reference to a period of time—

(a) in the case of the initial release of a prisoner serving an indeterminate sentence, applies as set out in the Rules; and

(b) in all other cases, applies as if it was a reference to such period of time as the chair shall in each case determine.

Part 2 General

Referral of cases

4. Where the Board is to consider the release of a prisoner serving a determinate sentence, the release following a recall of a prisoner serving an indeterminate sentence or is to advise the Secretary of

---

[3] 1997 c. 43; section 34(2) was amended by section 165(1) and paragraph 183 of Schedule 9 to the Powers of Criminal Courts (Sentencing) Act 2000 (c.6), section 230 and paragraph 3 of Schedule 18 to the Criminal Justice Act 2003 (c. 44) and by section 378 and Schedules 16 and 17 to the Armed Forces Act 2006 (c.52).

State, the case is deemed to be referred to the Board on the date it receives the information and reports specified in rule 7.

Appointment of panels

5.—(1) The Chairman shall appoint a single member of the Board to constitute a panel to deal with a case where the Board is to consider the initial release of a prisoner serving an indeterminate sentence.

(2) The Chairman shall appoint one or more members of the Board to constitute a panel to deal with a case where—

(a) the case is to be heard in accordance with Part 4 of these Rules;

(b) the Board is to consider the release of a prisoner serving a determinate sentence; or

(c) the Board is under a duty to give advice to the Secretary of State.

(3) The Chairman shall appoint one member of each panel to act as chair of that panel.

(4) In respect of a hearing in the case of a prisoner serving a life sentence or a sentence during Her Majesty's pleasure—

(a) an oral panel shall consist of or include a sitting or retired judge; and

(b) the sitting or retired judge shall act as chair of the oral panel.

(5) A person appointed under paragraph (1) may not in the same case sit on a panel appointed under paragraph (2)(a).

Representation

6.—(1) Subject to paragraph (2), a party may be represented by any person appointed by the party.

(2) The following may not act as a representative—

(a) any person who is detained or is liable to be detained under the Mental Health Act 1983[4];

(b) any person serving a sentence of imprisonment;

(c) any person who is on licence having been released from a sentence of imprisonment; or

(d) any person with a conviction for an offence which remains unspent under the Rehabilitation of Offenders Act 1974[5].

(3) Within 5 weeks of a case being referred to the Board, a party shall notify the Board and the other party of the name,

[4]1983 c.20.
[5]1974 c.53.

address and occupation of any person appointed to act as their representative.

(4) Where a prisoner does not appoint a person to act as their representative, the Board may, with the prisoner's agreement, appoint a person to do so.

Service of information and reports

7.—(1) The Secretary of State shall serve on the Board and, subject to rule 8, the prisoner or their representative—

(a) where a case relates to the initial release of a prisoner, the information specified in Part A of Schedule 1 to these Rules and the reports specified in Part B of that Schedule;

(b) where a case relates to the recall following release of a prisoner, the information specified in Part A of Schedule 2 to these Rules and the reports specified in Part B of that Schedule; and

(c) in either case, any other information which the Secretary of State considers relevant to the case.

(2) Where the Board has a duty to advise the Secretary of State, the Secretary of State shall serve on the Board and, subject to rule 8, the prisoner or their representative, any information or reports which the Secretary of State considers relevant to the case.

(3) The Secretary of State shall serve the information and reports mentioned in paragraph (1) within 8 weeks of the case being referred to the Board.

Withholding information or reports

8.—(1) The Secretary of State may withhold any information or report from the prisoner and their representative where the Secretary of State considers—

(a) that its disclosure would adversely affect—

(i) national security;

(ii) the prevention of disorder or crime; or

(iii) the health or welfare of the prisoner or any other person; and

(b) that withholding the information or report is a necessary and proportionate measure in the circumstances of the case.

(2) Where any information or report is withheld, the Secretary of State shall—

(a) record it in a separate document;

(b) serve it only on the Board; and

(c) explain to the Board in writing why it has been withheld.

(3) Where any information or report is withheld from the prisoner, the Secretary of State shall, unless the chair directs otherwise, serve it as soon as practicable on—
  (a) the prisoner's representative if the representative is—
    (i) a barrister or solicitor;
    (ii) a registered medical practitioner; or
    (iii) a person whom the chair directs is suitable by virtue of their experience or professional qualification; or
  (b) a special advocate who has been appointed by the Attorney General to represent the prisoner's interests.
(4) A prisoner's representative or a special advocate may not disclose any information or report disclosed in accordance with paragraph (3) without the consent of the chair.
(5) Where the chair decides that any information or report withheld by the Secretary of State under paragraph (1) should be disclosed to the prisoner or their representative, the Secretary of State may withdraw the information or report.
(6) If the Secretary of State withdraws any information or report in accordance with paragraph.
(7) Nobody who has seen that information or report shall sit on a panel which determines the case.

Representations by and evidence of the prisoner

9.—(1) A prisoner who wishes to make representations to the Board shall serve them on the Board and the Secretary of State within 12 weeks of the case being referred to the Board.
(2) Any documentary evidence that a prisoner wishes to present at their hearing shall be served on the Board and the Secretary of State at least 14 days before the date of the hearing.

Directions

10.—(1) Directions may be given, varied or revoked—
  (a) before the appointment of a panel, by a member of the Board; or
  (b) after the appointment of a panel, by the chair.
(2) Such directions may relate to—
  (a) the timetable for the proceedings;
  (b) the service of information or a report;
  (c) whether any information or report should be withheld;
  (d) the submission of evidence;
  (e) the attendance of a witness or observer.
(3) Within 7 days of being notified of a direction under paragraph (2)(c), either party may appeal against that direction to the Chairman, who shall notify the other party of the appeal.

(4) Within 7 days of being notified that a party has appealed under paragraph (3), the other party may make representations on the appeal to the Chairman.

(5) A party may apply in writing for a direction to be given, varied or revoked.

(6) An application under paragraph (5) shall—
   (a) specify any direction sought; and
   (b) be served on the other party.

(7) Where a party has applied in writing for a direction to be given, varied or revoked, either party may—
   (a) make written representations about the application;
   (b) where the chair thinks it necessary, and subject to rule 11(4)(b), make oral submissions at a directions hearing.

(8) The power to give directions may be exercised in the absence of the parties.

(9) The Board shall serve notice on the parties of any directions given, varied or revoked as soon as practicable.

Directions hearing

11.—(1) A chair may hold a directions hearing.

(2) A chair shall give the parties at least 14 days' notice of the date, time and place fixed for any directions hearing.

(3) A directions hearing shall be held in private.

(4) At a directions hearing, unless the chair directs otherwise—
   (a) the chair shall sit alone; and
   (b) a prisoner who is represented may not attend.

Adjournment

12.—(1) A chair may adjourn proceedings to obtain further information or for such other purpose as the chair considers appropriate.

(2) Where the chair adjourns a hearing without a further hearing date being fixed, the chair shall give the parties—
   (a) at least 3 weeks' notice of the date, time and place of the resumed hearing; or
   (b) such shorter notice period as the parties agree.

Panel decisions

13.—(1) Where a panel has been appointed under rule 5(2), a decision of the majority of the members of the panel shall be the decision of the panel.

(2) A panel that is unable to reach a decision in accordance with paragraph (1) shall be dissolved by the Chairman, who shall then appoint a new panel.

Appendix 3

Disclosure of information

14. Information about the proceedings and the names of persons concerned in the proceedings shall not be made public.

Release without a hearing

15.—(1) Where the Secretary of State refers a case to the Board relating to a prisoner serving a determinate sentence, the Board may make a decision without a hearing.

  (2) Where the Board has a duty to advise the Secretary of State with respect to any matter referred to it by the Secretary of State which is to do with the early release or recall of a prisoner, the Board may advise the Secretary of State without a hearing.

Part 3 Proceedings without a hearing relating to the initial release of a prisoner serving an indeterminate sentence

Consideration by single member

16.—(1) Within 14 weeks of a case being referred to the Board, a single member shall consider the case without a hearing.

  (2) The single member shall either—

  (a) decide that the case should be referred to an oral panel; or

  (b) make a provisional decision that the prisoner is unsuitable for release.

  (3) The decision of the single member shall be—

  (a) recorded in writing with reasons for the decision; and

  (b) provided to the parties within a week of the date of the decision

Provisional decision against release

17.—(1) Where a single member has made a provisional decision under rule 16(2)(b) that a prisoner is unsuitable for release, the prisoner may request that an oral panel hear the case.

  (2) A prisoner who requests a hearing shall, within 19 weeks of the case being referred to the Board, serve notice giving full reasons for their request on the Board and the Secretary of State.

  (3) If no notice has been served in accordance with paragraph (2) after the expiry of the period permitted by that paragraph, the provisional decision shall—

  (a) become final; and

  (b) be provided to the parties within 20 weeks of the case being referred to the Board.

(4) If notice is served in accordance with paragraph (2), a single member shall decide whether or not to hold a hearing.

(5) The single member who made the provisional decision under rule 16(2)(b) that a prisoner is unsuitable for release may not in the same case decide whether to grant a hearing requested by the prisoner under paragraph (1).

Consideration by an oral panel

18. Where a single member has referred a case to an oral panel for consideration under rule 16(2)(a) or where a hearing has been ordered pursuant to a request under rule 17(1), the case shall be considered by an oral panel within 26 weeks of the case being referred to the Board.

Part 4 Proceedings with a hearing

General provision

19.—(1) This Part of the Rules applies to hearings.

(2) Any reference in this Part of the Rules to a 'panel' is to an oral panel.

Notice of hearing

20.—(1) The hearing shall be held within 26 weeks of a case being referred to the Board.

(2) When fixing the date of the hearing the panel shall consult the parties.

(3) Within 5 working days of a case being listed, the Board shall notify the parties of the date on which the case is due to be heard.

(4) The panel shall give the parties—

(a) at least 3 weeks' notice of the date, time and place scheduled for the hearing; or

(b) such shorter notice as the parties agree.

(5) If applicable, the panel shall also give the parties notice that the hearing will be held via video link, telephone conference or other electronic means.

Notification of attendance by prisoner

21. A prisoner who wishes to attend their hearing shall notify the Board and the Secretary of State within 23 weeks of the case being referred to the Board.

Witness

22.—(1) A party who wishes to call a witness at a hearing shall make a written application to the Board, a copy of which shall be served on the other party, within 20 weeks of the case being referred to the Board.

(2) A written application to call a witness shall—
  (a) include the witness's name, address and occupation; and
  (b) explain why the witness is being called.

(3) A chair may grant or refuse an application to call a witness and shall communicate this decision to the parties.

(4) The chair shall give reasons in writing for any refusal to call a witness.

(5) Where the panel intends to call a witness, the chair shall notify the parties in writing within 21 weeks of the case being referred to the Board.

(6) Written notification from the panel that it intends to call a witness shall—
  (a) include the witnesses's name, address and occupation; and
  (b) explain why the witness is being called.

(7) Where a witness is called under paragraph (1) or (5), it shall be the duty of the person calling the witness to notify the witness at least 2 weeks before the hearing of the date of the hearing and the need to attend.

Observer

23.—(1) A party who wishes to be accompanied by an observer shall make a written application to the panel, a copy of which shall be served on the other party, within 20 weeks of the case being referred to the Board.

(2) A chair may grant or refuse an application for a party to be accompanied by an observer and shall communicate this decision to the parties.

(3) Before granting an application under paragraph (2), the Board shall obtain the agreement—
  (a) where the hearing is being held in a prison, of the prison governor or prison director; or
  (b) in any other case, of the person who has the authority to agree.

Location and privacy of proceedings

24.—(1) Subject to paragraph (2), a hearing shall be held at the prison where the prisoner is detained or at such other place as the chair, with the agreement of the Secretary of State, directs.

(2) Where a hearing is held in accordance with paragraph (3), paragraph (1) shall not apply.

(3) A chair may direct that a hearing is to be held via video link, telephone conference or other electronic means.

(4) A hearing shall be held in private.

(5) In addition to any witness and observer whose attendance has been approved in accordance with rule 22 or 23, the chair may—

    (a) admit any other person to the hearing; and

    (b) impose conditions on that person's admittance.

(6) At the hearing the parties may not challenge the attendance of any witness or observer whose attendance has been approved pursuant to rule 22 or 23.

Hearing procedure

25.—(1) At the beginning of the hearing the chair shall—

    (a) explain the order of proceeding which the panel proposes to adopt; and

    (b) invite each party present to state their view as to the suitability of the prisoner for release.

(2) The panel—

    (a) shall avoid formality in the proceedings;

    (b) may ask any question to satisfy itself of the level of risk of the prisoner; and

    (c) shall conduct the hearing in a manner it considers most suitable to the clarification of the issues before it and to the just handling of the proceedings.

(3) The parties shall be entitled to—

    (a) take such part in the proceedings as the panel thinks fit;

    (b) hear each other's evidence;

    (c) put questions to each other;

    (d) call a witness who has been granted permission to give evidence; and

    (e) question any witness or other person appearing before the panel.

(4) If, in the chair's opinion, any person at the hearing is behaving in a disruptive manner, the chair may require that person to leave.

(5) The chair may permit a person who was required to leave under paragraph (4) to return on such conditions as the chair may specify.

(6) A panel may produce or receive in evidence any document or information whether or not it would be admissible in a court of law.

(7) No person shall be compelled to give any evidence or produce any document which they could not be compelled to give or produce on the trial of an action.

Appendix 3

(8) The chair may require any person present to leave the hearing where evidence which has been directed to be withheld from the prisoner or their representative is to be considered.

(9) After all the evidence has been given, the prisoner shall be given an opportunity to address the panel.

The decision

26.—(1) The panel's decision determining a case shall be—

(a) recorded in writing with reasons;

(b) signed by the chair; and

(c) provided to the parties not more than 14 days after the end of the hearing.

(2) The recorded decision shall refer only to the matter which the Secretary of State referred to the Board.

Part 5 Miscellaneous

Time

27. Where the time prescribed by or under these Rules for doing any act expires on a Saturday, Sunday or public holiday, the act shall be in time if it is done on the next working day.

Transmission of documents etc.

28. Any document required or authorised by these Rules to be served or otherwise transmitted to any person may be transmitted by electronic means, sent by pre-paid post or delivered—

(a) in the case of a document directed to the Board or the chair, to the office of the Board; or

(b) in any other case, to the last known address of the person to whom the document is directed.

Error

29. Where there has been an error of procedure such as a failure to comply with a rule—

(a) the error does not invalidate any steps taken in the proceedings unless the panel so directs; and

(b) the panel may remedy the error.

Signed by the authority of the Secretary of State

J Djanogly
Parliamentary Under Secretary of State
8th December 2011   Ministry of Justice

Schedule 1 Rule 7

Information and reports for submission to the Board by the Secretary of State on a reference to the Board to determine the initial release of a prisoner

Part A Information relating to the prisoner

1. The full name of the prisoner.
2. The date of birth of the prisoner.
3. The prison in which the prisoner is detained, details of any other prisons in which the prisoner has been detained and the date and the reason for any transfer.
4. The date on which the prisoner was given the current sentence, details of the offence and any previous convictions.
5. The comments, if available, of the trial judge when passing sentence.
6. If available, the conclusions of the Court of Appeal in respect of any appeal by the prisoner against conviction or sentence.
7. The parole history, if any, of the prisoner, including details of any periods spent on licence during the current sentence.

Part B Reports relating to the prisoner

1. If available, the pre-trial and pre-sentence reports examined by the sentencing court on the circumstances of the offence.
2. Reports on a prisoner who was subject to a transfer direction under section 47 of the Mental Health Act 1983.[6]
3. Current reports on the prisoner's risk factors, reduction in risk and performance and behaviour in prison, including views on suitability for release on licence as well as compliance with any sentence plan.
4. An up-to-date risk management report prepared for the Board by an officer of the supervising local probation trust, including information on the following where relevant:
   (a) details of the home address, family circumstances and family attitudes towards the prisoner;
   (b) alternative options if the offender cannot return home;
   (c) the opportunity for employment on release;
   (d) the local community's attitude towards the prisoner (if known);
   (e) the prisoner's attitude to the index offence;

---

[6] 1983 c.20; section 47 was amended by sections 1 and 4 of the Mental Health Act 2007 (c. 12) and by sections 49(3) and 56(2) and Schedule 6 of the Crime (Sentences) Act 1997 (c.37).

    (f) the prisoner's response to previous periods of supervision;

    (g) the prisoner's behaviour during any temporary leave during the current sentence;

    (h) the prisoner's attitude to the prospect of release and the requirements and objectives of supervision;

    (i) an assessment of the risk of reoffending;

    (j) a programme of supervision;

    (k) if available, an up-to-date victim personal statement setting out the impact the index offence has had on the victim and the victim's immediate family;

    (l) a view on suitability for release; and

    (m) recommendations regarding any non-standard licence conditions.

Schedule 2 Rule 7

Information and reports for submission to the Board by the Secretary of State on a reference to the Board to determine the release of a recalled prisoner

Part A Information relating to the prisoner

1. The full name of the prisoner.
2. The date of birth of the prisoner.
3. The prison in which the prisoner is detained, details of other prisons in which the prisoner has been detained and the date and reason for any transfer.
4. The date on which the prisoner was given the current sentence, details of the offence and any previous convictions.
5. The parole history, if any, of the prisoner, including details of any periods spent on licence during the current sentence.
6. If available, the details of any sentence plan prepared for the prisoner which has previously been disclosed to the prisoner.
7. The details of any previous recalls of the prisoner including the reasons for such recalls and subsequent re-release on licence.
8. The statement of reasons for the most recent recall which was given to the prisoner, including the outcome of any criminal charges laid against the prisoner prior to or subsequent to the point at which they were recalled.

Part B Reports relating to the prisoner

1. Any reports considered by the Secretary of State in deciding to recall the prisoner.
2. If available, any pre-sentence report examined by the sentencing court on the circumstances of the offence.
3. Any details of convictions prior to the index offence.
4. A copy of the prisoner's licence at the point at which the Secretary of State decided to recall the prisoner.

Criminal Justice Act 2003

Schedule 15 Specified Offences For Purposes of Chapter 5 of Part 12

Section 224

Part 1 Specified Violent Offences

1 Manslaughter.
2 Kidnapping.
3 False imprisonment.
4 An offence under section 4 of the Offences against the Person Act 1861 (c 100) (soliciting murder).
5 An offence under section 16 of that Act (threats to kill).
6 An offence under section 18 of that Act (wounding with intent to cause grievous bodily harm).
7 An offence under section 20 of that Act (malicious wounding).
8 An offence under section 21 of that Act (attempting to choke, suffocate or strangle in order to commit or assist in committing an indictable offence).
9 An offence under section 22 of that Act (using chloroform etc to commit or assist in the committing of any indictable offence).
10 An offence under section 23 of that Act (maliciously administering poison etc so as to endanger life or inflict grievous bodily harm).
11 An offence under section 27 of that Act (abandoning children).
12 An offence under section 28 of that Act (causing bodily injury by explosives).
13 An offence under section 29 of that Act (using explosives etc with intent to do grievous bodily harm).
14 An offence under section 30 of that Act (placing explosives with intent to do bodily injury).
15 An offence under section 31 of that Act (setting spring guns etc with intent to do grievous bodily harm).
16 An offence under section 32 of that Act (endangering the safety of railway passengers).
17 An offence under section 35 of that Act (injuring persons by furious driving).
18 An offence under section 37 of that Act (assaulting officer preserving wreck).
19 An offence under section 38 of that Act (assault with intent to resist arrest).

20 An offence under section 47 of that Act (assault occasioning actual bodily harm).

21 An offence under section 2 of the Explosive Substances Act 1883 (c 3) (causing explosion likely to endanger life or property).

22 An offence under section 3 of that Act (attempt to cause explosion, or making or keeping explosive with intent to endanger life or property).

23 An offence under section 1 of the Infant Life (Preservation) Act 1929 (c 34) (child destruction).

24 An offence under section 1 of the Children and Young Persons Act 1933 (c 12) (cruelty to children).

25 An offence under section 1 of the Infanticide Act 1938 (c 36) (infanticide).

26 An offence under section 16 of the Firearms Act 1968 (c 27) (possession of firearm with intent to endanger life).

27 An offence under section 16A of that Act (possession of firearm with intent to cause fear of violence).

28 An offence under section 17(1) of that Act (use of firearm to resist arrest).

29 An offence under section 17(2) of that Act (possession of firearm at time of committing or being arrested for offence specified in Schedule 1 to that Act).

30 An offence under section 18 of that Act (carrying a firearm with criminal intent).

31 An offence under section 8 of the Theft Act 1968 (c 60) (robbery or assault with intent to rob).

32 An offence under section 9 of that Act of burglary with intent to--
(a) inflict grievous bodily harm on a person, or
(b) do unlawful damage to a building or anything in it.

33 An offence under section 10 of that Act (aggravated burglary).

34 An offence under section 12A of that Act (aggravated vehicle-taking) involving an accident which caused the death of any person.

35 An offence of arson under section 1 of the Criminal Damage Act 1971 (c 48).

36 An offence under section 1(2) of that Act (destroying or damaging property) other than an offence of arson.

37 An offence under section 1 of the Taking of Hostages Act 1982 (c 28) (hostage-taking).

38 An offence under section 1 of the Aviation Security Act 1982 (c 36) (hijacking).

39 An offence under section 2 of that Act (destroying, damaging or endangering safety of aircraft).

40 An offence under section 3 of that Act (other acts endangering or likely to endanger safety of aircraft).

41 An offence under section 4 of that Act (offences in relation to certain dangerous articles).

42 An offence under section 127 of the Mental Health Act 1983 (c 20) (ill-treatment of patients).

43 An offence under section 1 of the Prohibition of Female Circumcision Act 1985 (c 38) (prohibition of female circumcision).

44 An offence under section 1 of the Public Order Act 1986 (c 64) (riot).

45 An offence under section 2 of that Act (violent disorder).

46 An offence under section 3 of that Act (affray).

47 An offence under section 134 of the Criminal Justice Act 1988 (c 33) (torture).

48 An offence under section 1 of the Road Traffic Act 1988 (c 52) (causing death by dangerous driving).

49 An offence under section 3A of that Act (causing death by careless driving when under influence of drink or drugs).

50 An offence under section 1 of the Aviation and Maritime Security Act 1990 (c 31) (endangering safety at aerodromes).

51 An offence under section 9 of that Act (hijacking of ships).

52 An offence under section 10 of that Act (seizing or exercising control of fixed platforms).

53 An offence under section 11 of that Act (destroying fixed platforms or endangering their safety).

54 An offence under section 12 of that Act (other acts endangering or likely to endanger safe navigation).

55 An offence under section 13 of that Act (offences involving threats).

56 An offence under Part II of the Channel Tunnel (Security) Order 1994 (SI 1994/570) (offences relating to Channel Tunnel trains and the tunnel system).

57 An offence under section 4 or 4A of the Protection from Harassment Act 1997 (c 40) (putting people in fear of violence and stalking involving fear of violence or serious alarm or distress).

58 An offence under section 29 of the Crime and Disorder Act 1998 (c 37) (racially or religiously aggravated assaults).

59 An offence falling within section 31(1)(a) or (b) of that Act (racially or religiously aggravated offences under section 4 or 4A of the Public Order Act 1986 (c 64)).

59A An offence under section 54 of the Terrorism Act 2000 (weapons training).

59B An offence under section 56 of that Act (directing terrorist organisation).

59C An offence under section 57 of that Act (possession of article for terrorist purposes).

59D An offence under section 59 of that Act (inciting terrorism overseas).

60 An offence under section 51 or 52 of the International Criminal Court Act 2001 (c 17) (genocide, crimes against humanity, war crimes and related offences), other than one involving murder.

60A An offence under section 47 of the Anti-terrorism, Crime and Security Act 2001 (use etc of nuclear weapons).

60B An offence under section 50 of that Act (assisting or inducing certain weapons-related acts overseas).

60C An offence under section 113 of that Act (use of noxious substance or thing to cause harm or intimidate).

61 An offence under section 1 of the Female Genital Mutilation Act 2003 (c 31) (female genital mutilation).

62 An offence under section 2 of that Act (assisting a girl to mutilate her own genitalia).

63 An offence under section 3 of that Act (assisting a non-UK person to mutilate overseas a girl's genitalia).

63A An offence under section 5 of the Domestic Violence, Crime and Victims Act 2004 (causing or allowing a child or vulnerable adult to die or suffer serious physical harm).

63B An offence under section 5 of the Terrorism Act 2006 (preparation of terrorist acts).

63C An offence under section 6 of that Act (training for terrorism).

63D An offence under section 9 of that Act (making or possession of radioactive device or material).

63E An offence under section 10 of that Act (use of radioactive device or material for terrorist purposes etc).

63F An offence under section 11 of that Act (terrorist threats relating to radioactive devices etc).

64 An offence of--
   (a) aiding, abetting, counselling, procuring or inciting the commission of an offence specified in this Part of this Schedule,
   (b) conspiring to commit an offence so specified, or
   (c) attempting to commit an offence so specified.

65 An attempt to commit murder or a conspiracy to commit murder.

Part 2 Specified Sexual Offences

66 An offence under section 1 of the Sexual Offences Act 1956 (c 69) (rape).

67 An offence under section 2 of that Act (procurement of woman by threats).

Appendix 4

68 An offence under section 3 of that Act (procurement of woman by false pretences).

69 An offence under section 4 of that Act (administering drugs to obtain or facilitate intercourse).

70 An offence under section 5 of that Act (intercourse with girl under thirteen).

71 An offence under section 6 of that Act (intercourse with girl under 16).

72 An offence under section 7 of that Act (intercourse with a defective).

73 An offence under section 9 of that Act (procurement of a defective).

74 An offence under section 10 of that Act (incest by a man).

75 An offence under section 11 of that Act (incest by a woman).

76 An offence under section 14 of that Act (indecent assault on a woman).

77 An offence under section 15 of that Act (indecent assault on a man).

78 An offence under section 16 of that Act (assault with intent to commit buggery).

79 An offence under section 17 of that Act (abduction of woman by force or for the sake of her property).

80 An offence under section 19 of that Act (abduction of unmarried girl under eighteen from parent or guardian).

81 An offence under section 20 of that Act (abduction of unmarried girl under sixteen from parent or guardian).

82 An offence under section 21 of that Act (abduction of defective from parent or guardian).

83 An offence under section 22 of that Act (causing prostitution of women).

84 An offence under section 23 of that Act (procuration of girl under twenty-one).

85 An offence under section 24 of that Act (detention of woman in brothel).

86 An offence under section 25 of that Act (permitting girl under thirteen to use premises for intercourse).

87 An offence under section 26 of that Act (permitting girl under sixteen to use premises for intercourse).

88 An offence under section 27 of that Act (permitting defective to use premises for intercourse).

89 An offence under section 28 of that Act (causing or encouraging the prostitution of, intercourse with or indecent assault on girl under sixteen).

90 An offence under section 29 of that Act (causing or encouraging prostitution of defective).

91 An offence under section 32 of that Act (soliciting by men).

92 An offence under section 33 of that Act (keeping a brothel).

93 An offence under section 128 of the Mental Health Act 1959 (c 72) (sexual intercourse with patients).

94 An offence under section 1 of the Indecency with Children Act 1960 (c 33) (indecent conduct towards young child).

95 An offence under section 4 of the Sexual Offences Act 1967 (c 60) (procuring others to commit homosexual acts).

96 An offence under section 5 of that Act (living on earnings of male prostitution).

97 An offence under section 9 of the Theft Act 1968 (c 60) of burglary with intent to commit rape.

98 An offence under section 54 of the Criminal Law Act 1977 (c 45) (inciting girl under sixteen to have incestuous sexual intercourse).

99 An offence under section 1 of the Protection of Children Act 1978 (c 37) (indecent photographs of children).

100 An offence under section 170 of the Customs and Excise Management Act 1979 (c 2) (penalty for fraudulent evasion of duty etc) in relation to goods prohibited to be imported under section 42 of the Customs Consolidation Act 1876 (c 36) (indecent or obscene articles).

101 An offence under section 160 of the Criminal Justice Act 1988 (c 33) (possession of indecent photograph of a child).

102 An offence under section 1 of the Sexual Offences Act 2003 (c 42) (rape).

103 An offence under section 2 of that Act (assault by penetration).

104 An offence under section 3 of that Act (sexual assault).

105 An offence under section 4 of that Act (causing a person to engage in sexual activity without consent).

106 An offence under section 5 of that Act (rape of a child under 13).

107 An offence under section 6 of that Act (assault of a child under 13 by penetration).

108 An offence under section 7 of that Act (sexual assault of a child under 13).

109 An offence under section 8 of that Act (causing or inciting a child under 13 to engage in sexual activity).

110 An offence under section 9 of that Act (sexual activity with a child).

111 An offence under section 10 of that Act (causing or inciting a child to engage in sexual activity).

112 An offence under section 11 of that Act (engaging in sexual activity in the presence of a child).

113 An offence under section 12 of that Act (causing a child to watch a sexual act).

114 An offence under section 13 of that Act (child sex offences committed by children or young persons).

115 An offence under section 14 of that Act (arranging or facilitating commission of a child sex offence).

116 An offence under section 15 of that Act (meeting a child following sexual grooming etc).

117 An offence under section 16 of that Act (abuse of position of trust: sexual activity with a child).

118 An offence under section 17 of that Act (abuse of position of trust: causing or inciting a child to engage in sexual activity).

119 An offence under section 18 of that Act (abuse of position of trust: sexual activity in the presence of a child).

120 An offence under section 19 of that Act (abuse of position of trust: causing a child to watch a sexual act).

121 An offence under section 25 of that Act (sexual activity with a child family member).

122 An offence under section 26 of that Act (inciting a child family member to engage in sexual activity).

123 An offence under section 30 of that Act (sexual activity with a person with a mental disorder impeding choice).

124 An offence under section 31 of that Act (causing or inciting a person with a mental disorder impeding choice to engage in sexual activity).

125 An offence under section 32 of that Act (engaging in sexual activity in the presence of a person with a mental disorder impeding choice).

126 An offence under section 33 of that Act (causing a person with a mental disorder impeding choice to watch a sexual act).

127 An offence under section 34 of that Act (inducement, threat or deception to procure sexual activity with a person with a mental disorder).

128 An offence under section 35 of that Act (causing a person with a mental disorder to engage in or agree to engage in sexual activity by inducement, threat or deception).

129 An offence under section 36 of that Act (engaging in sexual activity in the presence, procured by inducement, threat or deception, of a person with a mental disorder).

130 An offence under section 37 of that Act (causing a person with a mental disorder to watch a sexual act by inducement, threat or deception).

131 An offence under section 38 of that Act (care workers: sexual activity with a person with a mental disorder).

132 An offence under section 39 of that Act (care workers: causing or inciting sexual activity).

133 An offence under section 40 of that Act (care workers: sexual activity in the presence of a person with a mental disorder).

134 An offence under section 41 of that Act (care workers: causing a person with a mental disorder to watch a sexual act).

135 An offence under section 47 of that Act (paying for sexual services of a child).

136 An offence under section 48 of that Act (causing or inciting child prostitution or pornography).

137 An offence under section 49 of that Act (controlling a child prostitute or a child involved in pornography).

138 An offence under section 50 of that Act (arranging or facilitating child prostitution or pornography).

139 An offence under section 52 of that Act (causing or inciting prostitution for gain).

140 An offence under section 53 of that Act (controlling prostitution for gain).

141 An offence under section 57 of that Act (trafficking into the UK for sexual exploitation).

142 An offence under section 58 of that Act (trafficking within the UK for sexual exploitation).

143 An offence under section 59 of that Act (trafficking out of the UK for sexual exploitation).

143A *An offence under section 59A of that Act (trafficking for sexual exploitation).

144 An offence under section 61 of that Act (administering a substance with intent).

145 An offence under section 62 of that Act (committing an offence with intent to commit a sexual offence).

146 An offence under section 63 of that Act (trespass with intent to commit a sexual offence).

147 An offence under section 64 of that Act (sex with an adult relative: penetration).

148 An offence under section 65 of that Act (sex with an adult relative: consenting to penetration).

149 An offence under section 66 of that Act (exposure).

150 An offence under section 67 of that Act (voyeurism).

151 An offence under section 69 of that Act (intercourse with an animal).

152 An offence under section 70 of that Act (sexual penetration of a corpse).

153 An offence of--

---

*not yet in force (inserted by the Protection of Freedoms Act 2012)

(a) aiding, abetting, counselling, procuring or inciting the commission of an offence specified in this Part of this Schedule,

(b) conspiring to commit an offence so specified, or

(c) attempting to commit an offence so specified.

Schedule 15b Offences Listed for the Purposes of Sections 224a, 226a and 246a

Part 1 Offences Under the Law of England and Wales Listed for the Purposes of Sections 224A(1), 224A(4), 226A and 246A

The following offences to the extent that they are offences under the law of England and Wales--

1 Manslaughter.

2 An offence under section 4 of the Offences against the Person Act 1861 (soliciting murder).

3 An offence under section 18 of that Act (wounding with intent to cause grievous bodily harm).

4 An offence under section 16 of the Firearms Act 1968 (possession of a firearm with intent to endanger life).

5 An offence under section 17(1) of that Act (use of a firearm to resist arrest).

6 An offence under section 18 of that Act (carrying a firearm with criminal intent).

7 An offence of robbery under section 8 of the Theft Act 1968 where, at some time during the commission of the offence, the offender had in his possession a firearm or an imitation firearm within the meaning of the Firearms Act 1968.

8 An offence under section 1 of the Protection of Children Act 1978 (indecent images of children).

9 An offence under section 56 of the Terrorism Act 2000 (directing terrorist organisation).

10 An offence under section 57 of that Act (possession of article for terrorist purposes).

11 An offence under section 59 of that Act (inciting terrorism overseas) if the offender is liable on conviction on indictment to imprisonment for life.

12 An offence under section 47 of the Anti-terrorism, Crime and Security Act 2001 (use etc of nuclear weapons).

13 An offence under section 50 of that Act (assisting or inducing certain weapons-related acts overseas).

14 An offence under section 113 of that Act (use of noxious substance or thing to cause harm or intimidate).

15 An offence under section 1 of the Sexual Offences Act 2003 (rape).

16 An offence under section 2 of that Act (assault by penetration).

17 An offence under section 4 of that Act (causing a person to engage in sexual activity without consent) if the offender is liable on conviction on indictment to imprisonment for life.

18 An offence under section 5 of that Act (rape of a child under 13).

19 An offence under section 6 of that Act (assault of a child under 13 by penetration).

20 An offence under section 7 of that Act (sexual assault of a child under 13).

21 An offence under section 8 of that Act (causing or inciting a child under 13 to engage in sexual activity).

22 An offence under section 9 of that Act (sexual activity with a child).

23 An offence under section 10 of that Act (causing or inciting a child to engage in sexual activity).

24 An offence under section 11 of that Act (engaging in sexual activity in the presence of a child).

25 An offence under section 12 of that Act (causing a child to watch a sexual act).

26 An offence under section 14 of that Act (arranging or facilitating commission of a child sex offence).

27 An offence under section 15 of that Act (meeting a child following sexual grooming etc).

28 An offence under section 25 of that Act (sexual activity with a child family member) if the offender is aged 18 or over at the time of the offence.

29 An offence under section 26 of that Act (inciting a child family member to engage in sexual activity) if the offender is aged 18 or over at the time of the offence.

30 An offence under section 30 of that Act (sexual activity with a person with a mental disorder impeding choice) if the offender is liable on conviction on indictment to imprisonment for life.

31 An offence under section 31 of that Act (causing or inciting a person with a mental disorder to engage in sexual activity) if the offender is liable on conviction on indictment to imprisonment for life.

32 An offence under section 34 of that Act (inducement, threat or deception to procure sexual activity with a person with a mental disorder) if the offender is liable on conviction on indictment to imprisonment for life.

33 An offence under section 35 of that Act (causing a person with a mental disorder to engage in or agree to engage in sexual activity by inducement etc) if the offender is liable on conviction on indictment to imprisonment for life.

34 An offence under section 47 of that Act (paying for sexual services of a child) against a person aged under 16.

35 An offence under section 48 of that Act (causing or inciting child prostitution or pornography).

36 An offence under section 49 of that Act (controlling a child prostitute or a child involved in pornography).

37 An offence under section 50 of that Act (arranging or facilitating child prostitution or pornography).

38 An offence under section 62 of that Act (committing an offence with intent to commit a sexual offence) if the offender is liable on conviction on indictment to imprisonment for life.

39 An offence under section 5 of the Domestic Violence, Crime and Victims Act 2004 (causing or allowing the death of a child or vulnerable adult).

40 An offence under section 5 of the Terrorism Act 2006 (preparation of terrorist acts).

41 An offence under section 9 of that Act (making or possession of radioactive device or materials).

42 An offence under section 10 of that Act (misuse of radioactive devices or material and misuse and damage of facilities).

43 An offence under section 11 of that Act (terrorist threats relating to radioactive devices, materials or facilities).

44 (1) An attempt to commit an offence specified in the preceding paragraphs of this Part of this Schedule ('a listed offence') or murder.

(2) Conspiracy to commit a listed offence or murder.

(3) Incitement to commit a listed offence or murder.

(4) An offence under Part 2 of the Serious Crime Act 2007 in relation to which a listed offence or murder is the offence (or one of the offences) which the person intended or believed would be committed.

(5) Aiding, abetting, counselling or procuring the commission of a listed offence.

Part 2 Further Offences Under the Law of England and Wales Listed for the Purposes of Sections 224A(4), 226A and 246A

45 Murder.
46 (1) Any offence that—
    (a) was abolished (with or without savings) before the coming into force of this Schedule, and
    (b) would, if committed on the relevant day, have constituted an offence specified in Part 1 of this Schedule.
    (2) 'Relevant day', in relation to an offence, means—
    (a) for the purposes of this paragraph as it applies for the purposes of section 246A(2), the day on which the offender was convicted of that offence, and
    (b) for the purposes of this paragraph as it applies for the purposes of sections 224A(4) and 226A(2), the day on which the offender was convicted of the offence referred to in section 224A(1)(a) or 226A(1)(a) (as appropriate).

Part 3 Offences Under Service Law Listed for the Purposes of Sections 224A(4), 226A and 246A

47 An offence under section 70 of the Army Act 1955, section 70 of the Air Force Act 1955 or section 42 of the Naval Discipline Act 1957 as respects which the corresponding civil offence (within the meaning of the Act in question) is an offence specified in Part 1 or 2 of this Schedule.
48 (1) An offence under section 42 of the Armed Forces Act 2006 as respects which the corresponding offence under the law of England and Wales (within the meaning given by that section) is an offence specified in Part 1 or 2 of this Schedule.
    (2) Section 48 of the Armed Forces Act 2006 (attempts, conspiracy etc) applies for the purposes of this paragraph as if the reference in subsection (3)(b) of that section to any of the following provisions of that Act were a reference to this paragraph.

Part 4 Offences Under the Law of Scotland, Northern Ireland or a Member State Other than the United Kingdom Listed for the Purposes of Sections 224A(4) and 226A

49 An offence for which the person was convicted in Scotland, Northern Ireland or a member State other than the United Kingdom and which, if committed in England and Wales at the time of the conviction, would have constituted an offence specified in Part 1 or 2 of this Schedule.

Part 5 Interpretation

50 In this Schedule 'imprisonment for life' includes custody for life and detention for life.

Index

Index

Index

Index

Index

Index

Index

Index

Index

Index

Index

Index

Index

Index

Index

Index

Index

Index

Index

Index

Index

Index